W9-ASU-096

Versailles, 1919

THE FORCES, EVENTS AND PERSONALITIES
THAT SHAPED THE TREATY

BY

Ferdinand Czernin

G. P. PUTNAM'S SONS
NEW YORK

This volume is dedicated to

THE MEMORY OF CHARLES SEYMOUR

President emeritus of Yale University

who served as one of Woodrow Wilson's experts at the Paris Peace Conference,
who, in collaboration with Edward House, wrote two of the most authoritative works on the Conference,
who arranged and took charge of the vast collection of papers gathered by Colonel House,
and who spent a great deal of his energy interpreting the Paris Peace Conference to several generations of American scholars.

President Seymour was good enough to encourage me to undertake the task of compiling this volume, took the trouble to read the first drafts of some of its chapters and generously told me that he "would be honored to write the introduction to this book."

It was not to be. Before the book was completed, President Seymour passed away.

May this volume be a small tribute to the memory of a great scholar and a gentle man.

FERDINAND CZERNIN

Library of Congress Catalog Card
Number: 64-10408

MANUFACTURED IN THE UNITED STATES OF AMERICA

Contents

ACKNOWLEDGMENTS

My thanks are due to:

President Herbert Hoover, for his permission to quote from *Years of Adventure;*

Mr. Bernard M. Baruch, for his encouragement and his permission to quote from *The Making of the Reparation and Economic Sections of the Treaty;*

The Carnegie Endowment for International Peace, for the extensive use of its library facilities and for permission to quote from *Reparations at the Paris Peace Conference,* by Philip Burnett, and from *The German Delegation at the Peace Conference,* by Alma Luckau;

The Council on Foreign Relations, and Mr. Donald Wasson, its librarian, for the use of its library facilities and for help in tracking down some of the more elusive material;

Miss Judith A. Schiff and her staff at the Historical Manuscript Section of the Sterling Memorial Library, Yale University, for the permission to use the invaluable collection of manuscripts and papers in her custody, and for double-checking my quotes from the manuscript of the House *Diary* and from the files of the House and Wiseman papers;

The Beaverbrook Foundation, London, for permission to quote from the British and American editions of David Lloyd George's *Memoirs*;

Messrs. Houghton Mifflin Company, Boston, for permission to quote from *The Intimate Papers of Colonel House*, by Charles Seymour;

Messrs. G. P. Putnam's Sons, New York, for permission to quote from *The Drafting of the Covenant,* by David Hunter Miller; and I also acknowledge with thanks permission to reprint from:

The Economic Consequences of the Peace, by John Maynard Keynes, copyright, 1920, by Harcourt, Brace and World, Inc.; renewed 1948, by Lydia Lopokova Keynes. Reprinted by permission of the publishers.

The Truth About the Treaty, by André Tardieu, copyright 1921 by The Bobbs-Merrill Company; 1948 by Madame Largenton Julia Angelique. Reprinted by permission of the publishers.

My Memoir, copyright 1939 by Edith Bolling Wilson; reprinted by permission of the publishers, The Bobbs-Merrill Company, Inc.

Woodrow Wilson and World Settlement, by Ray Stannard Baker, copyright 1922 by Doubleday and Company, Inc. Reprinted by permission of the publishers.

Introductory Remarks

DAVID LLOYD GEORGE, one of the "Big Four" primarily responsible for the Treaty of Versailles, has called that paper "the most abused and least perused document in history."

There are very good reasons why this should be. Inasmuch as the Treaty of Versailles, together with the other subsidiary treaties of the lesser French châteaux that the Paris Peace Conference also produced (Saint-Germain, Trianon, Neuilly and Sèvres), created the inter-World-War structures of Europe, Africa and Asia, those treaties had to take the blame and the abuse for all the discontent and unrest of that turbulent era. And as for being the "least perused document in history," that too is easily understood—the 80,000-word volume not only makes somewhat tedious and confusing reading, but its provisions, occasionally contradictory, often remain incomprehensible unless they are studied together with the records of the meetings, discussions, correspondence and negotiations from which they resulted. To understand the Treaty of Versailles it is not enough just to "peruse" the more than two hundred pages of the Treaty itself; it becomes necessary to burrow into mountains of documents, minutes of innumerable meetings and conferences, and piles of letters and memoranda before the document begins to take on a semblance of sense. In addition, there are the many diaries and memoirs written by almost every major, and by many a lesser, participant of the Peace Conference, all of which have to be scanned and evaluated for significant evidence.

The Paris Peace Conference is probably the most lavishly documented political gathering of all time. Almost every word that was spoken was recorded, every gesture made by the statesmen of the day has been noted and interpreted, nearly every one of their remarks and actions have been analyzed and criticized.

As every sentence mouthed at the Conference was spoken with a purpose, as all "evidence" contained in the papers which were presented to the Conference was presented to prove a point, and as the same facts are apt to look very different depending on the national viewpoint of the one who presents them, almost all documents connected with the Paris Peace Conference are naturally "biased" in the sense that they represent particular points of view.

Faced with the task of putting together a documentary account of the evolution of the five main clauses of the Treaty of Versailles, the author has therefore, whenever possible, fallen back upon primary documents, such as minutes of meetings, letters and memoranda written under the pressures of the day, or upon such secondary documents, if we may call them that, as diaries and letters written by the Conference's participants after they had had time to collect their thoughts and to reflect. But to knit together a coherent story he had, on occasion, to take recourse to writings penned after the event, to memoirs and books written some time after the Conference had passed into history.

Except for the author's conclusion and for some inevitable transition pieces to tie the documents together, every word in this book has been spoken or written by participants of the Paris Conference itself. The bridge material has been purged of all expressions of opinion, as far as possible, so as to present a truly documentary account of the proceedings.

Therein lies a certain danger for the reader: unless he remains permanently aware of whose viewpoint is being voiced at any given point he may be apt to take argument for fact or bias for truth. Both in the heat of discussion and in the slow burn of recollection, statesmen, like ordinary human beings, occasionally tend to paint in colors that will flatter their own profiles. Much of what has been written about the Treaty of Versailles in the making was written to prove that the author "was right" and "all the others were wrong." Some such writing inevitably has been included in this volume. *Caveat lector!*

Most books written about the Treaty of Versailles have been written to prove something. It is not the purpose of this volume to prove anything. It neither wishes to pass judgment on whether the Treaty of Versailles was "good" or "bad," whether a more Carthaginian peace or a more lenient treaty would have been "better" or "worse," nor is it its purpose to "prove" that Wilson, Lloyd George, Clemenceau, or any of the other actors in the drama were "right" or "wrong" in either their general approaches or in any particular instance.

This book simply attempts to show by documentary evidence how the five main, and most controversial, clauses of the Treaty of Versailles came to be written the way they were and what parallelograms of forces shaped them. By confining himself to so narrow a goal the author deliberately set himself certain limitations.

Harold Nicolson, the eminent British writer and diplomat who earned his diplomatic spurs working at the Paris Peace Conference and who later became one of the most astute chroniclers and analysts of the Conference, has succinctly sketched the difficulties all reporters of the Paris Conference have to encounter.

> Those writers who have ventured upon complete records of the Paris Peace Conference have tended to adopt one or another of three methods of treatment, striving thereby to find, through all the inchoate confusion, some clue to continuity, some consecutive thread of narrative. A few of them have chosen the chronological system and have sought to tell their story in terms of time. Others have divided their account under the heading of subjects, and have discussed each particular issue as a problem in itself. Others again have dramatized the whole negotiations in the form of a conflict of wills, and have achieved thereby a readable, yet essentially inaccurate, representation. Each of these three methods of treatment entails a falsification of values. The chronological method is apt to give an erroneous impression of continuity, and to omit the element of synchronisation as well as the element of fits and starts. The piecemeal treatment, though valuable for purposes of lucidity, ignores the interrelation of subjects and gives no account of the effect of obstruction in one area upon concession in another. The "conflict of wills" system errs on the side of oversimplification, and attributes to Wilson, Lloyd George and Clemenceau antagonistic as well as protagonistic positions which are often exaggerated.*

Because this volume deals with separate issues only, the author has been forced to adopt what Sir Harold has called "the piecemeal treatment" and take up each of his five subjects as "a problem in itself." In doing so he is fully aware that he is "sacrificing some interrelations of subjects" and, wherever possible, he has tried to indicate "the effects

* Harold Nicolson, *Peacemaking 1919* (Houghton Mifflin), pages 157-158.

of obstructions in one area upon concessions in another." But, much to his regret, he has had to ignore important side issues such as the problems of the Southern Tyrol, Fiume, the Dodecanese and Anatolia. He also has had to pass by all the global political and economic subjects the Paris Peace Conference dealt with that were not directly related to the issues under discussion.

Indirectly all of these issues did, of course, affect the Treaty of Versailles, be it only by sharpening the differences between the "Big Four," by ruffling tempers, by enhancing or damaging the standing of one or the other statesman and by setting precedents in the application of principles. But, rather than widen the scope of this presentation, it seems preferable to concentrate on the five subjects originally chosen, even at the cost of sacrificing some dramatic highlights.

* * *

A short chronological survey of the "Preliminary Peace Conference at Paris," as it was officially called, may be of some assistance to the reader. The Conference can be divided into six distinct phases:

1. The first five weeks (January 8 to February 14, 1919), during which the various committees were set up to wrestle with the respective problems of the Peace Treaties that had been assigned to them, while Woodrow Wilson concentrated on hammering out a Covenant of the League of Nations and whipping it through his committee.

2. The four weeks of Wilson's absence in the United States (February 15 to March 15, 1919). Four days after Wilson sailed for America, an assassin's bullet laid low Georges Clemenceau; at this time, also, Lloyd George departed for England to mend his political fences. During the absence of the Big Four the affairs of the Conference were in the hands of the second echelon, Colonel Edward House for the United States, Arthur Balfour and Robert Cecil for the United Kingdom, André Tardieu and Louis Loucheur for France. The French seized the opportunity of Wilson's absence to mount a general assault on the American position in an attempt to ram through a peace treaty on French terms. Because the French were joined by the British in this effort, Colonel House was in an awkward position and, conciliatory man that he was, he retreated from compromise to compromise.

3. The third phase (March 15th to 28th), which started with Wilson's return from America, saw some of the toughest struggles of the Conference as Wilson tried to regain lost ground and encountered

not only stubborn French resistance, but also difficulties with the British, Japanese and Italian representatives. This phase came to an abrupt end when Clemenceau, in a show of temper, called Wilson "pro-Boche" and angrily stalked out of a Big Four meeting.

4. During the fourth phase, which Ray S. Baker has called "the dark period" of the Conference, the Conference machinery ground to an almost complete halt as the French and American positions on all important questions seemed immovable and irreconcilable. Woodrow Wilson's health collapsed and, once again, Colonel House was in charge of conducting American policy at the Conference. Matters reached such an impasse that President Wilson even ordered the S.S. *George Washington* readied to take him back to Washington.

5. On April 12th, after two weeks of deadlock, a compromise was reached on the crucial problem of the Saar; and from then on compromise followed compromise until the treaty with Germany was finally knitted together for presentation to the German delegation on May 7th.

6. The last phase of the Peace Conference consisted of an exchange of innumerable notes between the president of the Peace Conference (Georges Clemenceau) and the German delegation. The Germans gained some important concessions, but, on the whole, the Treaty remained very much as it had been originally written. It was signed on June 28, 1919, exactly five years to the day after the fatal shots which ignited World War I had been fired at Sarajevo.

Only in its very last phase was the "Preliminary Peace Conference at Paris" a true peace conference in the sense that the belligerent parties came face to face with one another. The major part of the Conference was devoted to skirmishes in which the antagonists were not the enemies of the war, but the Allied and Associated Powers themselves. The primary task of the "Preliminary Conference" was to reach agreement on the peace terms that were to be imposed upon the enemy. The problem would have been comparatively simple if the Allies had been in a position to dictate their own terms. But Woodrow Wilson had injected a whole set of new values into the negotiations; moreover, he had managed to make the Allied Powers accept them as the basis for the peace to be made at the Conference. This book will attempt to show how the resulting difficulties were solved or compromised, and why the Treaty of Versailles took on the shape in which it was written into history.

* * *

One final remark. It seems hardly fair to let the reader judge the stature of the men of Versailles by their utterances frozen in dry verbatim minutes of meetings without, at the same time, stressing the manifold pressures these men were constantly subjected to, and without emphasizing the many aspects of every problem they continuously had to keep in mind. They are bound to appear far more bungling and incompetent than they really were. The author knows no way of remedying this distortion. He would only like to ask the reader to remember one thing—both author and reader, and every John, Ike and Harry for that matter, could be not only great but superlative statesmen if Providence granted them two things: complete removal from the pressures of the day, and at least forty years of hindsight.

I

The Armistice and the Pre-Armistice Agreement

ONE of the major difficulties confronting the architects of the Versailles Treaty was the fact that it was preceded by a pre-armistice agreement with the Germans which the Americans took very seriously, the British reluctantly acknowledged, and the French denied was ever made. In its dying gasp, German imperial diplomacy had scored a major success by foisting this agreement on its enemies in the hope of saving the German Reich from utter disaster.

By the end of the summer of 1918 the German Imperial Army had spent the last of its strength—after four years of a war that, according to the plans of the German General Staff, should have been won in six months. All German offensives had bogged down; the German defenses in France were being breached by the reserves which the Allies, thanks to the United States, were able to throw into the fray; and the morale of the Imperial Army was crumbling. Even the Imperial High Command had begun to realize that its cherished *Siegfrieden* (the victorious peace which would enable Germany to dictate her own terms) was no longer obtainable, and on September 10th stiff-necked General Ludendorff had had enough. He requested the German government "to make peace as soon as possible."

On September 15th Austria-Hungary sent a frantic peace appeal to President Wilson, who turned it down as insufficiently specific. But the desperate tone of the appeal was enough to convince the Allies that the collapse of the Central Powers could not be far off. On September 30th Bulgaria capitulated and signed an armistice, thereby completely wrecking General Ludendorff's nerves. The Imperial High Command on October 1st summoned the representatives of the Kaiser (Baron von Grünau) and the Foreign Office (Counselor of Legation von Lersner) to demand that peace proposals be made immediately. Just at that moment, however, Germany was without a government capable of acting. Prince Max of Baden, the Count Mirabeau of the German Revolution, was at this juncture trying to form a "democratic, constitutional government" under his leadership. The Imperial High Command had to agree to wait twenty-four hours. The following exchange of telegrams is self-explanatory:

The Imperial Counselor of Legation to the Foreign Office

GENERAL HEADQUARTERS, *October 1, 1918, 1* P.M.

General Ludendorff has just asked Baron von Grünau and myself in the presence of Colonel Heye *to transmit to Your Excellency his urgent request that our peace proposal shall be issued at once. Today the troops are holding their own; what may happen tomorrow cannot be foreseen.*

I pointed out the fact that it could effect no change in our position, whether our proposal was sent out today or within the next few days. Baron Grünau will likewise wire Your Excellency later as he wishes to consult with His Majesty.

LERSNER

GENERAL HEADQUARTERS, *October 1, 1918, 1.30* P.M.

To Major Baron von dem Bussche
for Vice Chancellor von Payer.

If by seven or eight o'clock tonight it is certain that Prince Max of Baden is going to form the Government, I will agree to the postponement until tomorrow forenoon.

If, on the other hand, the formation of the Government is in any way doubtful, I consider the dispatch of the declaration to the foreign Governments as imperative for tonight.

VON HINDENBURG

Note delivered October 1, 2 P.M., to His Excellency von Payer.

V. D. BUSSCHE

The Imperial Counselor of Legation to the Foreign Office

Confidential. GENERAL HEADQUARTERS, *October 1, 1918, 2* P.M.

General Ludendorff just asked me in the presence of Colonel Heye and Lersner to transmit to Your Excellency his urgent request to issue the peace proposal at once, and *not to hold it back until the formation of the new Government*, which might be delayed.

The troops still held their ground today, and we were in a respectable position, *but the line might be broken at any moment and then our proposal would come at the most unfavorable time. He said he felt like a gambler, and that a division might fail him any where at any time.*

I get the impression that they have all lost their nerve, here, and that, if things come to the worst, we can justify our action to the outside world by Bulgaria's behavior.

GRÜNAU

The Imperial Counselor of Legation to the Foreign Office

Urgent. GENERAL HEADQUARTERS, *October 1, 1918, 2.35* P.M.

His Majesty is of the opinion of Your Excellency that the step in question should be taken only by the new Government.

GRÜNAU

BERLIN, *October 1, 1918, 7.20* P.M.

1. Grünau.
2. Lersner.

New Government will probably be formed tonight, October 1. So the proposal can also go out tonight. *Military situation is strongest means of pressure on silly and arrogant parties.*

VON HINTZE

The Imperial Counselor of Legation to the Foreign Office

GENERAL HEADQUARTERS, *October 1, 1918, 9.45* P.M.

General Ludendorff requests that you inform him as soon as possible of the text of our peace proposal, and when it will go to Wilson.

He asks that the peace proposal also be communicated to the other enemy Powers.

The proposal must contain a demand that the enemy determine on a locality for the conduct of armistice negotiations at the front. Armistice commission: General von Beseler, Colonel von Winterfeld, Major Brinckmann, Major von Harbou, a captain, two naval officers, one representative of the Foreign Office, presumably Zeki Pasha and Lieutenant Field Marshal Baron Klepsch.

Should the armistice negotiations commence at once, I should, assuming that Your Excellency agrees to this, go with them as the representative of the Foreign Office, until Your Excellency has appointed a representative.

The Field Marshal will give the credentials to the military, the Imperial Chancellor presumably to the civil members.

LERSNER

The Imperial Counselor of Legation to the Foreign Office

GENERAL HEADQUARTERS, *October 1, 1918**

General Ludendorff told me that our proposal must be forwarded *immediately* from Berne to Washington. *The Army could not wait forty-eight hours longer.* He [word missing, probably "begged"] Your Excellency most urgently to make every effort to have the proposal issued in the *quickest possible manner.*

I showed him plainly that notwithstanding the greatest haste the enemy would hardly make a reply in less than a week. The General insisted that *everything depended* on the proposal being in the hands of the Entente by Wednesday night or early Thursday morning at the latest, and begs Your Excellency to leave no stone unturned to that end. He thinks that, in the interest of speed, the note might be sent by the Swiss Government in Swiss cipher to the persons addressed by wireless from Nauen.

LERSNER[1]

But the last thing Prince Max von Baden wanted was to have the new democratic government discredited from the outset by suing for peace the moment it got into power. He therefore pleaded for time. But the German High Command had no more

* Filed October 2, 12:10 A.M.

time to give and, on October 3rd, Field Marshal von Hindenburg dispatched this memorable telegram to the new Reichskanzler:

BERLIN, *October 3, 1918*

The Supreme Army Command persists in its request of Sunday, September 29, of this year, urging the immediate dispatch to our enemies of the peace proposal.

As a result of the collapse of the Macedonian front, entailing the weakening of our reserves in the west, and as a result of the impossibility of making good the very considerable losses sustained in the battles of the last few days, there exists, according to all human calculation, no further prospect of compelling the enemy to sue for peace.

Our opponents, for their part, can continuously bring new and fresh reserves into battle.

The German Army is still firm and in good order, and is victoriously repulsing all attacks. *But the situation is daily growing more acute, and may force the Supreme Army Command to very serious decisions.*

Under these circumstances it is imperative to bring the struggle to an end in order to spare the German people and their allies useless sacrifice. *Every day's delay costs the lives of thousands of brave soldiers.*

VON HINDENBURG,
General Field Marshal[2]

Prince Max was astute enough to realize that any appeal to the enemy as a whole would result in demands for German unconditional surrender, which, even at this stage, the Imperial High Command would not have accepted. But among the voices that reached German ears from across the trenches one had struck a chord in the war-weary hearts of the German people: that of President Woodrow Wilson, who kept calling for "a just peace" and "impartial justice," and whose "Fourteen Points," which he had proclaimed as a blueprint for the peace he envisaged, had kindled hopes of a new and better world in millions of despairing breasts. The Reichskanzler therefore decided to appeal to the prophet in the White House and, through the good services of the Swiss government, he sent his request for an armistice to the President of the United States.

The German Government requests the President of the United States of America to take steps for the restoration of peace, to notify all belligerents of this request, and to invite them to delegate plenipotentiaries for the purpose of taking up negotiations. The German Government accepts, as a basis for the peace negotiations, the program laid down by the President of the United States in his message to Congress of January 8, 1918, and in his subsequent pronouncements, particularly in his address of September 27, 1918.*

In order to avoid further bloodshed the German Government requests to bring about the immediate conclusion of an armistice on land, on water, and in the air.

MAX,
Prince of Baden, Imperial Chancellor[3]

The German appeal reached Washington on October 5th, and Congressional, press and public opinion was almost unanimous in urging President Wilson "not to fall into the German trap" and in demanding that the war go on to unconditional surrender. But the President, presented with the chance of remaking the world in accordance with his vision, kept his own counsel, and on October 8th Robert Lansing, his Secretary of State, sent the German government the American reply.

DEPARTMENT OF STATE, *October 8, 1918*

Before making reply to the request of the Imperial German Government, and in order that that reply shall be as candid and straightforward as the momentous interests involved require, the President of the United States deems it necessary to assure himself of the exact meaning of the note of the Imperial Chancellor.

Does the Imperial Chancellor mean that the Imperial German Government accepts the terms laid down by the President in his addresses to the Congress of the United States on the eighth of January last and in subsequent addresses, and that its object in entering into discussions would be only to agree upon the practical details of their application? The President feels bound to say with regard to the

* An obvious reference to Wilson's subsidiary point: "The impartial justice meted out must involve no discrimination between those to whom we wish to be just and those to whom we do not wish to be just. It must be a justice that plays no favorites and knows no standard but the equal rights of the several peoples concerned."

suggestion of an armistice that he would not feel at liberty to propose a cessation of arms to the governments with which the Government of the United States is associated against the Central Powers so long as the armies of those powers are upon their soil. The good faith of any discussion would manifestly depend upon the consent of the Central Powers immediately to withdraw their forces everywhere from invaded territory.

The President also feels that he is justified in asking whether the Imperial Chancellor is speaking merely for the constituted authorities of the Empire who have so far conducted the war. He deems the answer to these questions vital from every point of view.

Accept, Sir, etc. etc.

[signed] ROBERT LANSING[4]

The German government wasted no time and promptly dispatched its answer to the President's note on October 12th. Field Marshal von Hindenburg felt compelled to advise the Imperial Foreign Office that Germany's reply should contain the demand that Wilson obtain the consent of his Allies to his Fourteen Points of Peace. "Therein," he said, "I see a renewed assurance against more extensive demands by the Entente."[5] Prince Max hardly needed the Field Marshal's reminder, and the second German note contained the following sentence: "The German government believes that the governments of the Powers associated with the United States also accept the position taken by the President in his addresses."

The second American note was considerably tougher than the first. By drawing attention to Wilson's nineteenth point ("the destruction of all arbitrary power") it obviously intended to convey the message that "justice" might not be the "forgiveness" the Germans seemed to be expecting. But the German government showed no signs of taking the hint. Moreover, Wilson's pointed allusion to "the German people's ability to choose to alter the arbitrary powers which have hitherto controlled Germany" failed to convey the idea that the Kaiser's abdication was an essential condition for peace. The leading statesmen of the Reich were not yet ready to contemplate such a monstrous possibility.

The German Minister in Brussels reported that "an informant" had told him that "the two chief points without which the

President will not permit an armistice are 1) abdication of His Majesty and the Crown Prince, and 2) plain evidence of the superiority of Entente troops, by, for instance, conceding the occupation of the fortress of Metz."[6] Despite this report, Germany's third note to President Wilson tried to brush aside the point of the Kaiser's abdication by asserting that the German government was fully representative of the German people.

The Imperial High Command, having somewhat recovered its nerve, now attempted to interfere with the conduct of Germany's foreign policy. During the early morning hours of October 20th Hindenburg sent Prince Max the following message:

TO THE IMPERIAL CHANCELLOR

(transmitted by Colonel von Haeften):

The situation has not changed. Turkey has commenced separate negotiations. Austria-Hungary will follow soon. We shall very soon stand alone in Europe. The western front is showing the greatest tension. A break through is possible, although I do not fear it. By breaking off with the enemy in Belgium and by bringing up the promised reserves, a durable resistance might be organized which would protract the fight on the western front for some time, and, though it would not bring us a decisive victory, yet would prevent the worst. But even if we should be beaten, we should not really be worse off than if we were to accept everything at present.

The question must be asked: Will the German people fight for their honor, not only in words but with deeds, to the last man, and thereby assure themselves of the possibility of a new existence, or will they allow themselves to be forced to capitulate and thus delivered to destruction *before* making their last and final exertion?

By the sacrifice of the U-Boat war without any counter-concession, as agreed to by the note, we are adopting the latter course.

We should, in addition, most unfavorably influence the spirit of the Army, sorely tried in heavy fighting. Therefore, on this point, I cannot agree to the note. If the Government should adopt the attitude that it must reckon with Wilson's breaking off negotiations, it must also be determined to fight on to the bitter end for the sake of our honor.

In spite of the unusually serious situation of the Army, I can see no other way out, and I firmly hope that the Government will have the whole Fatherland behind it in coming to this serious determination. . . .

VON HINDENBURG,
Field Marshal[7]

General Ludendorff went even further and cabled the Foreign Office demanding that a paragraph be inserted in the note to the effect that "the German people find it impossible to dispense with a weapon forced upon it by its foes in a life and death struggle, if some equivalent is not supplied at once by the inauguration of a general armistice. Thus for reasons of equity and self-preservation the German Government will be forced to have recourse to this weapon again unless an armistice goes into effect within a brief period."[8]

The German Foreign Office, however, had sufficient backbone to inform the Quartermaster General that the note had already been dispatched by the time his request had reached Berlin and that "the additional clause would, however, have been impossible."

The third German note was sent on October 20th, and the American reply is dated October 23rd. Short of saying in so many words that "the Kaiser must abdicate before we will sign an armistice," Wilson's note could not have been more explicit with regard to the Kaiser's abdication. The Bavarian government drew Berlin's attention to the urgent necessity of an abdication and a Prince Hohenlohe, serving as councilor at the German Legation in Berne, Switzerland, cabled the German Foreign Office that "a confidential informant has informed me that the conclusion of the Wilson note of October 23 refers to nothing less than the abdication of the Kaiser as the only way to a peace which is more or less tolerable."[9]

But the Berlin government still could not conceive of such a possibility and, instead, sacrificed Ludendorff, who was given his walking papers on October 27th. The fourth German note proudly referred to that fact and intimated that now was the time for armistice terms to be presented.

Meanwhile President Wilson had informed his Associates (for reasons deeply rooted in American tradition the United States Government referred to its co-belligerents always as "Associated Powers," never as "Allies") of his negotiations with the German government and he now dispatched Colonel Edward M. House, his close friend and trusted political adviser, to Europe with what amounted to sweeping power of attorney.

KNOW YE, That reposing special Trust and Confidence in the Ability and Integrity of EDWARD M. HOUSE of Texas, I do appoint him a special Representative of the United States of America, in Europe in matters relating to the war, and do authorize and empower him to execute and to fulfill the duties of this Commission with all the Powers and Privileges thereunto of right appertaining to the pleasure of the President of the United States.

WOODROW WILSON[10]

The Colonel's most pressing task was to wring acceptance of the Fourteen Points from the Allied statesmen. Under his direction a group of experts, headed by Professor Isaiah Bowman, had been assembled to advise the President on all matters connected with the Peace Treaties. This group, known as "the American Inquiry," worked out a commentary on the Fourteen Points which became the official interpretation.

October, 1918

I. Open covenants of peace, openly arrived at, after which there shall be no private international understandings of any kind but diplomacy shall proceed always frankly and in the public view.

The purpose is clearly to prohibit treaties, sections of treaties or understandings that are secret, such as the Triple Alliance, etc.

The phrase "openly arrived at" need not cause difficulty. In fact, the President explained to the Senate last winter that the phrase was not meant to exclude confidential diplomatic negotiations involving delicate matters. The intention is that nothing which occurs in the course of such confidential negotiations shall be binding unless it appears in the final covenant made public to the world.

The matter may perhaps be put this way: It is proposed that in the future every treaty be part of the public law of the world; and that every nation assume a certain obligation in regard to its enforcement. Obviously, nations cannot assume obligations in matters of which they are ignorant; and therefore any secret treaty tends to undermine the solidity of the whole structure of international covenants which it is proposed to erect.

II. Absolute freedom of navigation upon the seas, outside territorial waters, alike in peace and in war, except as the seas may be closed in whole or in part by international action for the enforcement of international covenants.

This proposition must be read in connection with No. XIV, which proposes a League of Nations. It refers to navigation under the three following conditions:

1. General peace;
2. A general war, entered into by the League of Nations for the purpose of enforcing international covenants;
3. Limited war; involving no breach of international covenants.

Under "1" (General peace) no serious dispute exists. There is implied freedom to come and go on the high seas.

No serious dispute exists as to the intention under "2" (a general war entered into by the League of Nations to enforce international covenants). Obviously such a war is conducted against an outlaw nation and complete non-intercourse with that nation is intended.

"3" (A limited war, involving no breach of international covenants) is the crux of the whole difficulty. The question is, what are to be the rights of neutral shipping and private property on the high seas during a war between a limited number of nations when that war involves no issue upon which the League of Nations cares to take sides. In other words, a war in which the League of Nations remains neutral. Clearly, it is the intention of the proposal that in such a war the rights of neutrals shall be maintained against the belligerents, the rights of both to be clearly and precisely defined in the law of nations.

III. The removal, so far as possible, of all economic barriers and the establishment of an equality of trade conditions among all the nations consenting to the peace and associating themselves for its maintenance.

The proposal applies only to those nations which accept the responsibilities of membership in the League of Nations. It means the destruction of all special commercial agreements, each nation putting the trade of every other nation in the League on the same basis, the most favored nation clause applying automatically to all members of the League of Nations.

Thus a nation could legally maintain a tariff or a special railroad rate or a port restriction against the whole world, or against all the signatory powers. It could maintain any kind of restriction which it chose against a nation not in the League. But it could not discriminate as between its partners in the League.

This clause naturally contemplates fair and equitable understanding as to the distribution of raw materials.

IV. Adequate guarantees given and taken that national armaments will be reduced to the lowest point consistent with domestic safety.

"Domestic safety" clearly implies not only internal policing, but the protection of territory against invasion. The accumulation of armaments above this level would be a violation of the intention of the proposal.

What guarantees should be given and taken, or what are to be the standards of judgment have never been determined. It will be necessary to adopt the general principle and then institute some kind of international commission of investigation to prepare detailed projects for its execution.

V. A free, open-minded, and absolutely impartial adjustment of all colonial claims, based upon a strict observance of the principle that in determining all such questions of sovereignty, the interests of the populations concerned must have equal weight with the equitable claims of the government whose title is to be determined.

Some fear is expressed in France and England that this involves the reopening of all colonial questions. Obviously it is not so intended. It applies clearly to those colonial claims which have been created by the war. That means the German colonies and any other colonies which may come under international consideration as a result of the war.

The stipulation is that in the case of the German colonies the title is to be determined after the conclusion of the war by "impartial adjustment" based on certain principles. These are of two kinds: 1. "Equitable" claims: 2. The interests of the populations concerned.

What are the "equitable" claims put forth by Britain and Japan, the two chief heirs of the German colonial empire, that the colonies cannot be returned to Germany? Because she will use them as submarine bases, because she will arm the blacks, because she uses the colonies as bases of intrigue, because she oppresses the natives. What are the "equitable" claims put forth by Germany? That she needs access to tropical raw materials, that she needs a field for the expansion of her population, that under the principles of peace proposed, conquest gives her enemies no title to her colonies.

What are the "interests of the populations"? That they should not be militarized, that exploitation should be conducted on the principle of the open door, and under the strictest regulation as to labor conditions, profits and taxes, that a sanitary regime be maintained, that permanent improvements in the way of roads, etc., be made, that native organization and custom be respected, that the protecting authority be stable and experienced enough to thwart intrigue and corruption, that the protecting power have adequate resources in money and competent administrators to act successfully.

It would seem as if the principle involved in this proposition is that a colonial power acts not as owner of its colonies, but as trustee for the natives and for the interests of the society of nations, that the terms on which the colonial administration is conducted are a matter of international concern and may legitimately be the subject of international inquiry and that the peace conference may, therefore, write a code of colonial conduct binding upon all colonial powers.

VI. The evacuation of all Russian territory and such a settlement of all questions affecting Russia as will secure the best and freest cooperation of the other nations of the world in obtaining for her an unhampered and unembarrassed opportunity for the independent determination of her own political development and national policy and assure her of a sincere welcome into the society of free nations under institutions of her own choosing; and, more than a welcome, assistance also of every kind that she may need and may herself desire. The treatment accorded Russia by her sister nations in the months to come will be the acid test of their good will, of their comprehension of her needs as distinguished from their own interests, and of their intelligent and unselfish sympathy.

The first question is whether Russian territory is synonymous with territory belonging to the former Russian Empire. This is clearly not so, because Proposition XIII stipulates an independent Poland, a proposal which excludes the territorial re-establishment of the Empire. What is recognized as valid for the Poles will certainly have to be recognized for the Finns, the Lithuanians, the Letts, and perhaps also for the Ukrainians. Since the formulation of this condition, these subject nationalities have emerged, and there can be no doubt that they will have to be given an opportunity of free development.

The problem of these nationalities is complicated by two facts: 1. That they have conflicting claims: 2. That the evacuation called for in the proposal may be followed by Bolshevist revolutions in all of them.

The chief conflicts are (a) Between the Letts and Germans in Courland; (b) Between the Poles and the Lithuanians on the northeast; (c) Between the Poles and the White Ruthenians on the east; (d) Between the Poles and the Ukrainians on the southeast (and in Eastern Galicia). In this whole borderland the relation of the German Poles to the other nationalities is roughly speaking that of landlord to peasant. Therefore the evacuation of the territory, if it resulted in class war, would very probably also take the form of a conflict of nationalities. It is clearly to the interests of a good settlement that the real nation in each territory should be consulted rather than the ruling and possessing class.

This can mean nothing less than the recognition by the Peace Conference of a series of *de facto* Governments representing Finns, Esths, Lithuanians, Ukrainians. This primary act of recognition should be conditional upon the calling of National Assemblies for the creation of *de jure* Governments, as soon as the Peace Conference has drawn frontiers for these new states. The frontiers should be drawn so far as possible on ethnic lines, but in every case the right of unhampered economic transit should be reserved. No dynastic ties with German or Austrian or Romanoff princes should be permitted, and every inducement should be given to encourage federal relations between these new states. Under Proposition III the economic sections of the Treaty of Brest-Litovsk are abolished, but this Proposition should not be construed as forbidding a customs union, a monetary union, a railroad union, etc., of these states. Provision should also be made by which Great Russia can federate with these states on the same terms.

As for Great Russia and Siberia, the Peace Conference might well send a message asking for the creation of a government sufficiently representative to speak for these territories. It should be understood that economic rehabilitation is offered, provided a government carrying sufficient credentials can appear at the Peace Conference.

The Allies should offer this provisional government any form of assistance it may need. The possibility of extending this will exist when the Dardanelles are opened.

The essence of the Russian problem then in the immediate future would seem to be:

1. The recognition of Provisional Governments.
2. Assistance extended to and through these Governments.

The Caucasus should probably be treated as part of the problem of the Turkish Empire. No information exists justifying an opinion on the proper policy in regard to Mohammedan Russia—that is, briefly, Central Asia. It may well be that some power will have to be given a limited mandate to act as protector.

In any case the treaties of Brest-Litovsk and Bucharest must be cancelled as palpably fraudulent. Provision must be made for the withdrawal of all German troops in Russia and the Peace Conference will have a clean slate on which to write a policy for all the Russian peoples.

VII. Belgium, the whole world will agree, must be evacuated and restored, without any attempt to limit the sovereignty which she enjoys in common with all other free nations. No other single act will serve as this will serve to restore confidence among the nations in the laws which they have themselves set and determined for the government of their relations with one another. Without this healing act the whole structure and validity of international law is forever impaired.

The only problem raised here is in the word "restored." Whether restoration is to be in kind, or how the amount of the indemnity is to be determined is a matter of detail, not of principle. The principle that should be established is that in the case of Belgium there exists no distinction between "legitimate" and "illegitimate" destruction. The initial act of invasion was illegitimate and therefore all the consequences of that act are of the same character. Among the consequences may be put the war debt of Belgium. The recognition of this principle would constitute "the healing act" of which the President speaks.

VIII. All French territory should be freed and the invaded portions restored, and the wrong done to France by Prussia in 1871 in the matter of Alsace-Lorraine, which has unsettled the peace of the world for nearly fifty years, should be righted, in order that peace may once more be made secure in the interest of all.

In regard to the restoration of French territory it might well be argued that the invasion of Northern France, being the result of the illegal act as regards Belgium, was in itself illegal. But the case is not perfect. As the world stood in 1914, war between France and Germany was not in itself a violation of international law, and great insistence should be put upon keeping the Belgian case distinct and symbolic. Thus Belgium might well (as indicated above) claim reimbursement not only for destruction but for the cost of carrying on the war. France could not claim payment, it would seem, for more than the damage done to her northeastern departments.

The status of Alsace-Lorraine was settled by the official statement issued a few days ago. It is to be restored completely to French sovereignty.

Attention is called to the strong current of French opinion which claims "the boundaries of 1814" rather than of 1871. The territory claimed is the Valley of the Saar with its coal fields. No claim on grounds of nationality can be established, but the argument leans on the possibility of taking this territory in lieu of indemnity. It would seem to be a clear violation of the President's proposal.

Attention is called also to the fact that no reference is made to the status of Luxembourg. The best solution would seem to be a free choice by the people of Luxembourg themselves.

IX. A readjustment of the frontiers of Italy should be effected along clearly recognizable lines of nationality.

This proposal is less than the Italian claim, less of course, than the territory allotted by the Treaty of London, less than the arrangement made between the Italian Government and the Jugo-Slav State.

In the region of Trent the Italians claim a strategic rather than an ethnic frontier. It should be noted in this connection that Italy and Germany will become neighbors if German Austria joins the German Empire. And if Italy obtains the best geographical frontier she will assume sovereignty over a large number of Germans. This is a violation of principle. But, it may be argued that by drawing a sharp line along the crest of the Alps, Italy's security will be enormously enhanced and the necessity of heavy armaments reduced. It might, therefore, be provided that Italy should have her claim in the Trentino, but that the northern part, inhabited by Germans, should be completely autonomous, and that the population should not be liable to military service in the Italian army. Italy could thus occupy the uninhabited Alpine peaks for military purposes, but would not govern the cultural life of the alien population to the south of her frontier.

The other problems of the frontier are questions between Italy and Jugo-Slavia, Italy and the Balkans, Italy and Greece.

The agreement reached with Jugo-Slavs may well be allowed to stand, although it should be insisted for the protection of the hinterland that both Trieste and Fiume be free ports. This is essential to Bohemia, German Austria, Hungary as well as to the prosperity of the cities themselves.

Italy appears in Balkan politics through her claim to a protectorate over Albania and the possession of Valona. There is no serious objection raised to this, although the terms of the protectorate need to be vigorously controlled. If Italy is protector of Albania, the local life of Albania should be guaranteed by the League of Nations.

A conflict with Greece appears through the Greek claim to Northern Epirus (or what is now Southern Albania). This would bring Greece closer to Valona than Italy desires. A second conflict with Greece occurs over the Ægean Islands of the Dodekanese, but it is understood that a solution favorable to Greece is being worked out.

(Italy's claims in Turkey belong to the problem of the Turkish Empire.)

X. The peoples of Austria-Hungary, whose place among the nations we wish to see safeguarded and assured, should be accorded the freest opportunity of autonomous development.

This proposition no longer holds. Instead we have today the following elements:

1. CZECHO-SLOVAKIA. Its territories include at least a million Germans, for whom some provision must be made.

The independence of Slovakia means the dismemberment of the northwestern counties of Hungary.

2. GALICIA. Western Galicia is clearly Polish. Eastern Galicia is in large measure Ukrainian, (or Ruthenian), and does not of right belong to Poland.

There also are several hundred thousand Ukrainians along the north and northeastern borders of Hungary, and in parts of Bukowina (which belonged to Austria).

3. GERMAN AUSTRIA. This territory should of right be permitted to join Germany, but there is strong objection in France because of the increase of population involved.

4. JUGO-SLAVIA. It faces the following problems:

a. Frontier questions with Italy in Istria and the Dalmatian Coast; with Rumania in the Banat.

b. An internal problem arises out of the refusal of the Croats to accept the domination of the Serbs of the Serbian Kingdom.

c. A problem of the Mohammedan Serbs of Bosnia who are said to be loyal to the Hapsburgs. They constitute a little less than one third of the population.

5. TRANSYLVANIA. Will undoubtedly join Rumania, but provision must be made for the protection of the Magyars, Szeklers and Germans who constitute a large minority.

6. HUNGARY. Now independent, and very democratic in form, but governed by Magyars whose aim is to prevent the detachment of the territory of the nationalities on the fringe.

The United States is clearly committed to the programme of national unity and independence. It must stipulate, however, for the protection of national minorities, for freedom of access to the Adriatic and the Black Sea, and it supports a programme aiming at a Confederation of Southeastern Europe.

XI. Rumania, Serbia, and Montenegro should be evacuated; occupied territories restored; Serbia accorded free and secure access to the sea; and the relations of the several Balkan states to one another determined by friendly counsel along historically established lines of allegiance and nationality; and international guarantees of the political and economic independence and territorial integrity of the several Balkan states should be entered into.

This proposal is also altered by events. Serbia will appear as Jugo-Slavia with access to the Adriatic. Rumania will have acquired the Dobrudja, Bessarabia, and probably Transylvania. These two states will have 11 or 12 million inhabitants and will be far greater and stronger than Bulgaria.

Bulgaria should clearly have her frontier in the Southern Dobrudja as it stood before the Second Balkan War. She should also have Thrace up to the Enos-Midia line, and perhaps even to the Midia-Rodosto line.

Macedonia should be allotted after an impartial investigation. The line which might be taken as a basis of investigation is the southern line of the "contested zone" agreed upon by Serbia and Bulgaria before the First Balkan War.

Albania could be under a protectorate, no doubt of Italy, and its frontiers in the north might be essentially those of the London Conference.

XII. The Turkish portions of the present Ottoman Empire should be assured a secure sovereignty, but the other nationalities which are now under Turkish rule should be assured an undoubted security of life and an absolutely unmolested opportunity of autonomous development, and the Dardanelles should be permanently opened as a free passage to the ships and commerce of all nations under international guarantees.

The same difficulty arises here, as in the case of Austria-Hungary, concerning the word "autonomous."

It is clear that the Straits and Constantinople, while they may remain nominally Turkish, should be under international control. This control may be collective or be in the hands of one Power as mandatory of the League.

Anatolia should be reserved for the Turks. The coast lands, where Greeks predominate, should be under special international control, perhaps with Greece as mandatory.

Armenia must be given a port on the Mediterranean, and a protecting power established. France may claim it, but the Armenians would prefer Great Britain.

Syria has already been allotted to France by agreement with Great Britain.

Britain is clearly the best mandatory for Palestine, Mesopotamia and Arabia.

A general code of guarantees binding on all mandatories in Asia Minor should be written into the Treaty of Peace.

This should contain provision for minorities and the open door. The trunk railroad lines should be internationalized.

XIII. An independent Polish state should be erected which should include the territories inhabited by indisputably Polish populations, which should be assured a free and secure access to the sea, and whose political and economic independence and territorial integrity should be guaranteed by international covenant.

The chief problem is whether Poland is to obtain territory west of the Vistula which would cut off the Germans of East Prussia from the Empire, or whether Danzig can be made a free port and the Vistula internationalized.

On the east, Poland should receive no territory in which Lithuanians or Ukrainians predominate.

If Posen and Silesia go to Poland rigid protection must be afforded the minorities of Germans and Jews living there, as well as in other parts of the Polish state.

The principle on which frontiers will be delimited is contained in the President's words "indisputably." This may imply the taking of an impartial census before frontiers are marked.

XIV. A general association of nations must be formed under specific covenants for the purpose of affording mutual guarantees of political independence and territorial integrity to great and small states alike.

The question of a League of Nations as the primary essential of a permanent peace has been so clearly presented by President Wilson in his speech of September 27, 1918, that no further elucidation is required. It is the foundation of the whole diplomatic structure of a permanent peace.[11]

This analysis of the Fourteen Points was cabled to President Wilson who cabled his qualified approval on October 30th.

ANALYSIS OF FOURTEEN POINTS SATISFACTORY INTERPRETATION OF PRINCIPLES INVOLVED BUT DETAILS OF APPLICATION MENTIONED SHOULD BE REGARDED AS MERELY ILLUSTRATIVE AND I RESERVE FOR THE PEACE CONFERENCE. WOODROW WILSON[12]

Colonel House clarifies the question of how "official" these interpretations became by an entry in his diary fifteen months later.

. . . Each point was interpreted before the armistice was made and the interpretations filled many typewritten pages. . . . These interpretations were on the table day after day when we sat in Conference at Paris. Many times they [Clemenceau, Orlando, Lloyd George] asked the meaning of this or that point and I would read from the accepted interpretation.[13]

Equally as important as the original Fourteen Points, however, were the "subsequent," "complementary" and "explanatory" points the President made in his speeches in the course of 1918.

Address to Congress, February 11, 1918

15. That each part of the final settlement must be based upon the essential justice of that particular case and upon such adjustments as are most likely to bring a peace that will be permanent;

16. That peoples and provinces are not to be bartered about from sovereignty to sovereignty as if they were mere chattels and pawns in a game, even the great game, now forever discredited, of the balance of power; but that

17. Every territorial settlement involved in this war must be made in the interest and for the benefit of the populations concerned, and not as a part of any mere adjustment or compromise of claims amongst rival states; and

18. That all well-defined national aspirations shall be accorded the utmost satisfaction that can be accorded them without introducing new or perpetuating old elements of discord and antagonism that would be likely in time to break the peace of Europe and consequently of the world.

Address at Mount Vernon, July 4, 1918

19. The destruction of every arbitrary power anywhere that can separately, secretly, and of its single choice disturb the peace of the world; or, if it cannot be presently destroyed, at the least its reduction to virtual impotence.

(17) (Compare with No. 17 above.) The settlement of every question, whether of territory, of sovereignty, of economic arrangement, or of political relationship, upon the basis of the free acceptance of that settlement by the people immediately concerned, and not upon the basis of the material interest or advantage of any other nation or people which may desire a different settlement for the sake of its own exterior influence or mastery.

20. The consent of all nations to be governed in their conduct towards each other by the same principles of honor and of respect for the common law of civilized society that govern the individual citizens of all modern states in their relations with one another; to the end that

all promises and covenants may be sacredly observed, no private plots or conspiracies hatched, no selfish injuries wrought with impunity, and a mutual trust established upon the handsome foundation of a mutual respect for right.

(14) (Compare with No. 14 above.) The establishment of an organization of peace which shall make it certain that the combined power of free nations will check every invasion of right and serve to make peace and justice the more secure by affording a definite tribunal of opinion to which all must submit and by which every international readjustment that cannot be amicably agreed upon by the peoples directly concerned shall be sanctioned.

Address in New York City, September 27, 1918

(15) (Compare with No. 15 above.) The impartial justice meted out must involve no discrimination between those to whom we wish to be just and those to whom we do not wish to be just. It must be a justice that plays no favorites and knows no standard but the equal rights of the several peoples concerned;

21. No special or separate interest of any single nation or any group of nations can be made the basis of any part of the settlement which is not consistent with the common interest of all;

22. There can be no leagues or alliances or special covenants and understandings within the general and common family of the League of Nations.

23. And more specifically, there can be no special, selfish economic combinations within the League and no employment of any form of economic boycott or exclusion except as the power of economic penalty by exclusion from the markets of the world may be vested in the League of Nations itself as a means of discipline and control.

24. All international agreements and treaties of every kind must be made known in their entirety to the rest of the world.[14]

Meanwhile the Allied Commander in Chief was preparing the armistice terms. On October 26th Colonel House got an intimation of what was in store for the enemy.

Clemenceau gave me in the greatest confidence Marshal Foch's terms for an armistice. No one has seen it except himself, not even the President of the Republic. . . . Clemenceau expressed his belief, which was also that of Marshal Foch, that Germany was so thoroughly beaten she would accept any terms offered. . . . Lloyd George sent a rather peremptory telegram to Clemenceau. . . . It seems . . . Lloyd George received the impression that Clemenceau was weakening and was inclined to give Germany better terms than he, Lloyd George, thought should be offered. If George has anything worse in mind than Clemenceau, GOD help Germany.[15]

The Allied statesmen were faced with a problem: so far they had considered the "fourteen commandments" as a piece of clever and effective American propaganda, designed primarily to undermine the fighting spirit of the Central Powers, and to bolster the morale of the lesser Allies. Now, suddenly, the whole peace structure was supposed to be built up on that set of "vague principles," most of which seemed to them thoroughly unrealistic, and some of which, if they were to be seriously applied, were simply unacceptable.

Colonel House had hardly had time to settle down at 78, rue de l'Université and embrace Clemenceau and a couple of assorted Frenchmen, when he got the first indications of brewing trouble. He notes in his diary on October 28th:

Sir William Wiseman came around last night just as I was going to bed. He had just arrived from London with Lord Reading and he came to tell me what had happened in London during the past few days. The Cabinet have been having some stormy sessions over the President's peace terms. They rebel against the "Freedom of the seas," and they wish to include reparations for losses at sea.

I told Wiseman, and later Reading, that if the British were not careful they would bring upon themselves the dislike of the world. . . . I did not believe that the United States or any other country would willingly submit to Great Britain's complete domination of the seas, any more than to Germany's domination of the land, and the sooner the English recognized the fact the better it would be for them; furthermore, that our people, if challenged, would build a navy and maintain an army as great as theirs. We had more money, more men, and our natural resources were greater. Such a program would be popular in America and, should England give the incentive, the people would demand the rest.[16]

The next day, at a meeting at the Quai d'Orsay, the full fury of the storm broke. Clemenceau, flanked by Pichon, his Minister of Foreign Affairs of the moment, Lloyd George and his Foreign Secretary, Arthur Balfour, and Italy's Foreign Minister, Sonnino, faced Colonel House. The following discussion took place:

LLOYD GEORGE: If we agree to the terms of the armistice, do we not assume that we accept the Fourteen Points as stated by President Wilson? Germany has asked for an armistice on condition of President Wilson's Fourteen Points. If we send conditions across, it would appear that we accept those terms. Therefore we should consider whether we accept the Fourteen Points. I ask Colonel House whether the German Government is accepting terms of an armistice on the President's conditions of peace. The question is: Do we or do we not accept the whole of President Wilson's Fourteen Points? Should we not make it quite clear that we are not going in on the Fourteen Points of Peace?

CLEMENCEAU: . . . Have you ever been asked by President Wilson whether you accept the Fourteen Points? I have never been asked.

LLOYD GEORGE: I have not been asked either. What is your view, Colonel House? Do you think that if we agree to an armistice we accept the President's peace terms?

COLONEL HOUSE: That is my view.

PICHON: We can say to Germany that we are only stating terms of an armistice, not terms of peace.

BALFOUR: What we are afraid of is that we cannot say that we are merely interested in the terms of an armistice. For the moment, unquestionably, we are not bound by President Wilson's terms; but if we assent to an armistice without making our position clear, we shall certainly be so bound.

CLEMENCEAU: Then I want to hear the Fourteen Points.

SONNINO: Yes, and the five more and the others.

So Pichon started reading off the Fourteen Points.

To the First Point, the one providing for open covenants, openly arrived at, Clemenceau immediately objected.

CLEMENCEAU: I cannot agree never to make a private or secret agreement of any kind.

LLOYD GEORGE: I do not think it is possible so to limit oneself.

Colonel House read the interpretation his "Inquiry" had drawn up and which proved that the point did not mean what it said, but only that treaties and negotiations have to be made public *post factum,* if they were to have international acceptance.

This explanation seemed to satisfy the three Allied statesmen, and M. Pichon went on to Point Two (freedom of the seas).

LLOYD GEORGE: This Point we cannot accept under any conditions. It means that the power of blockade goes. Germany has been broken almost as much by blockade as by military methods. If this power is to be handed over to the League of Nations, and Great Britain were fighting for her life, no League of Nations could prevent her from defending herself. This power has prevented Germany from getting rubber, cotton, and food through Holland and the Scandinavian countries. Therefore it is my view that I should like to see this League of Nations established first before I let this power go. If the League is a reality, I might be willing to discuss the matter.

COLONEL HOUSE: In order to understand the question it is necessary to bear in mind not only this war but also future wars. Great Britain might find herself at war with some other power, possibly France; in the past war the sympathy of the United States has been with the Allies, because of Germany's abominable naval practices; in a future war if France did not resort to any of these practices and was the weaker naval power, the sympathy of the United States might be with France.

CLEMENCEAU: That doesn't really answer Mr. Lloyd George's question. Anyhow, we can't say whether any particular nation might behave badly or well in the future. It isn't to the point.

SONNINO: We all desire to see the League of Nations established in some form or other, but it must be remembered that nations, like animals, have different weapons. One animal has teeth, another tusks, another claws, and so it is with nations. Could we not inform President Wilson that we cannot see our way out on these questions, and deal only with the question of an armistice?

LLOYD GEORGE: It is impossible to make an armistice if doing so commits us to these conditions.

COLONEL HOUSE: The discussion is leading to this: that all negotiations with Germany and Austria up to this point will have to be wiped off the slate. The President would have no alternative but to tell the enemy that his conditions were not accepted by the Allies. The question would then arise whether America would not have to take up these matters directly with Germany and Austria.

CLEMENCEAU: That would amount to a separate peace between the United States and the Central Powers.

COLONEL HOUSE: It might.*

LLOYD GEORGE: If the United States made a separate peace, we would be sorry, but we could not give up the blockade, the power which enabled us to live. As far as the British Public is concerned, we will fight on.

CLEMENCEAU: Yes, I cannot understand the meaning of that doctrine, the Freedom of the Seas. War would not be war if there were Freedom of the Seas.

COLONEL HOUSE: It is for France, England and Italy to get together to limit their acceptance of the fourteen conditions; that would seem to be the first preliminary to working out the armistice.

The British Foreign Secretary, unruffled and calm as ever, rose to speak:

BALFOUR: We are overlooking the fact that there are large areas of agreement contained in the President's Fourteen Points, and most of us would be willing to agree to most of them. There may be points at issue, but I feel certain that on those we can arrive at a workable compromise. Germany is obviously intent on driving a wedge between the Allies and the Associated Powers, and we should make every effort to avoid that trap.

The fiery Welshman took his cue from his Foreign Secretary.

LLOYD GEORGE: Except for Point Two, I have no objections to raise. Let us all of us then go on with the terms of the armistice, and in the meantime each of us, France, Great Britain, and Italy make a draft of our reservations of the Fourteen Points and see tomorrow whether we cannot agree on a common draft.[17]

* In a cable to President Wilson, House says: "My statement had a very exciting effect on those present," as well it might since it amounted to a threat to break up the wartime coalition. (Ed.)

After a short period of desultory discussion, in the course of which Sonnino complained that Point Nine, giving Italy only "clearly recognizable lines of nationality," was totally unacceptable, and Clemenceau brought up the question of what was meant by Point Three, "equality of trade conditions," the meeting broke up, and the Allied statesmen dispersed to formulate their objections to the President's Fourteen Points of Peace.

Colonel House spent a restless night at 78, rue de l'Université. Although an open break among the Allies had not occurred, it had merely been postponed, unless he could somehow get the statesmen of Great Britain, France and Italy to drop their reservations. On the morrow an avalanche of Allied objections would descend upon him, and if he could not stem it, the result would be an almost flat rejection of the President's peace program. Having cabled a full report of the meeting to the "Governor"—the title by which the President was addressed by his most intimate admirers such as Colonel House and Joseph Tumulty, his secretary—he went to bed. He recorded in his diary:

> This morning, around three o'clock I was awakened . . . and I fell to thinking about the dilemma I was in with the three Prime Ministers. It then occurred to me that there was a way out of the difficulty. I would tell them that if they did not accept the President's Fourteen Points and other terms enunciated since January 8, I would advise the President to go before Congress and lay the facts before it, giving the terms which England, France and Italy insisted upon, and ask the advice of Congress whether the United States should make peace with Germany now that she has accepted the American terms, or whether we should go on fighting until Germany had accepted the terms of France, England, and Italy, whatever they might be. . . . I turned over and went to sleep, knowing I had found a solution to a very troublesome problem.[18]

The next morning House met a very much mellowed Lloyd George who had drafted a memorandum that differed greatly from the violent objections he had raised the preceding afternoon. He proposed that it serve as the Allied reply to the President. To the Colonel's surprise, Clemenceau raised no objection to the Prime Minister's draft. And when House tried his night-time inspiration on the Tiger, and asked him not to raise any objections, the French Premier pocketed the long list of reservations he had drawn up. Sonnino tried once again to raise the question of Point Nine, but was brushed off by the British and French Premiers, who pointed out that they were now dealing with the German, not the Austrian, Peace Treaty.

House's position was greatly bolstered by a cable from the President that fully endorsed his stand on the freedom of the seas problem.

REFERRING TO YOUR # 12 I FREELY AND SYMPATHETICALLY RECOGNIZE THE STRONG POSITION AND NECESSITIES OF GREAT BRITAIN WITH REGARD TO THE USE OF THE SEA FOR DEFENCE, BOTH AT HOME AND THROUGHOUT THE EMPIRE AND ALSO REALIZE THAT FREEDOM OF THE SEAS NEEDS CAREFUL DEFINITION AND IS FULL OF QUESTIONS UPON WHICH THERE SHOULD BE FULLEST DISCUSSION AND THE MOST LIBERAL EXCHANGE OF VIEWS. BUT I AM NOT CLEAR THAT THE ALLIES QUOTED IN YOUR # 12 DEFINITELY ACCEPT THE PRINCIPLE OF FREEDOM OF THE SEAS AND MEAN TO RESERVE ONLY SUCH AS FREE DISCUSSION AND LIMITATIONS. PLEASE INSIST THAT IT BE MADE CLEAR BEFORE I DECIDE WHETHER IT MUST BE ALTERED, OR GO AGAIN TO CONGRESS WHO WILL HAVE NO SYMPATHY OR WISH THAT AMERICAN LIFE AND PROPERTY BE SACRIFICED FOR BRITISH NAVAL CONTROL. I CANNOT RECEDE FROM MY POSITION TAKEN IN # 5, THOUGH, OF COURSE, I DEPEND ON YOUR DISCRETION TO INSIST AT THE RIGHT TIME AND IN THE RIGHT WAY ON TERMS 1, 2, 3, AND 14, AS ESSENTIALLY AMERICAN TERMS IN THE PROGRAM AND I CANNOT CHANGE WHAT OUR TROOPS ARE FIGHTING FOR OR CONSENT TO END WITH EUROPEAN ARRANGEMENTS OF PEACE. FREEDOM OF THE SEAS WILL NOT HAVE TO BE DISCUSSED WITH GERMANS IF WE AGREE AMONG OURSELVES BEFOREHAND, BUT WILL BE IF WE MUST. BLOCKADE IS ONE OF MANY THINGS WHICH WILL REQUIRE IMMEDIATE RE-DEFINITION IN VIEW OF THE MANY NEW CIRCUMSTANCES OF WARFARE DEVELOPED BY THIS WAR. THERE IS NO DANGER OF ITS BEING ABOLISHED.

WOODROW WILSON[19]

After censoring out the passage about sacrificing American lives to British naval control, House read the cable to a meeting on November 3rd. Lloyd George repeated that he could not and would not accept the principle of the freedom of the seas, and when Clemenceau suggested that there was no real harm in accepting it in principle, Lloyd George begged to disagree.

LLOYD GEORGE: I could not accept the principle of Freedom of the Seas. It has got associated in the public mind with the blockade. It's no good saying that I accept the principle. It would only mean that in a week's time another Prime Minister would be here who would say that he cannot accept this principle. The English people will not look at it. On this point the nation is absolutely solid. It's no use for me to say that I can accept when I know that I am not speaking for the British Nation.

HOUSE: Would you be willing to discuss the problem freely at the Peace Conference, if you can not accept the principle at this time? Or does your reservation imply a peremptory challenge of the President's position?

LLOYD GEORGE: This formula does not challenge the position of the U. S. in the least. All we say is that we reserve the freedom to discuss the point when we go to the peace conference. I don't despair of coming to an agreement.

HOUSE: I wish you would write something I could send to the President.[20]

Lloyd George obligingly produced the letter, which was all that Colonel House was able to get from him for the moment.

MY DEAR COLONEL HOUSE,

I write to confirm the statement I made in the course of our talk this afternoon at your house when I told you that "we were quite willing to discuss the freedom of the seas in the light of the new conditions which have arisen in the course of the present war." In our judgment this most important subject can only be dealt with satisfactorily through the freest debate and the most liberal exchange of views. I send you this letter after having had an opportunity of talking this matter over with the Foreign Secretary who quite agrees.

Ever sincerely

[signed] D. LLOYD GEORGE[21]

As it turned out, discussion of the freedom of the seas problem was carefully avoided at the Conference, and its solution, such as it was, was left to Anglo-American discussions during the twenties and thirties.

One more minor difficulty presented itself before the final Allied consent to the Fourteen Points could be cabled to Washington. M. Hymans, the Belgian Foreign Minister, seconded by Lloyd George, brought up Point Three (removal, as far as possible, of all economic barriers). Clemenceau however argued that the article was self-limiting, due to the "as far as possible" clause, and Hymans dropped his objections.

On November 4th the Supreme War Council finally accepted the text of the Allied reply to President Wilson. In a cable to the President Colonel House was able proudly to boast: ". . . we have won a diplomatic victory in getting the Allies to accept our principles. . . . This was done in the face of a hostile and influential junta in the U. S. and the thoroughly unsympathetic personnel constituting the Entente governments."[22]

The Colonel could not possibly know how Pyrrhic that victory would turn out to have been, but he was quite correct when he made this entry in his diary:

> I am glad the exceptions were made, for it emphasizes the acceptance of the Fourteen Points. Had they not dissented . . . they would have been in a better position to object to them at the Peace Conference.[23]

Lloyd George's reservations were incorporated in the vitally important American note to Germany of November 6, 1918.

> In my note of October 23rd, 1918, I advised you that the President had transmitted his correspondence with the German authorities to the Governments with which the Government of the United States is associated as belligerent, with the suggestion that, if those Governments were disposed to effect peace upon the terms and principles indicated, their military advisers and the military advisers of the United States be asked to submit to the Governments associated against Germany the necessary terms of such an armistice as would fully protect the interests of the people involved and ensure to the associated Governments the unrestricted power to safeguard and enforce the details of the peace to which the German Government had agreed, provided they deemed such an armistice possible from the military point of view.

The President is now in receipt of a memorandum of observations by the Allied Governments on this correspondence, which is as follows:

> "The Allied Governments have given careful consideration to the correspondence which has passed between the President of the United States and the German Government. Subject to the qualifications which follow they declare their willingness to make peace with the Government of Germany on the terms of peace laid down in the President's address to Congress on January 8, 1918, and the principles of settlement enunciated in his subsequent addresses. They must point out however, that clause two, relating to what is usually described as freedom of the seas, is open to various interpretations, some of which they could not accept. They must therefore, reserve to themselves complete freedom on this subject when they enter the peace conference.
>
> "Further, in the conditions of peace laid down in his address to Congress of January 8, 1918, the President declared that invaded territories must be restored as well as evacuated and freed, the Allied Governments feel that no doubt ought to be allowed to exist as to what the provision implies. By it they understand that compensation will be made by Germany for all damage done to the civilian population of the Allies and their property by the aggression of Germany by land, by sea, and from the air."

I am instructed by the President to say that he is in agreement with the interpretation set forth in the last paragraph of the memorandum, above quoted. I am further instructed by the President to request you to notify the German Government that Marshal Foch has been authorized by the Government of the United States and by the Allied Governments to receive properly accredited representatives of the German Government, and to communicate to them the terms of an armistice.

ROBERT LANSING[24]

This note, together with the German reply accepting the terms under which the German armies were to retire from occupied territories and under which Germany was to accept the Allied armistice terms, constitutes what became known as the "Pre-Armistice Agreement," a statement of principles upon which the peace treaty with Germany was to be drawn up. By most Allied as well as by German statesmen it was considered a binding contract, and a great many of the post-Treaty arguments were based on the contention that the Versailles Treaty did not conform to the Pre-Armistice Agreement.

In later years Clemenceau was heavily attacked in France for "having committed the unpardonable sin of accepting that Agreement instead of going on and signing the armistice in Berlin." He defended himself thus:

> . . . my duty was very simple. Mr. Wilson, when he sent us the American army, had put to us the famous Fourteen Points. Were we prepared to cease fighting on the day the Germans accepted these various points? If I had refused to reply in the affirmative it would have been nothing less than a breach of faith, and the country would have denounced me with one voice, while our soldiers would have disowned me, and with good reason. We, like our Allies, were unanimous for acceptance. It was France's peace, it was the Allies' peace. We had no right to risk another human life for another result. . . . After I had promised, with everyone's approval, to agree to President Wilson's conditions, conditions which were as wise as they were firm, was I likely to confront him with a refusal at the moment when he asked me to fulfill our engagements? I was not the man to turn traitor to myself as well as to my country. . . .[25]

These statements contrast queerly with the minutes of the London meeting with Colonel House at which Clemenceau denied having made any commitments to the President's Fourteen Points of Peace. The truth of the matter is that, prior commitments or not, neither he nor Lloyd George could afford to prolong the war one day longer than necessary for victory.

While these inter-Allied discussions were going on, Marshal Foch was busy drawing up the terms of the armistice itself. The Allied Commander in Chief was given a free hand as far as the strictly military terms of the armistice were concerned.

On October 30, 1918, House cabled the President from Paris.

> I ascertained that George and Clemenceau believed the terms of the armistice, both naval and military, were too severe and that they should be modified. George stated he thought it might be unwise to insist on the occupation of the east bank of the Rhine. Clemenceau

stated that he could not maintain himself in the Chamber of Deputies unless this was made a part of the armistice to be submitted to the Germans, and that the French army would also insist on this as their due after the long occupation of French soil by the Germans; but he gave us his word of honor that France would withdraw after the peace conditions had been fulfilled.* I am inclined to sympathize with the position taken by Clemenceau.[26]

Clemenceau and Foch both won their points, the terms were not modified and occupation of the left bank of the Rhine became part of the armistice terms.

Clemenceau scored one more important point during the discussion of the armistice terms. He insisted:

that there should be a clause in the Armistice demanding reparation for damages. To this Lloyd George objected that he was willing to insert a clause covering restitution of stolen property, but that reparation was rather a condition of peace. House added, and Sonnino agreed, that the subject was so large that it would threaten to hold up the Armistice indefinitely.

On the afternoon of November 2, Clemenceau returned to his demand for a reference to reparations in the Armistice. "It would not be understood in France," he said, "if we omitted such a clause. All I am asking is simply the addition of three words 'reparation for damages,' without other commentary."

"Can that be made a condition of the Armistice?" asked Hymans, representing Belgium.

"It is rather a condition of peace," said Sonnino.

"It is useless," said Bonar Law, "to insert in the Armistice a clause which cannot be immediately carried out."

"I wish only to make mention of the principle," returned Clemenceau. "You must not forget that the French people are among those who have suffered most; they would not understand our failure to allude to this matter."

"If you are going to deal with the question of reparation for damages on land, you must also mention the question of reparation for ships sunk," said Lloyd George.

"That is all covered in my formula of three words," said Clemen-

* Inasmuch as Clemenceau was determined that the left bank of the Rhine should be removed from German sovereignty by the terms of the peace treaty, he could afford to give this word of honor. (Ed.)

ceau, " 'reparation for damages,' and I beg the Council to comprehend the feeling of the French people."

"Yes, and of the Belgian," interjected Hymans. "And the Serbs," said Vesnitch. "Italians also," added Sonnino.

Once more Bonar Law objected that reparations was not properly a topic to be introduced into the Armistice clauses; that special mention was made of it as an underlying condition of peace in the note which was to be sent to President Wilson and that it was useless to repeat it.

But the insistence of Clemenceau carried the Council. At the close of the session an addition was made to the clause, which had momentous consequences. "It would be prudent," said Klotz, French Minister for Finance, "to put at the head of the financial section a clause reserving future claims of the Allies and I propose the following text: 'With the reservation that any future claims or demands on the part of the Allies remain unaffected.' " The clause was accepted, and upon this apparently innocent sentence was later based the French claim that, as regards reparations, they were not bound by the terms of the pre-Armistice agreement, but were authorized to insert in the conditions of peace any terms that seemed to them justified by circumstances.

Colonel House made no further objection to the French demand for the insertion of the topic of reparations in the Armistice. In fact it was he who at the close of the discussion, appreciating the insistence of Clemenceau, proposed the adoption of the French Prime Minister's formula. His feeling was that, although out of place in the Armistice, it was harmless and, as Clemenceau indicated, a sop to French sentiment. The basis for the peace, House argued, was to be found not in the Armistice clauses, which merely put an end to the war, but rather in the pre-Armistice correspondence between the Allies, President Wilson, and Germany, in which the principles of the settlement were carefully defined. But the references to reparations in the Armistice Convention were destined to return to plague the American delegates at the Peace Conference.[27]

The naval terms, which Marshal Foch had proposed, were actually modified at the insistence of the Allied statesmen, who feared that they might prevent Germany from signing the armistice. Lloyd George (of all people) proposed that instead of making Germany surrender all submarines and the whole High

Sea Fleet, only submarines and battle cruisers should be surrendered, leaving the battleships to be interned. With some modifications these were the terms which were ultimately accepted and which led to the internment of the High Sea Fleet at Scapa Flow.*

By November 5th the armistice terms had been agreed upon by the Allied leaders and President Wilson was asked to request the Germans to send parliamentaries to the Allied Commander in Chief, who would hand them the terms.

The most important points of the Armistice were:

A.—On the Western Front.

I.—Cessation of hostilities on land and in the air six hours after the signature of the Armistice.

II.—Immediate evacuation of the invaded countries:—Belgium, France, Luxembourg, as well as Alsace-Lorraine, so ordered as to be completed within fifteen days from the signature of the Armistice. German troops which have not evacuated the above-mentioned territories within the period fixed will be made prisoners of war. Joint occupation by the Allied and United States forces shall keep pace with evacuation in these areas. All movements of evacuation or occupation shall be regulated in accordance with a Note (Annexe No. 1), drawn up at the time of signature of the Armistice.

III.—Repatriation, beginning at once, to be completed within fifteen days, of all inhabitants of the countries above enumerated (including hostages, persons under trial, or convicted).

IV.—Surrender in good condition by the German Armies of the following war material:

5,000 guns (2,500 heavy, 2,500 field).

25,000 machine-guns.

3,000 trench mortars.

1,700 fighting and bombing aeroplanes—in the first place, all D 7's and all night-bombing aeroplanes.

The above to be delivered *in situ* to the Allied and United States troops in accordance with the detailed conditions laid down in the Note (Annexe 1) determined at the time of the signing of the Armistice.

* Where the German maintenance crews scuttled the vessels some weeks later, thus relieving the Peace Conference of a major bone of contention.

v.—Evacuation by the German Armies of the districts on the left bank of the Rhine. These districts on the left bank of the Rhine shall be administered by the local authorities under the control of the Allied and United States Armies of Occupation.

The occupation of these territories by Allied and United States troops shall be assured by garrisons holding the principal crossings of the Rhine (Mainz, Coblenz, Cologne), together with bridgeheads at these points of a 30-kilometre (about 19 miles) radius on the right bank, and by garrisons similarly holding the strategic points of the area.

A neutral zone shall be reserved on the right bank of the Rhine, between the river and a line drawn parallel to the bridgeheads and to the river and 10 kilometres (6¼ miles) distant from them, between the Dutch frontier and the Swiss frontier.

The evacuation by the enemy of the Rhine districts (right and left banks) shall be so ordered as to be completed within a further period of 16 days, in all 31 days after the signing of the Armistice.

All movements of evacuation and occupation shall be regulated according to the Note (Annexe 1) determined at the time of the signing of the Armistice. . . .

IX.—The right of requisition shall be exercised by the Allied and United States armies in all occupied territories, save for settlement of accounts with authorized persons.

The upkeep of the troops of occupation in the Rhine districts (excluding Alsace-Lorraine) shall be charged to the German Government. . . .

B.—Clauses relating to the Eastern Frontiers of Germany.

XII.—All German troops at present in any territory which before the war formed part of Austria-Hungary, Roumania, or Turkey, shall withdraw within the frontiers of Germany as they existed on 1st August, 1914, and all German troops at present in territories which before the war formed part of Russia, must likewise return to within the frontiers of Germany as above defined, as soon as the Allies shall think the moment suitable, having regard to the internal situation of these territories. . . .

XV.—Annulment of the treaties of Bucharest and Brest-Litovsk and of the supplementary treaties.

XVI.—The Allies shall have free access to the territories evacuated by the Germans on their Eastern frontier, either through Danzig or by the Vistula, in order to convey supplies to the populations of these territories or for the purpose of maintaining order.

C.—Clause relating to East Africa.

XVII.—Evacuation of all German forces operating in East Africa within a period specified by the Allies. . . .

E.—Naval Conditions.

XX.—Immediate cessation of all hostilities at sea, and definite information to be given as to the position and movements of all German ships.

Notification to be given to neutrals that freedom of navigation in all territorial waters is given to the Navies and Mercantile Marines of the Allied and Associated Powers, all questions of neutrality being waived.

XXI.—All Naval and Mercantile Marine prisoners of war of the Allied and Associated Powers in German hands to be returned without reciprocity.

XXII.—To surrender at the ports specified by the Allies and the United States all submarines at present in existence (including all submarine cruisers and minelayers), with armament and equipment complete. Those that cannot put to sea shall be deprived of armament and equipment, and shall remain under the supervision of the Allies and the United States. Submarines ready to put to sea shall be prepared to leave German ports immediately on receipt of a wireless order to sail to the port of surrender, the remainder to follow as early as possible. The conditions of this Article shall be completed within 14 days of the signing of the Armistice.

XXIII.—The following German surface warships, which shall be designated by the Allies and the United States of America, shall forthwith be disarmed and thereafter interned in neutral ports, or, failing them, Allied ports, to be designated by the Allies and the United States of America, and placed under the surveillance of the Allies and the United States of America, only care and maintenance parties being left on board, namely:

6 battle cruisers.
10 battleships.
8 light cruisers (including two minelayers).
50 destroyers of the most modern type.

All other surface warships (including river craft) are to be concentrated in German Naval bases, to be designated by the Allies and the United States of America, completely disarmed and placed under the supervision of the Allies and the United States of America. All vessels of the Auxiliary Fleet are to be disarmed. All vessels specified for internment shall be ready to leave German ports seven days after the signing of the Armistice. Directions for the voyage shall be given by wireless. . . .

XXVI.—The existing blockade conditions set up by the Allied and Associated Powers are to remain unchanged, and all German merchant ships found at sea are to remain liable to capture. The Allies and United States contemplate the provisioning of Germany during the Armistice as shall be found necessary.

XXVII.—All Aerial Forces are to be concentrated and immobilized in German bases to be specified by the Allies and the United States of America. . . .

XXX.—All merchant ships at present in German hands belonging to the Allied and Associated Powers are to be restored to ports specified by the Allies and the United States of America without reciprocity. . . .

XXXIII.—No transfers of German merchant shipping of any description to any neutral flag are to take place after signature of the Armistice.

F.—Duration of Armistice.

XXXIV.—The duration of the Armistice is to be 36 days, with option to extend. During this period, on failure of execution of any of the above clauses, the Armistice may be repudiated by one of the contracting parties on 48 hours' previous notice. It is understood that failure to execute Articles III and XVIII completely in the periods specified is not to give reason for a repudiation of the Armistice, save where such failure is due to malice aforethought.

To ensure the execution of the present convention under the most favourable conditions, the principle of a permanent International Armistice Commission is recognized. This Commission shall act under the supreme authority of the High Command, military and naval, of the Allied Armies.[28]

In the early morning hours of November 7th Marshal Foch received the following telegram:

THE GERMAN GOVERNMENT HAVING BEEN INFORMED BY THE PRESIDENT OF THE UNITED STATES THAT MARSHAL FOCH HAS BEEN AUTHORIZED TO RECEIVE THE ACCREDITED REPRESENTATIVES OF THE GERMAN GOVERNMENT TO COMMUNICATE TO THEM THE CONDITIONS OF THE ARMISTICE, HAS NOMINATED THE FOLLOWING REPRESENTATIVES: GENERAL OF INFANTRY VON GUNDEL, SECRETARY OF STATE ERZBERGER, AMBASSADOR COUNT OBERNDORFF, GENERAL VON WINTERFELDT, CAPTAIN VANSELOW OF THE IMPERIAL NAVY. THEY ASK TO BE INFORMED BY WIRELESS OF THE PLACE WHERE THEY CAN MEET MARSHAL FOCH. THE GERMAN GOVERNMENT WOULD BE GLAD IF, IN THE INTEREST OF HUMANITY, THE ARRIVAL OF THE GERMAN DELEGATION ON THE ALLIED FRONT SHOULD BE THE OCCASION FOR A PROVISIONAL SUSPENSION OF HOSTILITIES. GERMAN HIGH COMMAND[29]

Meanwhile the Kaiser had retired to Spa where the Headquarters of the German High Command were situated. Holed up in a gingerbread chalet, he steadfastly resisted the urgent telephonic pleas of his Chancellor who implored his monarch to abdicate and thereby give Germany a chance of obtaining acceptable peace terms. Even after his generals, including Field Marshal von Hindenburg, informed him that he could no longer depend on the support of his army, the Kaiser still could not bring himself to take the final step.

In Berlin the mounting tide of revolution finally forced Prince Max von Baden to make the public announcement that the Kaiser had abdicated. When the news of his kinsman's "treasonable act" reached the Kaiser he finally made up his mind and left by train for Holland.

At seven A.M. the same day the German plenipotentiaries reported at Rethondes in the Compiègne Forest as ordered by Marshal Foch. However, an important last-minute switch had been made in the makeup of the German delegation. The German Foreign Office substituted a civilian, Secretary of State Erzberger, for General von Gundel as head of the delegation. In later years, therefore, the German army faction was able to claim that the armistice had been the result of civilian treachery and not an honorable armistice concluded between army commanders.

Clemenceau has described what took place when the German delegates presented themselves at Rethondes.

The German delegates take places at the table.

Maréchal Foch asks the delegates the purpose of their visit. M. Erzberger replies that the delegation has come to receive the propositions of the Allied Powers so as to arrive at an armistice on land, on sea, and in the air, on all fronts and the colonies. Maréchal Foch replies that he has no proposition to make. Count Oberndorff asks how they should express themselves? He himself is not apt at phrases. He may say that the delegation asks for the conditions of the armistice.

Maréchal Foch replies that he has no conditions to offer. M. Erzberger reads the text of the last paragraph of President Wilson's note of November 6th which says that Maréchal Foch is authorized to make known the conditions of the armistice.

Maréchal Foch replies that he is authorized to make known these conditions *if* the German delegates ask for an armistice. "Do you ask for an armistice? If you ask for it, I can make known the conditions under which it can be obtained."

M. Erzberger and Count Oberndorff both declare that they ask for an armistice.

Maréchal Foch then declares that he will have the conditions read. As the text is rather long, the principal paragraphs will first be read by themselves. The entire text will then be handed to the delegates.

General Weygand reads the principal clauses of the armistice conditions.

General von Winterfeldt declares that he is entrusted with a special mission by the High Command and the German Government. He reads the following declaration:

"The armistice conditions we have just listened to demand careful examination. In view of our intention to reach a settlement the examination will be made as rapidly as possible; all the same, it will require a certain amount of time, so much more since it is necessary to consult with our Government and the High Command. During this time the struggle between our armies will continue and will demand necessarily numerous victims among the troops and the people, who will have fallen uselessly at the last minute and who might be saved for their families. In these circumstances the German Government and the High Military Command have the honor to revive the proposition they made day before yesterday by radio telegram, to wit, that Maréchal Foch might agree to fix immediately and for the entire front a provisional suspension of hostilities, to begin today at a certain hour and the details of which might be arranged as soon as possible."

Maréchal Foch replied: "I am General-in-Chief of the Allied Armies and Representative of the Allied Governments. The Governments have drawn up their conditions. Hostilities cannot cease before the signing of the armistice. I too am indeed anxious to reach a conclusion and I will help you as far as possible. But hostilities cannot cease before the signing of the armistice."

The German delegates made no observations with regard to either the bridgeheads or the fleet. Their line is to say that they will be overwhelmed by Bolshevism if we do not help them resist it, and that afterwards we shall be invaded by the same plague. They asked that they be permitted to retire more slowly from the left bank of the Rhine, saying that they must have the means to combat Bolshevism and to re-establish order. Foch replied that they could form their army on the right bank. They also objected that we were taking too many machine-guns and that they would have none left with which to fire on their compatriots. Foch replied that they still had their rifles. They also asked what we were going to do with the left bank of the Rhine. Foch answered that he did not know and that it was none of his business. Finally, they asked to be fed by us, saying that they would otherwise die of hunger. Foch replied that they should put their merchant marine in our pool and thus could be fed. They replied that they would prefer to receive *laisser-passer* for their own boats. They complained that we were taking much too many locomotives, considering that theirs were scattered everywhere. Foch replied that we were only asking for what they had taken from us. They are much depressed. From time to time a sob escaped from the throat of von Winterfeldt. . . .[30]

A heavy German artillery barrage prevented the delegates from getting back to the German lines until evening, but on November 9th General Headquarters in Spa were able to cable the gist of the armistice terms to the Foreign Office in Berlin. Hindenburg immediately cabled a vigorous protest against the armistice terms to the War Ministry in Berlin.

An attempt must be made to procure the modification of the following points in the Armistice terms.

1. Extension of the date of evacuation to two months, the greater part of this time being needed for the evacuation of the Rhine

Provinces, the Palatinate and Hesse, otherwise the Army will collapse, as the technical execution of the terms is absolutely impossible.

2. The right wing of the Army must be allowed to march through the corner of Maestricht.
3. Abandonment of neutral zones for reasons of internal order, at least must be restricted to ten kilometers.
4. Honorable capitulation of East Africa.
5. A considerable reduction must be effected in the railway material to be surrendered; otherwise industry will be seriously endangered. With regard to paragraph 7, only a small number of personnel can be left; more detailed arrangements required at this point.
6. Army only provided with 18,000 motor lorries, fifty percent available for use; surrender of number demanded would mean complete breakdown of Army supply system.
7. Only 1,700 pursuit-bombing aeroplanes in existence.
8. If there is to be one-sided surrender of prisoners of war, at least present arrangements as to treatment of latter must remain in force.
9. The blockade must be raised so far as food supplies are concerned. Commissioners to deal with regulations of food supplies are on the way.

If it is impossible to gain these points, it would nevertheless be advisable to conclude the agreement.

In case of refusal of points 1, 4, 5, 6, 8, 9, a fiery protest should be raised, and an appeal addressed to Wilson.

Please notify Government of outcome of these matters at earliest possible moment.

VON HINDENBURG[31]

The Chancellor, however, paid little heed to these protests and cabled the Armistice Commission:

You are authorized to sign the armistice. You will at the same time add the following declaration to the protocol: "The German Government will make every effort to execute the conditions imposed. The undersigned, however, conceive it to be their duty to call attention to the fact that execution of certain points of these conditions will plunge the population of the unoccupied parts of Germany into the misery of starvation. The abandonment of all provisions in the territories to be evacuated—provisions which were destined to feed the army—as well as the curtailment of the traffic facilities which is equal to an abstraction, while the blockade is at the same time maintained, makes the nourishment of the nation and any organized distribution impossible. The undersigned therefore request that they be allowed to negotiate on such alterations of these points as will ensure the question of nourishment." I also agree that the Supreme Army Command be permitted, through His Excellency Erzberger, to effect the capitulation of East Africa in an honorable manner, and furthermore to arrange for the march of our troops through the corner of Maestricht.

IMPERIAL CHANCELLOR[32]

On November 11th the Armistice documents were signed and at 11:55 A.M. the guns fell silent. After fifteen hundred and sixty-three days, for the first time, all was quiet on the Western Front.

II
Pre-Conference Positions

The leaders of the Allied and Associated Powers had agreed to make Wilson's Fourteen Points their basis for drawing up a peace treaty; it now remained for each of them to attain his individual war aims within the framework to which he had reluctantly agreed.

The French Position

The French were the first to produce a full-fledged peace program. In effect it had been ready in their Foreign Office ever since the days of Louis XIV. France's peace aims were very simple: guaranteed security for France. The peace which was to be hammered out would have to make quite sure that Germany would never again be able to menace her.

That meant, above all, pushing Germany back across the Rhine and permanently occupying strategic bridgeheads on the east bank of the river, as well as reducing Germany's territory and natural resources in the east. These had been France's goals ever since the war had started, but the Quai d'Orsay took great care to keep them secret. Early in 1916 the British government had suggested to its Allies that it might be a good idea to coordinate war aims, but France had been reluctant at the time to disclose her territorial ambitions for fear that the British might disapprove. The French Foreign Office wanted to make sure first that it had the support of some major ally, and M. Paul Doumerge, one of France's ablest diplomats, was therefore dispatched to St. Petersburg to get the approval of the Czar's government.

Imperial Russia proved as eager as France to conclude an agreement. In an exchange of notes between the two governments, Russia, in return for a completely free hand on its western frontiers, agreed to support France's territorial aspirations on the Rhine.

1. Alsace-Lorraine to be restored to France.
2. The frontiers are to be extended at least up to the limits of the former principality of Lorraine, and are to be drawn up at the discretion of the French Government so as to provide for the strategical needs and for the inclusion in French territory of the entire iron ore district of Lorraine and the entire coal district of the Saar Valley.
3. The rest of the territories situated on the left bank of the Rhine which now form part of the German Empire are to be entirely separated from Germany and freed from all political and economic dependence on her.
4. The territories on the left bank of the Rhine outside French territory are to be constituted an autonomous and neutral state, and are to be occupied by French troops until such time as the enemy states have completely satisfied all the conditions and guarantees indicated in the Treaty of Peace.[1]

As France's luck would have it, however, the Russian Revolution broke out within a month of the exchange of notes. As soon as the Bolsheviks got into power they threw open the Czarist Foreign Office archives and France's war aims became public knowledge. The British pricked up their ears and questions were asked in the House of Commons. Speaking for the Government, Mr. Arthur Balfour replied on December 19, 1917:

His Majesty's Government have never expressed their approval of this plan, nor do I believe it represents the policy of successive French Governments who have held office during the war. Never did we desire and never did we encourage the idea, that a bit of Germany should be cut off from the parent state and erected in some kind of . . . independent government on the left bank of the Rhine. His Majesty's Government were never aware that was seriously entertained by any French statesman.[2]

The Quai d'Orsay remained discreetly silent.

The defection of her Russian ally necessitated a slight change in France's plans. Inasmuch as Russia could no longer be relied upon to annex major portions of eastern Germany, a strong Polish state, the stronger the better, would have to be created from German, Austrian and Russian territories. This had the great advantage of conforming with the war aims of both Great Britain and the United States.

But to keep Germany from menacing French security again, territorial adjustments were not enough. The French program also included keeping Germany economically on a subsistence level for at least one generation, preferably for two or more. This was to be achieved by making Germany assume the total cost of the war, no matter how long it might take her to pay it; and by simultaneously depriving her of the main sources of her wealth, her coal and iron ore.

The French statesmen were fully aware that their program ran counter to the letter and the spirit of President Wilson's Fourteen Point Peace Program, to which France had subscribed by accepting the Pre-Armistice Agreement. But they put their faith in one of the subsequent "points"—the nineteenth—which Wilson himself had so strongly stressed in his fourth note to Germany: "All arbitrary power shall be reduced to virtual impotence." Surely, French diplomacy would be able to convince America and Britain that France remained in permanent peril unless Germany, an arbitrary power if ever they had seen one, was reduced to "virtual impotence." Regardless of what France's Allies might think of her program, her leaders were committed to it and they had the unqualified support of the French people.

Georges Clemenceau, the old Tiger, France's "civilian field marshal,"* was at the height of his popularity at the war's end. In spite of the many bitter enemies he had accumulated among French politicians, the French people stood solidly behind the man who, more than any other, represented the "win-the-war" spirit, and they had every faith that he would also win the peace for them. Clemenceau had a dictator-like grip on the country; he commanded a solid majority in the Chamber of Deputies and completely controlled the nation's press. With sovereign disregard for all political sensibilities, he picked his fellow delegates

* Mermeix (Gabriel Terrail).

to the Conference not from among the great names of France, but from among those on whose loyalty he could count and who could be relied upon to follow orders unquestioningly.

President Wilson's chief public relations officer and official biographer, Ray Stannard Baker, described the organization of the French Peace Conference team:

The French position at Paris was set forth and defended with matchless ingenuity and obstinacy. No matter what party a leader belonged to, or whether he was a statesman, a soldier, a diplomat, or a financier, he was first of all French—100% French!—and moved straight ahead securing French safety. Foch had a military plan of safety, Bourgeois a diplomatic plan, Loucheur and Klotz an economic plan (but the coordination between them was perfect), and Clemenceau was the supreme strategist of the entire campaign. If the French did not achieve all they sought at Paris, it was not for lack of sheer intelligence! The French had their entire programme worked out before the Peace Conference met. They were the first to place their memoranda in the President's hands. No other nation approached them—unless it was the Japanese—in diplomatic preparedness or singleness of purpose. The British seemed not prepared at all; always appeared to live from hand to mouth, diplomatically speaking, and yet never lost a trick, while the Italians were so divided in their inner councils as never to strike any clear note.[3]

Present-day students of history will have great difficulty in visualizing the wave of chauvinist hysteria which swept not only France but also England and, to a somewhat lesser extent, the United States, during the months which followed the high tension of World War I. While Woodrow Wilson and David Lloyd George had to buck that wave in pursuit of their peace programs, Georges Clemenceau could ride it as if he were on a surfboard.

On November 30th Clemenceau, Marshal Foch and General Weygand went to London to discuss the terms of the coming peace settlement with their British counterparts. After a triumphal tour of the English capital the French were to meet Lloyd George, Bonar Law, Balfour, and Field Marshal Sir Henry Wilson in Downing Street for an evening conference.

"But," Lloyd George relates:

Clemenceau had a social engagement which prevented his attendance. When I discovered the real topic which was to be raised, I realised why he was absent. The wily old politician, knowing our partiality for Foch and the debt of gratitude we owed him, deemed it advisable that the first introduction of French ideas as to the future of the Rhineland should be left to him.

This meeting is notable for being the first intimation given to the British Government that the French intended to secure control over all the territory on the left bank of the Rhine. As was his wont, Foch came straight to the point without wasting words:—

. . . Considering, however, only military necessities, whatever the form of government on the right bank of the Rhine might be, namely, an Empire, Republic or Confederation, there would be concentrated there from 55 to 75 million Germans, and these, if they wished, might endeavour to repeat the experience of 1914. In such an event, what would be the means of defence? If there were no material barrier set up, and no special precautions taken, the invasion of France, Luxembourg, and Belgium, might again be undertaken. More particularly, the Belgian coast would be easier for the enemy to reach, for they now realised the importance of it, and would endeavour to cut England from France. The natural barrier against such an invasion was the Rhine.

MR. LLOYD GEORGE asked what Marshal Foch proposed?

MARSHAL FOCH said that Germany ought to be limited to the right bank of the Rhine. Even so, she would have a population of some 60 millions. We had to consider, therefore, what arrangements should be made on the left bank of the Rhine. It was perfectly useless to rely on neutral States as barriers. Belgium and Luxembourg as neutrals really constituted no effective defence. Hence, there was nothing for it but to have an armed State ready to fight, if necessary, against Germany. He then considered the States on the left bank of the Rhine. France, Belgium, Alsace-Lorraine and Luxembourg would give an aggregate of 49 million inhabitants. If to these were added the Rhenish Provinces on the left bank of the river, there would be a population of 54,900,000. Practically, therefore, in case of a coalition of all the countries on the left bank of the Rhine, there would be 55 millions against 65 to 75 millions on the right bank. With this agglomeration of countries, namely, France, Belgium and Luxembourg, properly organised in a military sense, it would probably be practicable to hold the line of the Rhine. If, however, the line of the Rhine were forced by a surprise attack there would be a repetition of the war of 1914, and in this case it was absolutely essential that Great Britain should lend her assistance. Otherwise Germany would become the master of the whole of the West. Hence it was essential that there should be a permanent mutual assistance between all the countries of the West. France, Belgium, Luxembourg, the Rhine lands left of the river, and Great Britain—all organised for the defence of the Western front. We ought to prepare an Alliance, *including the Rhenish Provinces*, whether they were in an autonomous organisation or not (a question which he did not wish to discuss) which would provide forces fully organised to safeguard the position. The control of the organisation should be under Great Britain, France and Belgium.

MR. LLOYD GEORGE asked what he contemplated would be the political condition of the German Provinces on the left bank of the Rhine? Would they be independent, or who would govern them?

MARSHAL FOCH said that they would probably be independent. They might consist of one State or several States. All that he insisted on was that they should be included in an economic and military system. His object was not to annex or to conquer, but merely to profit by our experience and provide proper defence against the 75 million inhabitants on the right bank of the Rhine.

MR. LLOYD GEORGE asked Marshal Foch how he reconciled his proposals with President Wilson's Fourteen Points?

MARSHAL FOCH thought it could be arranged. We could defend it on the grounds that we have before us a political organisation which, in spite of treaties, Hague Conventions, etc., has launched on the world the late tremendous war. The signature of this nation to any treaty could not be trusted. As this was the case, it was necessary to take material precautions. The military barrier of the Rhine was the obvious precaution to take.

MR. LLOYD GEORGE asked what would be the position if the inhabitants of the left bank of the Rhine did not like this scheme and declared in favour of being joined to Germany?

MARSHAL FOCH said that they must be brought to our side by the attraction of our economic organisation. There would be another attraction, that it was better to be on the side of the victors than of the conquered.

Mr. Lloyd George asked whether Marshal Foch did not fear the danger of creating a new Alsace-Lorraine on the other side, which would in course of years result in a new war of revenge?

Marshal Foch said that, of course, he would take precautions to conciliate the feelings and interests of these people.

Mr. Bonar Law pointed out that Germany had said exactly the same thing. We ourselves had tried for years to conciliate the Irish.

Marshal Foch then handed Mr. Lloyd George a note he had himself prepared on this question, and asked him to read and study it. The whole problem was a very grave and large one and required mature consideration.

Mr. Lloyd George said that he would study Marshal Foch's memorandum very carefully. Anything that emanated from Marshal Foch would start with a predisposition in its favour. Nevertheless, we must be very careful not to create new problems in Europe.

Marshal Foch concurred in this consideration.

This is the first occasion when the differences between the British and French point of view about the future settlement of the territories on the left bank of the Rhine were revealed. But the fact that this was the first topic raised by the French at the first Conference held after the Armistice to discuss the Peace settlement, shows the importance they attached to it.

The first full Conference was held in Downing Street the following day. France was represented by M. Clemenceau and Marshal Foch, and Italy by Signor Orlando, the Italian Premier, and Baron Sonnino, the Foreign Secretary. Colonel House was to have represented the United States, but a serious illness which incapacitated him for some weeks detained him in Paris. America was thus unrepresented at these important preliminary conversations. It is rather characteristic of President Wilson's suspicious nature that he would not depute the task of representing his views, or even of reporting the views of the delegates of other nations, to the American Ambassadors in France or in London.[4]

From his bedside in the rue de l'Université, Colonel House cabled the President a report of the Downing Street Conference meetings. Of the private meeting between the British and Marshal Foch he, of course, had no knowledge. The Allied attempt to slip in the little word "indemnity" into the reparations resolution did not escape him in spite of his prone position.

PARIS, *December 5, 1918*

Sonnino, Lord Derby, and Clemenceau have each given me a separate account of the proceedings on December 2d and 3d at the conferences held in London between Lloyd George, Clemenceau, and Orlando. The following is a summary of these proceedings.

I. Meeting held December 2d at 11 A.M. . . .

Resolution (*b*). Establishment of Interallied Commission, Belgium, France, Great Britain, Italy, and the United States each to have three delegates thereon and Japan one delegate, to examine and report on amount enemy countries are able to pay for reparation and indemnity. Form of payment also to be considered. The Commission to meet in Paris provided the United States Government agrees. Each Government to compile its claims for reparation, which will be referred for examination by Interallied Commission to be nominated when claims are prepared. . . .

With respect to resolutions taken at meeting December 2d at 11 A.M., I am advising the Governments concerned: 1. That eliminating the word "indemnity" from Resolution (*b*) the United States agrees to resolution. . . .

With this exception I suggest that you authorize me to state that the United States agrees to these resolutions.

[signed] EDWARD HOUSE[5]

Woodrow Wilson concurred.

The French had thus been the first to lay their cards, or at least some of them, on the table. Lloyd George, however, remained icily noncommittal.

THE BRITISH POSITION

David Lloyd George was in a more difficult position than his French counterpart. The House of Commons had last been elected in 1910 and a new general election was mandatory; as Lloyd George himself said, "Someone had to go to the Peace Conference with authority from the people—to speak in their name." National elections were held in Britain on December 14, 1918. The two outstanding battle cries of Mr. Lloyd George's coalition during that election campaign were Mr. Barnes' "Hang the Kaiser" and Sir Eric Geddes' "Squeeze the lemon until you can hear the pips squeak."

The election, conducted at the height of England's chauvinistic frenzy, handed Lloyd George's coalition a resounding victory and burdened him with election promises that haunted him throughout the Paris Peace Conference. Lloyd George himself took a statesmanlike attitude during the election and, in one of his major campaign speeches, said:

> I am now coming to the reason why Germany should pay to the utmost limit of her capacity. Why have I always said "up to the limit of capacity"? Well, I will tell you at once. It is not right for the Government to raise any false hopes in the community, and least of all is it right to do so on the eve of an election. You have no right to mislead your public at any time, and I venture to claim that during the whole of this war I have never misled the public (cheers), and I am not going to do so now, whatever the result. (Cheers.) If I were to say to you, "Not merely ought Germany to pay, but we can expect every penny," I should be doing so without giving you the whole of the facts. Let me give you the facts. We consulted our financial advisers—not international financiers, those are not our financial advisers—(cheers)—I mean the financial advisers you get in every Government Department. They were doubtful. I will give you their reasons. Before the war it was estimated that the wealth of Germany was between 15,000 and 20,000 millions. That is the figure that was given as an estimate. The bill is 24,000 millions, so that if that estimate (of the total assets of Germany) was correct—that is, our estimate before the war—it is quite clear that, even if you take the whole of this wealth away—and you cannot do that, because there are 70,000,000 people who have got to work in order to make that wealth available—there would not be enough. . . .
>
> The British Imperial Committee . . . think that the assets of Germany, the wealth of Germany, have been under-estimated in the past —that she is wealthier, that she has a greater capacity, than we have given her credit for. There is no doubt that Germany herself thinks so. If that is so, you may find that the capacity will go a pretty long way. (Laughter.) . . . Let me summarize. First, as far as justice is concerned, we have an absolute right to demand the whole cost of the war from Germany. The second point is that we proposed to demand

the whole cost of the war. (Cheers.) The third point is that when you come to the exacting of it you must exact it in such a way that it does not do more harm to the country that receives it than to the country which is paying it. The fourth point is that the Committee appointed by the British Cabinet believe that it can be done. The fifth point is that the Allies, who are in exactly the same boat as we are, because they have also got a claim to great indemnities, are examining the proposal in conjunction with us. When the report comes it will be presented to the Peace Conference, which will put our demands together, and, whatever they are, they must come in front of the German war debt. (Cheers.) You may depend upon it that the first consideration in the minds of the Allies will be the interests of the people upon whom Germany has made war, and not the interests of the German people who have been guilty of this crime against humanity.[6]

Another celebrated Englishman, John Maynard Keynes, gives a slightly different version of the election campaign.

The progress of the General Election of 1918 affords a sad, dramatic history of the essential weakness of one who draws his chief inspiration not from his own true impulses, but from the grosser effluxions of the atmosphere which momentarily surrounds him. The Prime Minister's natural instincts, as they so often are, were right and reasonable. He himself did not believe in hanging the Kaiser or in the wisdom or the possibility of a great indemnity. On the 22nd of November he and Mr. Bonar Law issued their Election Manifesto. It contains no allusion of any kind either to the one or to the other, but, speaking, rather, of Disarmament and the League of Nations, concludes that "our first task must be to conclude a just and lasting peace, and so to establish the foundations of a new Europe that occasion for further wars may be for ever averted." In his speech at Wolverhampton on the eve of the Dissolution (November 24), there is no word of Reparation or Indemnity. On the following day at Glasgow, Mr. Bonar Law would promise nothing. "We are going to the Conference," he said, "as one of a number of allies, and you cannot expect a member of the Government, whatever he may think, to state in public before he goes into that Conference, what line he is going to take in regard to any particular question." But a few days later at Newcastle (November 29) the Prime Minister was warming to his work: "When Germany defeated France she made France pay. That is the principle which she herself has established. There is absolutely no doubt about the principle, and that is the principle we should proceed upon—that Germany must pay the costs of the war up to the limit of her capacity to do so."

At this stage the Prime Minister sought to indicate that he intended great severity, without raising excessive hopes of actually getting the money, or committing himself to a particular line of action at the Conference. . . . He could . . . shelter himself behind the wide discrepancy between the opinions of his different advisers, and regard the precise figure of Germany's capacity to pay as an open question in the treatment of which he must do his best for his country's interests. As to our engagements under the Fourteen Points he was always silent.

On November 30, Mr. Barnes, a member of the War Cabinet, in which he was supposed to represent Labor, shouted from a platform, "I am for hanging the Kaiser."

On December 6, the Prime Minister issued a statement of policy and aims in which he stated, with significant emphasis on the word *European*, that "All the European Allies have accepted the principle that the Central Powers must pay the cost of the war up to the limit of their capacity." . . .

The grossest spectacle was provided by Sir Eric Geddes in the Guildhall at Cambridge. An earlier speech in which, in a moment of injudicious candor, he had cast doubts on the possibility of extracting from Germany the whole cost of the war had been the object of serious suspicion, and he had therefore a reputation to regain. "We will get out of her all you can squeeze out of a lemon and a bit more," the penitent shouted, "I will squeeze her until you can hear the pips squeak"; his policy was to take every bit of property belonging to Germans in neutral and Allied countries, and all her gold and silver and her jewels, and the contents of her picture-galleries and libraries, to sell the proceeds for the Allies' benefit. "I would strip Germany," he cried, "as she has stripped Belgium."

On the same evening [December 9, 1918] the Prime Minister at Bristol withdrew in effect his previous reservations and laid down four principles to govern his Indemnity Policy, of which the chief were: First, we have an absolute right to demand the whole cost of the war; second, we propose to demand the whole cost of the war; and third, a Committee appointed by direction of the Cabinet believe that it can be done. Four days later he went to the polls.

The Prime Minister never said that he himself believed that Germany could pay the whole cost of the war. But the program became in the mouths of his supporters on the hustings a great deal more than concrete. The ordinary voter was led to believe that Germany could certainly be made to pay the greater part, if not the whole cost of the war. Those whose practical and selfish fears for the future the expenses of the war had aroused, and those whose emotions its horrors had disordered, were both provided for. A vote for a Coalition candidate meant the Crucifixion of Anti-Christ and the assumption by Germany of the British National Debt.[7]

Whether or not Lloyd George himself was responsible for the mood of the British public, the fact remains that the Coalition Government was voted back into power and Lloyd George was handed his ticket to Paris on the assumption that Germany would be made to pay the whole cost of the war, and that the Kaiser would be, if not hanged, at least severely punished.

Apart from the delightful prospect of witnessing the hanging of "Little Willie," their own Queen Victoria's grandson, and the anticipation of hearing the squeak of lemon pips, the British had few peace aims which had not already been satisfied by the war itself and by the terms of the Armistice. The German fleet was in Allied hands, as was its merchant marine and all the German colonies which the British intended to share with France and Japan. The war itself had eliminated Germany as a competitor on the world markets and heavy indemnities would keep her out for the foreseeable future, or so it was hoped. For the rest, Great Britain's main interest lay in getting a durable peace settlement which would contain as few seeds of war as possible, and in this respect her program closely paralleled Wilson's. A League of Nations, general disarmament, self-determination of nations, all were British aims as well as American.

Of course, if Wilson should again bring up that Freedom of the Seas question there would be trouble, and his idea of parceling out Germany's colonies as mandates to neutral countries would have to be quashed, and there might be some difficulties about the wartime treaties England had made to get Italy into the war and to enlist Japan's help in fighting the submarine menace in the Mediterranean, but those were problems which would have to be dealt with when and if they cropped up. On the whole, Lloyd George went to Paris in a fairly comfortable bargaining position, ideally suited to his mercurial temperament; forced to side with the French on some questions, able to go along with the Americans on others, he could let both protagonists woo his support and trade it for whatever the market would bear at any given moment.

The delegation Lloyd George took to Paris was dictated by the composition of the Coalition which he headed: there was Bonar Law, leader of the Unionist Party and Chancellor of the Exchequer; there was Arthur Balfour, Britain's elder statesman, now somewhat past his prime, a former Prime Minister and one of the creators of the Entente Cordiale, now Foreign Secretary; there was George N. Barnes, representative of British Labour, which had been admitted to the Establishment by Lloyd George's coalition; and there was Lord Milner, ex-High Commissioner for Egypt and South Africa, representing all that the British Empire ever stood for at its zenith. In addition, Lord Robert Cecil was there, throwing himself heart and soul into the making of the League; and a second echelon of experts included Lords Cunliffe and Sumner, for some reason dubbed "the heavenly twins" by their colleagues, representing the "City" at its most conservative, and Keynes and Montagu, their liberal counterparts. London was near enough to Paris that the leaders of the British delegation could, almost at a moment's notice, summon any additional help and brainpower they felt they needed.

THE AMERICAN POSITION

America's position and her war aims were universally known and almost as universally misinterpreted. Wilson's Fourteen Points had splattered around the globe like a burst of machine-gun bullets, and every nation, almost every individual in every nation, interpreted them to suit himself, stressing the points he liked, slurring over others, and ignoring the ones that went against his grain. There was sufficient lack of clarity in them and there were enough contradictions embodied in them to make this possible.

The Fourteen Points had the effect that political propaganda is designed to have; they aroused passionate hopes and they met with almost universal acclaim. But now that the war was over, the world was suddenly confronted with the realization that Wilson's Points had not solely been good propaganda; the President really meant them. The Germans and the United States between them had managed to commit the Allied Powers to the Fourteen Points as a basis for the peace to come. Now the statesmen and the peoples of the world started taking another, closer look at the Fourteen Points, the supplementary points of February 11th, the four additional points of July 4th, and the five complementary points of September 27th. They sat back and wondered how on earth the American President expected to translate them into reality.

On December 5, 1918, the "American Argosy," as Ray Stannard Baker, Wilson's press chief, called the President's expedition sailing on the SS *George Washington*, left America for Europe. The American argonauts were blissfully unaware that they were not destined to return with the Golden Fleece, and the President himself was supremely confident in spite of a severe setback he had just suffered at the hands of the American electorate; in the November elections the Democratic Party had lost control of both houses of Congress. That, in itself, would not have meant so much, for it is an accepted fact of American political life that midterm elections often go against the party in power. But what made the defeat at the polls such a stinging personal rebuke to the President was the fact that, two weeks before the election, he had issued a personal appeal to the American people to give him a "Democratic Congress" as a vote of confidence, which, he said, he needed "to be their unembarrassed spokesman at home and abroad."

Defeated by Wilson in his second try for the Presidency, Theodore Roosevelt had retired to Oyster Bay and from there the wounded Bull Moose let out a bellow which was heard around the world.

Our Allies and our enemies and Mr. Wilson himself should all understand that Mr. Wilson has no authority to speak for the American People at this time. . . . Mr. Wilson and his fourteen points and his four supplementary points and his five complementary points and all

> his utterances every which way have ceased to have any shadow of right to be accepted as expressive of the will of the American People. . . . Let the Allies impose their common will on the nations responsible for the hideous disaster which has almost wrecked mankind.[8]

Thus the President of the United States was the only delegate to the Paris Peace Conference who did not have the full and unreserved backing of the people of his own country. This did not make his job in Paris any easier. According to those closest to him at the time, however, his setback did not seem to bother the President, nor did he apparently see in it any portent of things to come.

As the "American Argosy" sailed past the Azores, Woodrow Wilson summoned his staff and outlined to them his concepts of the job ahead. No stenographic records were kept of the President's talk, but fortunately Professor Isaiah Bowman, Wilson's chief geographer and manager of Colonel House's "American Inquiry," kept extensive notes which capture the highlights of the President's briefing.

> After a few introductory remarks to the effect that he was glad to meet us, and that he welcomed the suggestion of a conference to give his views on the impending peace conference, the President remarked that *we would be the only disinterested people* at the peace conference, and that *the men whom we were about to deal with did not represent their own people.*
>
> He next mentioned the advisability of not leaving in purely political hands the question of the German indemnity, and went on to say that the matter should be studied by *a commission to determine the just claims of the Allies against Germany*, and that after such determination *Germany should be made to pay.* The President illustrated the difficulties of Allied action in imposing an indemnity by a reference to the Boxer question of a few years ago, and contrasted the attitude of the United States with that of Germany and the other European powers.
>
> As for the form of Poland's government and questions like that of the disposition of Danzig, he would only say that he was in favor of their having *any government they damned pleased*, and that he was for imposing upon them *no other provision* than those which applied to

individuals—the important thing is *what a person ought to have, not what he wants.**

The President pointed out that this was *the first conference in which decisions depended upon the opinion of mankind*, not upon the previous determinations and diplomatic schemes of the assembled representatives. With great earnestness he re-emphasized the point that unless the conference was prepared to follow the opinions of mankind and to express the will of the people rather than that of their leaders at the conference, we should soon be involved in *another breakup of the world, and when such a breakup came it would not be a war but a cataclysm.*

He spoke of the League to Enforce Peace, of the possibility of an international court with international police, etc., but added that such a plan could hardly be worked out in view of the fact that there was *to be only one conference* and it would be difficult to reach agreements respecting such matters; and he placed in opposition to this view of the work of the conference and of the project of a *League of Nations, the idea of covenants*, that is, agreements, pledges, etc., such as could be worked out in *general form* and agreed to and set in motion, and he particularly emphasized the importance of relying on *experience to guide subsequent action.*

As for the League of Nations, it implied political independence and *territorial integrity plus later alteration of terms and alteration of boundaries if it could be shown that injustice had been done or that conditions had changed.* And such alteration would be the easier to make in time as *passion subsided* and matters could be viewed in the light of justice rather than in the light of a peace conference at the close of a protracted war. He illustrated his point by the workings of the *Monroe Doctrine*, saying that what it had done for the western world the League of Nations would do for the rest of the world; and

* This last phrase seems to be contradictory of the previous sentence. As to this, Dr. Bowman wrote . . . as follows, under date of December 2, 1924:

> "The President was making two points, first that he was in favor of letting them have a wide area of liberty in which to play with reference to their form of Government; second, that so far as their outside relations were concerned he also wished to meet them halfway, but in dealing with them he wanted to set up the principle that the nationalistic desires of a particular people could not be always or fully satisfied though he did feel that the Peace Conference could give each nation what it ought to have. In the form in which my memorandum casts his thought there is room for misinterpretation. I hope this explanation makes it clear."

just as the Monroe Doctrine had developed in time to meet changing conditions, so would the League of Nations develop. In fact, he could not see how a treaty of peace could be drawn up or how both *elasticity and security could be obtained save under a League of Nations*; the opposite of such a course was to maintain the idea of the *Great Powers and of balance of power*, and such an idea *had always produced* only "*aggression and selfishness and war*"; the *people* are *heartily sick of such a course* and want the Peace Conference and the Powers to take an *entirely new course of action*.

He then turned to some specific questions and mentioned the fact that *England herself was against further extension of the British Empire*.

He thought that *some capital, as The Hague or Berne*, would *be selected for the League of Nations*, and that there would be organized in the place chosen a *Council of the League* whose members should be *the best men that could be found*. Whenever trouble arose it could be *called to the attention of the Council* and would be *given* thereby *the widest publicity*. In cases involving *discipline* there *was* the *alternative to war*, namely, the *boycott*; *trade*, including *postal and cable facilities*, could be *denied a state* that had been *guilty of wrong-doing*. Under this plan no *nation* would be *permitted to be an outlaw*, free to work out its evil designs *against a neighbor* or the world.

He thought that the *German colonies* should be *declared* the *common property* of the *League of Nations and administered by small nations*. The *resources* of each colony should be *available to all members of the League*, and in this and other matters involving international relations or German colonies or resources or territorial arrangements, the *world* would be *intolerable if only arrangement ensues*; that *this* is a *peace conference in which arrangements cannot be made in the old style*. Anticipating the difficulties of the Conference in view of the suggestion he had made respecting the desire of the people of the world for a new order, he remarked, "*If it won't work, it must be made to work*," because the world was faced by a task of terrible proportions and only the adoption of a cleansing process would recreate or regenerate the world. The *poison of Bolshevism* was *accepted readily* by the world because "*it is a protest against the way in which the world has worked*." It was to be our business at the Peace Conference to fight for a new order, "*agreeably if we can, disagreeably if necessary*."

We must *tell* the *United States the truth* about diplomacy, the Peace

Conference, the world. He here referred to the *censorship*, saying that he had arranged in the face of opposition from Europe for the *free flow of news to the United States*, though he doubted if there would be a similarly free flow to the peoples of other European countries; after a considerable effort he had secured the *removal of French and English restrictions on political news*. Thereupon he finished his reference to the frank conditions under which the Conference had to work and the necessity for getting the truth to the people by saying that *if* the *Conference did not settle things* on such a basis the Peace Treaty would not work, and "if it doesn't work right *the world will raise Hell*."

He stated that we should only go so far in *backing the claims of a given Power* as *justice required*, "and not an inch farther," and referred to a remodeled quotation from Burke: "*Only that government is free whose peoples regard themselves as free*."

The European *leaders* reminded one of the *episode in Philippopolis*—for the *space of two hours they cried*, "*Great is Diana of the Ephesians*"—to which the President appended in an aside, "*in the interest of the silversmiths*."

The President concluded the conference by saying that he hoped to see us frequently, and while he expected us to work through the Commissioners according to the organization plans of the Conference, he wanted us in case of emergency not to hesitate to bring directly to his attention any matter whose decision was in any way critical; and concluded with a sentence that deserves immortality: "*Tell me what's right and I'll fight for it; give me a guaranteed position*."[9]

President Wilson chose as his fellow delegates to the Peace Conference his Secretary of State, Robert Lansing, his personal friend and confidential adviser, Colonel Edward M. House, General Tasker H. Bliss, and a nominal Republican, Mr. Henry White, an experienced diplomat and former ambassador. Wilson's choice has been much criticized; particularly the absence of any member of the Senate has been blamed for the final rejection of the Treaty by that body. Against the advice of his best counselors, however, the President decided not to include any Republicans in his delegation, with the exception of Henry White, and he preferred to tackle the job with his own men.

To assist the delegates in their unfamiliar task, a whole shipload of experts was assembled to accompany the American delegation to Paris. It must be remembered that, while France had all the brainpower she could muster right at her beck and call, and Great Britain could and did summon any expert from London at a moment's notice, the American delegation had to bring everyone it was likely to need a distance of 3,000 miles across the ocean. The SS *George Washington* was loaded to the gunwales with brainpower and memoranda. Professors abounded: Shotwell, Seymour, Lord, Bowman; as did writers and public relations experts: Lippmann, Cobb; lawyers: Hunter-Miller, the Dulles brothers, Alan and John Foster; financial experts: Lamont, Baruch, Davis. There was no field of science and research which was not represented by some top experts. Ray Baker explains their need.

> The new way so boldly launched at Paris (so ineffectively carried out) was, first, to start with certain general principles of justice, such as those laid down by President Wilson and accepted by all the world; and, second, to have those principles applied, not by diplomats and politicians each eager to serve his own interests, but by dispassionate scientists—geographers, ethnologists, economists—who had made studies of the problems involved. It has often been charged that Wilson had no programme: this *was* his programme.
>
> The principles were before the world and had been generally accepted by it. The same specialists of the Inquiry who had aided Wilson in their formulation were accompanying him to Europe to assist in their application. The hold of the *George Washington* was crammed with the materials for scientific research on all the problems of the peace. . . . This was the American method, and it was more possible for America to practice it than for other nations because she had so few material interests to serve. It was pre-eminently President Wilson's method, and he used it, or endeavored to use it, at every turn.
>
> He saw in it the only calm, safe, sure basis upon which the peace could be made to rest; the only thing that would take it out of the realm of immediate passion, ambition, and fear.[10]

The very size and the vast amount of brainpower of the American staff proved somewhat self-defeating at the Conference. Wilson's request: "Tell me what's right—and I'll fight for it" rarely worked, for as often as not the experts, individualist all, disagreed and the President was forever struggling for that "guaranteed position" for which he had asked.

The Japanese Position

The only other power directly interested in the treaty with Germany was Japan, which aspired to several of Germany's colonies. Japan had concluded treaties with Great Britain assuring her possession of the German Pacific Island colonies north of the Equator and of a foothold in China's Shantung Province. While the United States had not been a party to these treaties, of which Washington had been ignorant until their existence was disclosed at the Paris Conference, Wilson was put in the unenviable position of either honoring those secret treaties or forcing Britain to treat them as "scraps of paper." For the first time in history Japan appeared on the scene as participant at a Conference of world-wide significance. Baker analyzes Japan's position.

Japan had two purposes at Paris:

First, a more complete recognition of her status as a great Power, equal to any other. From the very first she sought a place as one of the principal allied and associated powers and while so admitted, though against the judgment of France, she was not taken into the Supreme Council of Four, except when Far Eastern questions were discussed. This desire was also expressed in her demand that the Covenant of the League of Nations provide for "the equality of the nations and the just treatment of their nationals." It was also expressed in her steady pressure for representation on the Reparations Commission, the International Labour Board, and other similar arrangements.

Second, a recognition of her right to deal with China unhampered by the other powers. This was expressed in her insistent demand that the former German concessions in China be surrendered without condition to her, with the future disposition of these rich possessions left for decision solely between herself and China. She also demanded the ownership without restrictions of the former German islands in the North Pacific, according to her secret treaty with Great Britain and France.

In short, Japan desired all the advantages of full equality and co-operation with the other world powers in the Councils at Paris and in the League of Nations (indeed, she desired a special recognition of her racial equality), and on the other hand she wanted the right to play a lone hand in the Pacific, where her selfish interests were involved. These aims, pressed to their ultimate, were, of course, absolutely contradictory and self-destructive. A nation, no more than a man, can enjoy *all* the benefits of team-play and at the same time seize greedily upon *all* the spoils. And yet this paralyzing duality of purpose infected Paris like a wasting disease. No nation escaped it, no nation would listen to the President's warnings of the danger of such a course: that it was impossible with one foot in the Old Order and the other in the New to arrive anywhere. Thus France wanted for her security all the advantages of the new guarantees of the League, and at the same time all the advantages of the old militarism and the old diplomacy—an army on the Rhine. Even America was eagerly willing to accept all the advantages of the Versailles Treaty, and yet wished to retain and enjoy all the rights and privileges of isolation—a position utterly absurd.

This duality of interest goes to the core of the problem of the Far East: how far does Japan intend to pursue her own unrestricted way with China and indeed all eastern Asia, and how far does she intend to work in co-operation with America and other Western nations? Is China only a Japanese problem, or is it a world problem?

The same double-mindedness also extended to the delegates themselves, and in the case of certain nations—Italy, for example—resulted in a practical paralysis of efficient action. It was perhaps exhibited least of all by the Japanese and yet it was there and plainly evident at every turn. For Japan, like other nations, is torn by parties and divided as to aims. While the controlling element in Japan may have accepted, as has frequently been charged, the Prussian model in its foreign diplomacy, yet there are also liberal and democratic forces at work in Japan. Thus at Paris Baron Makino could be counted upon to support the new co-operative ideas; and he was deeply interested in the League of Nations. Very early in the Conference, January 22, we find him expressing his view of the League of Nations:

> Baron MAKINO . . . desired to say that Japan was sincerely desirous of co-operating with the Great Powers in this work, having for its object the future welfare of mankind.*

* Secret Minutes, Council of Ten, January 22.

Viscount Chinda, on the other hand, had his eye always on the islands and the rights in Shantung, and was sharp in his demands that the material interests of Japan be served. Yet the difference of attitude between Makino and Chinda never shook the Japanese unity of purpose, which was inexorably dictated from Tokyo. And at Tokyo the old military party or clique was in control.

Japan was in a stronger position to get what she wanted at Paris than any other nation except the United States. She had been little hurt, indeed much strengthened, by the war both economically and in military armament. Her only dangerous rival in the Far East, Germany, had been crushed. She was far distant from Europe and supreme in her own sphere. But more than this, she was, by virtue not only of her position but of her foresight, in an extraordinarily strong legal position. In the first place, she had her treaty of alliance (renewed in 1911) with Great Britain. She had also the secret agreements of 1917 with Great Britain and France (and Italy and Russia) under which her claims to the "disposal of Germany's rights in Shantung and possessions in the islands north of the equator on the occasion of the Peace Conference" were formally approved. These secret treaties were made before America came into the war. Japan had also the (partly) secret treaties with China of 1915 and 1918 providing for the future disposition of Shantung.

Finally, Japan had the powerful nine points of actual possession, both of Shantung and of the islands, with no real threat from any source except from weak and disorganized China.[11]

The brilliant French writer-diplomat, Gabriel Terrail, writing under the pseudonym Mermeix, thus describes the Japanese delegates and their position at Paris:

The Japanese delegates had been most carefully chosen. The Marquis Saionji, a former Prime Minister, headed the delegation, with Baron Makino, a former Secretary of State for Foreign Affairs, as his right hand man. Assisting these two were the Japanese ambassadors to Rome, Paris and London, Viscount Chinda, and Messrs. Matsui and Ijuin. Throughout the war the latter three diplomats had worked closely with the statesmen of the countries to which they had been accredited. They had made many personal contacts and some intimate friendships in their host countries, knew their statesmen well, and had a fair knowledge of those countries' problems and national affairs. They were a great help to the heads of their delegation.

Initially, Japanese delegates had seats in the Council of Ten, which was composed of Heads of Governments and Foreign Ministers. When . . . the Council of Ten was dissolved and its functions split up between the Council of Foreign Ministers and the Council of Four, Japan could no longer claim a seat in the latter, since it was made up exclusively of Heads of Governments. Japan, did, however, retain a seat in the Council of Foreign Ministers. In addition, representatives of the Mikado sat in most of the important, and in many of the less important, Peace Conference Commissions: . . . the Territorial Problems Commission, the Polish Affairs Commission, the Military Affairs Commission, the Naval Affairs Commission, the Danish Commission, the Belgian Commission, the Reparations Commission, the Labor Commission, the Post & Telegraph Commission, the War-Guilt Commission, and the Sanctions Commission.

Considering that the Japanese were members of that group of nations of the yellow race which, until so recently, had been regarded as "inferior" by Europeans, they had come a long way to be now sitting in on the discussions of such varied problems so far removed from their own sphere of interest, and to be included among the legislators of Europe.

But the Japanese delegates did not let this go to their heads. They did not behave like newcomers, but like real veterans of diplomacy. They took everything in their stride, and, far from behaving like upstarts, as so many of the delegates from the newly created European nations did, they acted as if they had been bred to diplomatic traditions.

Their tact was greatly admired by all, they never interfered in any problems which did not directly concern their own national interests, they neither threw their weight around nor demeaned themselves, but always wore an air of quiet reserve and soon acquired the respect and the sympathy of most of their colleagues.

Two Japanese delegates, Chindo and Makino, sat on President Wilson's own League of Nations Commission. Here they brought up the racial equality issue, which proved so embarrassing to the President.[12]

III

Organization of the Conference

It never occurred to the French that the Conference which would put an end to the war and avenge their defeat of 1871 might take place anywhere other than Paris. The British and Americans preferred some quiet, out-of-the-way city, and The Hague, Brussels, Basel, Geneva and Lausanne were all seriously considered at one time or another. But the French kept pressing for "the honor of the Conference," and, when Woodrow Wilson suddenly swung over to their point of view, Paris was settled upon as the site for the "Preliminary Peace Conference."

It seems as if Wilson did not fully comprehend what this decision entailed, for he continued to voice his hope that he would be asked to preside over the Conference. The moment Paris was chosen this became impossible; traditionally organizing and presiding over a conference is the job of the host country, and the French were not likely to relinquish the advantage this gave them.

Clemenceau had some uneasy moments over Wilson's decision to attend the Conference in person. With Wilson at the table, Clemenceau might not be able to preside at the Conference; his old antagonist Raymond Poincaré, then President of the Republic, seemed likely to claim the job as a matter of prestige. But when President Wilson did not "pull rank" and agreed to sit as an equal with the Prime Ministers, Clemenceau's election to the presidency of the Council became assured.

The consequences of holding the Conference at Paris have been noted by Harold Nicolson, then a young British third secretary, who worked at the Peace Conference at the Commission level.

In choosing that shell-shocked capital the rulers of the world committed a grave initial blunder. Since it was an inevitable blunder, I call it a misfortune. Yet Paris, in any circumstances, is too self-conscious, too insistent, to constitute a favourable site for any Congress of Peace. So long ago as 1814, Lord Castlereagh had noted this unsuitability. "Paris," he wrote to Bathurst, "was a bad place for business." This defect, in 1919, was very marked indeed. "We were hampered" records Dr. Charles Seymour in that admirable compilation, *The Intimate Papers of Colonel House*, "We were hampered by the atmosphere of Paris, where German guilt was assumed as a proved fact. Everyone was afraid of being called a pro-German." Subconsciously the shell-shock of Paris affected the nerves of all the delegates. "Paris," records Mr. Keynes, "was a nightmare and everyone there was morbid." Its very size, its many diversions, in themselves conspired against that intensive concentration which was essential if all that spate of knowledge and opinion was ever to be classified and arranged. We felt like surgeons operating in the ballroom with the aunts of the patient gathered all around.

Even to those who claimed the privilege of understanding Paris, that sombre and authoritative capital appeared, during those barbarian weeks, to have lost her dignity. . . .

Paris, gashed to her very soul, withdrew to lick her wounds. Her place was taken by the Compagnie des Grands Express Européens, or more accurately by the American Express Company. American military police stood side by side with the Policemen on the Champs Élysées. The uniforms of twenty-six foreign armies confused the monochrome of the streets. Paris, for those few weeks, lost her soul. The brain of Paris, that triumphant achievement of western civilisation, ceased to function. The nerves of Paris jangled in the air.

The French reacted to this barbarisation of their own foyer in a most unhelpful manner. Almost from the first they turned against the Americans with embittered resentment. The constant clamour of their newspapers, the stridency of their personal attacks, increased in volume. The ineptitude of the newspapers published in Paris in the English language has seldom been surpassed. The cumulative effect of all this shouting outside the very doors of the Conference produced a nervous and as such unwholesome effect. Our breakfast tables became a succession of intemperate yells.

The President himself was strangely sensitive to these forms of animosity. He did not mind so much when he was accused of theocracy, when he was abused for not visiting the devastated areas, or when he was openly arraigned as a pro-German or as a prophet obsessed by his Utopias. Alone with God and the People he could withstand, almost without wincing, these assaults upon him. What he minded were the funny little jokes which the French papers would make about him, the persistent cloud, not of incense, but of ridicule with which they perfumed his path. Every incident that occurred (and there were many incidents) was used by the French press to expose the President in a ridiculous light. To the presbyterian, persecution is a crown of glory, and opposition is an opportunity vouchsafed by God. It is the quiet of the constant smile which goads them to desperation. Mr. Wilson suffered most acutely under the gay lampoons of Paris. This addition to his many preoccupations, these bright shavings flaming around the slow fire of his despair, are not to be underestimated as factors in his final collapse. The President had come to Paris armed with power such as no man in history had possessed: he had come fired with high ideals such as have inspired no autocrat of the past: and Paris, instead of seeing in him the embodiment of the philosopher-king, saw in him a rather comic and highly irritating professor. The cumulative effect of these sharp little pin-pricks was far greater than has been supposed.

The choice of Paris, therefore, became one of the most potent of our misfortunes.[1]

Once it was decided to hold the Conference at Paris, the French Foreign Office, an old hand at diplomatic procedure, started organizing with a will. Invitations to attend the "Preliminary Peace Conference"* went out to thirty-two nations and the staff of the Quai d'Orsay was kept busy drawing up detailed plans and agendas.

Before Woodrow Wilson sailed for Europe, the French ambassador to Washington, M. Jusserand, handed him the French

* It is worthy of note that the Paris Peace Conference assembled under the official title of "Preliminary Conference of Peace" and retained that title until March 1919.

program for the Conference. This paper surprisingly lacked the usual French finesse and contained some unflattering remarks about the League of Nations and the President's Fourteen Points. Among other things, it said that ". . . those principles of President Wilson which are not sufficiently defined in their character to be taken as a basis for a concrete settlement . . . will resume their full strength in the matter of future settlement of public law, and this will remove one of the difficulties that might obstruct the Allies" and ". . . nor the President's fourteen propositions which are principles of public law can furnish a concrete basis for the labors of the Congress."[2] The French obviously had not learned how to handle the President, and Woodrow Wilson discarded the document. This was a pity, for the paper contained the suggestion that a set of preliminary peace terms be imposed upon the enemy immediately, without discussion, and that subsequently a Congress should be called at which both enemy and neutral powers would be represented. It also contained the proposal that all secret treaties should be immediately canceled. Had President Wilson adopted this last suggestion alone, it would have saved him considerable headaches and some embarrassment at the Conference. As it was, the Jusserand memorandum was filed away and never received any United States response.

Two aspects of the Conference presented an immediate problem; one concerned the nature of the Conference and the other concerned its participants. In Nicolson's words:

> The first of these points was whether the Treaty should be preliminary or final. The second of these points was whether the Treaty should be imposed or negotiated—in other words whether the enemy should be allowed, at the last moment, to attend and speak at the Conference, or whether all discussion should from first to last be barred.
>
> It is a strange, but indisputable fact, that neither of these two important points of procedure were discussed or decided in the early stages of the Conference. During January, February and the first half of March—for a period, that is of more than ten weeks—the rulers of the world were completely unaware whether the Treaty which they were discussing was to be negotiated or imposed. It may seem strange indeed that this essential consideration should not have been exam-

ined from the outset and from the outset decided. Yet in fact the problem was shelved throughout that period as something which was too painful to raise immediately, as something which would settle itself.

The original idea had certainly been that there would be a preliminary Treaty the terms of which would be settled in advance as between the victorious Powers. This Treaty, which would be imposed upon the beaten enemy, was to have contained merely the terms of military and naval disarmament, as well as the main lines of the future territorial settlement. All other details were to be elaborated at a subsequent "Congress" at which the enemy would be represented and at which they would have occasion to advance counter proposals.

At a later stage it was suggested that a "General Act" should be drafted by the Conference embracing the essentials of all the Treaties of Peace with the four enemy Powers. So late as March 19, President Wilson was still undecided whether he desired a Preliminary or Final Treaty. He was assured by Mr. Lansing and the jurists that even a Preliminary Treaty would have to be ratified by the Senate, and he was thus afraid that they would grasp at this power of ratification in order to refuse acceptance of the ensuing Covenant of the League. "At this statement," records Mr. Lansing, "the President was evidently much perturbed." During Mr. Wilson's absence in the United States, the idea was mooted that a preliminary treaty might be drafted and signed under the guise of a "Final Armistice." On February 22 it was decided even that the main items of such an Armistice might be prepared against the President's return, and the Military and Naval advisers to the Council were instructed to cast it immediately into shape. Yet by the time these clauses had finally been drafted and approved, the President had himself returned to Paris. It was then discovered that the territorial and other clauses had in the interval advanced to a stage at which, with a little further drafting, they also could be embodied in the Treaty of Peace. The whole theory of a Preliminary Peace was thereafter, and as it were by chance, abandoned.

This hesitation between the conception of a Preliminary and a Final Treaty has a direct bearing upon the question of enemy representation. The Germans are to this day convinced that it was from the outset the deliberate intention of the Allies to exclude their representatives from any share in the Peace discussions. In actual fact, this point, as other points of a similar nature, swirled as a small straw upon the gathering waters of the Conference. In November 1918 Colonel House had solemnly allotted five seats at the impending Congress to the

Representatives of Germany. At that date, and until March, it was taken for granted by all who laboured in Paris that once the Allies had agreed among themselves as to the terms to be offered to Germany the Conference would cease to be a "Conference" and become a "Congress"—or in other words that we should then enter upon the second phase of our labours, namely negotiation on the terms of the eventual settlement with our late enemies, and in the presence of the neutral Powers.

How came it that this estimable idea faded, as the weeks wore on, from our immediate consciousness? History will refuse to believe that we "forgot about the enemy." She will attribute to us motives and a state of awareness which were certainly not ours at the time. It is difficult to explain the exclusion of our enemies from the discussion except in terms which will appear incredible, or at least far-fetched. Yet I seriously believe that the following were the stages by which the necessity of consulting with our enemies receded into the background of our minds.

Subconsciously we thought in terms of a "Conference" of Allies, followed by a "Congress" of all belligerents and neutrals. The former conception became identified with the expression "Preliminary Treaty": the latter took the word-form of "Final Treaty." The "Preliminary Treaty" would be imposed by force upon the defeated enemy: the "Final Treaty" would be a matter of world negotiation and world consent.

As the Conference progressed, as more and more of the technical Committees produced their recommendations in the form of articles which were ready for immediate insertion in a final document—the conception of a Preliminary Treaty merged gradually into the conception of one final Treaty covering the whole. It had always been assumed that the essential articles—such as those providing for German disarmament and the main territorial cessions—would figure in the Preliminary Treaty and would therefore be, not negotiated, but imposed. It had also been supposed that what might be called the secondary articles—and especially the economic if not also the financial clauses—would be a matter for discussion. Yet when the Preliminary Treaty was abandoned, and the Final Treaty took its place, the latter inherited from the former this original idea of imposition versus negotiation. And all this happened before many of us had realised exactly what had occurred.

I do not contend that we drifted into imposing, rather than negotiating, a Treaty in a mood of complete unawareness. Obviously there were certain deliberate factors which impelled us to that decision. In the first place President Wilson's insistence upon the inclusion of the Covenant, in any form of Treaty, delayed our deliberations beyond the moment when a Preliminary Treaty was either sensible or necessary. In the second place the absence of the President and Mr. Lloyd George, coupled with the attempted assassination of M. Clemenceau, entailed at a vital moment the suspension of the supreme direction of the Conference, and an accumulation in the interval of much completed material. In the third place Marshal Foch feared that the conclusion of the Preliminary Treaty would lead to even more rapid demobilisation on the part of Great Britain and the United States, after which there would be little hope of negotiating any peace at all. And in the fourth place the acute disagreements which, during those weeks, developed as between the Allies themselves produced a feeling amounting to terror lest the presence in the divided counsels of Europe of so disruptive an element as our late enemies would lead to even more alarming disintegration.

The fact remains, in any case, that throughout the early stages of the Conference the directing Powers never allowed it to be known whether the Treaty which was being prepared was a final text to be imposed upon Germany, or a mere basis of agreement as between the Allies for eventual negotiation with Germany at a final Congress. This omission on their part was most serious and has not, except by Mr. Keynes, been sufficiently stressed. Many paragraphs of the Treaty, and especially in the economic sections, were in fact inserted as "maximum statements" such as would provide some area of concession to Germany at the eventual Congress. This Congress never materialised; the last weeks of the Conference flew past us in a hysterical nightmare; and these "maximum statements" remained unmodified and were eventually imposed by ultimatum. Had it been known from the outset that no negotiations would ever take place with the enemy, it is certain that many of the less reasonable clauses of the Treaty would never have been inserted.[3]

Originally scheduled to convene on December 18th, the Conference did not formally open until January 18, 1919. The intervening month was taken up by Wilson's triumphal state visits to France, England and Italy, and by Allied attempts to feel out this American Man of Destiny, who was, after all, still an unknown quantity.

The first five committees were not appointed until January 25th, and the territorial committees, charged with fixing the future frontiers of Europe, did not come into being until the beginning of February. Nicolson comments:

> This delay of more than nine weeks between the signature of the armistice and the first serious attempt to get down to business will certainly remain as one of the most unanswerable criticisms of the Paris Conference. It is therefore necessary to consider the causes, psychological and other, by which it was occasioned. Two phases of delay must be distinguished from each other. There was first the delay between the Armistice and the meeting of the Conference. There was secondly the delay, after the Conference had assembled, in getting down to practical work. . . .
>
> I have consulted many of the important figures at the Conference on this very problem. "Why," I have asked them, "was the Conference postponed from December 18 till January 18?" "Oh," they answer, "there was Christmas, of course: and we wanted a holiday: besides it was necessary to allow emotions to die down: and after all, we had to take stock of the situation. Russia, you remember, was in turmoil: and so was Germany. We thought that if we waited a little things might settle down."[4]

Woodrow Wilson, from the outset, rejected all the plans drawn up by the French Foreign Office and insisted that the talks between the Allied statesmen be conducted on an informal basis and all the important decisions of the Conference be made by a small council composed of representatives of the five major Allied Powers. As it was, that council came into being almost automatically as soon as Wilson sat down in conference with the representatives of the "Associated Powers." Colonel House has described the haphazard way in which the Council of Ten (Supreme Council) originated.

> Upon the arrival of Lloyd George in Paris, a meeting of the Supreme War Council was held January 12, at the Quai d'Orsay. France was represented by Clemenceau and Pichon, Great Britain by Lloyd

George and Balfour, Italy by Orlando and Sonnino, the United States by Wilson and Lansing. Though ostensibly an informal conversation among plenipotentiaries of the four leading Powers, the meeting was the occasion of the significant decision to add only the representatives of Japan to the Supreme Council and to exclude all others from the major decisions of the Peace Conference. Thus the Council of Ten sprang from the Supreme War Council. There also came to Paris the representatives of Belgium, Serbia, Rumania, Greece and the other States—32 in all—which had fought against the Central Powers or had broken off diplomatic relations with them. Obviously it was impossible for all to have equal part in determining the conditions of peace. To each, seats and a vote were allotted in the Plenary Sessions of the Conference. Representatives of those states which had remained neutral during the war, and yet had interests to safeguard or to advance at the Peace Conference, were permitted to attend only those sessions which were arranged for discussion of their claims, whenever they were specially summoned by the five chief Powers. . . .

But there was considerable dispute before the five principal Powers finally assigned places in the Conference to each state in accordance with its military strength and its share in the war. Five seats were given to each of the five chief Powers; three apiece were assigned to Belgium, Serbia and Brazil; two each to Canada, Australia, South Africa, India, China, Czechoslovakia, Poland, Greece, the Hejaz, Portugal, Rumania and Siam; one each to New Zealand, Bolivia, Cuba, Ecuador, Guatemala, Haiti, Honduras, Liberia, Nicaragua, Panama, Peru and Uruguay. Many delegates were thus left out, but the panel system was adopted so that all Powers could use their plenipotentiaries in rotation if they desired. Representatives of the British Dominions, for example, more than once shared in important decisions of the Supreme Council by reason of their membership in the panel of the British Empire. Other work was found for excess members of several delegations on commissions and sub-committees. When the Plenary Assembly of the Conference met for the first time on January 18 it proved to be only a body of approval merely passing upon actions that had already been determined in the Supreme Council. Clemenceau was elected president of the Conference. A secretariat-general previously selected by the Supreme Council was appointed. A drafting committee was approved, on which had been placed only representatives of the five chief Powers. The Smaller Powers endeavoured to protest against such rigid control by the Five. But at the second

Plenary Session on January 25 Clemenceau bluntly dismissed their objections with allusion to the 12,000,000 soldiers behind the Five Powers.[5]

The place that the small powers were to have at the Conference presented quite a problem, and Nicolson explains the role which they were finally assigned to play.

In the first place the Supreme Council of the Conference had inherited the status, and with it the methods of thought, of the old Supreme War Council. They had fallen . . . into the habit of supposing that their agenda would be imposed by events and not evolved by processes of their own forethought and selection. A good illustration of this method of approach is furnished by their relations with the smaller Powers. They realised, and quite rightly, that discussions between the whole twenty-seven States represented in Paris would degenerate into a farce. They saw from the first that the Five Great Powers would have to constitute their "Council of Ten" as representing a force of twelve million fully armed soldiers and sailors. They realised that the smaller Powers would for this reason have to be excluded from the direction of the Conference. They recognised the fact that these smaller Powers would resent such exclusion. And they decided, therefore, that something should be done to salve, not only the personal feeling of the minor Representatives in Paris, but the nationalist expectations of their Chambers and electorates at home. From the very outset, therefore, a method had to be devised such as would enable the delegates of the smaller Powers to pretend that they were in fact playing some sort of part in the deliberations of the Supreme Council. This method took two forms. In the first place the delegates of the smaller or the succession States were asked to put in writing the territorial and other concessions which they desired to obtain from the Treaty of Peace. In the second place these delegates were each invited in turn orally to expound before the Supreme Council the arguments upon which their claims were based. This entailed a wastage of time and a falsification of proportion. There were in fact fourteen such "auditions" in February alone, and each absorbed many hours. Inevitably, also, the smaller Powers produced memoranda of claims which were far in excess of their real expectations. Inevitably in expounding these claims orally before the Council they merely repeated what had been written in their Statements, and diminished the powers of resistance which those old gentlemen, in that hot and stuffy room, were able to maintain. This initial wastage of time and energy is a point to which any historian should direct his attention. It gave to the members of the Supreme Council the impression that they were doing valuable and constructive work. Yet in fact they were doing nothing more than suffer, with varying degrees of courtesy, an exhausting and unnecessary imposition. . . .

The desire to mitigate the somewhat artificial resentment of the smaller Powers at being excluded from the supreme direction of the Conference led to a falsification of approach, and to a consequent confusion of secondary with major purposes. I now come to the farce of the Plenary Sessions. The smaller Powers were given to understand that the recommendations of the territorial and other Committees of the Conference would be submitted to a Plenary Session at which they would have the opportunity to state their views. In practice, the representatives of these Powers were too intelligent to take this promise very seriously. Yet we of the Committees were less sceptical. We believed that our recommendations would, in the last resort, be submitted to some final form of discussion, in which the interested parties would have their say. We were never for one instant given to suppose that our recommendations were absolutely final. And we thus tended to accept compromises, and even to support decisions, which we ardently hoped would not, in this last resort, be approved. I do not believe that it would in fact have been possible to revise the recommendations of the Committees either in the Council of Ten, nor yet in that of Four, nor yet in Plenary Conference. Mr. Lloyd George's revision of the recommendations of the Polish Committee, although wholly justified, produced in itself an outburst. Yet the fact remains that *we* should have been told that our recommendations were likely to be approved without further discussion, and the smaller Powers should have been told that in effect the Committees would constitute the final court of appeal. Here again was an imprecision of function which produced unfortunate results.[6]

André Tardieu sheds some further light on the question.

I have just mentioned the various groups who made these decisions: Council of Foreign Ministers, Council of Ten, Council of Four. Why so many? Why so interlocking? The former a question of procedure, the latter a question of principle. Both need answer.

And first of all why did not all the Powers summoned to Paris take part in the elaboration of the Peace? There were twenty-seven Allied Powers and four Enemy Powers. The admission of the latter to the preparatory discussions was not even suggested. There remained the Allies. Could they all be asked to sit? Evidently not. First because it would have been a regular parliament, the debates of which would have been interminable; then also because the positions of the various countries were not equal. The Big Nations had been accused of thrusting the smaller ones aside. But not to mention those who, without any act of war, had merely broken off diplomatic relations with Germany, nor those who, having declared war, had furnished no military effort, could it be maintained that, in the difficult work of giving expression to victory, the right of initiative should not be in some measure dependent upon the sacrifices made? Among the victors some had given everything, their soil, their blood, their treasure, not only to defend their own liberties but to win liberty for others. These latter on the contrary, despite the endurance of long sufferings, owed their resurrection entirely to the former. A classification was thus essential, and how can one challenge the justice of the distinction made, by a protocol pregnant with reality, between the Powers of general and those of restricted interest? It enhanced the clearness and moderation of the debates. Moreover it was only just. Those who had borne the fearful burden of war were entitled to the privilege of determining, in accordance with the war aims accepted by all and in the interest of all, the general lines of the peace. M. Clemenceau at the second plenary sitting of the Conference, January 25, 1919, dealt with the question frankly on the occasion of a discussion on the composition of the commissions.

"Sir Robert Borden," he said, "head of the Canadian delegation, has in very friendly manner reproached the Great Powers with having made the decision. Yes, we decided in the matter of the commissions; as we decided to call the present Conference; and as we decided to invite the representatives of interested nations.

"I make no secret of it. A Conference of the Great Powers is being held in an adjoining room. The Five Great Powers whose action it is desired should be justified before you today, are in a position to furnish that justification.

"A few moments ago, the Prime Minister of Great Britain reminded me that the day the war came to a close, the principal Allies had twelve million soldiers fighting on the fields of battle. That is a title.

"We have lost, killed and wounded, by millions, and if we had not had present to our minds the great question of the League of Nations, we might have been selfishly led to consult ourselves alone. Who can say that we should not have been justified?

"Such was not our wish. We called together the entire assembly of the interested nations. We called them together not to impose our will upon them, not to make them do that which they do not want, but to ask their cooperation. That is why we invited them here. Yet we must ascertain how this cooperation is to be organized.

"Experience has taught me that the more numerous committees are, the less chance there is of getting things done. Now, behind us stands a very great, very august, and at times very imperious force called public opinion. It will not ask us if such or such a state was represented on such or such a commission. That is of no interest to anybody. Public opinion will ask us what we have done. It is my duty to direct our work so that we may get things done."

Thus ordered, the Conference deprived no one of the right of being heard. All the countries represented, no matter how small, participated in the labours of the commissions, either as members or as witnesses. All were heard by the Great Powers, and the number of these hearings exceeds three hundred. But the direction of the work remained in the hands of those who had won the war. It was thus that on January 12, 1919, the body known as the Council of Ten met; it was composed of the heads of Governments and Ministers of Foreign Affairs of the United States, the British Empire, France, Italy and Japan. This Council sat twice daily from January 12 to March 24, dealing both with the peace and with such urgent problems of world politics as could not be left unsolved: application and renewals of the Armistice; food supplies for Europe; Russian affairs. The Council listened to the claims of the small nations. It settled the clauses of the disarmament of Germany. That having been done, it suddenly realized that six weeks had passed, that the end was not yet in sight and that with its ten members assisted by several dozen experts no headway was being made. Little by little everybody had got into the habit of making speeches. Matters were constantly being adjourned. That perfect frankness essential to obtain results was difficult in the presence of so large an audience. When anything leaked out, each delegation blamed the other for it. These were the reasons—and there was none other—why it was decided to narrow the circle. Thus the Council of Four, increased to five when the Japanese delegate was present, was formed and it was assisted in some of the less important matters by the Council of Five made up of the Ministers of Foreign Affairs.[7]

Thus the Supreme Council (sitting as the Council of Ten to begin with and as the Council of Four later on) and the Plenary Session sat side by side, almost constituting two separate conferences. The Supreme Council reserved the right to deal with all territorial questions and all matters of general policy, while the Plenary Conference was deputized to handle such matters as the League of Nations, Reparations, War Guilt, Disarmament, Ports, Harbors and Waterways, International Labor Organization and other matters of lesser importance. In actual practice even the committees subject to the authority of the Plenary Conference reported their findings to the Supreme Council rather than to their parent body, and the Plenary Sessions of the Conference, of which few were held during the whole duration of the Conference, were reduced to rubber-stamping the decisions of the Supreme Council.

Because the Conference was being held in Paris, the General Secretariat was set up under French direction and, at Clemenceau's suggestion, M. Dutasta was appointed Secretary General. Dutasta's main qualification for the job seems to have been his infinite capacity to absorb Clemenceau's abuse. He proved a somewhat inefficient, timid and bungling individual, and he was soon overshadowed by the supreme efficiency of Maurice Hankey, the Secretary of the British Delegation.

The Paris Peace Conference naturally drew a large number of the world's most highly paid press correspondents to the French capital. They expected this Conference to produce the first of a series of "open covenants openly arrived at," but were to be gravely disappointed. The very author of that stirring phrase himself insisted upon complete secrecy of all discussions, and it was only with difficulty that Clemenceau prevailed upon him to permit the Plenary Sessions of the Conference to be made public. This arrangement left the members of the fourth estate totally dissatisfied, and the newsmen of Paris had to rely upon news leaks, unintentional or deliberate, as the case might be. The best reporters soon established connections that enabled them to give the world amazingly accurate reports of what went on at secret meetings.

The French were particularly adept at leaking news when it suited their purpose. The Council of Ten fell victim to this practice when Lloyd George finally lost his Welsh temper and refused to sit any longer in such leaky surroundings. The Council of Ten was then superseded by the Council of Four, composed solely of Clemenceau, Lloyd George, Orlando and Wilson, while the Foreign Ministers of the five Allied Powers and the Staff were relegated to a Council of Five which was given only minor assignments and routine matters.

The problem of language produced a minor skirmish when Wilson and Lloyd George challenged France's claim to the exclusive use of French as the official language of the Conference. Ever since Latin had been discarded as the language of international intercourse French had taken its place, and the French put up a valiant struggle to maintain the exclusivity of their language as the international tongue. Wilson, however, put forth a strong argument stating that while French might have been the traditional language of European diplomacy, English had become the language of Pacific diplomacy, and finally a compromise was reached by which both English and French were recognized as official languages of the Conference, with French texts taking precedence in case of dispute. By enabling the Anglo-American members of the drafting committees to see that French and English texts were properly coordinated, this compromise worked out quite satisfactorily. But in 1919 the art of translation had not reached the state of perfection which, thanks to the League and United Nations, it has attained today, and the constant translations back and forth between French and English greatly retarded the work of the Conference.

IV

The Covenant

All the statesmen preparing to attend the Paris Peace Conference knew of President Wilson's overriding interest in the League of Nations. Few, however, had any clear concept of what he had in mind, inasmuch as he had never spelled out his ideas in detail and all his public utterances had been confined to generalities. In fact, Wilson himself would have preferred to arrive at the conference table without any blueprint committing him to specifics. He had publicly announced his principles and he knew the concepts he had in his own mind. He would have greatly preferred to remain at liberty to apply them to situations as he met them.

But, obviously, more than that was required: the British had set up a parliamentary commission (the Phillimore Commission) to work out a draft for a League of Nations and unless the President wanted to let Lloyd George steal his thunder he had to produce a plan of his own. Accordingly, Colonel House and his American Inquiry had been instructed to work out an American draft of a Covenant of the League of Nations. Gradually, and in close cooperation with their British counterparts, they groped their way toward a proposal which would encompass Woodrow Wilson's ideas.

By the time the President sailed for Europe, he and Colonel House had drafted and redrafted the constitution of the League several times. The later drafts had been coordinated with the Phillimore report and many of the latter's ideas were incorporated in the American paper. Some weeks later President

Wilson himself gave a good description of the genealogy of his League constitution at an informal meeting of Allied Leaders.

PRESIDENT WILSON observed that he had himself drawn up a constitution of a League of Nations. He could not claim that it was wholly his own creation. Its generation was as follows: He had received the Phillimore Report, which had been amended by Colonel House and re-written by himself. He had again revised it after having received General Smuts' and Lord Robert Cecil's reports. It was therefore a compound of these various suggestions. During the week he had seen M. Bourgeois, with whom he found himself to be in substantial accord on principles. A few days ago he had discussed his draft with Lord Robert Cecil and General Smuts, and they had found themselves very near together.[1]

As soon as Woodrow Wilson arrived in Europe he made it very clear to the statesmen of the Old World that he regarded the League of Nations as the keystone of his Peace Program, that he wished it to be the first item on the Conference agenda, and that he would press for it to be made "an integral part of the Treaty of Peace." He stated his position to the British during his visit to London in December of 1918 and Lloyd George dutifully reported it to the Imperial Cabinet.

The President had opened at once with the question of the League of Nations and had given the impression that that was the only thing that he really cared much about. There was nothing in what he said which would in the least make it difficult for us to come to some arrangement with him. His mind was apparently travelling in very much the direction of the proposals advocated by Lord Robert Cecil and General Smuts. He had no definite formal scheme in his mind, and was certainly not contemplating anything in the nature of giving executive powers to the League of Nations. The question of Germany's inclusion had not been raised, but was not apparently contemplated by him as a matter for the immediate future. What he was anxious about was that the League of Nations should be the first subject discussed at the Peace Conference. Both Mr. Lloyd George and Mr. Balfour were inclined to agree, on the ground that this would ease other matters, such as the questions of the "Freedom of the Seas," the disposal of the German colonies, economic issues, etc. The President, having attained his object, could then say that these matters could be left to be worked out by the League of Nations. There was also the consideration that the President might have to go back to America before the Conference concluded, and would wish to be able to say that he had achieved his purpose of creating the League of Nations.

LORD CURZON added that the President had, on another occasion, given him as a reason for beginning with the League of Nations, that the question of giving a mandate to certain Powers in certain territories could not be settled unless there was a League of Nations to give it.[2]

While the President found full understanding and cooperation among the statesmen of Great Britain, his plans for a League of Nations ran into skepticism and ridicule among the French. Clemenceau, for one, did not believe in the League. As early as November 1917 he had warned the Chamber of Deputies: "You think that you will be able to solve everything with the magic formula of a League of Nations. But first of all one must know what it means. . . . I do not think that a League of Nations will be the necessary outcome of this war."[3]

As soon as Wilson arrived in Paris (in mid-December) he discussed his ideas with Clemenceau, who was polite but skeptical. Colonel House, who was present at the interview, described the meeting.

The President . . . desired to . . . take up the most important subject with Clemenceau—the League of Nations. . . . During the hour and a half we were there together the President did nearly all the talking . . . Clemenceau expressed himself, in a mild way, in agreement with the President. He thought a League of Nations should be attempted, but he was not confident of success, either of forming it or of its being workable after it was formed.[4]

Ten days later, while Wilson was in England, Clemenceau poked fun at the President's ideas in the Chamber of Deputies, to the applause and laughter of the august body; with his unmatched ability to give meanings to words by a gesture of the hand or the lift of an eyebrow he said:

With regard to international guarantees . . . I will say that if France is permitted to establish her own defence . . . I, personally, will joyfully accept any additional supplementary guarantees that may be offered to us. . . . I would be lying if I said that I immediately agreed with him (Wilson) on all points. As I remarked a little while ago, America is far removed from the frontiers of Germany. I have, perhaps, pre-occupations which, I would not say are exactly foreign to him, but which do not affect him as closely as they do a man who, for four years, has watched his country being devastated by an enemy who stood within a few days' march of Paris. . . . Mr. Wilson has a broad mind, open and elevated. He is a man who inspires respect by the simplicity of his words and the noble artlessness of his spirit. (Applause, laughter and interruptions from the far left)

M. RENAUDEL: This is abominable. This is a bad joke.

M. CLEMENCEAU: I only meant it as high praise.

M. ALBERT THOMAS: Mr. President of the Council, if there are any divergencies between the policies of certain of our great Allies and our own, perhaps they rest in a more ardent and more immediate faith in the realisation of this common ideal.

M. CLEMENCEAU: I am not at all sure of that.

M. ALBERT THOMAS: Ah, Mr. President of the Council, how little the new spirit seems to inspire you, as yet.[5]

Only the liberals and the far left of the French political spectrum seemed to fall in with Wilson's ideas. The rest of France was hypnotized by the idea of "French security."

According to Colonel House, Clemenceau became converted to the idea of the League of Nations barely two weeks later. The Colonel notes in his diary that he presented the French Prime Minister with the following argument.

In the present war England voluntarily came to France's aid. She was not compelled to do so. The United States did likewise without compulsion. I asked whether or not in the circumstances France would not feel safer if England and America were in a position where they would be compelled to come to the aid of France in the event another outlaw nation like Germany should try to crush her. Under the old plan, the shadow and the spectre of another war would haunt her. If she lost this chance which the United States offered through the League of Nations, it would never come again because there would never be another opportunity. Wilson was an idealist, but our people were not all of his mind. Wilson could force it through because, with all the brag and bluster of the Senate, they would not dare defeat a treaty made in agreement with the Allies and thereby continue alone a war with Germany, or make a separate peace. The old man seemed to see it all and became enthusiastic. He placed both his hands upon my shoulders and said: "You are right. I am for the League of Nations as you have it in mind, and you may count upon me to work with you."[6]

If Clemenceau really was converted to the American concept of the League of Nations, the subsequent actions of the French delegation hardly confirmed this. Most of the time of the League of Nations Commission was occupied with warding off French attempts to convert the League into a Grand Alliance of victorious powers to enforce the terms of the Peace Treaty. On the other hand, it can be argued that this was precisely the view of the League that Colonel House had outlined to the ferocious old lord of the jungle.

The "Preliminary Peace Conference" opened in Plenary Session on January 18, 1919. Wilson was scheduled to leave for the United States on February 15th, so he had less than a month in which to get his Covenant approved by the Conference. At the second Plenary Session, a week later (January 25th), Lloyd George presented the League of Nations resolution.

The Conference, having considered the proposals for the creation of a League of Nations, resolves that:—

(*a*) It is essential to the maintenance of the world settlement, which the associated nations are now met to establish, that a League of Nations be created to promote international co-operation, to ensure the fulfilment of accepted international obligations, and to provide safeguards against war.

(*b*) This League should be created as an integral part of the general treaty of peace, and should be open to every civilised nation which can be relied on to promote its objects.

(*c*) The members of the League should periodically meet in international Conference, and should have a permanent organisation and secretariat to carry on the business of the League in the intervals between the Conferences.

The Conference therefore appoints a Committee representative of the associated Governments to work out the details of the constitution and functions of the League.[7]

Lloyd George himself describes Georges Clemenceau's official reaction.

In the course of the discussion M. Clemenceau, who is supposed to have been the most inveterate of the passive resisters to the idea of a League of Nations, made a very remarkable speech in support of the League:—*

. . . He would at once take up the question of a League for the preservation of Peace. He greatly favoured such a League, and he was prepared to make all sacrifices to attain that object. If it was insisted upon, he would assent to a League with full powers to initiate laws, but he would ask that his objections be recorded, as he had no confidence in such a scheme. He might be too conservative—that being a fault of age. In a speech which he had made to the Chamber of Deputies a few days ago he had stated that if, before the war, the great powers had made an alliance pledging themselves to take up arms in defence of any one of them who might be attacked there would have been no war. Today they had not only five nations in agreement, but practically the whole world. If the nations pledged themselves not to attack anyone without the consent of the members of the League, and to defend any one of them who might be attacked, the peace of the world would be assured. Such an alliance might well be termed a League of Nations. Such procedures and tribunals as might be thought necessary could be added. He would accept all these. If Mr. Lloyd George were to promise that he would accept these two conditions, the League of Nations would be created in less than three days.[8]

The League of Nations resolution was quickly adopted and a League of Nations Commission was set up. To the surprise of everyone and to the dismay of those who had hoped to sidetrack

* The Prime Minister obviously missed the subtle irony in Clemenceau's endorsement. (Ed.)

the League, Woodrow Wilson himself took over as chairman of the Commission. By this simple move the Conference's whole weight was shifted to the League of Nations Commission, which became the center of all Conference activity for the succeeding three weeks.

To give the President a chance to attend Supreme Council meetings, and so as not to interfere with the schedules of other commissions which were being set up, it was decided to hold all sessions of the League of Nations Commission in the evening.

Colonel House and Lord Robert Cecil, the two foremen of the American and British League of Nations construction crews, and their staffs labored hard to get a joint Covenant draft ready for the Commission which convened on February 3, 1919. The French, as usual, had done all their homework a long time before; their draft had been gathering dust in a drawer at the Quai d'Orsay since June 18th, five months before the signing of the Armistice. Because it was actually a plan to set up, under the name of a League of Nations, a military alliance to preserve the status quo that a peace treaty would establish, the French plan was doomed in the eyes of both the British and the Americans. When the Commission convened the Anglo-American draft* was adopted as a "basis for discussion" while the French paper was brushed aside. During the following four months all French efforts in the Commission were concentrated on molding the Covenant into the form of their original proposal:

I.

Statement of the Principles to Be taken as Basis of the League of Nations.

The problem of the League of Nations is one which forces itself upon the consideration of every Government. Historically, the idea is a very old one, which took shape when the civilized States assembled at the two Hague Conferences in 1899 and 1907. Practically, during the present war, it has been taken up afresh under various forms by the Allied Governments in their official declarations, by President Wilson in his note of December, 1916, and even by our enemies in their replies to the Papal Note of the 16th August, 1917. It is, there-

* For full text of Anglo-American draft see page 140ff.

fore, impossible to avoid the study of the question; it can and must be considered quite apart from the questions which form the subject proper of the Treaty of Peace.

1. In declaring that a sense of justice and honor compelled them to carry on the war thrust upon them by the aggressive action of the Central Powers until a joint and decisive victory had been gained, the Allies intend to convey that one of the results of that victory should be (a) to protect the world in future against any recurrence of the employment of brute force and attempts on the part of any nation to obtain universal supremacy, and (b) to establish the reign of justice on sure foundations throughout the world.

They declare that, in order to secure conditions which will exclude the existence of a mere dangerous truce and guarantee real peace, it is necessary to provide for the contractual and permanent organization of international relations, by the constitution between States of the association to which universal public opinion has given the name of "the League of Nations."

2. The object of the League of Nations shall not be to establish an international political State. It shall merely aim at the maintenance of peace by substituting Right for Might as the arbiter of disputes. It will thus guarantee to all States alike, whether small or great, the exercise of their sovereignty.

3. The scope of the League of Nations is universal, but, by its very nature, it can only extend to those nations which will give each other all necessary guarantees of a practical and legal nature, and which, in loyal fulfillment of their given word, solemnly undertake to be bound by certain rules in order to maintain peace by respecting Right, and to guarantee the free development of their national life.

Consequently, no nations can be admitted to the League other than those which are constituted as States and provided with representative institutions such as will permit their being themselves considered responsible for the acts of their own Governments.

4. The League of Nations shall be represented by an international body, composed of the responsible heads of Governments or of their delegates.

This international body shall have the following powers:

(1) It shall organize an international tribunal.
(2) It shall effect the amicable settlement of disputes between the States members of the League by means of mediation, preceded,

if necessary, by an enquiry in the terms of The Hague Convention of 1907.

(3) In the event of an amicable settlement proving impossible, it will refer the matter to the International Tribunal, if the question at issue is open to a legal decision; otherwise it shall itself decide the matter.

(4) It shall enforce the execution of its decisions and those of the International Tribunal; at its demand every nation shall be bound, in agreement with the other nations, to exert its economic, naval, and military power against any recalcitrant nation.

(5) Every nation shall likewise be bound, at the demand of the International Body, to exert, in common accord with the other nations, its economic, naval, and military power against any nation which, not having become a member of the League of Nations, shall attempt, by any means whatsoever, to impose its will on another nation.

5. The International Tribunal shall pronounce on all questions submitted to it, either by the International Body or by a State having any dispute with another.

It shall decide and pronounce upon questions of law at issue between States, on the basis of custom or of international conventions, as well as of theory and jurisprudence.

In cases of violation of such law, it shall order the necessary reparation and sanctions.

Part II deals with economic, legal and diplomatic sanctions while Part III comes to the heart of the French proposal.

III.

Military Sanctions.

(i) INTERNATIONAL FORCES.

The execution of the military sanctions on land or at sea shall be entrusted either to an international force, or to one or more Powers members of the League of Nations, to whom a mandate in that behalf shall have been given.

The International Body shall have at its disposal a military force supplied by the various member States of sufficient strength:

(1) to secure the execution of its decision and those of the International Tribunal;

(2) to overcome, in case of need, any forces which may be opposed to the League of Nations in the event of armed conflict.

(ii) STRENGTH OF INTERNATIONAL CONTINGENTS.

The International Body shall determine the strength of the international force and fix the contingents which must be held at its disposal.

Each of the member States shall be free to settle as it deems best the conditions under which its contingent shall be recruited.

The question of the limitation of armaments in each of the member States will be dealt with elsewhere.

(iii) PERMANENT STAFF.

A permanent international Staff shall investigate all military questions affecting the League of Nations. Each State shall appoint the officer or officers who shall represent it, in a proportion to be determined later.

The Chief and Deputy Chiefs of Staff shall be appointed for a period of three years by the International Body, from a list submitted by the member States.

(iv) FUNCTIONS OF THE PERMANENT STAFF.

It shall be the duty of the permanent International Staff to deal, under the supervision of the International Body, with everything relating to the organization of the joint forces and the eventual conduct of military operations. It will in particular be charged with the task of inspecting international forces and armaments in agreement with the military authorities of each State, and of proposing any improvements it may deem necessary, either in the international military organization or in the constitution, composition, and methods of recruiting of the forces of each State.

The Staff shall report the result of its inspections, either as a matter of routine or at the request of the International Body. Military instructions shall be given in each member State in accordance with rules designed to procure, as far as possible, uniformity in the armaments and training of the troops destined to act in concert.

The International Body shall be entitled, at any time, to require that the member States introduce any alteration into their national system of recruiting which the Staff may report to be necessary.

(V) COMMANDER-IN-CHIEF AND CHIEF OF GENERAL STAFF.

When circumstances shall so require, the International Body shall appoint, for the duration of the operations to be undertaken, a Commander-in-chief of the international forces.

Upon his appointment, the Commander-in-chief shall nominate his Chief of General Staff and the officers who are to assist him.

The powers of the Commander-in-chief and his Chief of General Staff shall cease when circumstances become such that an armed conflict is no longer to be feared, or when the object of the military operations has been attained.

In either case, the date at which the powers of the Commander-in-chief and the General Staff shall cease shall be fixed by a decision of the International Body.

IV.

Scope and Functions of the International Body.

Public opinion among civilized nations, which regards The Hague Conferences as a step towards the recognition and application of the principles of justice and equity as guarantees of the security of States and the well-being of their peoples, is unanimously demanding a fresh effort in the same direction. Although it has seen arbitration applied in cases of ever-increasing importance, and likewise the creation of an international judicial organization and the institution of a system of enquiry and mediation, it still considers as indispensable the establishment of more concrete guarantees, in order that peace may be secured by the reign of organized justice.

The question thus arises of the institution of a permanent International Body to carry into effect the real aims of the League of Nations.

There is no question of making the League of Nations a super-State, or even a Confederation. Any such idea is rendered impossible by respect for the sovereignty of States, by the diversity of national traditions and of political and judicial standards, by the differences in systems of administration and opposition of economic interests; but public opinion among the free nations would be disappointed if the result of the present crisis were not to be the institution of an International Body capable of contributing, by constant vigilance and the exercise of sufficient authority, to the maintenance of peace.

In conformity with the statement of principles adopted by the Commission on the 18th January, this body, constituted in the form of an International Council, will derive its authority from the reciprocal undertaking given by each of the member nations to use its economic, naval, and military power in conjunction with the other members of the League against any nation contravening the Covenant of the League.[9]

With their plan shelved in favor of the Anglo-American draft, the French resorted to offering amendments that would make the resulting Covenant conform to their concepts. They made extended use of this tactic, which they pursued with admirable pertinacity. Their first attempt was extraordinarily successful; when Article 8* came up for discussion, the French objected to the sentence suggesting an end to compulsory military service, a concept as dear to the French heart as it was repulsive to Anglo-American thinking.

Mr. Bourgeois pointed out the inability of France to agree to the abolition of compulsory military service, which appeared to France to be a fundamental issue of democracy, and was a corollary of universal suffrage.

After remarks by Mr. Orlando and Mr. Larnaude, President Wilson proposed to delete the last clause of the first paragraph relative to the possibility of abolishing compulsory military service and to substitute for it the following: "The Executive Council shall also determine for the consideration and action of the several Governments what military equipment and armament is fair and reasonable in proportion to the scale of forces laid down in the programme of disarmament; and these limits, when adopted, shall not be exceeded without the permission of the Body of Delegates."

This amendment was adopted.

Upon the proposal of President Wilson, which was likewise accepted, the last paragraph of this Article was changed as follows: "The High Contracting Parties further agree that munitions and implements of war should not be manufactured by private enterprise, and direct the Executive Council to advise how this practice can be dispensed with; and further agree that there shall be full and frank publicity as to all national armaments and military or naval programmes."

* For text of Article 8 see page 146.

Baron Makino proposed that in the first clause of this Article, in the third line, the words "national safety" should be substituted for the words "domestic safety."

This suggestion was adopted.

Article 8, as amended, was adopted.[10]

But, as the French kept hammering away at the Anglo-American draft, the Commission hardened; and, as Wilson's concepts commanded an overwhelming majority in the Commission, the French amendments were invariably defeated, usually by a vote of 12 to 3. Nevertheless, the French came back again and again, and throughout ten exhausting afternoon and evening sessions M. Bourgeois stuck to his guns, stating and restating the French case for a League that would amount to a military alliance of the victorious powers, a concept neither the British nor the Americans were able to accept.

Excerpts from the minutes of the eighth meeting of the League of Nations Commission (February 11, 1919) will serve as well as any others to demonstrate the perseverance and agility of French diplomacy:

Mr. Bourgeois read the following note, and asked that it be inserted in the minutes:

"I had thought of asking the Drafting Committee to reconsider the text of Article 14. Then I was told that our mandate was limited to only three articles, and I was convinced that this was so. Nevertheless, I ask that I may record the following observations:

"It was understood that in this first reading we would not consider ourselves bound by what had been provisionally adopted before, and that is all the more necessary since there are certain articles whose import cannot be measured without discussing the provisions of certain later articles.

"According to the Draft which has just been adopted for Articles 12 and 13, even in case of an unanimous agreement, if a Power, acting in bad faith, and being the possessor of the thing in dispute, refuses to abide by the judgment of the arbitrators or the decision of the Executive Committee, the League of Nations is not legally bound to ensure the fulfilment of the decree. In view of the necessary consequences, it is imperative that stronger provisions be introduced in order to protect a State acting in good faith against a State which is acting in bad faith.

"Otherwise it would happen that nations faithful to their international obligations would suffer as the result of an organisation effective in appearance, but in reality a trap for nations of good faith.

"Our Commission certainly does not want this, and indeed it would be too much in conflict with the principles of justice so forcibly expressed by President Wilson.

"I feel all the more impelled to offer these observations now for the reason that since we have been working here a trend of opinion has developed revealing a spirit of uneasiness to which I must call your attention.

"Our colleagues representing Great Britain and the United States have very justly called attention to the serious consideration which they must give to the public opinion of their nations, and to the necessity that their Governments should not be involved in sacrifices beyond those which are at the same time demanded and delimited by the very principles of the League of Nations.

"In the presence of these evidences of uneasiness, shall we not together examine carefully the articles which we adopted at the time of the first reading? In this way we can make whatever changes are necessary in order to secure the unqualified approval of the public opinion of our respective countries. I shall deal with the following three points:—

"1. Article 11, as it is now drawn, limits the application of its sanction to violations of Article 10. It therefore does not make any provision to secure the execution of the decrees of arbitration contemplated in Article 11, nor for the unanimous decisions of the Executive Council referred to in Article 13.

"Yesterday, Articles 11 and 13 were sent back to us for re-drafting. Article 14, however, was not sent; yet the new draft of these two articles calls for a corresponding change in Article 14.

"In order that the provisions of Articles 11 and 13 may be rendered effective beyond all doubt, it is necessary that, under some form to be agreed upon, they should be backed by sanctions.

"And so I propose to add to Article 14, after these words in the second paragraph, 'To be used to protect the Covenants of the League,' the two following paragraphs:—

> " 'In case one of the contesting parties, after having followed the procedure prescribed under Article 10, should not accept the verdict of the tribunal, or a decision unanimously rendered by the Execu-

tive Council or by the Body of Delegates, the Council shall ask the Associated Governments to apply appropriate sanctions from among those enumerated in the first paragraph of this article.

" 'In the case of a recommendation made by majority vote, where the dispute might terminate in a resort to force by the interested parties, the Executive Council shall submit the question to the Governments themselves.'

"2. The observations which precede must likewise involve a reexamination of the text of Article 8, relating to the reduction of armaments. The substitution of the words 'national safety' for the words 'domestic safety,' which was adopted at the suggestion of the Japanese Delegate, ought to involve certain modifications with a view to insuring a practical realisation of the words of President Wilson:—

" 'A force must be created, a force so superior to that of all nations or to that of all alliances, that no nation or combination of nations can challenge or resist it.'

"In order that the international force should be what President Wilson desires, it must be so great that no single force can defeat it. And so, I believe that we must organise a control of troops and armaments of such a kind as definitely to put a stop to preparation for fresh wars on the part of nations acting in bad faith, and to protect honest nations against every sudden attack; for such a thing would indicate a real failure in the organisation of law.

"In Article 8 then, the following words should be inserted after the words, 'The Executive Council shall formulate plans for effecting such reduction':—

" 'It will establish an international control of troops and armaments, and the High Contracting Parties agree to submit themselves to it in all good faith. It will fix the conditions under which the permanent existence and organisation of an international force may be assured.'

"I may recall that at the meeting of the 6th February, in respect to this Article 8, I insisted that in the determination of what troops and what armaments each nation should have, on the one hand to preserve its national security and on the other hand to bear its share in maintaining an international force, it would be necessary to introduce two distinct elements, and that with the factor of power in the case of each

State should be considered also the factor of risk which each State may have to run by reason of its geographical situation and the nature of its frontier.

"President Wilson clearly recognised this necessity when, speaking from the platform of the French Chamber of Deputies, he pronounced those splendid words, for which I here thank him: 'The frontier of France is the frontier of the world's liberty.' I ask then, that following the words 'The Executive Council shall formulate plans for effecting such reduction,' this clause be added:—

> " 'Having due regard, in determining the number of troops, not only to the relative strength of the different States, but also to the risks to which they are exposed by their geographical situation and the nature of their frontiers.'

"I offer this as a new amendment to Article 8.

"3. My third amendment, which concerns Article 6, goes back to quite a different thought. I mentioned it to you when first we discussed this Article. It relates to the conditions which shall govern the admission of a new State into the League of Nations. To my mind the veto of one nation would not be desirable, providing the majority be two-thirds. We have all stated here that mutual good faith ought to be the basis and constitute the strength of an international organisation. Guarantees of uprightness are indispensable. The associated States ought to be free States, fortified with institutions which will safeguard them in the enjoyment of liberty.

"If they have previously committed acts in defiance of law, acts of violence, acts of barbarity or crimes, they must first be required to make reparations and to pay the price which justice demands. Briefly, it is necessary that every one of the associated States be at the same time cleansed of its past and free for the future. That is the spirit of the following amendment, which will give to the League of Nations its high moral position in the eyes of the world.

"I would modify the second paragraph as follows:—

> " 'Furthermore no nation shall be admitted into the League unless it has representative institutions which permit of its being considered as itself responsible for the acts of its own Government; unless it is in a position to give effective guarantees of its sincere intention to abide by its agreement; and unless it conforms to those principles

which the League shall formulate regarding naval and military forces and armaments.'

"The French Senators and Deputies who compose the parliamentary group of arbitration, consisting of members favourably disposed toward the League of Nations, have already taken steps to acquaint us with their anxiety regarding those matters of which I have just spoken. If we should not take formal precautions in the matter of controlling armaments, this group of men would feel that we were exposing our country to grave risks unless guarantees were given on that point, and it would oppose the plan all the more vigorously."

Mr. Larnaude supported these views, and held that they could not create difficulties. He insisted on the idea of the geographical risk, which is of such great importance for nations like Poland, the Czecho-Slovak Republic, Roumania, Belgium, France, &c. The control of munitions of war, and of other manufactures which might conceal potential preparations for war, lay at the very basis of the League of Nations, unless one wished the nations of good faith to be the victims of the others.

President Wilson: We must make a distinction between what is possible and what is not. No nation will consent to control. As for us Americans, we cannot consent to control because of our Constitution. We must do everything that is possible to ensure the safety of the world. Some plan must be worked out by which every country shall have a sufficient force, first, to maintain its national security, secondly, to contribute to international safety.

It may be admitted that France should maintain a force proportionately more considerable than other nations, on account of the geographical risk that has been mentioned, but as to the construction of an unified military machine in time of peace, that is quite another question. This war made apparent the absolute necessity of the unity of command, and this unity of command constituted an immense advantage which had a decisive influence on the very issue of the war, but the unity of command only became possible because of the immediate and imminent danger which threatened civilisation. To propose to realise unity of command in time of peace, would be to put forward a proposal that no nation would accept. The Constitution of the United States forbids the President to send beyond its frontiers the national forces. If the United States maintained an army, there would always be a certain inevitable delay in sending it to the States where it might be required. And it is possible that the Germans may gather together once more their military power. If the militarist madness has not been destroyed in Germany by this war, a new menace may threaten us, but this menace will not develop suddenly. The economic condition of Germany will make that impossible.

As for us, if we organise from now onwards an international army, it would appear that we were substituting international militarism for national militarism. Some eminent Frenchmen have already told me that they would not accept what the American Constitution forbids me to accept. I know how France has suffered, and I know that she wishes to obtain the best guarantees possible before she enters the League, and everything that we can do in this direction we shall do, but we cannot accept proposals which are in direct contradiction to our Constitution.

The argument which has been most employed against the League of Nations in America, is that the army of the United States would be at the disposal of an international council, that American troops would thus be liable to be ordered to fight at any moment for the most remote of causes and this prospect alarms our people. There is therefore no other course open to us but to accept some system compatible at once with our Constitution and with the views of our public opinion.

Mr. Bourgeois said that he need not add that France was ready to become a member of the League of Nations, the principles of which, as laid down in the draft Covenant, were in accordance with those which she herself had always fought for, but she required the organisation of international action to be considered and clearly defined. He thought there was a misunderstanding with regard to the word "control." President Wilson had alluded to the command of an international army, and to the difficulties that would be raised as to the admission of a single chief placed at the head of all the armies of the nations in the League. But what was most important of all was to have some means of verifying the quantities of armaments produced by each nation, and that could only be done if every State in the League undertook not to surpass certain limits, and to allow that the extent of its manufactures should be verified. This verification was indispensable in order to avoid that a State should secretly produce arms and munitions. He used the word control, therefore, only in the sense of the French words "surveillance" or "vérification."

So far as the international army was concerned it was not a question of a permanent army, but simply of making some provision for a military organisation to be given to national contingents so that they could be rapidly co-ordinated against an aggressive State. If one could not do that the League became nothing but a dangerous façade. France held the frontier of the Rhine, which President Wilson had called the frontier of liberty. She was therefore obliged to maintain a considerable force even in time of peace, and she could never be tranquil unless it were certain that, in case of attack, she could count on the effective help of the other members of the League, and that she would not have to wait for their support for months, or perhaps for years; unless this were certain France would be again exposed to a sudden attack and would think that the League was nothing but a trap.

It appeared, therefore, necessary for the safety of the members of the League who were particularly exposed to attack to provide some organisation for the international forces which would be ready to come into operation whenever affairs took a critical turn. He did not hold in any way to his wording, but simply to the double idea which he had expressed to the verification or surveillance of armaments and of a certain organisation to provide for cases in which the utilisation of national contingents might be required. He asked, therefore, for the insertion in the convention of a formula which would give public opinion the sense of security which it demanded. It was necessary that the idea of the League of Nations should engender a feeling of confidence in order to obtain universal acceptance.

President Wilson: In this discussion we have so far left on one side an essential element. Our principal safety will be obtained by the obligation which we shall lay on Germany to effect a complete disarmament. It is said that she will be able to prepare again in secret, but I ask, what part of the German military preparation was secret before this war? We knew the number of their soldiers, their plan of attack, and the extent of their armaments. In reality no serious preparation for war can be made in secret. There is nothing to be feared from a large number of men; the danger lies rather in the quantity of machines and of munitions which have been manufactured, and these things cannot be accumulated in secret. I am convinced that we shall carry out the effective disarmament of Germany, and in that case we shall enjoy on that side a period of safety, for it will be impossible for Germany to accumulate anew reserves of munitions and of the machinery of war.

Lord Robert Cecil observed that the French proposals seemed to be summed up in three principal points:—

1. National security must be considered in relation to the geographical position of States. One could meet this preoccupation by adding to the articles words of this sort: "Having special regard to the situation and circumstances of certain States." This was a matter which could be put right by the draughtsmen.

2. The word "control" might lead to a misunderstanding. It might be preferable to use the word "inspection." In any case the French amendment had for its object to make certain of two things: (*a*) that no State should have an army greater than a permitted maximum, and (*b*) that every State should have a force equal to the minimum imposed by the League. The second of these points seemed to him extremely delicate, and the people of Great Britain would have many objections to accepting a control which insisted on a certain number of British soldiers being maintained under arms. He did not think that this proposal could be adopted.

3. The French amendment indicated the necessity of an organisation which would permit of the immediate utilisation of the military forces of the members of the League. In this form the proposal departed from our conception of the League, which did not include an international force, but some less strict arrangement might be adopted which would permit of the preparation of agreements on the subject whenever the need for it should be felt. Thus a result could be obtained if we were content to accept some provision such as the following: "A permanent Commission shall be established to advise the League of Nations on naval and military questions."

Mr. Larnaude: Several nations which have taken part in this war are afraid of having made sacrifices in vain. The protection which results from the existence of a League of Nations will perhaps become a guarantee of safety, but within what period of time? Perhaps within a hundred years. By that time the militarist spirit will no doubt have disappeared, but at the present moment we are emerging from a terrible war. Can it be thought that we shall pass immediately from the state of intensive militarism in which we live to a state of practical disarmament?

Today we are in a period of transition. We must have national contingents always ready to reassure the States within the League. The sacrifice which is asked of each State will be negligible beside this. The idea of an international force is bound up with the very idea of the League of Nations, unless one is content that the League should be a screen of false security.

President Wilson: It must not be supposed that any of the members of the League will remain isolated if it is attacked, that is the direct contrary of the thought of all of us. We are ready to fly to the assistance of those who are attacked, but we cannot offer more than the condition of the world enables us to give.

Mr. Larnaude: If the Treaty of Peace gives us absolute guarantees that Germany will be virtually disarmed, and will not be able to build up her armaments again, then we shall feel safer.

Mr. Bourgeois: The dilemma has been put to us in the following manner: Is France prepared to enter into a League of Nations such as is defined in the Covenant, that is to say, without the organisation of an international army, or would she prefer to stand alone?

We must equally call your attention to the fact that we are ourselves disposed to submit to the corresponding obligations, that is to say, to our armies, and our military preparations being controlled by the League. Other nations say they cannot consent to this control. Nevertheless, there can be no rule of justice and of safety among the different nations of the world if every State can at its will prepare an attack. Opposition to the essential principles of the League of Nations does not therefore come from our side.

President Wilson: The only method by which we can achieve this end lies in our having confidence in the good faith of the nations who belong to the League. There must be between them a cordial agreement and goodwill. Take a new State which is going to enter this League, Poland. We have confidence in Poland, we hope that she will co-operate willingly in our efforts, and that she will take the necessary measures to secure her safety, and also to make the principles of the League respected. I therefore ask the French Delegation to consider this question again, for I think that any control, by whatever name it may be called, will be too offensive to be adopted. All that we can promise, and we do promise it, is to maintain our military forces in such a condition that the world will feel itself in safety. When danger comes, we too will come, and we will help you, but you must trust us. We must all depend on our mutual good faith.

Mr. Bourgeois: France is ready to accept some system of control, and considers that in accepting it she would surrender no portion of her dignity. It is a common measure of mutual guarantee which has nothing offensive in it, since it would apply equally to all the Great Powers, and since it is made by common accord amongst them all. We are dealing with everyone on the footing of perfect equality, and we do not think that this step would involve any sacrifice of independence. I ask therefore with insistence that something should be done in this matter, which cannot be left outside our Covenant; something that will give to public opinion the feeling of safety which it demands. Without that any scheme for a League of Nations will simply arouse general distrust.

It was agreed that the matter should be considered again by the Drafting Committee.

(*The Meeting adjourned.*)[11]

Besides coping with the French attempts to rewrite the Covenant to suit their conceptions, the Commission was faced with another, most delicate, problem. Colonel House meticulously sketches in the background.

February 4, 1919: . . . Baron Makino and Viscount Chinda came for advice what Japan had best do regarding the race question. There is a demand in Japan that the Peace Conference through the League of Nations, should express some broad principles of racial equality. Chinda and Makino do not desire to bring it up themselves if they can avoid doing so. I advised them to prepare two resolutions, one which they desired, and another which they would be willing to accept in lieu of the one they prefer. Chinda and Makino said: "On July 8th at Magnolia you expressed to Viscount Ishii sentiments which pleased the Japanese Government, therefore we look upon you as a friend and we have come for your advice."

February 5, 1919: . . . I showed the President the drafts that Baron Makino and Viscount Chinda had brought this afternoon. The resolution they wanted we discarded at once, but the resolution which they had prepared as a compromise the President thought might do by making a slight change, which he did in his own handwriting. Later in the evening I showed Chinda what we had prepared, and he seemed to think it would be satisfactory. He wished to first discuss it with his colleagues.

February 6, 1919: . . . Viscount Chinda brought another draft covering the race question. He found, after consultation with his legal adviser, that the one we agreed upon was practically meaningless. The one he brought today will not be accepted by either our people or the British Colonies. The Japs are making the adoption of a clause regarding immigration a sine qua non of their adhesion to the League of

Nations. I have a feeling that it can be worked out by a satisfactory compromise which will in no way weaken the American or British Dominion's position and yet will satisfy the amour-propre of the Japanese.

February 9, 1919: . . . a good many callers today, including Viscount Chinda and Baron Makino, who came again upon the inevitable race question. I have placed them "on the backs" of the British, for every solution which the Japanese and I have proposed, Hughes of the British Delegation objects to.

February 12, 1919: . . . Viscount Chinda called again to say that he could get nothing definite from the British and that he intended to present a resolution himself which would be more drastic than the one the President and I agreed to accept. His idea is that while it will not be adopted, it will be an explanation to his people in Japan. He thanked me warmly for the interest I had taken and said ". . . his government and people would always remember my consideration and sympathy."[12]

Article 21 (nondiscrimination on the grounds of religion) came up for discussion in the meeting on February 13th. The following exchange of opinions took place.

Lord Robert Cecil read Article 21.

Colonel House wished to make known to the Commission the importance which President Wilson attached to the inclusion of this article.

Mr. Larnaude, while appreciating the importance which might attach to a proclamation of the inviolability of the human conscience and the exercise of religion, nevertheless thought it difficult to include a clause on the matter. In any case, the anxieties of President Wilson related to countries which were not members of the actual League.

Baron Makino: I wish to add the clause:—

> "The equality of nations being a basic principle of the League of Nations, the High Contracting Parties agree to accord, as soon as possible, to all alien nationals of States members of the League, equal and just treatment in every respect, making no distinction, either in law or fact, on account of their race or nationality."

directly after the end of the article as it stands.[13]

In support of his amendment Baron Makino made a strong and dignified appeal.

> It is not necessary to dwell on the fact that racial and religious animosities have constituted a fruitful source of warfare among different peoples throughout history, often leading to deplorable excesses. . . . I am aware of the difficult circumstances that stand in the way of acting on the principle embodied in this clause, but I do not think it insurmountable if sufficient importance is attached to the consideration of serious misunderstanding between different peoples which may grow to an uncontrollable degree. . . . What was deemed impossible before is about to be accomplished. The creation of this League itself is a notable example. If this organization can open a way to the solution of the question, the scope of the work will become wider and enlist the interest of a still greater part of humanity.
>
> As a result of this war, the wave of national and democratic spirit has extended to remote corners of the world, and has given additional impulse to the aspirations of all peoples; this impulse once set in motion . . . cannot be stifled, and it would be imprudent to treat this symptom lightly. . . .

Lord Robert Cecil remarked that this subject had been dealt with in long and difficult discussions. It was a question which had raised extremely serious problems within the British Empire. It was a matter of a highly controversial character, and in spite of the nobility of thought which inspired Baron Makino, he thought that it would be wiser for the moment to postpone its examination.

Mr. Koo stated that the Chinese Government and people were deeply interested in the question brought up by Baron Makino, adding that he was naturally in full sympathy with the spirit of the proposed amendment. But pending the receipt of instructions from his Government, he would reserve his right of discussion for the future, and request that the reservation be recorded in the Minutes.

Mr. Venizelos was of the opinion that questions of race and religion would certainly be dealt with in the future by the League of Nations, but that it would be better for the moment not to allude to them.

Several members of the Commission agreed with this view.

Colonel House said that he would inform President Wilson of the opinion of the Commission on this matter, and that in any case he would reserve the right of the President to raise the question again at the Conference.

With this reservation, Article 21 was dropped from the Covenant.[14]

Under the same date Colonel House notes in his diary:

. . . We passed [dropped?] article XXI of the old draft because Baron Makino was insistent upon the race clause going in if the religious clause was retained. I could not agree to eliminate the religious clause without first giving the President a chance to express himself, but tentatively promised that it should be withdrawn, in which event Baron Makino promised to withdraw, for the moment, the race amendment which neither the British nor we could take in the form in which he finally presented it. Makino agreed upon a form the other day which the President accepted, and which was mild and as inoffensive as possible, but even that the British refused. . . . I understand that all the British Delegation were willing to accept the form the President, Makino and Chinda had agreed upon, excepting Hughes of Australia. He has been the stumbling block.[15]

By February 14th, the day before Wilson's departure for America, the Covenant of the League was ready to be presented to the Plenary Session of the Conference. Although Woodrow Wilson could not claim exclusive copyright to the idea of the Covenant, it was due to his energy, single-mindedness and occasional ruthlessness that the Covenant was whipped through committee in less than two weeks. Moreover, it was entirely through his efforts that the original Anglo-American draft emerged from committee almost unchanged, that most of the French amendments were successfully beaten off, that the racial equality amendment was sidetracked, and that in substance, as well as in spirit, the Covenant presented to the Plenary Session on February 14th was almost identical to the draft presented to the Commission eleven days earlier.

The Japanese had been prevailed upon not to make any public statement at the Plenary Session, even though their racial equality amendment had been so ignominiously discarded; but the irrepressible M. Léon Bourgeois could not refrain from making a lengthy speech in which he restated all the French objections. He couched his remarks in the most diplomatic and conciliatory form, yet managed to indicate that the French were not in the least satisfied with the Covenant as it stood. In a welter of congratulatory speeches, the Covenant was approved by the Plenary Session, and President Wilson proudly announced: "A living thing is born."

Woodrow Wilson had achieved what he set out to do, but at a heavy price; he had made more enemies than he would be able to handle. All the important nations present at the Conference were bitterly disappointed: the French never forgave Wilson for overriding all their objections and amendments; the British, and particularly the British Dominions, were annoyed at being refused their share of the spoils; the Japanese blamed Wilson for the Commission's refusal to go along with their racial equality amendment; and, though the Plenary Session gave unanimous approval to the Covenant, it did so more in the spirit of "Let's get that nonsense over with and get down to serious business" than in any spirit of enthusiasm.

President Wilson may not have fully realized the prevailing sentiment. His mind was already preoccupied with the troubles awaiting him on the other side of the Atlantic. Before leaving Paris he had cabled the members of the Senate and House Foreign Affairs Committees requesting that they postpone discussion of the Covenant until his arrival in Washington. He also invited the Senators to dinner at the White House to discuss the subject with him.

When the President landed in Boston on February 24th, he found that the Senate had disregarded his request and was debating the League of Nations. Senators Lodge, Borah, and Reed and the irreconcilables were making headlines across the nation by mercilessly tearing the Covenant to shreds. The dinner party at the White House, too, was a failure. Senators Borah and Fall sent their regrets; Knox and Lodge sat through the proceedings like cigar store Indians, never opening their mouths; and Senator Brandegee of Connecticut cross-examined the President like a prosecuting attorney, and came away saying to the press: "I feel like I've just had tea with the mad hatter." The American press on the whole seemed anti-League, and the only comfort Wilson could find was that a public opinion poll conducted by the *Literary Digest* seemed to indicate a 2 to 1 sentiment *for* the League of Nations throughout the country.

Just minutes before the Senate adjourned on March 4th, thirty-nine senators (more than enough to defeat the Covenant) signed a round robin which said that "the Covenant was not acceptable in the form now proposed." Before boarding the *George Washington* for his return to Paris, in a speech at the Metropolitan Opera House in New York, the President, without mentioning the round robin, threw down the following challenge to his opponents in the Senate:

Gentlemen on this side will find the Covenant not only in it, but so many threads of the treaty tied to the Covenant that you cannot dissect the Covenant from the treaty without destroying the whole vital structure.[16]

Many of the President's friends, among them some of the most ardent supporters of the League of Nations idea, found much fault with the Covenant and urged him to amend the document before submitting it to the Senate. The President's old friend, Senator Hitchcock of Nebraska, Democratic Leader of the Senate pro tempore, wrote him a letter urging this course upon him.

March 4, 1919

MY DEAR MR. PRESIDENT:

A number of republican Senators who signed Lodge's manifesto on the league of nations constitution will, in my opinion, vote for it nevertheless if it is a part of the peace treaty. A still larger number will give it support if certain amendments are made. The following I would mention as likely to influence votes in the order given:

First, a reservation to each high contracting party of its exclusive control over domestic subjects.

Second, a reservation of the Monroe doctrine.

Third, some provision by which a member of the league can, on proper notice, withdraw from membership.

Fourth, the settlement of the ambiguity in Article 15.

Fifth, the insertion on the next to the last line of first paragraph of Article 8, after the word "adopted," of the words "by the several governments."

Sixth, the definite assurance that it is optional with a nation to accept or reject the burdens of a mandatory.

I wish you a safe journey.

Yours truly,
[*sd*] G. M. HITCHCOCK

THE PRESIDENT,
The White House.[17]

Very similar advice came from Republicans. Ex-President Taft, a strong supporter of the League of Nations idea, sent the President a cable via Tumulty, his secretary.

The White House,
Washington, March 18, 1919

PRESIDENT WILSON, Paris:

Following from William H. Taft:

"If you bring back the treaty with the League of Nations in it make more specific reservations of the Monroe Doctrine, fix a term for the duration of the League, and the limit of armament, require expressly unanimity of action of Executive Council and body of Delegates, and add to Article 15 a provision that where the Executive Council of the Body of Delegates finds the difference to grow out of an exclusively domestic policy, it shall recommend no settlement, the ground will be completely cut from under the opponents of the League in the Senate. Addition to Article 15 will answer objection as to Japanese immigration, as well as tariffs under Article 21. Reservation of the Monroe Doctrine might be as follows:

"Any American State or States may protect the integrity of American territory and the independence of the Government whose territory it is, whether a member of the League or not, and may, in the interests of the American peace, object to and prevent the further transfer of American territory or sovereignty to any power outside the Western Hemisphere.

"Monroe Doctrine reservation alone would probably carry the treaty, but others would make it certain,

(Signed) "WILLIAM H. TAFT."

TUMULTY[18]

Senator Henry Cabot Lodge of Massachusetts, who, together with Senator Borah, led the fight against the Covenant, outlined the major objections to the document in his debate with Lowell (March 19, 1919).

. . . As I have said, my first constructive criticism is that we should have a revision of the language and form of the draft.

I now come to what seems to me a very vital point indeed, and that is the Monroe Doctrine. I shall not undertake to trace the history of the Doctrine or its development since Mr. Monroe first declared it. But in its essence it rests upon the proposition of separating the Americas from Europe in all matters political. It rests on the differentiation of the American hemisphere from Europe, and therefore I have found it difficult to understand an argument first advanced with more confidence, perhaps, than it is now,—that we preserve the Monroe Doctrine by extending it. The Monroe Doctrine was the invisible line that we drew around the American hemisphere. It was the fence that we put around it to exclude other nations from meddling in American affairs, and I have never been able to get it through my head how you can preserve a fence by taking it down.

The Monroe Doctrine is the corollary of Washington's foreign policy declared in the Farewell Address. I am not going to base any argument upon it, but it is a mistake to consider the policy laid down by Washington and Monroe as ephemeral and necessarily transient. As Mr. Wilson well said, Washington's Doctrine was not transient. It may be wrong; the time may have come to discard it; but it is not ephemeral because it rests on two permanent facts,—human nature and geography.

Human nature, you may say, has changed. When you study the history of the past as far as we have a history there is a curious similarity in it at all stages. But one thing is certain,—not even the wisest and the most optimistic of reformers can change the geography of the globe. They say communication has quickened enormously. The Atlantic Ocean is not what it was as a barrier, or the Pacific either, I suppose. But do not forget that even under modern conditions the silver streak, the little channel only twenty miles wide, was England's bulwark and defense in this last war. Do not underrate the three thousand miles of Atlantic. It was on that that the Monroe Doctrine, the corollary of Washington's policy, rested. . . .

The Monroe Doctrine has been expanded. A resolution was passed unanimously in the Senate a few years ago stating that the United States would regard it as an act of hostility for any corporation or association of any other nation to take possession of Magdalena Bay, being a post of great strategic, naval and military advantage. That did not rest on the Monroe Doctrine. It rested on something deeper than that. It rested on the basis of the Monroe Doctrine, the great law of self-preservation. They say that if we demand the exclusion of the Monroe Doctrine from the operation of the League, they will demand compensation. Very well. Let them exclude us from meddling in Europe. That is not a burden that we are seeking to bear. We are ready to go there at any time to save the world from barbarism and tyranny, but we are not thirsting to interfere in every obscure quarrel that may spring up in the Balkans. Mr. Taft says that the Covenant "should be made more definite by a larger reservation of the Monroe Doctrine."

I agree entirely. I offer that as my third constructive criticism, that there should be a larger reservation of the Monroe Doctrine, and when the leading advocate of this draft takes that position it seems to me it cannot be a very unreasonable one.

There is the question of immigration which this treaty reaches under the nonjusticiable questions. I am told and I believe (I have followed it through all the windings) that a final decision could only be reached by unanimity, and it is said that the League would not be unanimous. I think that highly probable, but I deny the jurisdiction. I cannot personally accede to the proposition that other nations, that a body of men in executive council where we as a nation have but one vote, shall have any power, unanimous or otherwise, to say who shall come into the United States.

It must not be within the jurisdiction of the League at all. It lies at the foundation of national character and national well-being. There should be no possible jurisdiction over the power which defends this country from a flood of Japanese, Chinese, and Hindu labor.

The tariff is involved in the article for the boycott. The coastwise trade is involved in Article 21. I think we ought to settle our own import duties. They say it is a domestic question. So it is, so is immigration, but they are domestic questions with international relations.

Moreover—and I know some people think this is a far-fetched objection, but having other nations meddle with our tariff runs up against a provision of the Constitution. The Constitution provides that all revenue bills shall originate in the House of Representatives. Now I do not offer that as a final objection. No doubt we could amend our Constitution to fit the League, but it would take some time, and I think it is better to steer clear of the Constitution in cases like that. And I offer an amendment, already proposed by Senator Owen of Oklahoma, an ardent Democrat and a supporter of the League, to exclude international questions of the character of immigration and the tariff from the jurisdiction of the League. I present that as a fourth constructive criticism. . . .

Then comes Article 10. That is the most important article in the whole treaty. That is the one that I especially wish the American people to consider, take it to their homes, their firesides, discuss it, think of it. If they command it the treaty will be ratified and proclaimed with that in it. But think of it first, think well. This article pledges us to guarantee the political independence and the territorial integrity against external aggression of every nation a member of the League.

Now, guarantees must be fulfilled. They are sacred promises—it has been said only morally binding. Why, that is all there is to a treaty between great nations. If they are not morally binding they are nothing but "scraps of paper." If the United States agrees to Article 10 we must carry it out in letter and spirit; and if it is agreed to I should insist that we did so, because the honor and the good faith of our country would be at stake.

Now, that is a tremendous promise to make. I ask the fathers and mothers, the sisters and the wives and the sweethearts, whether they are ready yet to guarantee the political independence and territorial integrity of every nation on earth against external aggression, and to send the hope of their families, the hope of the nation, the best of our youth, forth into the world on that errand?

If they are, it will be done. If the American people are not ready to do it that article will have to go out of the treaty or be limited. If that League with that article had existed in the Eighteenth Century, France could not have assisted this country to win the Revolution. If that League had existed in 1898 we could not have interfered and rescued Cuba from the clutches of Spain; we should have brought a war on with all the other nations of the world.[19]

In Paris the atmosphere had undergone a marked change during the President's four-week absence. News of the Senate debates, Senator Lodge's round robin, and the attacks by the

American press, creating the impression that Wilson had been unable to sell the League to his own people, plus the additional fact that, in Paris itself, the Supreme Council was discussing peace terms with never a mention of the League of Nations, all combined to create the general impression that "the League is dead." Woodrow Wilson saw his prize achievement slipping from his grasp and he decided to meet the situation head on. He issued the following statement:

March 15, 1919

The President said today that the decision made at the Peace Conference at its plenary session, January 25, 1919, to the effect that the establishment of a League of Nations should be made an integral part of the Treaty of Peace, is of final force and that there is no basis whatever for the reports that a change in this decision was contemplated.

The resolution on the League of Nations, adopted January 25, 1919, at the plenary session of the Peace Conference, was as follows:

1. It is essential to the maintenance of the world settlement, which the associated nations are now met to establish, that a League of Nations be created to promote international co-operation, to insure the fulfillment of accepted international obligations, and to provide safeguards against war.

2. This League should be treated as an integral part of the general Treaty of Peace, and should be open to every civilized nation which can be relied upon to promote its objects.

3. The members of the League should periodically meet in international conference, and should have a permanent organization and secretariat to carry on the business of the League in the intervals between the conferences.[20]

Having disposed of that part of the business, Wilson then had to make up his mind what to do about the amendments proposed by the Senate. For a few days he hesitated. Colonel House outlined in his diary the problems facing the President.

March 16, 1919: . . . a conference with the President and Lord Robert Cecil. We were together for an hour and a half going over the Covenant of the League of Nations and discussing how it should be amended, if at all. I am in favor of some amendments and some clarifications. By doing this it will make the Covenant a better instrument and will meet many of the objections of our Senate. The President, with his usual stubbornness in such matters, desires to leave it as it is, saying that any change will be hailed in the United States as yielding to the Senate, and he believes it will lessen rather than increase the chances of ratification. Of course, I totally disagreed and so did Lord Robert, but rather more diplomatically than I.

March 18, 1919: [After-Dinner Conference with the President and Robert Cecil tonight.] Our meeting was fairly successful. We agreed on a number of changes. I found the President more reasonable than he was the other day as to meeting the wishes of the Senate, but we found it nearly impossible to write what the Senate desires into the Covenant, and for reasons which are entirely sufficient. We are perfectly willing to adopt them if the rest of the world would accept them, and if they do not cause more difficulties than they cure. If a special reservation of the Monroe Doctrine is made, Japan may want a reservation made regarding a sphere of influence in Asia, and other nations will ask for similar concessions, and there is no telling where it would end. If a statement is made that it is not intended to interfere in domestic affairs, this would please our Senators from the Pacific Slope, but it would displease all the Senators of pro-Irish tendencies, for they would declare that it was done at the instance of the English in order to keep the Irish question forever out of the League of Nations.

We are not trying to act in an arbitrary way but are sincerely desirous of meeting the views of those Senators who really have serious objections, but who do not understand our difficulties. No one can understand them without being here to formulate the Covenant as we have.[21]

By the next morning the President had made up his mind; he would reconvene the League of Nations Commission and present the various amendments the U. S. Senate demanded. He well knew that he would be opening the door to a flock of amendments that would come swarming from the four corners of the earth, but he saw no alternative. As far as the French were concerned, there was hope that they might now desist from putting forward their old amendments, inasmuch as Clemenceau had frankly admitted to Robert Cecil that they had only done so to exert pressure in the Supreme Council. Cecil had so informed the Colonel.

March 8, 1919

DEAR COLONEL HOUSE,

I saw Clemenceau this morning. If all Frenchmen were like him how easy our business would be.

He said to me two things: In the first place that Bourgeois' insistence on the military amendments was by his orders, and that he did it merely in order to say that he had tried every means to obtain security for his country before asking for guarantees on the frontier.—If it had been possible for the League to guarantee him military assistance in an effective way that would have been a great security for him.—But, if not, then he was quite satisfied to accept that refusal and to use it as an argument in favor of guarantees of another nature.

That seemed to me a perfectly legitimate attitude. It is only a pity it was not made clear at the outset.

I told him that I had guessed that that was the real meaning of Bourgeois' amendments, and that I felt sure that if he (Clemenceau) had been a member of the Commission he would have put them forward in a very different way. He laughed and said that he had never agreed with Bourgeois in his life, but that in this case he had acted on his (Clemenceau's) instigation. . . .[22]

Clemenceau having admitted that much, it seemed reasonable to assume that the French would not revert again to their old tactics. However, Colonel House must have been left somewhat uneasy by a visit he had from M. Léon Bourgeois.

March 16, 1919: I consented to be bored with Léon Bourgeois for an hour today. He wished to talk about his amendments to the League. They were the same old amendments that were turned down practically unanimously by the Committee. He brought them forth again this morning just as fresh and enthusiastically as if the matter had never been finally settled. What he wants, that is what the French want, is to make the League an instrument of war instead of an instrument of peace. Also to make it a league against Germany and for the benefit of France. They desire to create a general staff with authority to plan all sorts of military defences, invasions and whatnot.[23]

The Colonel's forebodings proved justified, for the French put up the same old fight to the very last session of the Commission. But they were not the only ones to make life difficult for the President. The most serious trouble came from an unexpected quarter. David Hunter Miller recounts:

Early in the afternoon of March 24, Mr. Close, one of Mr. Wilson's Secretaries, came to my office and handed me three amendments written on the President's typewriter, which he said the President wanted ready for the evening meeting, in English and in French, all on one paper. The French text was prepared in my office. As Wilson wrote them, the amendments were as follows:

Add to Article X the following paragraph:

Nothing in this Covenant shall be deemed to deny or affect the right of any American State or states to protect the integrity of American territory and the independence of any American government whose territory is threatened, whether a member of the League or not, or, in the interest of American peace, to object to or prevent the further transfer of American territory or sovereignty to any power outside the Western Hemisphere.

Add to Article XV the following paragraph:

If the difference between the parties shall be found by the Executive Council or by the Body of Delegates to be a question which by international law is solely within the domestic legislative jurisdiction of one of the parties, it shall so report, and shall make no recommendation as to its settlement.

Add to Article XXIV the following paragraph:

After the expiration of ten years from the ratification of the Treaty of Peace of which this Covenant forms a part any State a member of the League may, after giving one year's notice of its intention, withdraw from the League, provided all its international obligations and all its obligations under this Covenant shall have been fulfilled at the time of its withdrawal.

These amendments of Wilson covered the first three points of the Hitchcock letter and also followed Taft's dispatch of March 18 . . . from which indeed the language of the proposed additions to Articles 10 to 15 (the Monroe Doctrine and domestic questions) was largely taken. . . .

Just before the meeting in the evening Colonel House told me to have the mimeographed copies of the President's amendments cut up, so as to leave out the Monroe Doctrine amendment, and to have only the remaining parts of the sheets distributed.[24]

The last-minute change had become necessary, for Lloyd George suddenly conceived the idea of emulating the French, and had applied pressure in the League of Nations Commission to gain a point in a totally unrelated field. He had refused to accept the American Monroe Doctrine Amendment unless the President agreed to scrap the United States Naval Building Program.

Wilson therefore decided not to offer the Monroe Doctrine Amendment until this matter had been disposed of. All the other American amendments, however, were duly proposed and passed at the thirteenth meeting of the Commission (March 26th). The French proved unexpectedly cooperative and the "withdrawal amendment," which had threatened to create difficulties, emerged from the discussion in far sounder shape than it had entered.

David Hunter Miller records the story.

A real discussion took place over Wilson's Article regarding withdrawal. It came up in connection with Article 24 (formerly 26) which provided for the amendment of the Covenant by three-fourths of the Members of the League, including all the Powers on the Council. Cecil proposed to change "three-fourths" to "a majority" and Wilson then introduced his withdrawal amendment [see above].

The French reaction to this proposal was not exactly what had been expected. While Larnaude objected to the clause, he objected more to the fixing of a ten year period preliminary to any right of withdrawal than to the right of withdrawal itself; and Bourgeois was even willing to accept withdrawal on two years' notice *if* the ten year period was eliminated. The difference in the point of view between the American legal mind here and the French legal mind is very striking. We would say that a clause binding the parties absolutely for ten years and then giving a right of withdrawal on notice was more stringent than a clause simply giving a right of withdrawal on notice. I venture to say that to the average English or American lawyer such a proposition would seem to be beyond debate. The reasoning, however, is wrong, because it looks more at words than at the psychology of human beings. As the continental jurists pointed out, the fixing of a ten year period would be regarded by the world as a trial term at the end of which the League would presumably break up, or at least might break up; and Bourgeois said, regarding the draft which he suggested, which read thus:

> Nul Etat faisant partie de la Société des Nations n'a le droit de s'en retirer sans s'être acquitté de ses obligations et sans un préavis de deux ans.

and which according to our point of view would give an almost unqualified right of withdrawal on two years' notice, that it consecrated the principle of perpetuity and at the same time maintained the right of withdrawal. I believe his observation to be fundamentally sound; events indeed have almost proved it. Under the existing provisions, withdrawal from the League is a very serious matter, to be raised by a State for very special reasons only, peculiar to itself, and subject to discussion and reasoning and perhaps retraction of resignation. If there were a definite binding period applicable to all States it might very well, as Orlando suggested, bring about a collective suggestion of more or less general withdrawal. Indeed, one of Orlando's later phrases seems to me of very high rank among diplomatic *bons mots*: "L'important n'est pas tant d'être libre que de se croire libre." His whole remarks here, as the French minutes have them, are worth quoting:

> La liberté est essentielle dans toutes les manifestations humaines. Mais l'important n'est pas tant d'être libre que de se croire libre. Si les Etats ont la conviction qu'il leur suffit de donner un préavis pour sortir de la Société, il est bien vraisemblable qu'ils n'useront pas de cette faculté. Au contraire, s'ils ont l'impression qu'ils portent une chaîne, il pourra se produire des ruptures brutales. Sans doute, comme le dit M. Larnaude, nous voulons fonder un nouveau droit, mais il faut pour cela plus qu'un traité et qu'une déclaration. Il faut créer des moeurs, des habitudes, une force intérieure qui soutiennent l'édifice que nous construisons. La fixation d'un délai de dix ou vingt ans parait contre-indiquée au point de vue psychologique: mieux vaut ne pas assigner un terme à la Société et admettre simplement la faculté réglementée de s'en retirer. . . .

Signor Orlando said that . . . M. Larnaude's objection could be met within the text. The proposal to fix a definite time limit had the disadvantage that all withdrawals might come together. He considered that President Wilson's amendment should be accepted with an additional amendment, so as to mean that any member might withdraw after two years' notice.

President Wilson said that he would abandon the time limit and substitute two years' notice.

M. Larnaude was not convinced. He thought that it was being assumed that the League was going to be something tyrannical and that States would be anxious to get out of it. This impression might produce very serious effects. Countries not belonging to the League might ally themselves against it. We wanted, not to make a Treaty on the old lines, but to strike out a new line and provide a substitute for the old order of international relations. He thought that giving notice by a Great Power would throw the League into confusion. While we are trying to establish the League, let us be thorough.

President Wilson said that he did not entertain the smallest fear that any State would take advantage of the proposed clause. Any State which did so would so become an outlaw. It would be breaking up an arrangement on which we must assume that the world has set its heart.

The sovereignty of their own country was the fetish of many public men. If they entered into a permanent arrangement they would feel that they were surrendering this sovereignty; the most precious thing they had, the thing for which they were willing to fight and to lay down their lives.

Too technical an aspect should not be given to ideas which were sound at bottom. He blamed lawyers for having given too rigid an interpretation to international agreements in the past.

America was keener on her sovereignty than most countries. Americans would have to be assured that they were not permanently giving up the sovereignty of their State.

He thought that the clause would have no practical effects, while its omission might have very serious results. The time would come when men would be just as eager partisans of the sovereignty of mankind as they were now of their own national sovereignty.

It was necessary to give way to current prejudices, but he thought that the initial obstacle which lay in the way of the League, the idea that nationality came before international co-operation, might be overcome. We should make concessions to a sense of independence of will. We must not give the people the chance of saying that we were surrendering it forever.

He himself would be in a very singular, a very awkward position if the amendment was not passed, as he had himself been in a minority of one in the earlier meetings of the Commission as an anti-secessionist. He had never been a believer in secession, though he came from a Southern State.

No State having entered would have a moral right to withdraw, since by entering it would have conferred a benefit upon mankind. States would have a legal right, that was all that he proposed to admit.

He had assured his colleagues in America that everyone took it that the right to secede was assured. He was afraid that the Senate would not come in if they thought that they had not got it.

M. Bourgeois said that all that was wanted was not to fix a definite time limit. There should be a negative instead of a positive formula: something of the following kind:

> "No State may withdraw without being quit of its obligations and having given notice."

This would leave the right to withdraw, and would also ensure that states might not do so except on terms that would not damage the League.

Lord Robert Cecil said that the rule of International Law was that if no definite term was fixed withdrawal was illegal. Denunciation was illegal unless expressly provided for.

President Wilson recapitulated the arguments in favour of a positive term for the benefit of the French authorities.

M. Larnaude said that for some time past national sovereignty had been a fiction. The question of the cessation of military service was one which was keenly discussed in every hamlet, in every cottage, in all France. If the people of France thought that the League was to last ten years only, they would think that it was already bankrupt. He repeated his assertion that the League was not an ordinary Treaty.

M. Vesnitch said that the quintessence of the League was that it was to be a League of Liberty. It should be as elastic as possible. The properties of an ideal organization should be retained. No chains should be laid upon States entering the League. The same questions as the President stated would be asked in America would be asked in many countries.

M. Reis said that we had already been widely accused of having laid violent hands upon national independence. We should do all that we could to remove that impression.

Signor Orlando said that the Meeting was in agreement that the general delay should be abolished.

M. Venizelos said that the Meeting did not agree. He wanted a term of twenty years fixed, but he would accept fifteen or even ten. The essential thing was that some security should be obtained.

M. Larnaude said that he thought that the term should be suppressed. Nations leaving the League should be compelled to say why.

Signor Orlando said that motives would always be found. He thought that liberty of action was essential. He himself lived the life of a prisoner. The difference was that he did it voluntarily. M. Larnaude had said that we were going to establish a new conception of Right. If we were going to do that, we must have confidence.

President Wilson agreed with M. Larnaude's hopes and ambitions. We must make a start. If the Senate was not given a chance of retiring, the difficulty of inducing them to come in might be so great that it would be impossible to start the League. Once it was started he was convinced that the United States would stay in till the last.

M. Bourgeois adhered to the principle that Nations should have to find justification for leaving the League.

M. Venizelos agreed that two years' notice without a time limit would suffice.

M. Vesnitch thought that it would not be necessary to retain the clause compelling retiring members of the League to have fulfilled their obligations.

The result was the adoption of the withdrawal clause in the following form: . . .

> Any State, a member of the League, may, after giving two years' notice of its intention, withdraw from the League, provided all its international obligations and all its obligations under this Covenant shall have been fulfilled at the time of its withdrawal.[25]

Only the Monroe Doctrine Amendment remained to be disposed of and intense behind-the-scenes activity developed to clear away Lloyd George's roadblock. House, Balfour and Cecil jointly worked out a toned-down version of the amendment, which the President reluctantly approved. But even that was turned down by the British Prime Minister. David Hunter Miller, who took an active part in these negotiations, recounts:

At Colonel House's request I went over to the Hotel Astoria and saw Robert Cecil. . . . He said, however, that the whole question was in a sense out of his hands; that he had spoken to Mr. Balfour about it, and that Balfour had thought that he should speak to Lloyd George, which he had done, and Lloyd George raised two objections to including any mention of the Monroe Doctrine; first, it would be very hard to explain in Great Britain, where the people would say that so far as America was concerned this was an element embodying concession; and second, he gave the original objection made by the President that a Doctrine specifically applicable to only one part of the world should not be contained in the Covenant. Accordingly, Cecil suggested that the only thing that could be done was for Lloyd George to speak to the President on the subject. . . .

There was of course nothing real in the objections raised by Lloyd George. He cared nothing whatever about the recognition of the Monroe Doctrine; but he was trying to bargain about it so as to get an agreement with Wilson on the subject of naval building.

The minutes of the American Commissioners of March 27 contain a reference to this matter. . . . Colonel House was not present, so Mr. White recounted to Mr. Lansing and General Bliss the information which Colonel House had imparted to him:

> Mr. White stated that he had just had a conference with Colonel House, and that he later had given him certain bits of information with regard to the President and the President's attitude upon certain current questions. The President had been unable to have the proposed amendment with regard to Article 10 of the Covenant of the League of Nations passed which safeguarded the Monroe Doctrine because Lloyd George was opposed to it. Lloyd George felt that the insertion of such an Article would be giving to the United States a special prerogative, and would likewise localize the League of Nations. Moreover, Lloyd George had not yet been able to reach a satisfactory agreement with the President in regard to the shipbuilding program of the two countries, and that was undoubtedly his fundamental objection to making a concession to the United States. Colonel House had observed that in view of the fact that Lord Robert Cecil and Mr. Balfour were both willing to pass the amendment in question, the President had decided to see Mr. Lloyd George personally in the hope of getting him finally to consent to it.[26]

All these efforts were in vain, however, and Colonel House notes in his diary on March 27th:

. . . I had the President also in my room for a few minutes before the meeting [of the League of Nations Commission]. I was to tell him that the draft for the article on the Monroe Doctrine, which Balfour, Cecil and I had agreed upon, was refused by Lloyd George, therefore Cecil asked me to urge him not to present it. . . . Lloyd George told Cecil he had no intention of having the Covenant in the Treaty and he did not intend to sign any Covenant for a League of Nations until he had a complete understanding with the President concerning the United States naval building programme.[27]

From March 24th to April 10th every effort was made to try to reach an understanding with Lloyd George. Finally, President Wilson decided to call the Prime Minister's bluff.

David Miller recounts:

That afternoon I saw Colonel House at 2:30. I told him that I had an appointment with Cecil at 3:30. He said that Cecil had told him that morning that the letter that he (House) had written about the naval program was not satisfactory to Lloyd George. House told Cecil that the two questions of the insertion of the Monroe Doctrine clause and the naval program had nothing to do with each other and that he would take the position that he had taken in everything over here; that the United States was not going to bargain but was going to take the position it believed to be right; that these were the instructions he had given to everybody when the question of bargaining had been brought up; that he did not want the letter on the naval program back, because it represented the policy of the United States; that the American amendment on the Monroe Doctrine would be presented at tonight's session, and the British could oppose it if they saw fit. He said that Cecil was very much impressed by what he said and seemed very much upset, and had said that he was disposed to quit the whole thing. House told him that the matter was too important for him to leave, that he (Cecil) was one of the few available rafts floating in the sea that could be used at all.[28]

On April 10th, at the fourteenth session of the League of Nations Commission, the Monroe Doctrine Amendment was at last presented. Britain's mercurial Prime Minister threw in his hand as soon as his bluff was called, but the representatives of the Continental and South American Powers were baffled by the American attempt to incorporate the Monroe Doctrine in the Covenant. Throughout Europe the Monroe Doctrine was looked upon as the most isolationist formulation of American foreign policy since Washington's Farewell Address. To them it seemed to say: "East is East, and West is West." To incorporate that doctrine in the charter of an organization that would bring the United States out of its isolation seemed not only illogical but dangerous. Besides, the Monroe Doctrine had never been more than a strictly American statement of her own foreign policy and had not been recognized by any European power. By permitting its insertion in an international treaty, European governments would be giving it official sanction, which they had studiously withheld for almost a hundred years. Wilson's interpretation of the League as "an expansion of the Monroe Doctrine to cover the whole world" puzzled European statesmen as much as it puzzled American politicians.

Ray S. Baker explains the President's reasoning.

. . . The Monroe Doctrine . . . It had been of the utmost importance in the President's thinking from the very beginning, and he not only did not wish to destroy its essential principle, but considered that he was extending and making it more powerful. For this reason he probably underestimated the pother at home, and failed to evaluate properly the demand for the specific mention of the Doctrine in the Covenant. . . . He considered the Monroe Doctrine as one of the most vital fundamental American policies; and the whole development of his programme for a "new order" may, indeed, be viewed as a generalization of the Monroe Doctrine in its positive aspect.

It must be borne in mind that there are two complementary propositions in the Monroe Doctrine: the first, positive, directed against European intervention in the American continents; the second, negative, against American intervention in Europe.

The latter proposition is more commonly associated with Washington's Farewell Address, "avoid entangling alliances," but it is contained also in Monroe's Message, and any unqualified assertion or repudiation of the Monroe Doctrine involves it. These two principles have formed for a century the bulwark of American isolation. Our sense of national safety has rested upon our isolation. Therefore, any proposal to change the Monroe Doctrine in any way, even to enlarge its application, naturally awakened American fears and anxieties.

The essential positive principle of the Monroe Doctrine, under which the United States assumed to protect the weaker South and Central American republics—the principle of the responsibility of the strong for the safety and welfare of the weak—had taken a powerful hold upon the President. It was to him a fundamental moral principle. It was the only principle that would save great and powerful nations from the snares and pits of imperialism.

He therefore wished to extend and emphasize this principle. He had been a strong advocate of the Pan-American Union projected in 1916 for drawing all the states of the Western Hemisphere into closer relationships. He had suggested as a basis of this union a mutual guarantee of "territorial integrity and political independence" (and these words became afterward the heart of Article X). Round this guarantee was to be built up a permanent organization for the peaceable conduct of all the affairs of North and South America.

What more natural than to extend this central idea of the Monroe Doctrine, with the mutual guarantees, to the proposed world league? The President told the Senate, January 22, 1917:

> I am proposing, as it were, that the nations should with one accord adopt the doctrine of President Monroe as the doctrine of the world.

Clearly enough this was not "scrapping the Monroe Doctrine," as his enemies charged, but giving it a broader development. And if all nations came into one league, with mutual guarantees of peace and protection, the negative proposition of the Monroe Doctrine, providing against our intervention in European affairs, would entirely lose its importance. We would step out of our isolation, and take our place in world affairs under the ægis of our own great international principle set forth in the Monroe Doctrine.

"We still read Washington's immortal warning against 'entangling alliances' with full comprehension and an answering purpose," he said in his address of September 27, 1918. "But only special and limited alliances entangle and we . . . hope for a general alliance which will avoid entanglements."

Elsewhere he referred to the League as a "disentangling alliance."

The Monroe Doctrine was a statement of methods, not of ends, and if the ends were as well served, and in larger measure, by a league of nations, surely one could regard its new application as an interpretation rather than a contradiction of these classical American principles.

President Wilson thus saw no essential conflict between the guarantees of Article X and the essential purpose of the Monroe Doctrine. He told friends on the *George Washington* that specific mention of the Monroe Doctrine was "mere repetition."[29]

The debate on the Monroe Doctrine Amendment is highly revealing and instructive. The reactions of Mr. Reis (Brazil) and Mr. Koo (China) are of particular interest, mainly for what they do not say: Mr. Koo fears Japan's "regional understandings" in the Far East, and Mr. Reis tries to get the President to formulate the Monroe Doctrine. Since the stenographic notes, from which the minutes of the meeting were composed, are somewhat more extensive than the minutes themselves, the former are quoted below.

President Wilson: Article 10. I have an amendment to propose to this Article which reads as follows:

> "Nothing in this Covenant shall be deemed to affect the validity of international engagements such as treaties of arbitration or regional understandings like the Monroe Doctrine for securing the maintenance of peace."

M. Koo: I do not wish to be understood as opposing the introduction of this amendment. I approve of it in principle, but I should like to suggest that the Monroe Doctrine should be named specifically and alone in this Article and not made one of the class of "regional understandings."

M. Larnaude: Before accepting this amendment, I should like very much to have a clear definition of what the Monroe Doctrine is. Every time the liberty of Europe has been threatened, the United States has either acted upon the right or reserved the right to come to Europe in defense of her liberty. Does the United States amendment intend to consecrate or to change this policy?

M. Reis: My difficulty of approving of this amendment is that I find no text of the Doctrine which is referred to. I, therefore, cannot commit my home government to an approval of something which is vague and unspecified. We all know of the letter from Jefferson to Monroe; we know that the Monroe Doctrine was framed to oppose the idea of the Holy Alliance going to America and introducing its ideas there; we know of the attitude of President Grant and we know of the various interpretations which have been put upon the Doctrine in Pan-American meetings. I know, however, of no definite existing text to approve. All of us are glad that America decided to come to Europe and participate in this war, nevertheless that action of hers would seem to be rather contradictory to the Monroe Doctrine.

Lord Robert Cecil: I wish to say something about this amendment, not to oppose its adoption but to explain its meaning, and I would like to have my remarks recorded in the procès-verbal. I understand this to mean, oddly enough, exactly what it says:

> "Nothing in this Covenant shall be deemed to affect the validity of" various international engagements.

It gives to these engagements no sanction or validity which they have not hitherto enjoyed. It accepts them as they are. And in particular it accepts the Monroe Doctrine as it is, a doctrine which has never been expressed in terms. Indeed, it is well to leave it undefined and as an example, because if we attempted to state it we might be extending or limiting its application. Yet in spite of the fact that it has never been definitely formulated, it would not be common sense to deny that such a doctrine has existed and has been acted upon.

What I would understand this amendment to say is what I believe to be implicit in the Covenant without saying. It says what I believe to be true, that nothing in the Covenant interferes with international understandings like the Monroe Doctrine. It makes no understanding or alleged understanding either more valid or less valid. It accepts them as they are.

M. Reis: Is there anything in the Covenant which conflicts with the Monroe Doctrine? Would it, for example, permit the United States to go to Europe or Europe to go to the United States?

President Wilson: May I answer Mr. Reis' question in this way. The Covenant provides that the members of the League will mutually defend each other in respect of their political and their territorial integrity. This Covenant is therefore the highest tribute to the Monroe Doctrine, for it is an international extension of that principle by which the United States said that it would protect the political independence and territorial integrity of other American States. By it the United States served notice on the rest of the world that it would defend any South American country against political or territorial attack.

When you try to understand what the Monroe Doctrine means, you should not study theoretical interpretations which have been placed upon it, but actions which have been taken thereunder. I am certain that no actions under this doctrine will be found to be inconsistent with the general principles of the Covenant.

When I was in America my colleagues asked whether the acceptance of the Covenant by America would destroy the principles of the Monroe Doctrine. I replied that it was nothing but a confirmation and extension of the Monroe Doctrine, and explained to them why this was so. They then asked me if this were so, whether there would be any objection to making a specific statement to that effect in the text. It is by way of concession to this reasonable request that I am asking the Commission to state definitely something which is already implicitly taken care of.

M. Koo observed that as the amendment stood, the word "understandings" was in the plural and appeared to be too broad. It would cover all kinds of understandings, good, bad and indifferent. If there were no serious objections he would like to have the words "regional understandings like" struck out and the word "of" substituted therefor.

M. Larnaude: It seems unnecessary to make a specific mention of the Monroe Doctrine. And it seems very much out of harmony with the rest of the document, since it is the only reference in the document to a particular country.

Article 20 provides that all the States which enter the League are bound to make their international engagements conform to the spirit of the League. If they are not inconsistent, they can stand. If, therefore, there is nothing in the Monroe Doctrine inconsistent with the Covenant, it will not be affected.

M. Reis: I should like to add at the end of President Wilson's amendment the words "so far as the Monroe Doctrine is not inconsistent with the League."

M. Larnaude: It would certainly be very unfortunate if the Monroe Doctrine should be interpreted to mean that the United States could not participate in any settlement of European affairs decided upon by the League.

M. Orlando: M. Larnaude will remember that the United States came to participate in this war.

M. Larnaude: And we will never forget it.

M. Orlando: If they came to Europe to participate in this war under the principles of the Monroe Doctrine, and without any League sanction, then more so would they come to Europe in similar circumstances if they were members of the League.

M. Reis: I should like permission to read the two capital sentences of President Monroe on this subject.

President Wilson: In answer to several objections which have been made, I would like to point out that if, for any reason, the Monroe Doctrine should take a line of development inconsistent with the principles of the League, the League would be in a position to correct this tendency. If there is any feeling that the word "regional" is too large I am ready to strike that word out, because I think myself that the word "region" is perhaps hardly applicable to so large a territory as the Western Hemisphere.

Lord Robert Cecil: I agree, Mr. President.

M. Bourgeois: If this amendment is written into the Covenant under Article 10, will it be in conflict with Article 20?

President Wilson: Not at all.

M. Bourgeois: Then why put it into the Covenant?

Lord Robert Cecil: Perhaps M. Bourgeois will permit me to explain again what I thought was quite clear by this time. In Article 5 we inserted a clause saying that the decisions of the Assembly and of the Council must be unanimous unless otherwise provided for.

All of us felt that there could be no question about this principle but there had been so much misunderstanding about it, that it seemed best to make a definite reference to it. Similarly this amendment proposes to make another implicit principle perfectly clear, that the validity of the Monroe Doctrine is not affected by anything in this Covenant.

M. Koo: I am in complete accord with President Wilson and Lord Robert Cecil in wishing to have the Monroe Doctrine specifically mentioned here, because I believe that this doctrine has been tested for a century and has been found to have contributed greatly to the development of the ideas of liberty and peace throughout the world. But as to the retention of the words "regional understandings" or even "understandings," I should like very much to see them omitted. Unless Lord Robert Cecil has some other understanding of a similar nature in mind, it would appear better to confine the amendment to the specific mention of the Monroe Doctrine.

As it is now worded, while it does not add anything to the validity of all existing understandings, it does appear to uphold all those which might otherwise become obsolete or fall into desuetude. Besides, the present wording appears also to include any understandings which may be made in the future of whatever nature. This would hardly be advisable, as one could not be sure of the understandings which might be made in five or ten years from now. For these reasons, I should like to see these words omitted but in case Lord Robert Cecil has some reason for still desiring to retain the word "understandings" then I would like to add after it the words "hitherto commonly accepted."

Lord Robert Cecil: So far as the British Empire is concerned there *are* other understandings. For example there is the ancient understanding concerning Arabia, and the new understanding with regard to the Kingdom of the Hedjaz, whereby Great Britain is to direct their foreign relations.

M. Koo: Both of these will fall into the category of "hitherto commonly accepted understandings."

Lord Robert Cecil: The wording suggested by M. Koo might raise difficulties as to what was or was not commonly accepted. In this way it might question or limit the validity of existing understandings. As the Article now reads it does not enlarge or detract from their validity. It gives another (?) understanding and (?) validity which it has not already got.

M. Koo: I agree fully with Lord Robert Cecil so far as a reference to the Monroe Doctrine is concerned. I should be glad to see it mentioned; but I should prefer to have it mentioned alone and to avoid use of such a broad word as "understandings."

Lord Robert Cecil: It would be a very dangerous and unfortunate thing to state it specifically, inasmuch as the French Delegation has already entered its objection to this procedure. And I feel myself that the Monroe Doctrine should be used merely as an illustration and as an example of similar understandings.

President Wilson: Any understanding which infringes upon the territorial integrity or political independence of any States would be inconsistent with the Covenant. Any State which signs the Covenant obligates itself immediately to abrogate such inconsistent understandings.

The inclusion of this reference to the Monroe Doctrine is in effect nothing but a recognition of the fact that it is not inconsistent with the terms of the Covenant.

M. Larnaude: If it is not inconsistent with the terms of the Covenant it seems to me very unnecessary to refer to it.

President Wilson: I again assure M. Larnaude that if the United States signs this document it is solemnly obliged to render aid in European troubles when the territorial integrity of European States is threatened by external aggression.

M. Orlando: I should like to remind M. Larnaude that if the United States came to Europe to participate in this war and that such action was consistent with the Monroe Doctrine, it will be quite ready to come when it has accepted additional obligations of membership in the League.

President Wilson: Will M. Larnaude please explain whether he really doubts whether the United States will live up to its obligations if it becomes a signatory to the Covenant of the League?

M. Larnaude: My only question is with regard to the significance of the Monroe Doctrine. I think that it should be definitely expressed in words.

President Wilson: I think that it is completely explained.

M. Bourgeois: If this amendment is introduced there will be two separate groups of States under the Covenant, the United States on the one hand and the European States on the other.

President Wilson: We certainly hope that other States of the American Continent, like Brazil, for example will come in at once. More than that we anticipate that practically all the States in the world will become members. In such a world League it seems out of place to talk about two groups.

Lord Robert Cecil: I think, Mr. President, that I see what is troubling the French Delegation. This amendment has been introduced as an addition to Article 10, the Article which they believe to be of the greatest importance to France. They are probably troubled because they fear that your amendment may limit the protection which is afforded by Article 10. If you were willing, for example, that it should be placed under Article 20, I think that their misapprehensions would be taken care of.

President Wilson: I am quite willing to have it go in under Article 20.

M. Larnaude: Yes, put it at the end of Article 20 and add an explanation by way of a footnote which should be part of the Covenant which states exactly what the Monroe Doctrine is.

(General objections from the Commission to M. Larnaude's suggestion.)

M. Vesnitch: As far as an explanation of the Monroe Doctrine is concerned it seems to me that it is clearly divided into two parts: The first part looks toward the protection of American States; the second part looks toward the abstention of America from European affairs. I do not think it can be questioned that the first part of the doctrine is its essence and that the second part of the doctrine is anything but a corollary of the first. The best evidence of this interpretation is in the fact that the United States did participate in this great European settlement in spite of the Monroe Doctrine.

President Wilson: I think it might be helpful for the discussion if I should give something of the history which lies behind the Monroe Doctrine. At a time when the world was in the grip of absolutism, one of the two or three then free States of Europe suggested to the United States that they should take some political step to guard against the spread of absolutism to the American Continent. Acting upon this suggestion, the principles of the Monroe Doctrine were laid down, and from that day to this proved a successful barrier against the insinuation of absolutism into North and South America.

The question now arises, whether you are going to penalize the United States for her adoption of this policy, when you are engaged upon the drafting of a document which is the logical, historical extension of the Monroe Doctrine to the whole world. A hundred years ago we said, "the absolutism of Europe shall not come to the American Continent," and we preserved that principle through all these years. Then there came a time when the liberty of Europe was threatened by the spectre of a new absolutism. America came and came gladly to help in the preservation of European liberty. America was proud to come in such a cause.

Are you now going to debate this issue, are we going to scruple on words when the United States is ready to sign a Covenant which makes her forever a part of the movement for liberty? This is not a little thing, this is a great thing. Gentlemen, you cannot afford to deprive America of the privilege of joining with you in this movement.

M. Koo: I should be glad if after the word "understandings" the following phrase could be added: "which are not inconsistent with the terms hereof like the Monroe Doctrine."

Lord Robert Cecil: This addition seems to be wholly unnecessary and rather redundant, inasmuch as the meaning of the words suggested by M. Koo is already implied.

M. Koo: The main purpose of this amendment, as I understand it, is to mention the Monroe Doctrine in the Covenant. If so, the amendment which I propose, though already implied, would make the meaning still clearer, and it would add further prestige to the Monroe Doctrine by thus characterizing it.

President Wilson: I agree with Lord Robert Cecil that this additional phrase is unnecessary, because the effect of Article 20 is to abrogate the understandings which are inconsistent with the terms of the Covenant.

M. Larnaude: I have no doubt that the United States would come again to the aid of Europe if it were threatened by absolutism. The question, however, is, whether the United States would come as quickly to our help if we should happen to be in a struggle with a country quite as liberal as our own.

Lord Robert Cecil: M. Larnaude is clearly wrong in his interpretation of the way in which the Monroe Doctrine has been applied. I think that if he will consult diplomatic history he will find that the Monroe Doctrine has never in a single instance been in effect as a guide of the policy of American participation in Europe, but always with regard to European interference in American affairs. When American statesmen or international lawyers make any objection to the interference of America in European affairs they never have done it on the basis of the Monroe Doctrine, but always on the basis of Washington's Farewell Address.

President Wilson: Is it conceivable that M. Larnaude wants the United States to say that she will not repudiate her obligations?

M. Reis: If this is the explanation of the Monroe Doctrine then I am ready to approve of this inclusion.

President Wilson: If the article is accepted by the Commission, a logical place can be found for it in the text.

The amendment was then adopted.[30]

The Monroe Doctrine Amendment came under renewed attack from the French at the twentieth, the final, meeting of the Commission. They proposed an amendment which, in essence, said that the Monroe Doctrine would not be considered incompatible with the Covenant as long as it did not prevent member nations from living up to their obligations. There were heated words on both sides; Wilson and Larnaude clashed and the President defended the sincerity of America's adherence to the League. He stated:

I understand that the French intend to publicly oppose this Article. That would create a most unfortunate impression on the other side of the water. . . .

To M. Larnaude:

It seems to me that all your objections are similar in the thought they express, namely, that they all really question the validity of the adherence of the United States to the Covenant. . . .

I respectfully urge that in phraseology of that sort we are casting suspicion upon the good faith of the United States in signing this Doctrine. I mean that any language of that sort is susceptible of that interpretation. How could the United States consciously sign this Doctrine if the Monroe Doctrine was incompatible with it? It is inconceivable. You see, the whole object of this mentioning of the Monroe Doctrine is to relieve a state of mind and misapprehension on the other side of the water; relieve the minds of certain conscientious public men in the United States who want to be assured that there is no intention in this League to interfere with the Doctrine, which if they all knew to be inconsistent with the Covenant, they would not in the same breath ask for an explanation like this and ask to be admitted with a League which was inconsistent with a situation like this.[31]

The French amendment was beaten down and the Monroe Doctrine Amendment as proposed by the President became part of the Covenant and, in consequence, of the Peace Treaty.

The final meeting of the Commission ended on a somewhat shameful note: the Japanese managed to put both the British and the Americans in a most embarrassing position. They had toned down their "racial equality amendment" to the point where it didn't even mention the naughty word "race," but simply asked for recognition of "the principle of equality of nations and the just treatment of their nationals." William Hughes, Australia's fiery premier, had threatened to create a world-wide scandal if any Japanese equality amendment were passed, and Wilson himself could not overlook the effect such an amendment would have on the Pacific Coast. He was finally forced to bend parliamentary procedures to kill the Japanese request.

David Miller gives a succinct résumé of the sad proceedings.

> Toward the close of the meeting the Japanese brought forward their final proposal for race equality by way of an amendment to the Preamble; its text, as it was laid on the table . . . was this:
>
> > (To be inserted in the Preamble after "relations between nations," and before "by the firm establishment," etc.)
> >
> > . . . by the endorsement of the principle of equality of nations and just treatment of their nationals,
>
> The presentation of this proposal by the Japanese delegates was very admirably done. Baron Makino read a carefully prepared statement, which the minutes have in full. Viscount Chinda also spoke. It seemed as if they were supported by the feelings of almost every one present. Lord Robert Cecil refused to accept the amendment and stood on his refusal, acting, as he said, under instructions from his Government. It seemed to me at the time that Cecil felt that he was performing a difficult and disagreeable duty. After making his statement Cecil sat with his eyes fixed on the table, and took no part in the subsequent debate. The minutes condense a good deal what was said; but Orlando, Bourgeois, Larnaude, Venizelos, Kramář and Koo all spoke in favor. Indeed, the form of the proposal was such that to formulate any objection to its language was not an easy task. No one could very well say that he objected to the principle of equality of Nations or that he favored unjust treatment of any nationals; but however unobjectionable the words, as words, might be, their very vagueness could only mean that they were a sort of curtain behind which was the question of White Australia and of immigration of Eastern peoples into countries which regarded the possibility of such immigration as impossible to discuss.
>
> From the standpoint of the terms of the proposals, the matter was very well put by Venizelos, who
>
> > reminded the Commission that he had been largely responsible for the disappearance of the religious liberty clause from the Covenant. He had thought that if this clause were cut out the difficulty

relative to the racial question would likewise be eliminated. Today, however, the question had appeared in a different light and Japan had taken her stand upon another ground; they were talking not of the equality of races, but of the equality of nations themselves and of just treatment of their nationals. It would be very difficult to reject such a proposal especially since Baron Makino had carefully pointed out that his proposal did not involve any State in the obligation to pass any measures whatever with respect to immigration. If the Japanese amendment were accepted and were written into the Preamble, a clause relative to religious liberty might also be introduced.

The other view was stated in a phrase by Colonel House. While this Japanese proposal was up, he wrote for the President the following note:

> The trouble is that if this Commission should pass it, it would surely raise the race issue throughout the world.

Mr. Wilson spoke on the matter, not directly against the Japanese idea, but rather suggesting the inadvisability of putting the amendment into the Covenant. However, his words speak best for themselves and thus they were taken down by an American stenographer:

> Gentlemen, it seems to me that it is wisest that we should be perfectly candid with one another in a matter of deep importance like this. The trouble is not that any one of us wishes to deny the equality of nations or wishes to deny the principle of just treatment of nationals of any nation. The trouble is not with our decisions here, but with the discussions which would certainly be raised in the Plenary Council if the words suggested were introduced into this Covenant. My own interest, let me say, is to quiet discussion that raises national differences and racial prejudices. I would wish them, particularly at this juncture in the history of the relations of nations with one another, to be forced as much as possible into the background. We here have no choice as to the part that is to be played by others of our colleagues of the Conference of Peace in the discussion of matters of this sort. It is not only in this room, but elsewhere, that attention has been drawn to this and similar suggestions, and those very suggestions have set burning flames of prejudice, which it would be very unwise to allow to flare out in

the public view in the Plenary Conference. It is in my own mind for the purpose of quieting these prejudices, of letting them play no part in the discussions connected with the establishment of this League, that I am looking at this whole matter. How can you treat on its merits in this quiet room a question which will not be treated on its merits when it gets out of this room? It is a question altogether of the wisest thing to do, not a question of our sentiments towards each other or of our position with regard to the abstract statement of the equality of nations. This League is obviously based on the principle of equality of nations. Nobody can read anything connected with its institution or read any of the articles in the Covenant itself, without realizing that it is an attempt —the first serious and systematic attempt made in the world to put nations on a footing of equality with each other in their international relations. It is recognized everywhere that this is an attempt, a most hopeful attempt, to secure for those nations which could not successfully protect themselves if attacked by the stronger nations of the world, the support of strong nations of the world in their defense. It is a combination of moral and physical strength of nations for the benefit of the smallest as well as the greatest. That is not only a recognition of the equality of nations, it is a vindication of the equality of nations. No one could question, therefore, the principle upon which this Covenant is based, and I think we ought to approach the present question which has been raised, in what I must call the very impressive [statement] by Baron Makino, from the point of view of what it is wisest to do in connection with the discussion which will attend the institution of this great League. I know from my own knowledge of their attitude and character that these considerations apply strongly to the very thoughtful men who represent Japan at this table. In presenting this matter they are doing their duty; they are doing it with conscious solemnity. But, I am saying what I have just said with a view of avoiding the very embarrassments which I think they have in mind. I offer these suggestions with the utmost friendship, as I need not assure my Japanese colleagues, and with a view to the eventual discussion of these articles.

The amendment was pressed to a vote, but only the affirmative vote was taken; the objection of Cecil prevented its adoption despite the fact that the majority of the Commission were recorded in the affirmative. My notes show that the eleven votes* in favor of the proposals were cast as follows: by Japan, France and Italy, two each; and by Brazil, China, Greece, Yugoslavia and Czecho-Slovakia. The minutes, speaking of the vote, say that eleven votes out of seventeen were recorded in favor of the amendment. The two members of the Commission who were absent were Smuts and Hymans. The negative vote was not taken, so the American delegation and also the other three delegates present, from Portugal, Poland and Roumania, were not formally recorded. Of these last, only Dmowski, according to the minutes, had spoken during the debate.

Mr. Wilson's statement on the vote was taken down as follows:

> I will put the question to a vote. All in favor of incorporating the phrase will be kind enough to raise their hand. I have counted eleven.
>
> It has been our practice to make the vote unanimous when incorporating a provision unless those who have entered (voted?) are willing to let a provision be incorporated as (with?) a reservation on their part.
>
> I think there are too serious objections on the part of some of us to make that possible.

In other words, Wilson ruled in this case that unanimity was necessary when an objection was finally pressed. Larnaude dissented from this ruling, claiming that it was not in accordance with previous rulings; but Wilson sustained his ruling, saying:

> I think that M. Larnaude is mistaken. I follow the course of saying that then the proposition was adopted if there was no objection. In several cases, the French delegates have merely made a reservation; have stated that they would not insist upon their objection. Whenever an objection has been insisted upon, I felt obliged to say that it has not been adopted. At least one objection is insisted upon by one of the Governments concerned. I am obliged to say that it is not adopted.

Regardless of any question of procedure, it was clear that the objection of the British Delegation was of such a character that, notwithstanding the views of the United States or of any other delegations, the Japanese proposal could not become part of the Covenant.

* A majority of the nineteen members of the Commission.

Wilson closed the discussion with the following words:

> I have gone on the principle that any objection insisted upon was an obstacle to the adoption. I do not think that anybody will ever interpret the result of this evening's discussion as a rejection on our part of the principle of equality of nations.[32]

On April 29, 1919, the new, revised Covenant was presented to the Plenary Session of the Conference and received its approval. It was now a different document from the one that had been given the nod by the Plenary Session six weeks earlier. It had undergone some changes, but, on the whole, it still maintained the basic concept of the original Anglo-American proposal. The most important changes had not been made to accommodate "Old World Imperialists" but "New World Senators" who disagreed with the new course of American Foreign Policy.

Texts of the Three Successive Versions of the Covenant

ANGLO-AMERICAN DRAFT OF COVENANT PRESENTED TO LEAGUE OF NATIONS COMMISSION.

PREAMBLE

In order to secure international peace and security by the acceptance of obligations not to resort to the use of armed force, by the prescription of open, just and honorable relations between nations, by the firm establishment of the understandings of international law as the actual rule of conduct among governments, and by the maintenance of justice and a scrupulous respect for all treaty obligations in the dealings of organized peoples with one another, and in order to promote international cooperation, the Powers signatory to this Covenant adopt this constitution of the League of Nations.

TEXT OF THE COVENANT AS ADOPTED AT THE PLENARY SESSION OF FEBRUARY 14 AND TAKEN BY PRESIDENT WILSON TO AMERICA (PRINTED)

COVENANT.

PREAMBLE.

In order to promote international coöperation and to secure international peace and security by the acceptance of obligations not to resort to war, by the prescription of open, just and honourable relations between nations, by the firm establishment of the understandings of international law as the actual rule of conduct among governments, and by the maintenance of justice and a scrupulous respect for all treaty obligations in the dealings of organized peoples with one another, the Powers signatory to this Covenant adopt this constitution of the League of Nations.

FINAL TEXT OF THE COVENANT OF THE LEAGUE OF NATIONS AS IT APPEARS IN THE TREATY OF VERSAILLES.

THE COVENANT OF THE LEAGUE OF NATIONS.

THE HIGH CONTRACTING PARTIES,

In order to promote international coöperation and to achieve international peace and security

by the acceptance of obligations not to resort to war,

by the prescription of open, just and honourable relations between nations,

by the firm establishment of the understandings of international law as the actual rule of conduct among Governments, and

by the maintenance of justice and a scrupulous respect for all treaty obligations in the dealings of organised peoples with one another,

Agree to this Covenant of the League of Nations.

ARTICLE I.

The action of the High Contracting Parties under the terms of this Covenant shall be effected through the instrumentality of meetings of Delegates representing the H. C. P., of meetings at more frequent intervals of an Executive Council representing the States more immediately concerned in the matters under discussion, and of a permanent international Secretariat to be established at the capital of the League.

ARTICLE II.

Meetings of the Body of Delegates shall be held from time to time as occasion may require for the purpose of dealing with matters within the sphere of action of the League.

Meetings of the Body of Delegates shall be held at the capital of the League or at such other place as may be found convenient and shall consist of not more than two representatives of each of the H. C. P.

An ambassador or minister of one of the H. C. P. shall be competent to act as its representative.

All matters of procedure at meetings of the Body of Delegates, including the appointment of committees to investigate

ARTICLE I.—The action of the High Contracting Parties under the terms of this Covenant shall be effected through the instrumentality of meetings of a Body of Delegates representing the High Contracting Parties, of meetings at more frequent intervals of an Executive Council, and of a permanent international Secretariat to be established at the Seat of the League.

ARTICLE II.—Meetings of the Body of Delegates shall be held at stated intervals and from time to time as occasion may require for the purpose of dealing with matters within the sphere of action of the League. Meetings of the Body of Delegates shall be held at the Seat of the League or at such other place as may be found convenient and shall consist of representatives of the High Contracting Parties. Each of the High Contracting Parties shall have one vote but may have not more than three representatives.

ARTICLE 1.—The original Members of the League of Nations shall be those of the Signatories which are named in the Annex to this Covenant and also such of those other States named in the Annex as shall accede without reservation to this Covenant. Such accession shall be effected by a Declaration deposited with the Secretariat within two months of the coming into force of the Covenant. Notice thereof shall be sent to all other Members of the League.

Any fully self-governing State, Dominion or Colony not named in the Annex may become a Member of the League if its admission is agreed to by two-thirds of the Assembly, provided that it shall give effective guarantees of its sincere intention to observe its international obligations, and shall accept such regulations as may be prescribed by the League in regard to its military, naval, and air forces and armaments.

Any Member of the League may, after two years' notice of its intention so to do, withdraw from the League, provided that all its international obligations and all its obligations under this Covenant shall have been fulfilled at the time of its withdrawal.

particular matters, shall be regulated by the Body of Delegates and may be decided by a majority of those present at the meeting.

ARTICLE III.

The representatives of the States members of the League directly affected by matters within the sphere of action of the League will meet as an Executive Council from time to time as occasion may require.

The United States of America, Great Britain, France, Italy and Japan shall be deemed to be directly affected by all matters within the sphere of action of the League. Invitations will be sent to any Power whose interests are directly affected, and no decision taken at any meeting will be binding on a State which was not invited to be represented at the meeting.

Such meetings will be held at whatever place may be decided on, or failing any such decision at the capital of the League, and any matter affecting the interests of the League or relating to matters within its sphere of action or likely to affect the peace of the world may be dealt with.

ARTICLE III.—The Executive Council shall consist of representatives of the United States of America, the British Empire, France, Italy, and Japan, together with representatives of four other States, members of the League. The selection of these four States shall be made by the Body of Delegates on such principles and in such manner as they think fit. Pending the appointment of these representatives of the other States, representatives of   shall be members of the Executive Council.

Meetings of the Council shall be held from time to time as occasion may require and at least once a year at whatever place may be decided on, or failing any such decision at the Seat of the League, and any matter within the sphere of action of the League or affecting the peace of the world may be dealt with at such meetings.

Invitations shall be sent to any Power to attend a meeting of the Council at

ARTICLE 2.—The action of the League under this Covenant shall be effected through the instrumentality of an Assembly and of a Council, with a permanent Secretariat.

ARTICLE 3.

1. The Assembly shall consist of Representatives of the Members of the League.

2. The Assembly shall meet at stated intervals and from time to time as occasion may require at the Seat of the League or at such other place as may be decided upon.

3. The Assembly may deal at its meetings with any matter within the sphere of action of the League or affecting the peace of the world.

4. At meetings of the Assembly each Member of the League shall have one vote, and may have not more than three Representatives.

ARTICLE 4.

1. The Council shall consist of Representatives of the Principal Allied and Associated Powers, together with Representatives of four other Members of the League. These four Members of the League shall be selected by the Assembly from time to time in its discretion. Until

ARTICLE IV.

The permanent Secretariat of the League shall be established at   , which shall constitute the capital of the League. The Secretariat shall comprise such secretaries and staff as may be required, under the general direction and control of a Chancellor of the League by whom they shall be appointed.

The Chancellor shall act as Secretary at all meetings of the Body of Delegates or of the Executive Council.

The expenses of the Secretariat shall be borne by the States members of the League in accordance with the distribution among members of the Postal Union of the expenses of the International Postal Union.

which matters directly affecting its interests are to be discussed and no decision taken at any meeting will be binding on such Power unless so invited.

ARTICLE IV.—All matters of procedure at meetings of the Body of Delegates or the Executive Council including the appointment of Committees to investigate particular matters shall be regulated by the Body of Delegates or the Executive Council and may be decided by a majority of the States represented at the meeting.

The first meeting of the Body of Delegates and of the Executive Council shall be summoned by the President of the United States of America.

the appointment of the Representatives of the four Members of the League first selected by the Assembly, Representatives of Belgium, Brazil, Spain and Greece shall be members of the Council.

2. With the approval of the majority of the Assembly, the Council may name additional Members of the League whose Representatives shall always be members of the Council; the Council with like approval may increase the number of Members of the League to be selected by the Assembly for representation on the Council.

3. The Council shall meet from time to time as occasion may require, and at least once a year, at the Seat of the League, or at such other place as may be decided upon.

4. The Council may deal at its meetings with any matter within the sphere of action of the League or affecting the peace of the world.

5. Any Member of the League not represented on the Council shall be invited to send a Representative to sit as a member at any meeting of the Council during the consideration of

ARTICLE V.

Representatives of the H. C. P. and officials of the League when engaged on the business of the League shall enjoy diplomatic privileges and immunities, and the buildings occupied by the League or its officials or by representatives attending its meetings shall enjoy the benefits of extraterritoriality.

ARTICLE VI.

Admission to the League of States who are not signatories of this Covenant re-

ARTICLE V.—The permanent Secretariat of the League shall be established at which shall constitute the Seat of the League. The Secretariat shall comprise such secretaries and staff as may be required, under the general direction and control of a Secretary-General of the League, who shall be chosen by the Executive Council; the Secretariat shall be appointed by the Secretary-General subject to confirmation by the Executive Council.

The Secretary-General shall act in that capacity at all meetings of the Body of Delegates or of the Executive Council.

The expenses of the Secretariat shall be borne by the States members of the League in accordance with the apportionment of the expenses of the International Bureau of the Universal Postal Union.

ARTICLE VI.—Representatives of the High Contracting Parties and officials of the League when engaged on the business

matters specially affecting the interests of that Member of the League.

6. At meetings of the Council, each Member of the League represented on the Council shall have one vote, and may have not more than one Representative.

ARTICLE 5.

1. Except where otherwise expressly provided in this Covenant or by the terms of the present Treaty, decisions at any meeting of the Assembly or of the Council shall require the agreement of all the Members of the League represented at the meeting.

2. All matters of procedure at meetings of the Assembly or of the Council, including the appointment of Committees to investigate particular matters, shall be regulated by the Assembly or by the Council and may be decided by a majority of the Members of the League represented at the meeting.

3. The first meeting of the Assembly and the first meeting of the Council shall be summoned by the President of the United States of America.

ARTICLE 6.

1. The permanent Secretariat shall be established at the Seat of the League.

quires the assent of not less than two-thirds of the Body of Delegates.

No State shall be admitted to the League except on condition that its military and naval forces and armaments shall conform to standards prescribed by the League in respect of it from time to time.

ARTICLE VII.

The H. C. P. undertake to respect and preserve as against external aggression the territorial integrity and existing political independence of all States members of the League.

of the League shall enjoy diplomatic privileges and immunities, and the buildings occupied by the League or its officials or by representatives attending its meetings shall enjoy the benefits of extraterritoriality.

ARTICLE VII.—Admission to the League of States not signatories to the Covenant and not named in the Protocol hereto as States to be invited to adhere to the Covenant requires the assent of not less than two-thirds of the States represented in the Body of Delegates, and shall be limited to fully self-governing countries including Dominions and Colonies.

No State shall be admitted to the

The Secretariat shall comprise a Secretary General and such secretaries and staff as may be required.

2. The first Secretary General shall be the person named in the Annex; thereafter the Secretary General shall be appointed by the Council with the approval of the majority of the Assembly.

3. The secretaries and staff of the Secretariat shall be appointed by the Secretary General with the approval of the Council.

4. The Secretary General shall act in that capacity at all meetings of the Assembly and of the Council.

5. The expenses of the Secretariat shall be borne by the Members of the League in accordance with the apportionment of the expenses of the International Bureau of the Universal Postal Union.

ARTICLE 7.

1. The Seat of the League is established at Geneva.

2. The Council may at any time decide that the Seat of the League shall be established elsewhere.

3. All positions under or in connection with the League, including the Secretariat, shall be open equally to men and women.

	League unless it is able to give effective guarantees of its sincere intention to observe its international obligations, and unless it shall conform to such principles as may be prescribed by the League in regard to its naval and military forces and armaments.	4. Representatives of the Members of the League and officials of the League when engaged on the business of the League shall enjoy diplomatic privileges and immunities. 5. The buildings and other property occupied by the League or its officials or by Representatives attending its meetings shall be inviolable.
ARTICLE VIII. The H. C. P. recognize the principle that the maintenance of peace will require the reduction of national armaments to the lowest point consistent with domestic safety and the enforcement by common action of international obligations; and the Executive Council shall formulate plans for effecting such reduction. It shall also inquire into the feasibility of abolishing compulsory military service and the substitution therefor of forces enrolled upon a voluntary basis and into the military and naval equipment which it is reasonable to maintain. The H. C. P. further agree that there shall be full and frank publicity as to all national armaments and military or naval programmes.	ARTICLE VIII.—The High Contracting Parties recognize the principle that the maintenance of peace will require the reduction of national armaments to the lowest point consistent with national safety and the enforcement by common action of international obligations, having special regard to the geographical situation and circumstances of each State; and the Executive Council shall formulate plans for effecting such reduction. The Executive Council shall also determine for the consideration and action of the several governments what military equipment and armament is fair and reasonable in proportion to the scale of forces laid down in the programme of disarmament; and these limits, when adopted, shall not be exceeded without the per-	ARTICLE 8. 1. The Members of the League recognise that the maintenance of peace requires the reduction of national armaments to the lowest point consistent with national safety and the enforcement by common action of international obligations. 2. The Council, taking account of the geographical situation and circumstances of each State, shall formulate plans for such reduction for the consideration and action of the several Governments. 3. Such plans shall be subject to reconsideration and revision at least every ten years. 4. After these plans shall have been adopted by the several Governments, the limits of armaments therein fixed shall

ARTICLE IX.

Any war or threat of war, whether immediately affecting any of the H. C. P. or not, is hereby declared a matter of concern to the League, and the H. C. P. reserve the right to take any action that may be deemed wise and effectual to safeguard the peace of nations.

It is hereby also declared and agreed to be the friendly right of each of the H. C. P. to draw the attention of the Body of Delegates or of the Executive Council to any circumstances anywhere which threaten to disturb international peace or the good understanding between nations upon which peace depends.

ARTICLE X.

The H. C. P. agree that should disputes arise between them which cannot be adjusted by the ordinary processes of diplomacy, they will in no case resort to armed force without previously submitting the questions and matters involved either to arbitration or to inquiry by the Executive Council and until three months after the award by the arbitrators or a recommendation by the Executive Council; and that they will not even then

mission of the Executive Council.

The High Contracting Parties agree that the manufacture by private enterprise of munitions and implements of war lends itself to grave objections, and direct the Executive Council to advise how the evil effects attendant upon such manufacture can be prevented, due regard being had to the necessities of those countries which are not able to manufacture for themselves the munitions and implements of war necessary for their safety.

The High Contracting Parties undertake in no way to conceal from each other the condition of such of their industries as are capable of being adapted to war-like purposes or the scale of their armaments and agree that there shall be full and frank interchange of information as to their military and naval programmes.

ARTICLE IX.—A permanent Commission shall be constituted to advise the League on the execution of the provisions of Article VIII and on military and naval questions generally.

ARTICLE X.—The High Contracting Parties undertake to respect and preserve as against external aggression the terri-

not be exceeded without the concurrence of the Council.

5. The Members of the League agree that the manufacture by private enterprise of munitions and implements of war is open to grave objections. The Council shall advise how the evil effects attendant upon such manufacture can be prevented, due regard being had to the necessities of those Members of the League which are not able to manufacture the munitions and implements of war necessary for their safety.

6. The Members of the League undertake to interchange full and frank information as to the scale of their armaments, their military, naval and air programmes and the condition of such of their industries as are adaptable to war-like purposes.

ARTICLE 9.

A permanent Commission shall be constituted to advise the Council on the execution of the provisions of Articles 1 and 8 and on military, naval and air questions generally.

ARTICLE 10.

The Members of the League undertake to respect and preserve as against external aggression the territorial integrity and existing political independence of all

resort to armed force as against a member of the League which complies with the award of the arbitrators or the recommendation of the Executive Council.

ARTICLE XI.

The H. C. P. agree that whenever any dispute or difficulty shall arise between them which they recognize to be suitable for submission to arbitration and which cannot be satisfactorily settled by diplomacy, they will submit the whole subject matter to arbitration and will carry out in full good faith any award or decision that may be rendered.

ARTICLE XII.

The Executive Council will formulate plans for the establishment of a Permanent Court of International Justice and this Court will be competent to hear and determine any matter which the parties recognize as suitable for submission to it for arbitration under the foregoing Article.

torial integrity and existing political independence of all States members of the League. In case of any such aggression or in case of any threat or danger of such aggression the Executive Council shall advise upon the means by which this obligation shall be fulfilled.

ARTICLE XI.—Any war or threat of war, whether immediately affecting any of the High Contracting Parties or not, is hereby declared a matter of concern to the League, and the High Contracting Parties reserve the right to take any action that may be deemed wise and effectual to safeguard the peace of nations.

It is hereby also declared and agreed to be the friendly right of each of the High Contracting Parties to draw the attention of the Body of Delegates or of the Executive Council to any circumstances affecting international intercourse which threaten to disturb international peace or the good understanding between nations upon which peace depends.

Members of the League. In case of any such aggression or in case of any threat or danger of such aggression the Council shall advise upon the means by which this obligation shall be fulfilled.

ARTICLE 11.

1. Any war or threat of war, whether immediately affecting any of the Members of the League or not, is hereby declared a matter of concern to the whole League, and the League shall take any action that may be deemed wise and effectual to safeguard the peace of nations. In case any such emergency should arise the Secretary General shall on the request of any Member of the League forthwith summon a meeting of the Council.

2. It is also declared to be the friendly right of each Member of the League to bring to the attention of the Assembly or of the Council any circumstance whatever affecting international relations which threatens to disturb international peace or the good understanding between nations upon which peace depends.

ARTICLE XIII.

If there should arise between States members of the League any dispute likely to lead to a rupture, which is not submitted to arbitration as above, the H. C. P. agree that they will refer the matter to the Executive Council; either party to the dispute may give notice to the Chancellor of the existence of the dispute, and the Chancellor will make all necessary arrangements for a full investigation and consideration thereof. For this purpose the parties agree to communicate to the Chancellor statements of their case with all the relevant facts and papers.

Where the efforts of the Council lead to the settlement of the dispute a statement shall be prepared for publication indicating the nature of the dispute and the terms of settlement, together with such explanations as may be appropriate. If the dispute has not been settled, a report by the Council shall be published, setting forth with all necessary facts and explanations the recommendations which the Council think just and proper for the settlement of the dispute. If the report is unanimously agreed to by the members of the Council, other than the parties to the dispute, the H. C. P. agree that none

ARTICLE XII.—The High Contracting Parties agree that should disputes arise between them which cannot be adjusted by the ordinary processes of diplomacy, they will in no case resort to war without previously submitting the questions and matters involved either to arbitration or to inquiry by the Executive Council and until three months after the award by the arbitrators or a recommendation by the Executive Council; and that they will not even then resort to war as against a member of the League which complies with the award of the arbitrators or the recommendation of the Executive Council.

In any case under this Article, the award of the arbitrators shall be made within a reasonable time, and the recommendation of the Executive Council shall be made within six months after the submission of the dispute.

ARTICLE XIII.—The High Contracting Parties agree that whenever any dispute or difficulty shall arise between them which they recognize to be suitable for submission to arbitration and which cannot be satisfactorily settled by diplomacy, they will submit the whole subject matter to arbitration. For this purpose the Court

ARTICLE 12.

1. The Members of the League agree that if there should arise between them any dispute likely to lead to a rupture, they will submit the matter either to arbitration or to inquiry by the Council, and they agree in no case to resort to war until three months after the award by the arbitrators or the report by the Council.

2. In any case under this Article the award of the arbitrators shall be made within a reasonable time, and the report of the Council shall be made within six months after the submission of the dispute.

ARTICLE 13.

1. The Members of the League agree that whenever any dispute shall arise between them which they recognise to be suitable for submission to arbitration and which cannot be satisfactorily settled by diplomacy, they will submit the whole subject-matter to arbitration.

2. Disputes as to the interpretation of a treaty, as to any question of international law, as to the existence of any fact which if established would constitute a breach of any international obligation, or as to the extent and nature of the

of them will go to war with any party which complies with its recommendations. If no such unanimous report can be made, it shall be the duty of the majority to issue a statement indicating what they believe to be the facts and containing the recommendations which they consider to be just and proper.

The Executive Council may in any case under this Article refer the dispute to the Body of Delegates. The dispute shall be so referred at the request of either party to the dispute. In any case referred to the Body of Delegates all the provisions of this Article relating to the action and powers of the Executive Council shall apply to the action and powers of the Body of Delegates.

ARTICLE XIV.

Should any of the H. C. P. be found by the League to have broken or disregarded its covenants under Article X, it shall thereby *ipso facto* be deemed to have committed an act of war against all the other members of the League, which shall immediately subject it to the severance of all trade or financial relations, the prohibition of all intercourse between

of arbitration to which the case is referred shall be the court agreed on by the parties or stipulated in any Convention existing between them. The High Contracting Parties agree that they will carry out in full good faith any award that may be rendered. In the event of any failure to carry out the award, the Executive Council shall propose what steps can best be taken to give effect thereto.

ARTICLE XIV.—The Executive Council shall formulate plans for the establishment of a Permanent Court of International Justice and this Court shall, when established, be competent to hear and determine any matter which the parties recognize as suitable for submission to it for arbitration under the foregoing Article.

reparation to be made for any such breach, are declared to be among those which are generally suitable for submission to arbitration.

3. For the consideration of any such dispute the court of arbitration to which the case is referred shall be the court agreed on by the parties to the dispute or stipulated in any convention existing between them.

4. The Members of the League agree that they will carry out in full good faith any award that may be rendered, and that they will not resort to war against a Member of the League which complies therewith. In the event of any failure to carry out such an award, the Council shall propose what steps should be taken to give effect thereto.

ARTICLE 14.

The Council shall formulate and submit to the Members of the League for adoption plans for the establishment of a Permanent Court of International Justice. The Court shall be competent to hear and determine any dispute of an international character which the parties thereto submit to it. The Court may also give an advisory opinion upon any dis-

their nationals and the nationals of the covenant-breaking State, and the prevention, so far as possible, of all financial, commercial, or personal intercourse between the nationals of the covenant-breaking State and the nationals of any other State, whether a member of the League or not.

It shall be the duty of the Executive Council in such a case to recommend what effective military or naval force the members of the League shall severally contribute to the armed forces to be used to protect the covenants of the League.

The H. C. P. agree, further, that they will mutually support one another in the financial and economic measures which are taken under this Article in order to minimize the loss and inconvenience resulting from the above measures, and that they will mutually support one another in resisting any special measures aimed at one of their number by the covenant-breaking State, and that they will afford passage through their territory to the forces of any of the H. C. P. who are co-operating to protect the covenants of the League.

ARTICLE XV.—If there should arise between States members of the League any dispute likely to lead to a rupture, which is not submitted to arbitration as above, the High Contracting Parties agree that they will refer the matter to the Executive Council; either party to the dispute may give notice of the existence of the dispute to the Secretary-General, who will make all necessary arrangements for a full investigation and consideration thereof. For this purpose the parties agree to communicate to the Secretary-General, as promptly as possible, statements of their case with all the relevant facts and papers, and the Executive Council may forthwith direct the publication thereof.

Where the efforts of the Council lead to the settlement of the dispute, a statement shall be published indicating the nature of the dispute and the terms of settlement, together with such explanations as may be appropriate. If the dispute has not been settled, a report by the Council shall be published, setting forth

pute or question referred to it by the Council or by the Assembly.

ARTICLE 15.

1. If there should arise between Members of the League any dispute likely to lead to a rupture, which is not submitted to arbitration in accordance with Article 13, the Members of the League agree that they will submit the matter to the Council. Any party to the dispute may effect such submission by giving notice of the existence of the dispute to the Secretary General, who will make all necessary arrangements for a full investigation and consideration thereof.

2. For this purpose the parties to the dispute will communicate to the Secretary General, as promptly as possible, statements of their case with all the relevant facts and papers, and the Council may forthwith direct the publication thereof.

3. The Council shall endeavour to effect a settlement of the dispute, and if such efforts are successful, a statement shall be made public giving such facts and explanations regarding the dispute and the terms of settlement thereof as the Council may deem appropriate.

ARTICLE XV.

In the event of disputes between one State member of the League and another State which is not a member of the League, or between States not members of the League, the H. C. P. agree that the State or States not members of the League shall be invited to become *ad hoc* members of the League, and upon acceptance of any such invitation, the above provisions shall be applied with such modifications as may be deemed necessary by the League.

Upon such invitation being given the Executive Council shall immediately institute an inquiry into the circumstances and merits of the dispute and recommend such action as may seem best and most effectual in the circumstances.

In the event of a Power so invited refusing to become *ad hoc* a member of the League, and taking any action against a State member of the League which in the case of a State member of the League would constitute a breach of Article X, the provisions of Article XIV shall be applicable as against the State taking such action.

If both parties to the dispute when so invited refuse to become *ad hoc* members

with all necessary facts and explanations the recommendation which the Council think just and proper for the settlement of the dispute. If the report is unanimously agreed to by the members of the Council other than the parties to the dispute, the High Contracting Parties agree that they will not go to war with any party which complies with the recommendation and that, if any party shall refuse so to comply, the Council shall propose the measures necessary to give effect to the recommendation. If no such unanimous report can be made, it shall be the duty of the majority and the privilege of the minority to issue statements indicating what they believe to be the facts and containing the recommendations which they consider to be just and proper.

The Executive Council may in any case under this Article refer the dispute to the Body of Delegates. The dispute shall be so referred at the request of either party to the dispute, provided that such request must be made within fourteen days after the submission of the dispute. In any case referred to the Body of Delegates all the provisions of this Article and of Article XII relating to the action and

4. If the dispute is not thus settled, the Council either unanimously or by a majority vote shall make and publish a report containing a statement of the facts of the dispute and the recommendations which are deemed just and proper in regard thereto.

5. Any Member of the League represented on the Council may make public a statement of the facts of the dispute and of its conclusions regarding the same.

6. If a report by the Council is unanimously agreed to by the members thereof other than the Representatives of one or more of the parties to the dispute, the Members of the League agree that they will not go to war with any party to the dispute which complies with the recommendations of the report.

7. If the Council fails to reach a report which is unanimously agreed to by the members thereof, other than the Representatives of one or more of the parties to the dispute, the Members of the League reserve to themselves the right to take such action as they shall consider necessary for the maintenance of right and justice.

8. If the dispute between the parties is claimed by one of them, and is found

of the League, the Executive Council may take such action and make such recommendations as will prevent hostilities and will result in the settlement of the dispute.

powers of the Executive Council shall apply to the action and powers of the Body of Delegates.

by the Council, to arise out of a matter which by international law is solely within the domestic jurisdiction of that party, the Council shall so report, and shall make no recommendation as to its settlement.

9. The Council may in any case under this Article refer the dispute to the Assembly. The dispute shall be so referred at the request of either party to the dispute, provided that such request be made within fourteen days after the submission of the dispute to the Council.

10. In any case referred to the Assembly, all the provisions of this Article and of Article 12 relating to the action and powers of the Council shall apply to the action and powers of the Assembly, provided that a report made by the Assembly, if concurred in by the Representatives of those Members of the League represented on the Council and of a majority of the other Members of the League, exclusive in each case of the Representatives of the parties to the dispute, shall have the same force as a report by the Council concurred in by all the members thereof other than the Representatives of one or more of the parties to the dispute.

ARTICLE XVI.

The H. C. P. entrust to the League the general supervision of the trade in arms and ammunition with the countries in which the control of this traffic is necessary in the common interest.

ARTICLE XVI.—Should any of the High Contracting Parties break or disregard its covenants under Article XII, it shall thereby *ipso facto* be deemed to have committed an act of war against all the other members of the League, which hereby undertake immediately to subject it to the severance of all trade or financial relations, the prohibition of all intercourse between their nationals and the nationals of the covenant-breaking State, and the prevention of all financial, commercial, or personal intercourse between the nationals of the covenant-breaking State and the nationals of any other State, whether a member of the League or not.

It shall be the duty of the Executive Council in such case to recommend what effective military or naval force the members of the League shall severally contribute to the armed forces to be used to protect the covenants of the League.

The High Contracting Parties agree, further, that they will mutually support one another in the financial and economic measures which are taken under this Article, in order to minimize the loss and inconvenience resulting from the above measures, and that they will mutually support one another in resisting

ARTICLE 16.

1. Should any Member of the League resort to war in disregard of its covenants under Articles 12, 13 or 15, it shall *ipso facto* be deemed to have committed an act of war against all other Members of the League, which hereby undertake immediately to subject it to the severance of all trade or financial relations, the prohibition of all intercourse between their nationals and the nationals of the covenant-breaking State, and the prevention of all financial, commercial or personal intercourse between the nationals of the Covenant-breaking State and the nationals of any other State, whether a Member of the League or not.

2. It shall be the duty of the Council in such case to recommend to the several Governments concerned what effective military, naval or air force the Members of the League shall severally contribute to the armed forces to be used to protect the covenants of the League.

3. The Members of the League agree, further, that they will mutually support one another in the financial and economic measures which are taken under this Article, in order to minimise the loss and inconvenience resulting from the above

ARTICLE XVII.

The H. C. P. agree that in respect of territories which formerly belonged to the German Empire or to Turkey and which are inhabited by peoples unable at present to secure for themselves the benefits of a stable administration, the well being of these peoples constitutes a sacred trust for civilization and imposes upon the States members of the League the obligation to render help and guidance in the development of the administration. They recognize that all policies of administration or economic development should be based primarily upon the well considered interests of the peoples themselves, upon the maintenance of the

any special measures aimed at one of their number by the covenant-breaking State, and that they will afford passage through their territory to the forces of any of the High Contracting Parties who are coöperating to protect the covenants of the League.

ARTICLE XVII.—In the event of disputes between one State member of the League and another State which is not a member of the League, or between States not members of the League, the High Contracting Parties agree that the State or States not members of the League shall be invited to accept the obligations of membership in the League for the purposes of such dispute, upon such conditions as the Executive Council may deem just, and upon acceptance of any such invitation, the above provisions shall be applied with such modifications as may be deemed necessary by the League.

Upon such invitation being given the

measures, and that they will mutually support one another in resisting any special measures aimed at one of their number by the covenant-breaking State, and that they will take the necessary steps to afford passage through their territory to the forces of any of the Members of the League which are co-operating to protect the covenants of the League.

4. Any Member of the League which has violated any covenant of the League may be declared to be no longer a Member of the League by a vote of the Council concurred in by the Representatives of all the other Members of the League represented thereon.

ARTICLE 17.

1. In the event of a dispute between a Member of the League and a State which is not a Member of the League, or between States not Members of the League, the State or States not Members of the League shall be invited to accept the obligations of membership in the League for the purposes of such dispute, upon such conditions as the Council may deem just. If such invitation is accepted, the provisions of Articles 12 to 16 inclusive shall be applied with such modi-

policy of the open door and of equal opportunity for all the H. C. P. in respect of the use and development of the economic resources of the territory. No military or naval forces shall be formed among the inhabitants of the territories in excess of those required for purposes of defense and of internal police.

ARTICLE XVIII.

The H. C. P. will work to establish and maintain fair hours and humane conditions of labor for all those within their several jurisdictions and they will exert their influence in favor of the adoption and maintenance of a similar policy and like safeguards wherever their industrial and commercial relations extend. Also they will appoint Commissions to study conditions of industry and labor in their international aspects and to make recommendations thereon, including the extension and improvement of existing conventions.

Executive Council shall immediately institute an inquiry into the circumstances and merits of the dispute and recommend such action as may seem best and most effectual in the circumstances.

In the event of a Power so invited refusing to accept the obligations of membership in the League for the purposes of such dispute, and taking any action against a State member of the League which in the case of a State member of the League would constitute a breach of Article XII, the provisions of Article XVI shall be applicable as against the State taking such action.

If both parties to the dispute when so invited refuse to accept the obligations of membership in the League for the purposes of such dispute, the Executive Council may take such action and make such recommendations as will prevent hostilities and will result in the settlement of the dispute.

ARTICLE XVIII.—The High Contracting Parties agree that the League shall be entrusted with the general supervision of the trade in arms and ammunition with the countries in which the control of this traffic is necessary in the common interest.

fications as may be deemed necessary by the Council.

2. Upon such invitation being given the Council shall immediately institute an inquiry into the circumstances of the dispute and recommend such action as may seem best and most effectual in the circumstances.

3. If a State so invited shall refuse to accept the obligations of membership in the League for the purposes of such dispute, and shall resort to war against a Member of the League, the provisions of Article 16 shall be applicable as against the State taking such action.

4. If both parties to the dispute when so invited refuse to accept the obligations of membership in the League for the purposes of such dispute, the Council may take such measures and make such recommendations as will prevent hostilities and will result in the settlement of the dispute.

ARTICLE 18.

Every treaty or international engagement entered into hereafter by any Member of the League shall be forthwith registered with the Secretariat and shall as soon as possible be published by it. No such treaty or international engage-

ARTICLE XIX.

The H. C. P. agree that they will make no law prohibiting or interfering with the free exercise of religion, and that they will in no way discriminate, either in law or in fact, against those who practice any particular creed, religion, or belief whose practices are not inconsistent with public order or public morals.

ARTICLE XIX.—To those colonies and territories which as a consequence of the late war have ceased to be under the sovereignty of the States which formerly governed them and which are inhabited by peoples not yet able to stand by themselves under the strenuous conditions of the modern world, there should be applied the principle that the well-being and development of such peoples form a sacred trust of civilization and that securities for the performance of this trust should be embodied in the constitution of the League.

The best method of giving practical effect to this principle is that the tutelage of such peoples should be entrusted to advanced nations who by reason of their resources, their experience or their geographical position, can best undertake this responsibility, and that this tutelage should be exercised by them as mandataries on behalf of the League.

The character of the mandate must differ according to the stage of the development of the people, the geographical situation of the territory, its economic conditions, and other similar circumstances.

Certain communities formerly belong-

ment shall be binding until so registered.

ARTICLE 19.

The Assembly may from time to time advise the reconsideration by Members of the League of treaties which have become inapplicable and the consideration of international conditions whose continuance might endanger the peace of the world.

ARTICLE 20.

1. The Members of the League severally agree that this Covenant is accepted as abrogating all obligations or understandings *inter se* which are inconsistent with the terms thereof, and solemnly undertake that they will not hereafter enter into any engagements inconsistent with the terms thereof.

2. In case any Member of the League shall, before becoming a Member of the League, have undertaken any obligations inconsistent with the terms of this Covenant, it shall be the duty of such Member to take immediate steps to procure its release from such obligations.

ARTICLE 21.

Nothing in this Covenant shall be deemed to affect the validity of international engagements, such as treaties of arbitration or regional understandings

ing to the Turkish Empire have reached a stage of development where their existence as independent nations can be provisionally recognized subject to the rendering of administrative advice and assistance by a mandatory power until such time as they are able to stand alone. The wishes of these communities must be a principal consideration in the selection of the mandatory power.

Other peoples, especially those of Central Africa, are at such a stage that the mandatary must be responsible for the administration of the territory subject to conditions which will guarantee freedom of conscience or religion, subject only to the maintenance of public order and morals, the prohibition of abuses such as the slave trade, the arms traffic, and the liquor traffic, and the prevention of the establishment of fortifications or military and naval bases and of military training of the natives for other than police purposes and the defense of territory, and will also secure equal opportunities for the trade and commerce of other members of the League.

There are territories, such as Southwest Africa and certain of the South Pacific Islands, which, owing to the sparse-

like the Monroe doctrine, for securing the maintenance of peace.

ARTICLE 22.

1. To those colonies and territories which as a consequence of the late war have ceased to be under the sovereignty of the States which formerly governed them and which are inhabited by peoples not yet able to stand by themselves under the strenuous conditions of the modern world, there should be applied the principle that the well-being and development of such peoples form a sacred trust of civilisation and that securities for the performance of this trust should be embodied in this Covenant.

2. The best method of giving practical effect to this principle is that the tutelage of such peoples should be entrusted to advanced nations who by reason of their resources, their experience or their geographical position can best undertake this responsibility, and who are willing to accept it, and that this tutelage should be exercised by them as Mandatories on behalf of the League.

3. The character of the mandate must differ according to the stage of the development of the people, the geographical

ness of their population, or their small size, or their remoteness from the centres of civilization, or their geographical contiguity to the mandatory state, and other circumstances, can be best administered under the laws of the mandatory state as integral portions thereof, subject to the safeguards above-mentioned in the interests of the indigenous population.

In every case of mandate, the mandatory state shall render to the League an annual report in reference to the territory committed to its charge.

The degree of authority, control, or administration to be exercised by the mandatory State shall if not previously agreed upon by the High Contracting Parties in each case be explicitly defined by the Executive Council in a special Act or Charter.

The High Contracting Parties further agree to establish at the seat of the League a Mandatory Commission to receive and examine the annual reports of the Mandatory Powers, and to assist the League in ensuring the observance of the terms of all Mandates.

situation of the territory, its economic conditions and other similar circumstances.

4. Certain communities formerly belonging to the Turkish Empire have reached a stage of development where their existence as independent nations can be provisionally recognised subject to the rendering of administrative advice and assistance by a Mandatory until such time as they are able to stand alone. The wishes of these communities must be a principal consideration in the selection of the Mandatory.

5. Other peoples, especially those of Central Africa, are at such a stage that the Mandatory must be responsible for the administration of the territory under conditions which will guarantee freedom of conscience and religion, subject only to the maintenance of public order and morals, the prohibition of abuses such as the slave trade, the arms traffic and the liquor traffic, and the prevention of the establishment of fortifications or military and naval bases and of military training of the natives for other than police purposes and the defence of territory, and will also secure equal opportunities for the trade and commerce of

ARTICLE XX.

The H. C. P. will agree upon provisions intended to secure and maintain freedom of transit and just treatment for the commerce of all States members of the League.

ARTICLE XXI.

The H. C. P. agree that any treaty or International engagement entered into between States members of the League shall be forthwith registered with the Chancellor and as soon as possible published by him.

ARTICLE XXII.

The H. C. P. severally agree that the present Covenant is accepted as abrogating all obligations *inter se* which are inconsistent with the terms hereof, and solemnly engage that they will not hereafter enter into any engagements inconsistent with the terms hereof.

In case any of the Powers signatory

ARTICLE XX.—The High Contracting Parties will endeavor to secure and maintain fair and humane conditions of labor for men, women, and children both in their own countries and in all countries to which their commercial and industrial relations extend; and to that end agree to establish as part of the organization of the League a permanent Bureau of Labor.

ARTICLE XXI.—The High Contracting Parties agree that provision shall be made through the instrumentality of the League to secure and maintain freedom of transit and equitable treatment for the commerce of all States members of the League, having in mind, among other things, special arrangements with regard to the necessities of the regions devastated during the war of 1914–1918.

ARTICLE XXII.—The High Contracting Parties agree to place under the control of the League all international bureaux already established by general treaties if the parties to such treaties consent. Furthermore, they agree that all such international bureaux to be constituted in future shall be placed under the control of the League.

---

other Members of the League.

6. There are territories, such as South-West Africa and certain of the South Pacific Islands, which, owing to the sparseness of their population, or their small size, or their remoteness from the centres of civilisation, or their geographical contiguity to the territory of the Mandatory, and other circumstances, can be best administered under the laws of the Mandatory as integral portions of its territory, subject to the safeguards above mentioned in the interests of the indigenous population.

7. In every case of mandate, the Mandatory shall render to the Council an annual report in reference to the territory committed to its charge.

8. The degree of authority, control, or administration to be exercised by the Mandatory shall, if not previously agreed upon by the Members of the League, be explicitly defined in each case by the Council.

9. A permanent Commission shall be constituted to receive and examine the annual reports of the Mandatories and to advise the Council on all matters relating to the observance of the mandates.

hereto or subsequently admitted to the League shall, before becoming a party to this Covenant, have undertaken any obligations which are inconsistent with the terms of this Covenant, it shall be the duty of such Power to take immediate steps to procure its release from such obligations.

ARTICLE XXIII.—The High Contracting Parties agree that every treaty or international engagement entered into hereafter by any State member of the League, shall be forthwith registered with the Secretary-General and as soon as possible published by him, and that no such treaty or international engagement shall be binding until so registered.

ARTICLE 23.—Subject to and in accordance with the provisions of international conventions existing or hereafter to be agreed upon, the Members of the League:

(a) will endeavour to secure and maintain fair and humane conditions of labour for men, women, and children, both in their own countries, and in all countries to which their commercial and industrial relations extend, and for that purpose will establish and maintain the necessary international organizations;

(b) undertake to secure just treatment of the native inhabitants of territories under their control;

(c) will entrust the League with the general supervision over the execution of agreements with regard to the traffic in women and children, and the traffic in opium and other dangerous drugs;

(d) will entrust the League with the general supervision of the trade in arms and ammunition with the countries in which the control of this traffic is necessary in the common interest;

(e) will make provision to secure and

Article XXIV.—It shall be the right of the Body of Delegates from time to time to advise the reconsideration by States members of the League, of treaties which have become inapplicable, and of international conditions, of which the continuance may endanger the peace of the world.

maintain freedom of communications and of transit and equitable treatment for the commerce of all Members of the League. In this connection, the special necessities of the regions devastated during the war of 1914–1918 shall be borne in mind;

(f) will endeavour to take steps in matters of international concern for the prevention and control of disease.

Article 24.—There shall be placed under the direction of the League all international bureaux already established by general treaties if the parties to such treaties consent. All such international bureaux and all commissions for the regulation of matters of international interest hereafter constituted shall be placed under the direction of the League.

In all matters of international interest which are regulated by general conventions but which are not placed under the control of international bureaux or commissions, the Secretariat of the League shall, subject to the consent of the Council and if desired by the parties, collect and distribute all relevant information

ARTICLE XXV.—The High Contracting Parties severally agree that the present Covenant is accepted as abrogating all obligations *inter se* which are inconsistent with the terms thereof, and solemnly engage that they will not hereafter enter into any engagements inconsistent with the terms thereof.

In case any of the Powers signatory hereto or subsequently admitted to the League shall, before becoming a party to this Covenant, have undertaken any obligations which are inconsistent with the terms of this Covenant, it shall be the duty of such Power to take immediate steps to procure its release from such obligations.

ARTICLE XXVI.—Amendments to this Covenant will take effect when ratified by the States whose representatives compose the Executive Council and by three-fourths of the States whose representatives compose the Body of Delegates.

and shall render any other assistance which may be necessary or desirable.

The Council may include as part of the expenses of the Secretariat the expenses of any bureau or commission which is placed under the direction of the League.

ARTICLE 25.—The Members of the League agree to encourage and promote the establishment and coöperation of duly authorised voluntary national Red Cross organisations having as purposes the improvement of health, the prevention of disease and the mitigation of suffering throughout the world.

ARTICLE 26.—Amendments to this Covenant will take effect when ratified by the Members of the League whose Representatives compose the Council and by a majority of the Members of the League whose Representatives compose the Assembly.

No such amendment shall bind any Member of the League which signifies its dissent therefrom, but in that case it shall cease to be a Member of the League.

V

German Colonies

Wilson's Point 5:

> *A free, open-minded and absolutely impartial adjustment of all colonial claims, based upon the strict observance of the principle that in determining all such questions of sovereignty, the interests of the population concerned must have equal weight with the equitable claims of the government whose title is to be determined.*

By the time the Conference opened, all of Germany's colonies had been conquered and occupied by one or another of the Allied Powers who, by mutual, albeit secret, agreements, had already parceled these colonies out among themselves. The beneficiaries of these agreements were Japan, France, Great Britain and her Dominions. When President Wilson visited England in December of 1918 all the Premiers of Britain's Dominions were assembled in London, impatiently waiting to have him confirm them in the possession of these territories.

Lloyd George broached the matter with the President, but he did not get very far. The British Prime Minister reported his impressions of the interview to the Imperial War Cabinet, where his report met with some angry comments by Australia's irascible Premier, William Hughes:

> As regards the German colonies, the President agreed that they could not be returned to Germany, and that they should be put under

some Power acting as a mandatory. Mr. Lloyd George had impressed upon him the distinction between the German colonies conquered by the British Dominions and adjacent to them, and those in the conquest of which the forces of the Empire as a whole had shared. He had expressed our [Great Britain's] willingness to leave German East Africa at the disposal of the League of Nations, and to accept all the conditions imposed by the League if we were entrusted with a mandate for its administration. In the other category he had put German South-West Africa as the strongest case, pointing out that it would be quite impossible to separate from the South African Union what was essentially part of the same country. The President did not seem prepared to contest that contention, but of his own accord retorted that the position of Australia with regard to the Pacific colonies was not quite the same. Mr. Lloyd George and Mr. Balfour had endeavoured to put the case as strongly as they could for Australia, on the grounds of security, but the President had answered that a case on similar grounds might be made for every other captured territory. In answer to the argument that we had definitely promised to Japan the islands in the Northern Pacific, and that it would be impossible to deny to Australia and New Zealand what was given to Japan, the President had shown that he was by no means prepared to accept the Japanese treaty, and was doubtful whether Japan could be admitted there even in the capacity of a mandatory Power. They had not succeeded in moving him from that position.

MR. BONAR LAW, who was present at that part of the discussion, said that President Wilson had remarked in that connection that he regarded it as his function to act as a buffer to prevent disagreeable things, such as the Japanese retention of the islands, being carried out.

LORD CURZON suggested that President Wilson ought not to be regarded as a sole arbiter in these matters; he would be only one of a party round the Conference Table.

MR. LLOYD GEORGE agreed. He was only reporting the President's views, and had in no sense accepted them as final. With regard to the Colonies, he had left the matter by telling the President that the question would have to be fought out at the Conference, where the Dominions would be able to present their own case.

MR. HUGHES said that if we were not very careful, we should find ourselves dragged quite unnecessarily behind the wheels of President Wilson's chariot. He readily acknowledged the part which America had played in the war. But it was not such as to entitle President

Wilson to be the god in the machine at the peace settlement, and to lay down the terms on which the world would have to live in the future. The United States had made no money sacrifice at all. They had not even exhausted the profits which they had made in the first two and a half years of the war. In men, their sacrifices were not even equal to those of Australia. Relatively their sacrifices had been nothing like as much as those of Australia. America had neither given the material nor the moral help which entitled her to come before France. If M. Clemenceau took the line which President Wilson seemed to be taking, he (Mr. Hughes) might be prepared to say, "You have a right to speak." He hoped that Great Britain and France, which had both sacrificed so much, would defend their own interests, and not let their future be decided for them by one who had no claim to speak even for his own country. Mr. Lloyd George had received an overwhelming vote from his fellow-countrymen, not only in recognition of what he had done but because of their confidence that he would see to it that their sacrifices had not been made in vain. In taking up that line at the Peace Conference, Mr. Lloyd George would have not only all England, but more than half America behind him. He and M. Clemenceau could settle the peace of the world as they liked. They could give America the respect due to a great nation which had entered the war somewhat late, but had rendered great service. It was intolerable, however, for President Wilson to dictate to us how the world was to be governed. If the saving of civilisation had depended on the United States, it would have been in tears and chains today.[1]

Under heavy pressure from the Dominion Premiers, Lloyd George raised the question of the German colonies in the Supreme Council on January 23rd. Ray S. Baker, Wilson's chief press officer, gives a vivid, though somewhat overly dramatized, picture of the proceedings.

Lloyd George precipitated the discussion of the disposition of the German colonies. He did this in spite of the fact that the council had already accepted (January 13) the President's "list of subjects for discussion," in which the League of Nations was first, followed by reparations and territorial questions, with "colonies" last of all.

It was an exceedingly bold and clever tactical move, calculated in the first place to get the Allies what they wanted, and in the second, to test out the capacities and fighting qualities of this American leader.

For President Wilson was the great unknown factor at Paris. While everyone knew what he had said, no one knew yet what he would do. Was he merely an inspirational preacher who had caught the enthusiasm of the world, or did he mean business? How much of a fighter was he?

Lloyd George, Clemenceau, Sonnino, had long been working together, and knew one another well. They had met in conference and decided military problems of the first magnitude; they had faced political crises together, and they had negotiated—as we now know more definitely than we did at the time—regarding many of the coming settlements of the peace, both those founded upon the earlier secret treaties and those which had arisen since American interposition in the war had assured ultimate victory to the allied arms.

But not one of the principal leaders except Mr. Balfour had previously met face to face this American President who had exercised so powerful a moral leadership in the world. They had willingly accepted him as the grand strategist of the diplomacy of the last year of the war, for he represented the strength of America, and his principles, widely accepted by the restive liberals and radicals of all Europe, had provided as powerful a unifying influence in the allied countries as it was corrosive in the Central Empires. But the time had come now for employing the tactics of diplomacy as contrasted with its strategy. And the struggle was now among themselves: not with a foreign enemy. What would Wilson do? Was this America, full of strange ideas and new principles, to sit in with the family of Europe as an honoured guest, politely accepting its ancient customs? Or was America to be like the rich and powerful pioneer son, returned from far lands, who had just saved the old home from foreclosure and now proposed to banish the antique furniture and change the plumbing?

When, therefore, Lloyd George proposed on January 23 that the colonial matters be discussed, M. Clemenceau of France and Signor Sonnino of Italy instantly agreed—as though it had all been understood beforehand.

It was perfectly plain to the President what this swift and astonishingly clever shift in tactics meant. In no other way could they more shrewdly drive forward their own ideas of the peace settlement as opposed to those of the President. In no other case than this relatively simple one of the distribution of the spoils of war, already in their hands, could the allied nations present such a united front. Here were hundreds of islands dotted throughout the Pacific Ocean, a great slice of China and vast areas in Africa inhabited by 13,000,000 people—the former German colonies—to be "divided up." . . . These were the most tangible spoils of war, and most easily disposed of. A distribution now would leave all the parties feeling that they had "got something definite" and in diplomatic good-humour to attack harder problems. Indeed, the reason given by Lloyd George for suggesting this action was that "Oriental questions and colonial questions were less involved [than European questions], and to economize time he suggested that these matters be tackled at once."

The President immediately objected—all the quotations here used are made directly from the Secret Minutes—arguing that:

> the world's unrest arose from the unsettled condition of Europe, not from the state of affairs in the East, or in the Colonies, and that the postponement of these questions would only increase the pressure on the Delegates of the Peace Conference. He would therefore prefer to set in process immediately all that was required to hasten a solution of European questions.

As a result of this discussion the President apparently won his point, for it

> was then decided that the Secretary General should ask all Delegations representing Powers with territorial claims to send to the Secretariat their written statements within 10 days.

The President, however, was profoundly disturbed. It was clear enough now that he was to have shrewd opponents—the shrewdest in the world. They were not going to fight him on his main contentions. That would have been poor tactics. It was the familiar policy which he himself described later in the Council of "acceptance in principle, but negation in detail."

In short, after a settlement had been completely made on the order of the old diplomacy and according to the provisions of the secret treaties, and each nation had got all it could get materially, strategically, and politically, there was to be a pious statement of "principles leading to justice, morals, and liberty" and a discussion of the organization of a society of nations!

But the President determined to settle *this* war according to the new principles which had been accepted at the Armistice. They were to be applied now. The League of Nations was not to be relegated to some vague future congress but brought at once into being. It is not at all troublesome to suffer idealists in the world, provided they are not determined upon applying their ideals immediately!

But the first principle of successful diplomacy, as of war, is attack —swift and unexpected attack. While President Wilson thought he had succeeded in getting the discussion of colonial claims postponed, he had not counted upon the mercurial Lloyd George.[2]

The President's tactics gained him a respite of no more than twenty-four hours, for the very next day the Dominion Premiers, whose claims had been burning holes in their pockets for weeks, presented themselves in person to the Supreme Council.

Perhaps the figures among them that stood out most impressively at first glance were Massey of New Zealand, a great shaggy, rough-hewn bulk of a man; and Smuts of South Africa, the youngest and most distinguished of the group in the uniform of a Lieutenant General of the British Army. Hughes of Australia, a small, deaf, rather dried-up old man with an electric ear phone, and Borden of Canada, the "handsomest man at the Peace Conference," completed the group. . . . They had come to present their claims for the possession of most of the former German colonies which . . . had been captured by Dominion troops. Mr. Lloyd George made a brief statement showing that the German colonial policy had been a bad one— "in Southwest Africa they had deliberately pursued a policy of extermination."

> All he would like to say on behalf of the British Empire as a whole was that he would be very much opposed to the return to Germany of any of these Colonies. . . .
>
> President WILSON said that he thought all were agreed to oppose the restoration of the German Colonies.
>
> M. ORLANDO, on behalf of Italy, and Baron MAKINO, on behalf of Japan, agreed.
>
> (There was no dissentient and this principle was adopted. . . .)

In this brief and summary way all the German colonies were alienated from German control. The Allies already had military and political sanctions for this alienation; and they felt that the maladministration of these Colonies by Germany gave them moral sanctions. . . .

The next question was to decide what to do with these vast derelict populations of more or less helpless native people. . . .

Mr. Lloyd George was at his best in presenting and dramatizing such a situation as this. Vigorously on his feet, with his leonine head thrown back, and his arguments pouring from him in a colourful torrent, he was an engaging and persuasive figure. He now presented three possible methods of future control of the colonies. The first was internationalization or direct administration by the League of Nations—and this he rejected without argument. . . . The second was "that one nation should undertake the trusteeship on behalf of the League as mandatory"—the idea already widely discussed as a part of the League of Nations scheme. The third was frank, old-fashioned annexation—and this was what the British Dominions wanted and wanted at once—and in this policy of annexation Mr. Lloyd George supported them. . . .

"He would like," he said, "the Conference to treat the territories as part of the Dominions which had captured them."

He was as vigorous and vivid in his arguments now for this solution, which President Wilson a little later called a "mere distribution of the spoils," as he had been vigorous and vivid in January, 1918, when the shibboleth "self-determination" was sweeping the world and he had pressed its application further than President Wilson had ever thought of doing—to the native tribes of Africa. On January 5, 1918, he had said to the Trade Union Congress which was vigorously supporting the principle of "no annexations":

> With regard to the German colonies, I have repeatedly declared that they are held at the disposal of a conference whose decisions must have primary regard to the wishes and interests of the native inhabitants of such colonies.

At that time he had vividly imagined these colonies as somehow controlling their own destinies, but in the present argument, where he had a wholly different purpose to serve, he saw some of them with equal vividness as "cannibal colonies, where people were eating each other."

The Dominion Prime Ministers then presented their cases, one after another: First, Mr. Hughes of Australia who wanted New Guinea and other islands; then Mr. Massey of New Zealand, who wanted Samoa; and then General Smuts of South Africa, who wanted German Southwest Africa. They were all frankly for outright annexation and their arguments were based practically upon the same premises:

1. The cost and losses of the Dominions in the war, and the fact that Dominion or British troops were now in possession.

2. The strategic security and military necessity of the Dominions. "Any strong power controlling New Guinea," said Mr. Hughes, "controlled Australia." "Samoa," argued Mr. Massey of New Zealand, "was of great strategic importance, and the key to the Pacific," and therefore it should be controlled absolutely by New Zealand.

3. Each Dominion argued that the interests of the natives would be secure under a policy of direct annexation. The Dominions were democracies: "They were doing their best for civilization in that part of the world." Mr. Massey mentioned the fact that "there were six native Members in the New Zealand Parliament today."

General Smuts made a slightly different case, for he showed that German Southwest Africa was practically "a desert country without any product of great value," and because of its small population a mandatory system would not work practically as well as direct annexation.

After these statements the discussion was adjourned in order to give the Congress full opportunity for considering the claims of the Dominion Premiers and the arguments advanced by them in support of them.[3]

Three days later (January 27th) the Japanese had finished typing out their claims and Baron Makino appeared before the Supreme Council to present the demands of the Empire of the Rising Sun.

The Japanese were always brief and to the point.

> The Japanese Government [said Baron Makino] feels justified in claiming from the German Government the unconditional cession of:
>
> (a) The leased territory of Kiauchau together with the railways and other rights possessed by Germany in respect of Shantung province.
>
> (b) All of the islands in German possession in the Pacific Ocean north of the equator together with the rights and properties in connection therewith.

He then related how Japan, upon the outbreak of the war, after "consultation with the British Government conformably with the agreement of 1911," had taken Shantung, and later the Pacific Islands, from the Germans and was now in possession of them.*

In this first statement the Japanese asked only for the complete acquisition of the former German possessions and said nothing either of Chinese rights or of the mandatory system. On the following day six Japanese were present and three Chinese, and Dr. Wellington Koo made an eloquent representation of the Chinese case.

> Mr. KOO said . . . he was the spokesman of one quarter of the human race. The Chinese delegation would ask the Peace Conference for the restoration to China of the leased territory of Kiauchau, the railway in Shantung and all other rights Germany possessed in that province before the war. . . . The history of the lease to Germany was doubtless familiar. The Lease had been extorted by force. . . . The pretext . . . was the accidental killing of two missionaries. . . . On the principles . . . accepted by this Conference, China had a right to the restoration of these territories.

He spoke then of the fact that Shantung was the Holy Land of the Chinese, the home of Confucius, with a great hold upon the affections of the Chinese, that it was already crowded with 36,000,000 people and, therefore not suitable for colonization, and finally, that its control meant the virtual control also of China and the capital of China.

> Baron MAKINO said that he had listened with great attention to what had fallen from his Chinese colleagues concerning the direct restoration of Kiauchau to China. . . . There was, however, one point he wished to make clear. Japan was in actual possession of the territory under consideration. It had taken it by conquest from Germany. Before disposing of it to a third party it was necessary that Japan should obtain the right of free disposal from Germany.
>
> President WILSON pointed out that the Council was dealing with territories and cessions previously German without consulting Germany at all.
>
> Baron MAKINO said that the work now in hand was one of preparation for the presentment of the case to Germany. It followed therefore that the cession of Kiauchau would have to be agreed upon by Germany before it was carried out. What should

* Secret Minutes, Council of Ten, January 27.

take place thereafter had already been the subject of an interchange of views with China.

The "interchange of views" here referred to by Makino—the famous notes of 1915 and 1918 . . . were not laid before the Council until April.

But Mr. Koo returned to his contention that China wished Shantung restored directly, not indirectly, to her. "It was always easier to take one step than two, if it led to the same place."

He claimed that "China's entry into the war had completely altered her status," and that she was no longer bound by the agreements with Japan.

In short, here was the issue clearly joined: China was suspicious and fearful of Japan and wanted Shantung and everything in it returned to her directly; Japan demanded the "unconditional cession" of these possessions from Germany but recalled her pledge to restore Kiauchau later to China. China was thus strong for basing her rights on international action and sought future security in international sanctions. Japan, on the other hand, based her claims on the secret agreements with China (the secret agreement of 1917 with the Allies had not yet come out in the Councils) and desired a free hand in the Pacific.[4]

On January 28th the French were heard from; M. Simon, minister for the colonies, argued with French passion and logic for "annexation, pure and simple."

It now remained . . . to consider the question of the government to be given to these territories, which had become ownerless. There were three possible solutions:—

1. Internationalisation, pure and simple.
2. A mandate given to one of the Powers by the League of Nations.
3. Annexation, pure and simple, by a Sovereign Power.

Mr. Lloyd George had frankly condemned the first system in the course of the conversation of 24th January, when he had said that it could not be adopted in regard to backward countries. . . .

The second system consisted in the appointment of a mandatory by the League of Nations. The Dominions had raised very strong objections to this system, and these objections were supported by France. . . .

The mandatory system consisted in empowering one nation to act on behalf of another. Every mandate was revocable, and there would therefore be no guarantee for the continuance of any. . . .

Another question occurs: Who would be the mandatory? Would it be a little nation, without colonising traditions, capital or men; or would the mandatory be a large nation whose presence would be a danger and compel the adjoining nations to organise for defence, as Mr. Hughes said in regard to New Guinea? This same remark applied to the Cameroons and to the Congo. . . .

He (M. Simon) could not, therefore, favour the system of a mandate to be given to one Power by the League of Nations. . . .

For a long time France had used all her strength for the purpose of exploring and developing the territories of Northern Africa, and the whole world had been able to enjoy the benefits to be derived therefrom.

France had spent 9 milliards of francs on the Mediterranean coast, 626 millions on West Africa, and 272 millions on Equatorial Africa. When the efforts made by France for the civilisation of Northern Africa were considered, full confidence would be felt that she would be able to carry out the same programme in Equatorial Africa. That was his reply to President Wilson's third condition.

France relied on these facts that day, in asking to be allowed to continue her work of civilisation in tropical Africa, and he hoped the delegates would give her the means of doing so by recognising her right to sovereignty in those regions, subject to the assurances he had outlined.[5]

Lloyd George comments:

This powerful statement of the anti-mandate case, following as it did the criticisms directed by the Dominions, provoked President Wilson to a statement which threatened a break-up of the Conference:—

PRESIDENT WILSON observed that the discussion so far had been, in essence, a negation in detail—one case at a time—of the whole principle of mandatories. The discussion had been brought to a point where it looked as if their roads diverged. He thought it would be wise to discontinue this discussion for a few hours—say until the next day, as he feared that otherwise it might lead to a point where it would appear as though they had reached a serious disagreement, and this he particularly wished to avoid.[6]

According to Ray S. Baker:

It also developed presently that the Belgians expected a piece of German East Africa, and that Italy had certain other provisional claims based upon the secret treaty of London. A little later, when she discovered what was going on, Portugal also lifted up a piping treble, but no one paid any attention.[7]

President Wilson was shocked, pained and angered by the attitude he encountered, and took no great pains to disguise his feelings.

He did not mince words in expressing his opinion . . . in the Council —sitting a little forward in his chair, speaking in a steady, rather low voice, with his eyes fixed for a moment on Lloyd George, then on Clemenceau:

> The world would say that the Great Powers first portioned out the helpless parts of the world, and then formed a League of Nations. The crude fact would be that each of these parts of the world had been assigned to one of the Great Powers. He wished to point out, in all frankness, that the world would not accept such action: it would make the League of Nations impossible and they would have to return to the system of competitive armaments, with accumulating debts and the burden of great armies.[8]

Earlier (on January 27th) he had said in the Supreme Council:

The basis of this idea was the feeling which had sprung up all over the world against further annexation. Yet, if the Colonies were not to be returned to Germany (as all were agreed), some other basis must be found to develop them and to take care of the inhabitants of these backward territories. It was with this object that the idea of administration through mandatories acting on behalf of the League of Nations arose. . . . Some institution must be found to carry out the ideas all had in mind, namely, the development of the country for the benefit of those already in it and for the advantage of those who would live there later. . . .

The purpose was to serve the people in undeveloped parts, to safeguard them against abuses such as had occurred under German administration and such as might be found under other administrations. Further, where people and territories were undeveloped, to assure their development so that, when the time came, their interests, as they saw them, might qualify them to express a wish as to their ultimate relations—perhaps lead them to desire their union with the mandatory power. . . .

In the first place, the League of Nations would lay down certain general principles in the mandate, namely, that districts be administered primarily with a view to the betterment of the conditions of the inhabitants. Secondly, that there should be no discrimination against members of the League of the Nations so as to restrict economic access to the resources of the districts. . . . All countries would pay the same duties, all would have the same right of access. . . .

If the process of annexation went on, the League of Nations would be discredited from the beginning. Many false rumours had been set about regarding the Peace Conference. Those who were hostile to it said that its purpose was merely to divide up the spoils. If they justified that statement in any degree, that would discredit the Conference.[9]

Woodrow Wilson's refusal to have mandates awarded before the League of Nations had become operative, and his insistence that all German colonies be treated as League mandates, caused considerable bad feeling among the aspirants to these territories who had expected their "just claims" to be awarded with dispatch. In vain did Colonel House try to persuade the British to prevail upon their Dominions to accept his chief's proposals, even using the quaint argument that "the President would agree that the peoples concerned should be able to vote themselves part of Australia or South Africa, thereby cancelling the mandate."[10] The Colonel's own account of his conciliatory efforts reads:

January 27th, 1919: Interesting and valuable meeting with Lord Robert Cecil this afternoon. Sir William Wiseman and David Miller were present. Lord Robert and I practically differed not at all, and yet there were some strong points of difference between his draft and ours. This is because, so he tells me, he could not get his views adopted. We argued at considerable length, especially upon the question of the German colonies, and whether or not the mandatory principle should be applied to them. I contended for it strongly and he accepted it, but objected to the clause by which a colony could by applying to the League of Nations ask for a change of Mandatory Power. This he thought impractical and said the Dominions would not consent. I made him see that it was best for Great Britain as a whole to take what we had proposed rather than what the Dominions proposed. The result I thought would be presumably the same and in the end the Mandatory Power would in a short time persuade the colony to annex itself.

While we were discussing this particular feature, Lloyd George, the President, and the Prime Ministers of the Dominions were discussing the same question at the Quai d'Orsay but upon different lines. Lloyd George and the President finally had a private conference. Balfour takes practically the same view that Lord Robert does, and which nearly agrees with my own.

I urged Lord Robert to commit the Prime Minister and Mr. Balfour to the Covenant of the League of Nations which he and I have so nearly agreed upon. When this is done, I promised to take it up with the President.[11]

Both in the Supreme Council and in the League of Nations Commission, the issue had become deadlocked and the President was deeply worried. He seriously considered making the issue public and acquainting the world with British and French "imperialist aims." A note that Colonel House dropped off to Wilson, and a telephone conversation between him and the President, which the Colonel duly records in his diary, give a fair picture of Wilson's state of mind.

PARIS, *January* 28, 1919

DEAR GOVERNOR:

I believe the entire British delegation, including the other Dominion representatives, are opposed to Hughes in his claim for annexation as opposed to the mandatory system. Either Hughes claims the Pacific Islands by right of conquest and as a reward for Australia's services in the war, or he must accept the mandatory of the League of Nations for the better government of the backward people of the Pacific Islands. It is doubtful if public opinion in Australia is really behind Hughes, and if he persists in his claim the best solution would be to tell him the whole arguments on both sides must be published in order that the world may judge Australia's claims, but so far as the Conference is concerned his proposal strikes at the whole idea of the League of Nations and cannot be accepted.

Affectionately yours

E. M. HOUSE[12]

January 28, 1919: The President called me over the private wire at 9:30 and I have just had a twenty-minute talk with him. He is much disturbed at the turn of things this afternoon. The French and British are demanding that if the "mandatory" is used by the League of Nations as to the German colonies, it shall be used immediately and the different Powers designated now rather than later. The President asked my advice as to procedure. He had in mind to tell them that if they maintained their attitude he intended to give both sides to the public. In lieu of this I suggested that he tell them that he did not believe they voiced the opinion of the Conference as a whole, and that it was his purpose at the next general meeting to bring the matter before the Conference and ask for an opinion. My purpose in this is that, since proceedings of the General Conference are public, he will get exactly the same publicity as he would by the method he suggested and there could be no criticism by the Powers.[13]

Alarmed by the President's blackening mood, Lloyd George took a hand in breaking the deadlock. He recounts:

I spent a great part of the next two days in consultations with the Dominion Premiers. I urged them not to take the responsibility of wrecking the Conference on a refusal to accept a principle which Great Britain was quite ready to see applied to much more extensive and important territories in East Africa. Sir Robert Borden was as usual very helpful in abating the pugnacity of Mr. Hughes and Mr. Massey. General Botha took, as he generally did, a broad and conciliatory view and at last I obtained general agreement to a series of propositions which I intended to submit to the Congress at their adjourned discussion on the subject.[14]

Lloyd George obviously here referred to the "Smuts resolution," the paper Jan Smuts, soon to be Premier of South Africa, had drawn up and which, in the end, did form the basis of a general compromise. The Smuts resolution reads as follows:

1. Having regard to the record of the German administration in the colonies formerly part of the German Empire, and to the menace which the possession by Germany of submarine bases in many parts of the world would necessarily constitute to the freedom and security of all nations, the Allied and Associated Powers are agreed that in no circumstances should any of the German colonies be restored to Germany.

2. For similar reasons, and more particularly because of historic oppression by the Turks of all subject peoples and the terrible massacres of Armenians and others in recent years, the Allied and Associated Powers are agreed that Armenia, Syria, Mesopotamia, Palestine, and Arabia must be completely severed from the Turkish Empire. This is without prejudice to the settlement of other parts of the Turkish Empire.

3. The Allied and Associated Powers are agreed that advantage should be taken of the opportunity afforded by the necessity of disposing of these colonies and territories formerly belonging to Germany and Turkey which are inhabited by peoples not yet able to stand by themselves under the strenuous conditions of the modern world, to apply to these territories the principle that the well-being and development of such peoples form a sacred trust of civilisation, and that securities for the performance of this trust should be embodied in the constitution of the League of Nations.

4. After careful study they are satisfied that the best method of giving practical effect to this principle is that the tutelage of such peoples should be entrusted to advanced nations who, by reason of their resources, their experience or their geographical position, can best undertake this responsibility, and that this tutelage should be exercised by them as mandatories on behalf of the League of Nations.

5. The Allied and Associated Powers are of opinion that the character of the mandate must differ according to the stage of development of the people, the geographical situation of the territory, its economic conditions and other similar circumstances.

6. They consider that certain communities formerly belonging to the Turkish Empire have reached a stage of development where their existence as independent nations can be provisionally recognised subject to the rendering of administrative advice and assistance by a

mandatory power until such time as they are able to stand alone. The wishes of these communities must be a principal consideration in the selection of the mandatory power.

7. They further consider that other peoples, especially those of Central Africa, are at such a stage that the mandatory must be responsible for the administration of the territory subject to conditions which will guarantee the prohibition of abuses such as the slave trade, the arms traffic and the liquor traffic, and the prevention of the military training of the natives for other than police purposes, and the establishment of fortifications of military and naval bases, and will also secure equal opportunities for the trade and commerce of other members of the League of Nations.

8. Finally they consider that there are territories such as South West Africa and the Pacific Islands which, owing to the sparseness of their population, or their small size, or their remoteness from the centres of civilisation, or their geographical contiguity to the mandatory state, and other circumstances, can best be administered under the laws of the mandatory state as if they were integral portions thereof, subject to the safeguards above mentioned in the interests of the indigenous population.

In every case of mandate, the mandatory state shall render to the League of Nations an annual report in reference to the territory committed to its charge.[15]

The British wanted to make sure that President Wilson would accept the Smuts resolution before they badgered their recalcitrant Dominion Premiers into subscribing to it. Jan Smuts therefore called on Colonel House.

January 29, 1919: General Smuts came to see me at 10:30 in order to see whether we could not get together on the colonies question. He had drafted a paper which he said Lloyd George and some of them approved, but which they had not offered Hughes and Massey. They did not want to present the paper unless they knew it was satisfactory to the President and me. When I read it I saw they had made great concessions from the position they took yesterday, and I told him that with a few slight verbal changes I was ready to accept it.[16]

By accepting the mandate principle, the Smuts resolution went a long way toward pacifying the President. By providing three different types of mandates, and by placing South-West Africa and the Pacific Islands in the third category, which was to be "administered as an integral part of the mandatory power," Smuts gave both his own South Africa and his fellow Dominions all they asked for—sovereign rights in the mandated territories, limited only by the obligation to file annual reports with the League. That evening Wilson had a meeting with his Commissioners while Lloyd George held a meeting with the British Empire Delegation.

House describes the meeting of American Commissioners.

The President came tonight and had a meeting with the Commissioners, and among other subjects discussed was this memorandum. He was not ready to accept it as a whole or at once.[17]

The meeting of the Empire Delegation was heated, but Lloyd George got the Dominion Premiers to agree to the Smuts resolution in the hope that this would satisfy the President and induce him to agree to an immediate distribution of mandates. By next morning (January 30th) President Wilson had made up his mind to accept the Smuts proposals, but he steadfastly refused to confirm either the Dominions or Japan as mandatories in the colonial possessions they occupied. This refusal set off fireworks in the Council of Ten, where Wilson clashed head on with the combustible William Hughes of Australia.

With the detailed discussion of the provision of Mr. Lloyd George's resolutions came further arguments and objections from Mr. Massey and Mr. Hughes, still in favour of direct annexation. At length, the discussion grew so acrid that President Wilson turned upon Mr. Hughes and Mr. Massey.

President WILSON asked if he was to understand that New Zealand and Australia had presented an ultimatum to the Conference. They had come there and presented their cases for annexation of New Guinea and Samoa. Was he now to understand that this was the minimum of their concession? That their agreement upon a plan depended upon that concession? And that if they could not get that definitely now, they proposed to do what they could to stop the whole agreement?

Mr. Hughes was very deaf, and laboured under the disadvantage of not hearing the arguments of the other side of the case.

> Mr. HUGHES replied that President Wilson had put it fairly well, and that that was their attitude, subject to the reservation which he had stated that morning. . . . For the present that represented the maximum of their concession in that direction.

But in spite of this defiance both Hughes and Massey finally said they expected to accept the resolution. While the Dominions thus permitted the question of mandates to go to the League of Nations Commission, they were sore enough.[18]

Great Britain, its Dominions, France and Japan were all assured of eventual possession of the German colonies they had conquered, and President Wilson had retained the right to delay the award of the mandates until the League was definitely set up. Actually mandates were not awarded until April 12, 1919, after the revised Covenant had been sanctioned by the Plenary Session of the Peace Conference. Then, and only then, did the conquering powers obtain legal possession of their spoils.

In the Council of Ten the Smuts resolution ran into stormy weather as soon as Paragraph Seven came up for discussion. Arguing French security, the French demanded the right to raise native troops in their mandated territories.

M. PICHON said that France could not renounce the right of raising volunteers in the countries under her administration, whatever they might be. The Germans had recognized the importance of the support France had received from her Colonies. Before powerful American troops came to aid, France had resisted with her own forces for a long time, together with the British Armies, and it was certain, but for the help she had received from her Colonial Possessions, the situation would have been very critical. It was necessary that France should be empowered to recruit not conscripts, but volunteers from all colonial territories under her control. That was absolutely necessary for her future security.

President WILSON enquired if this referred to the territories controlled as mandatory states as well as to the present colonies.

M. CLEMENCEAU said that . . . if France was not to be permitted to raise volunteers in the territories under her administration, the people of France would greatly resent any such arrangement and would have a grievance against the Government.

Mr. LLOYD GEORGE pointed out that as regards tropical colonies, at the beginning of this war, Great Britain had native forces in Uganda and Nigeria and other places, and the French also had forces in Senegal and other territories, but these forces were intended solely for the defense of those territories. They had never raised, armed and equipped great forces for carrying on big offensive operations outside those territories.

M. CLEMENCEAU observed that nevertheless the right to raise forces did exist.

Mr. LLOYD GEORGE said that there was nothing in the clause under review to prevent volunteer forces being raised. The words used were: "For other than police purposes and the defense of territory." He really thought those words would cover the case of France. There was nothing in the document which would prevent her doing exactly the same thing as she had done before. What it did prevent was the kind of thing the Germans were likely to do, namely, to organize great black armies in Africa, to be used for the purpose of clearing everybody else out of that country. . . .

M. CLEMENCEAU said that if France had the right in the event of a great war to raise troops in African territories under her control, he would ask for nothing more.

Mr. LLOYD GEORGE replied that France would have exactly the same rights she had previously enjoyed. The resolution proposed by him was only intended to prevent a mandatory from drilling all the natives and from raising great armies.

M. CLEMENCEAU said that he did not want to do that. All that he wished was that the matter should be made quite clear, and he did not want anybody to come and tell him afterwards that he had broken away from the agreement. If this clause meant that France had the right to raise troops in the African territories under her control in case of a general war, he was satisfied.

Mr. LLOYD GEORGE said that so long as M. Clemenceau did not train big nigger [sic] armies for the purposes of aggression, that was all the clause was intended to guard against.

M. CLEMENCEAU said that he did not want to do that. He therefore understood that Mr. Lloyd George's interpretation was adopted.

President WILSON said that Mr. Lloyd George's interpretation was consistent with the phraseology.

M. CLEMENCEAU said that he was quite satisfied.[19]

Although Clemenceau said that he was quite satisfied, he wasn't really, and on various occasions the French raised the same question again. Even in the final drafting of the treaty they tried to slip into the French text a sentence which would have permitted the raising of troops for overseas service. When an alert drafting committee caught the discrepancy and Clemenceau was accused of trying to "juggle the text" he shamefully blamed an unlucky subordinate for the "error," which was duly corrected.

The colonial debate in the Council of Ten had another consequence which almost led to the transfer of the Peace Conference from Paris. Ray Baker recounts the incident.

. . . The French, when they could not get the President to accept their blunt idea of "annexation pure and simple" in the secret conferences, began a red-hot attack upon him outside in the press, especially in those newspapers which act notoriously as instruments of the French Foreign Office. They began to comment bitterly upon the President and his "impractical ideals." Although the proceedings behind the muffled doors at the Quai d'Orsay were supposed to be absolutely secret—so that American correspondents could get next to nothing at all concerning what was going on—the French papers were evidently fully informed. Certain British papers also published quite completely an account of the controversy between Mr. Wilson and Mr. Hughes of Australia which lost nothing in emphasis and dramatic importance nor, it may be said, in the essential truth of the facts stated, because the proceedings had been secret. Mr. Hughes gave out interviews with scarcely veiled attacks upon Mr. Wilson.

On January 30 the President protested against these attacks, as he said, "in unaffected good-humour," but as a "question of privilege."

It was stated [he said] that, as regards President Wilson's ideals, he (President Wilson) did not know how his ideals would work. If these articles continued to appear, he would find himself compelled to publish his own views. So far he had only spoken to people in that room and to members of the American Delegation, so that nothing had been communicated to the Press regarding President Wilson's views, either by himself or by his associates. . . . Nevertheless the time might come when he would be compelled against his own wishes to make a full public exposé of his views.

At once the direct attacks in the French press ceased, for the French desired no public appeal by the President upon this issue of their annexationist programme; but from that time onward, in a certain number of the papers, there was an underlying subtle spirit of criticism of the President. This constant, clever, witty opposition, so evasive as not to be easily met—the kind of criticism by innuendo of which the French are past masters—read every day by all those connected with the Peace Conference, had a profound influence in making the President's task more difficult. There were those in the American commission who suggested the removal of the Conference to some neutral city like Geneva, to escape this atmosphere.[20]

By the end of January, all the colonial problems save one had been disposed of. This last problem, Japan's claims to the former German holdings in China's Shantung Province, was not tackled until the very last days of the Conference. The Japanese demands placed Wilson on the horns of a fearful dilemma. On the one hand, accession to the demands would bring down upon him the wrath of powerful interests in the United States, and might lead to China's refusal to participate in the peace settlement; on the other hand, refusal of these claims would not only offend Britain and France, who were treaty-bound to support the Japanese claims, but would very likely drive Japan into the arms of Soviet Russia and Germany, a prospect that constantly haunted Wilson's thoughts.

Ray S. Baker tells the story.

The Japanese presented their . . . territorial demands, with a kind of cold determination. They presented to the Conference what was practically an ultimatum.

> The Japanese delegation [declared Viscount Chinda] were under an express order in the case that the question [of Shantung] was not settled . . . they were not allowed to sign the treaty.*

They not only demanded a settlement exactly on the lines they had laid down, but they insisted upon immediate action.

* Secret Minutes, Council of Four, April 22.

President Wilson knew that the entire weight of the struggle, in this crisis, would rest upon him, that the influence of both Lloyd George and Clemenceau, who were indeed bound by the secret agreements of 1917, would be against him. . . .

For nearly a hundred years Western nations—especially Great Britain, France, and Russia—had been steadily encroaching upon China, seizing territory and exploiting the resources for their own benefit. . . .

When the World War broke out in 1914, Japan realized her new opportunity. . . . She issued an ultimatum to Germany demanding the surrender of Kiauchau, but promising to return it to China, to whom, of course, it really belonged. When nothing happened Japan, assisted by Great Britain, captured the port. Instead of returning it to China, however—she had made no promise as to time!—she took over the Shantung railroad and enforced a control in the province more extensive and drastic than Germany had ever attempted. . . .

In January, 1915, the Japanese, still eagerly improving the opportunities presented by the preoccupation of Europe, presented to China the famous or infamous "Twenty-one Demands," part of which were kept secret from the outside world. These demands, if accepted entire, would have made China practically a vassal of Japan. When China objected, Japan sent a forty-eight-hour ultimatum (on May 7), and China was forced to submit to a large proportion of them. And one of them gave Japan a secure foothold in the vast rich provinces of Manchuria. . . .

As to Shantung, its disposal was provided for in two sets of agreements between Japan and China, one concluded on May 25, 1915, the other September 24 and 28, 1918.

Japan, in these agreements, provided that when, after the war, she was free to dispose of the territory she had taken from Germany she would restore it to China upon certain conditions, the principal ones being that Kiauchau should be a free port, that Japan should have a concession there, and that the important Shantung railroad should become a joint Chino-Japanese enterprise with a "police force" directed by the Japanese. In short, while the Japanese were agreeing to return Kiauchau to China they were actually demanding—so the Chinese assert—more rights than the Germans ever had. The Chinese, with painful awareness of what Japan had already done in Korea, at Port Arthur, and in Manchuria, had no confidence whatever in Japanese policies and feared being left at the mercy of Japan.

Early in 1917 Japan took still another advantage of the war in Europe to assure herself of her new possessions and rights. Before she would grant her naval assistance against the ravages of the German and Austrian submarines in the Mediterranean she extorted the profoundly important secret agreements with Great Britain and France (February, 1917) under which these great nations agreed to support her claims in regard to the disposal of Germany's rights in Shantung and also agreeing that Japan was to have all the former German islands north of the equator, and Great Britain all of those south of the equator. . . .

Japan feared that the European aggressions meant a diminishing opportunity for her own expanding ambitions. She considered that she had better warrant for claiming China as her natural sphere of influence than any Western nation. If America had a Monroe Doctrine to keep all other nations out of South America, why could not Japan assert a similar doctrine as to eastern Asia? She also began playing the game of grab in 1894 when she first entered Korea, which she finally swallowed whole in 1910. Her victory in the Russo-Japanese War of 1904-05 enormously increased her own self-confidence and added to her prestige. In 1905 she succeeded to the Russian sphere of influence at Port Arthur and has steadily extended her power there.

The actual struggle in the Council of Four began on April 21 at the very time . . . that the Italian crisis was also acute. Baron Makino and Viscount Chinda went to President Wilson's house in the Place des États-Unis on the morning of that day and held a long conference. . . . The Japanese stood absolutely upon their original demands regarding Shantung and the Pacific islands. President Wilson, on his part, proposed a number of modifications.

First, as he reported to the "Four," he had made the suggestion that Mr. Lansing had already made at the Council of Foreign Ministers that all claims in the Pacific should be ceded to the allied and associated powers as trustees, leaving them to make fair and just dispositions.

Second, "he had reminded the Japanese delegates that it had been understood that Japan was to have a mandate for the islands in the North Pacific although he had made a reserve in the case of the island of Yap, which he himself considered should be international."

Third, and here he made a suggestion that touched the other Allies to the quick, that all "spheres of influence in China be abrogated"—

not only Japanese but British and French. He said "the interest of the world in China was the 'open door.' " The Japanese, as the President remarked, "replied that they were ready to do this," but there was no response from either Lloyd George or Clemenceau. While they were willing enough to help get Japan out of China, they were unwilling to purchase her abandonment of her position by renunciations of their own spheres of influence!

> Mr. LLOYD GEORGE suggested that it [Shantung] ought to be ceded to the League of Nations.
>
> President WILSON said that the Japanese were too proud to accept this solution . . . to be perfectly fair to the Japanese he thought they would interpret this as a challenge of their good faith. He had put it to the Japanese representatives that the peace of the Far East depended more on Chino-Japanese relations than on anything else. China was full of riches. It was clearly to the advantage of Japan to take the most generous position towards China and to show herself as a friend. The interest of the world in China was the "open door." The Japanese had assented and expressed benevolent intentions.
>
> Mr. LLOYD GEORGE pointed out that it was the triumph of the Great Powers in the West that enabled Japan to make this arrangement. He felt strongly that Japan should be in the same position as other States. Otherwise other nations could insist on the same right.*

On the next day the Japanese themselves came to the Council and Baron Makino again set forth the Japanese claims, described the agreements of 1915 and 1918 with China, asserted that the declaration of war by China had not abrogated them, and that China had "actually received the advance of 20,000,000 yen according to the terms of the above agreements."

Baron Makino then handed around a draft of the clauses which the Japanese delegation wished to have inserted in the Peace Treaty with Germany and which ultimately became, with little change, Articles 156, 157, and 158 of that treaty.**

* Secret Minutes, Council of Four, April 21.

** Following is the text of Articles 156, 157, and 158 of the Treaty:

Up to this time Lloyd George and Clemenceau had taken practically no part in the discussion. The President turned to them now and said that they had heard from the Japanese and that "he [President Wilson] had laid what was in his own mind before all present." He now wanted to know the "impression formed by Mr. Lloyd George and M. Clemenceau."

It is significant that in all these discussions at Paris, the old secret treaties sooner or later emerged. Up to this time nothing had been said in the Councils regarding the secret agreement of February, 1917. Lloyd George now produced it and the following conversation took place:

> Mr. LLOYD GEORGE said that so far as Great Britain was concerned they were in the same position towards Japan as towards

---

ARTICLE 156

Germany renounces, in favour of Japan, all her rights, title, and privileges—particularly those concerning the territory of Kiauchau, railways, mines and submarine cables—which she acquired in virtue of the Treaty concluded by her with China on March 6, 1898, and of all other arrangements relative to the Province of Shantung.

All German rights in the Tsingtao-Tsinanfu Railway, including its branch lines, together with its subsidiary property of all kinds, stations, shops, fixed and rolling stock, mines, plant and material for the exploitation of the mines, are and remain acquired by Japan, together with all rights and privileges attaching thereto.

The German State submarine cables from Tsingtao to Shanghai and from Tsingtao to Chefoo, with all the rights, privileges and properties attaching thereto, are similarly acquired by Japan, free and clear of all charges and encumbrances.

ARTICLE 157

The movable and immovable property owned by the German State in the territory of Kiauchau, as well as all the rights which Germany might claim in consequence of the works or improvements made or of the expenses incurred by her, directly or indirectly, in connection with this territory, are and remain acquired by Japan, free and clear of all charges and encumbrances.

ARTICLE 158

Germany shall hand over to Japan within three months from the coming into force of the present Treaty, the archives, registers, plans, title-deeds and documents of every kind, wherever they may be, relating to the administration, whether civil, military, financial, judicial or other, of the territory of Kiauchau.

Within the same period Germany shall give particulars to Japan of all treaties, arrangements or agreements relating to the rights, title or privileges referred to in the two preceding articles.

Italy. They had a definite engagement with Japan, as recorded in the Note of the British Ambassador at Tokyo, dated 16th February, 1917. Hence, so far as Great Britain was concerned, there was a definite engagement . . . the Japanese Government had undertaken to support the British claims south of the Equator, and the British Government had undertaken to support the Japanese claims in the islands north of the Equator. . . .

Baron MAKINO said that Japan had expressed her willingness to support the British claims.

But here Lloyd George, by again advancing his suggestion that Shantung be assigned as a mandate under the League of Nations, attempted to use his familiar device of postponement. To this the Japanese at once responded in most vigorous terms:

Viscount CHINDA asked if it was merely proposed to postpone this question: to put it in abeyance? The Japanese . . . had a duty to perform to China in this matter, and they could not carry out their obligation to China unless Kiauchau was handed over to them. They were under an express instruction from their Government that unless they were placed in a position to carry out their obligation to China they were not allowed to sign the Treaty. Consequently, they had no power to agree to a postponement.

Baron MAKINO said that if the Treaty were ignored, it would be a very serious matter for Japan. . . .

President WILSON pointed out that, as had happened in many instances, he was the only one present whose judgment was entirely independent. His colleagues were both bound by treaties, although perhaps he might be entitled to question whether Great Britain and Japan had been justified in handing round the islands in the Pacific. This, however, was a private opinion. . . . He was so firmly convinced that the Peace of the Far East centred upon China and Japan that he was more interested from this point of view than any other. . . . He was anxious that Japan should show to the world as well as to China that she wanted to give the same independence to China as other nations possessed; that she did not want China to be held in manacles. What would prejudice the peace in the Far East was any relationship that was not trustful. . . . What he feared was that Japan, by standing merely on her treaty rights, would create the impression that she was thinking more of her rights than of her duties to China. The world would never have peace based on treaty rights only unless there were also recognized to be reciprocal duties between States. Perhaps he was going a little too fast in existing circumstances, but he wished to emphasize the importance in future that States should think primarily of their duties towards each other. The central idea of the League of Nations was that States must support each other even when their interests were not involved. When the League of Nations was formed then there would be established a body of partners covenanted to stand up for each other's rights. The position in which he would like to see Japan, already the most advanced nation in the Far East with the leadership in enterprise and policy, was that of the leader in the Far East standing out for these new ideas. There could be no finer nor more politic role for her. That was what he had to say as the friend of Japan. . . . What he was after was to attain a more detailed definition as to how Japan was going to help China as well as to afford an opportunity for investment in railways, etc. He had hoped that by pooling their interest the several nations that had gained a foothold in China (a foothold that was to the detriment of China's position in the World) might forego the special position they had acquired and that China might be put on the same footing as other nations, as sooner or later she must certainly be. He believed this to be to the interest of everyone concerned. There was a lot of combustible material in China and if flames were put to it the fire could not be quenched, for China had a population of four hundred million people. It was symptoms of that which filled him with anxiety. Baron Makino and Viscount Chinda knew how deep-seated was the feeling of reverence of China towards Shantung which was the most sacred Chinese Province and he dreaded starting a flame there because this reverence was based upon the very best motives and owing to the traditions of Confucius and the foundations of intellectual development. He did not wish to interfere with treaties. As Mr. Lloyd George had remarked earlier, the war had been undertaken partly in order to establish the sanctity of treaties. Although he yielded to no one in this sentiment there were cases he felt where treaties ought not to have been entered into.

Baron MAKINO, referring to President Wilson's remarks in regard to the larger ideas of international relationship, said that the best opinion of Japan was at that point of view. For China, the best opinion in Japan wanted equal opportunities or the "open door."

He had convinced himself of this and was very glad of it, for he felt it would be to the advantage of both countries. He recalled, however, that international affairs in China had not always been conducted on very just lines. (Mr. LLOYD GEORGE interjected that this was undoubtedly the case.) . . . The best opinion, however, in Japan based itself on fairness and justice. Before he left Japan he had had a conversation with one of their elder statesmen, who had remarked to him that Japan would have to enter into a good many joint undertakings with China and must content herself to share equally, half in half, in them. . . . He had himself shared his views.

President WILSON said that he was satisfied on that point and he hoped Baron Makino would not interpret him to have expressed any doubts. He wanted that principle, however, to be shown in a concrete way to China.*

On the same afternoon, although the Japanese objected, the Chinese appeared before the Four. In an introductory statement the President again reviewed the Chino-Japanese notes of 1915 and 1918, reading aloud the agreement of the Chinese Minister in 1918. He then set forth the difficulties of the situation:

The Chinese delegation would see, President Wilson continued, the embarrassing position which had been reached. Mr. Lloyd George and M. Clemenceau were bound to support the claims of Japan. Alongside of them the Chinese had their exchange of notes with Japan. He reminded Mr. Koo that when urging his case before the Council of Ten at the Quai d'Orsay, he had maintained that the war cancelled the agreement with the German Government. It did not, however, cancel the agreement between China and the Japanese Government, which had been made before the war. What he had himself urged upon the Japanese was that, as in the case of the Pacific Islands, the leased territory of Kiauchau should be settled by putting it into the hands of the Five Powers as Trustees. He did not suggest that treaties should be broken, but that it might be possible, in conference, to bring about an agreement by modifying the Treaty. He also proposed to them that all governments should renounce the special rights they had acquired in China, so as to put China in a position free from the special limitations which had been imposed upon her. The Japanese were not willing to have

* Secret Minutes, Council of Four, April 22.

Kiauchau handed over to the Five Powers, and the British and French Governments were embarrassed by their treaties. When he pressed the Japanese for explanations of the meaning of their agreement, they had replied that the exploitation of two coal-mines and one iron-mine had not proved a successful venture, and were now bound up with the railway. They stated, however, that they would withdraw the civil administration; that they would maintain troops only on the termini of the railway; and that if a general agreement was reached, they would withdraw their extra-territoriality. They urged that they wanted a community of interest with the Chinese in the railway, and the only reserve they made was for a residential district in Kiauchau.

Mr. Koo said that the Treaties of 1915 and the subsequent exchange of notes were all part and parcel of one transaction. He hoped he had made this clear before the Council of Ten. He felt that the Treaties and notes which had been exchanged after Japan had delivered an ultimatum stood outside of the regular procedure and course of Treaties. They dealt with matters arising out of the war.

Mr. Lloyd George asked what ultimatum he referred to.

President Wilson asked if Mr. Lloyd George had never heard of the twenty-one points.

Mr. Lloyd George said he had not.

Mr. Koo then explained the tangle of treaties in which China was struggling.

Mr. Lloyd George asked if they had not appealed to the United States of America.

President Wilson said they had and the United States had intervened in regard to the infringement of sovereignty and political independence. The whole transaction, however, had been kept extremely secret and the United States only learnt of it in a roundabout way.

Mr. Koo said that secrecy had been imposed [upon China] by Japan under severe penalties. . . . For the last four years since they had captured Kiauchau, Japanese troops had penetrated far into the Province of Shantung. . . . The Chinese Government had protested, and asked the Japanese to withdraw, but they had refused and had established troops 250 miles up the railway and extended their control.

After Mr. Koo had stated his case, Mr. Lloyd George said that "the real question was whether the [Chinese] treaty with Japan was better for China than [the transference to Japan of] Germany's rights." . . . The Chinese . . . said that "both alternatives were unacceptable" . . . and [they] wished Shantung—which was their own territory—returned directly to them. . . .

> President WILSON [said that] . . . whatever arrangements were made both Japan and China would be members of the League of Nations, which would guarantee their territorial integrity and political independence. That is to say, that these matters would become the concern of the League and China would receive a kind of protection that she had never had before and other nations would have a right which they had never had before to intervene. Before, it had been, comparatively speaking, none of our business to interfere in these matters. The Covenant, however, laid down that whatever affected the peace of the world was a matter of concern to the League of Nations and to call attention to such was not an hostile but a friendly act. He, himself, was prepared to advocate at the Council of the League and at the Body of Delegates that the special position occupied by the various nations in China should be abandoned. Japan declared that she was ready to support this. There would be a forum for advocating these matters. The interests of China could not then be overlooked. He was stating this as an element of security for China in the future if the powers were unable to give her what she wanted now, and he asked the Chinese delegates to think the matter over.

In response Mr. Koo made an earnest statement. He

> said that he could not lay too much emphasis on the fact that the Chinese people were now at the parting of the ways. The policy of the Chinese Government was co-operation with Europe and the United States as well as with Japan. If, however, they did not get justice, China might be driven into the arms of Japan. There was a small section in China which believed in Asia for the Asiatics and wanted the closest co-operation with Japan. The position of the Government, however, was that they believed in the justice of the West and that their future lay there. If they failed to get justice there, the consequential reaction might be very great.

President Wilson responded by again showing the "quandary in which the Powers" found themselves, the entanglement of old treaties ("we could not undo past obligations"), and that the "undoing of the trouble" depended on all the nations uniting to secure justice.

> Mr. Koo said he believed prevention to be better than cure. He thought that the object of the peace was to undo unfortunate engagements.
>
> Mr. Lloyd George said the object of the war was not that. The war had been fought as much for the East as for the West. China also had been protected by the victory that had been won. If Germany had won the war and had desired Shantung or Pekin, she could have had them. The very doctrine of the mailed fist had been propounded in relation to China. The engagements that had been entered into with Japan had been contracted at a time when the support of that country was urgently needed. He would not say that the war could not have been won without this support. But he could say that Kiauchau could not have been captured without Japanese support. It was a solemn treaty and Great Britain could not turn round to Japan now and say "All right, thank you very much. When we wanted your help, you gave it, but now we think that the treaty was a bad one and should not be carried out." Within the treaties he would go to the utmost limits to protect the position of China. On the League of Nations he would always be prepared to stand up for China against any oppression, if there was oppression. China was a nation with a very great past and, he believed, with a still greater future. It would, however, be of no service to her to regard treaties as von Bethmann Hollweg had regarded them, as mere scraps of paper to be turned down when they were not wanted.
>
> M. Clemenceau said that Mr. Koo could take every word that Mr. Lloyd George had said as his also.*

In this crisis President Wilson was confronted by the greatest difficulties; for he was just then also at the height of the Italian struggle. On April 23 he had issued his bold message to the world regarding the disposition of Fiume, . . . and on the next day the Italian delegation departed from Paris with the expectation that their withdrawal would either force the hand of the Conference or break it up. While this crisis was at its height the Belgian delegation, which had long been restive over the non-settlement of Belgian claims for reparations, became insistent. They had no place in the Supreme Council and they

* Secret Minutes, Council of Four, April 22, afternoon session.

were worried lest the French and British—neither of whom could begin to get enough money out of Germany to pay for its losses—would take the lion's share and leave Belgium unrestored. It looked, indeed, as though the Conference was breaking down. The Japanese chose this critical moment (April 24) to send a most peremptory letter, signed by Marquis Saionji, head of their delegation, demanding a "definite settlement of this question . . . with the least possible delay."

The President knew that if he stood stiffly for immediate justice to China, he would have to force Great Britain and France to break their pledged word with Japan. Even if he succeeded in doing this, he still would have to face the probability, practically the certainty, that the Japanese would withdraw from the Conference and go home.

He felt convinced that the Japanese meant what they said, that they had orders from their government.

"They are not bluffers," he said to me, "and they will go home unless we give them what they should not have."*

. . . With Japan out of the association of Western nations there was . . . the possibility . . . that she would begin building up alliances of her own in the east—possibly with Germany and Russia. Indeed, if the truth were told, this was probably the most important consideration of all in shaping the final decision. . . .

On April 25, only Wilson, Lloyd George, and Clemenceau being present, the problem came up again. Clemenceau presented three documents, the demand of Saionji, already referred to, for an immediate settlement, a report of a committee of experts (E. T. Williams for America, Jean Gout for France, and Ronald Macleay for Great Britain) giving the opinion that while it "would be more advantageous to China" if Japan inherited the rights of Germany in Shantung than to be accorded the basis of the Chino-Japanese agreements of 1915 and 1918, "either course presents serious disadvantages for China"; and finally a new and strong demand by China in which she made four proposals:

1. That the German rights be renounced to the Five Powers for restoration to China. This was the original American proposal.
2. Japan to leave Shantung within a year.
3. China to agree to pay all the costs of Japanese military operations in capturing Tsingtao.

* In this opinion, some of the President's advisers, notably E. T. Williams and S. K. Hornbeck, were not in agreement.

4. China to agree to open the whole of Kiauchau Bay as a commercial port with a special quarter for foreign residence.

President Wilson said that "this question was almost as difficult as the Italian question," and asked "if the British and French were bound to transfer Kiauchau and Shantung to Japan."

> Mr. LLOYD GEORGE said that sooner or later they were.
> M. CLEMENCEAU agreed.

But Mr. Lloyd George now said that Mr. Balfour had made a proposal along the lines already suggested by Wilson that while "we were bound to transfer the German rights . . . to Japan . . . we should like to talk over the terms on which Japan would hand them back to China. That proposal would meet the Japanese sentiments of pride."

Here again the President reverted to his old suggestion that *all* the powers renounce their rights in China. He said the Japanese "were willing to discuss this with the other powers." If all went out, Japan would go, too. He said "his object was to take the chains off China." But here Lloyd George objected; he said "the British Government could not agree."

"We could not allow other nations to co-operate in the Yangtse-kiang," he said, "since we had not sufficient capital ourselves for development. The reason we could not do so was because we should have to allow the Japanese in."*

Here again was the nub of the matter!

Balfour was requested to confer with the Japanese delegates, and at the same time the President turned in every direction to see if there were not some way out of the difficulty. He had a conference with the American Commission on April 26 and asked Mr. Lansing to see the Japanese. That very day Lansing (with E. T. Williams, the American adviser on Far Eastern affairs) met Viscount Chinda who, according to the record of the conversation, was even stiffer in "insisting upon the exact fulfilment of the treaty with China" than he had been in the Council of Four. Chinda told Lansing flatly that the Japanese delegates "had instructions from home that if the German rights were not renounced in favour of Japan, the Japanese delegates were not to sign the Treaty."

The three days, April 28, 29, and 30, were the crucial days of the struggle.

Mr. Balfour had conferred with Baron Makino and presented a

* Secret Minutes, Council of Four, April 25.

memorandum to the Three, showing, as President Wilson remarked, a "decided approach in the Japanese attitude."

> President WILSON [said] he had told the United States delegation that his line was this:—"If Japan will return Kiauchau and Shantung to China and relinquish all sovereign rights and will reduce her claims to mere economic concessions foregoing all military rights, I would regard it as returning these possessions to China on better terms than Germany had held them."
>
> Mr. BALFOUR said that there was no doubt whatsoever that Japan was returning these territories to China on incomparably better terms than Germany had held them.
>
> President WILSON said his experts did not agree.
>
> Mr. BALFOUR said that the United States' experts had not heard the Japanese case. The same had applied to his expert, Mr. Macleay. . . .
>
> Mr. BALFOUR continued that the Japanese Government now in power was not the same government as had made the Treaty of 1915 with China. He honestly believed that this Government intended adopting a more liberal policy and had been influenced by what the Japanese representatives had learned in Paris.*

Up to the very last hour of the final decision on April 29, the President was strongly hopeful of finding some more liberal solution. The present writer saw him frequently during these days and knows how he took the problem to heart. He had asked me to gather certain information for him which I did, from the Chinese and the American experts, E. T. Williams and S. K. Hornbeck, and took up to him before the critical meeting of the Three on April 29. He examined the material and the maps carefully.

"There is no possible doubt," I find in my diary of that day, "as to where the President's sympathies lie: he is for the Chinese . . . I made as strong a case as I could for the Chinese position, urging some postponement, at least. The President pointed out how inextricably the whole matter was tied up with old treaties, how Great Britain felt herself bound to Japan and how, with Italy already out, Belgium bitterly discontented, the defection of Japan might not only break up the Peace Conference but destroy the League of Nations."

When the Japanese delegates came in a little later to the Council of Three there was another involved discussion, covering all the old

* Secret Minutes, Council of Four, April 28.

ground. Viscount Chinda did not wish to go so far in making concessions and in defining Japanese intentions as Baron Makino had gone with Mr. Balfour. The President fought for a clearer agreement as to what Japan meant by the control of the police and whether it was to be in the hands of the Japanese Government or in that of the railroad directorate upon which the Chinese were also represented.

The President well knew that public opinion in the United States would be against such concessions to the Japanese. His commissioners and his experts were all strong on that point. General Bliss, whose judgment the President greatly trusted, wrote a letter to him on that very day opposing the plan to "abandon the democracy of China to the domination of the Prussianized militarism of Japan."

The President knew that he was likely to find American public opinion against him. In the Council of Three and in the presence of the Japanese:

> President WILSON said it was extremely difficult for him in the face of public opinion in the United States of America to assent to any part of the arrangement. He was seeking a way to make it possible for him to agree, and it was not a simple matter. Public opinion in the United States did not agree to the transfer of the concession. He was bound to tell the Japanese representatives that. He was trying to see all views and to find a way out. In these circumstances it greatly increased his difficulty, if there were even an appearance of unusual control insisted on, particularly if the transfer of rights to Japan was greater than those exercised by Germany.*

The actual and final declaration or agreement by the Japanese, which, while it was not to be a part of the Treaty itself, was a supplementary understanding, was made on the morning of April 30. . . .

> In reply to questions by President Wilson—the Japanese Delegates declared that:
>
> "The policy of Japan is to hand back the Shantung peninsula in full sovereignty to China retaining only the economic privileges granted to Germany and the right to establish a settlement under the usual conditions at Tsingtao.
> The owners of the Railway will use special Police only to ensure security for traffic. They will be used for no other purpose.

* Secret Minutes, Council of Four, April 29.

The Police Force will be composed of Chinese and such Japanese instructors as the Directors of the Railway may select will be appointed by the Chinese Government."

Viscount CHINDA made it clear that in the last resort, if China failed to carry out the agreements—if, for example, she would not assist in the formation of the Police Force or the employment of Japanese Instructors, the Japanese Government reserved the right to fall back on the Agreements of 1915 and 1918.[21]

That was all that President Wilson was able to salvage. The final Shantung settlement gave Japan all that she had demanded, and all she gave in return was a declaration, not included in any treaty, promising restoration of sovereignty to China, provided the latter "cooperated" with Japan. Ray Baker records Wilson's reaction to the settlement.

I saw the President at 6:30 as usual and he went over the whole ground (of the Japanese settlement) with me at length. He said he had been unable to sleep the night before for thinking of it. Anything he might do was wrong. He said the settlement was the best that could be had out of a dirty past. . . . The only hope was to keep the world together, get the League of Nations with Japan in it and then try to secure justice for the Chinese not only as regarding Japan but England, France, Russia, all of whom had concessions in China. If Japan went home there was the danger of a Japanese-Russian-German alliance, and a return to the old "balance of power" system in the world, on a greater scale than ever before. He knew his decision would be unpopular in America, that the Chinese would be bitterly disappointed, that the Japanese would feel triumphant, that he would be accused of violating his own principles, but, nevertheless, he *must* work for world order and organization against anarchy and a return to the old militarism.[22]

The Chinese were more than "bitterly disappointed." Their request to be allowed to sign the treaty "with reservations" was turned down by the Big Four, and they chose not to sign the treaty. Instead they issued a statement in which they submitted "their case to the impartial judgment of the world."

VI

Germany's Eastern Frontiers

Early in January 1918, an "American Inquiry" team, composed of David Hunter Miller, Walter Lippman and S. E. Menzes (Colonel House's brother-in-law) drew up a set of suggestions to help President Wilson formulate his Fourteen Points. One of these suggestions read:

> An independent and democratic Poland shall be established. Its boundaries shall be based on a fair balance of national and economic considerations, giving due weight to the necessity of adequate access to the sea. The form of Poland's government and its economic and political relations shall be left to the determination of the People of Poland acting through their chosen representatives.
>
> The subject of Poland is by far the most complex of all the problems to be considered. The present distribution of Poles is such as to make their complete unification impossible without separating East Prussia from Germany. This is probably not within the bounds of practical politics. A Poland which consists essentially of Russian and perhaps Austrian Poland would probably secure its access to the sea through the Vistula river and the canals of Germany which run to Hamburg and Bremen. This relationship would very probably involve both the economic subjection of Poland and the establishment of an area of great friction. If Russia is to remain weak the new Poland will lie in an exceedingly exposed position. The experiment must no doubt be made, however, but in order to assure it a fair start it is necessary to insist at the outset upon the democratic basis for the Polish state. Unless this is loyally observed, the internal friction of Poles, Ruthenians, and Jews is likely to render Poland impotent in the presence of Germany.[1]

From this recommendation Wilson's thirteenth point evolved.

All the Allied and Associated Powers were agreed upon the necessity of creating a Polish state. "A big and strong, very, very strong" Poland was, in Pichon's words, essential for the security of France, for she needed a powerful ally to take the place of Russia at Germany's back. Not only could Germany be weakened by making her surrender territory to the new state, but a strong Poland would also be able to stand guard on Germany's eastern frontiers.

As there were no primary British interests involved, the British, for once, were able to "stand on principles," an opportunity Lloyd George did not let go by. While the creation of Poland itself posed no problem, the two stipulations in Wilson's thirteenth point, "founding a Polish State on territory indisputably inhabited by Poles," and "providing Poland with a free and secure access to the sea," both presented very grave difficulties indeed.

Incorporating territory indisputably inhabited by Poles in the new state automatically awarded Poland the two former German provinces of Posen and West Prussia, where Polish populations largely predominated. However, this cut off the largely German-populated province of East Prussia from Germany proper and created a new geopolitical concept: the corridor. Although the corridor gave Poland access to the sea, that access was neither free nor secure, for it left the country without a harbor to service its needs. The Poles, strongly supported by the French, who had no scruples about any "self-determination for Germans," had an easy solution: incorporation of all of East Prussia in the Polish state. This solution was presented to the Peace Conference by the Polish delegate on January 28th. Lloyd George tells the story.

. . . M. Dmowski suggested that in reaching the settlement of the territory to belong to Poland, we should start from the date 1772, before the first partition. This did not mean that she must be reconstituted with the same boundaries as then existed, but this must be the point of departure, and the boundaries should be rectified according to present conditions. . . .

In settling the boundaries of Poland, the principle of including within those boundaries only those territories where the Poles were in a large majority must not be accepted altogether. In the West, Poland could not be satisfied with the historical boundaries of 1772. For instance, Silesia was lost in the fourteenth century, but today 90 per cent of the population, owing to the national revival, had kept its language and was strongly Polish. . . .

The whole territory of Eastern Germany was not naturally German but was Germanised. . . . Ethnographically, the limits of Poland were irregular, and he pointed to the fact that some wrong would have to be done in East Prussia. Either a small island of Germans must be left in the midst of Polish territory, or the large Polish population must remain under Germany. His suggestion was that this small island of German people should be made a Republic with its capital at Königsberg. He maintained that it would be more just to expose a small Germanised country to infiltration by Poles, than to deprive all Poland of economic independence and to expose it to German aggression. Summing up the question of what is, or what is not, Polish territory, he said that a rough definition would be that such territory as had been oppressed by anti-Polish laws was Polish territory. From the point of view of the preservation of peace, it was evident that if the coast belonged to one nation and the land to another, there would be mutual tendency to conquest. This had been fully appreciated by the Germans, with the result that was apparent in their policy, which had aimed at the gradual absorption of Polish lands, and pointed out the colonisation schemes not only in German Poland but also in Russian Poland, and in this connection he quoted Herr Bebel, the Socialist Democrat, in his work *Die Frau*: "Our task is not to colonise Africa, but to colonise the Vistula." It could not be expected that this idea of absorbing Poland would die amongst the Germans. Therefore, he urged that the frontiers should be so arranged that Poland should no longer be exposed to this danger. . . .

Whilst the delegates of the Great Powers were occupied with deciding the outlines of the Peace Treaty with Germany, their deliberations were constantly interrupted by reports of armed conflict in every corner of the vast battle area of the War, from the Pacific shores to the Black Sea and the Baltic, and from the frozen rivers of Siberia to the sunny shores of the Adriatic. There were scores of little wars going on—some conducted with a savagery which looked as if man had reverted to the type of barbarian he was in the ferocious days of Tamerlane and Attila. . . . The emancipated races of Southern Europe were at each other's throats in their avidity to secure choice bits of the carcases of dead Empires. Pole and Czech were fighting over Teschen. The Poles and the Ukrainians had both pounced on Galicia, whilst Roumanians and Serbs were tearing up Hungary and Austria. Poles and Lithuanians had their fangs on the same cities and forests. Where races were mixed near frontiers, the snarling and clawing were deafening. The Congress could not get on with its work for the uproar. These areas were the mangrove swamps where the racial roots were so tangled and intermingled that no peacemakers could move inside them without stumbling. The resurrected nations rose from their graves hungry and ravening from their long fast in the vaults of oppression. . . . The Supreme Council did its best to persuade and pacify. At the meeting of the Congress on the 24th of January:—

PRESIDENT WILSON read the following communication, which he suggested should be published and transmitted by wireless telegraphy to all parts of the world:—

"The Governments now associated in conference to effect a lasting peace among the nations are deeply disturbed by the news which comes to them of the many instances in which armed force is being made use of, in many parts of Europe and the East, to gain possession of territory, the rightful claim to which the Peace Conference is to be asked to determine. They deem it their duty to utter a solemn warning that possession gained by force will seriously prejudice the claims of those who use such means. It will create the presumption that those who employ force doubt the justice and validity of their claim, and purpose to substitute possession for proof of right and set up sovereignty by coercion rather than by racial or national preference and natural historical association. They thus put a cloud upon every evidence of title they may afterwards allege and indicate their distrust of the Conference itself. Nothing but the most unfortunate results can ensue. If they expect justice they must refrain from force, and place their claims in unclouded good faith in the hands of the Conference of Peace."

(This was agreed to.) . . .

No one gave more trouble than the Poles. Having once upon a time been the most formidable military Power in Central Europe—when Prussia was a starveling Duchy—there were few provinces in a vast area inhabited by a variety of races that Poland could not claim as being historically her inheritance of which she had been reft. Drunk with the new wine of liberty supplied to her by the Allies, she fancied herself once more the resistless mistress of Central Europe. . . .

In Pilsudski the Poles . . . found a leader well fitted for the task of enforcing a claim which did not rest on justice but upon force, and with whom patriotism was the only judge of right. . . . From the moment he attained supreme power he devoted the whole of his mind and character to a policy of territorial expansion by force of arms. Protests of inhabitants went unheard and unheeded. The opposition of the Supreme Council and the admonitions of President Wilson were equally disregarded by this fierce and ruthless patriot.

There were two circumstances which encouraged Pilsudski's aggressions. The first was that a greater Poland suited French policy—and the greater the better. French foreign policy has always been swayed by one paramount aim—the weakening of Germany and the strengthening of its potential opponents. This victory was the supreme opportunity for achieving that purpose. French statesmen had always in their minds the fact that Germany had a warlike population more than half again as numerous as that of France. Their first object was to reduce the disparity by carving as many provinces out of Germany as they could find a decent pretext for taking away. It accounts for their anxiety to sever from the dominion of the Reich the whole of Silesia and the territories on the left bank of the Rhine without regard to ethnological or democratic considerations. But even if the whole of that mutilation had been accomplished, there would still have remained a preponderance of 50 per cent of Germans. To meet this sinister contingency France encouraged the creation of powerful States on the eastern and southern frontiers of the Reich, which would owe their origin and their permanent security to the friendship of France. Therefore a great Poland was one of the principal desiderata of French military strategy. A few million men—Ukrainians, Lithuanians and White Russians—incorporated into Poland meant so much more strength added to the eastern frontiers of France.

The second circumstance which favoured Pilsudski's grasping raids was the hold which the Poles had on the American delegation, owing to the existence of a powerful Polish vote in the United States. This had been thoroughly roused to activity during the War by the efforts of another notable Pole—Paderewski. This great artist had thrown up his musical career and devoted himself to the task of stirring up the Poles of America to a sense of the opportunity offered to them by the

War to recover their national independence. He developed oratorical powers of a high order and his seductive personality made a great impression on the President and his entourage. The President came to Europe an enthusiastic pro-Pole. He did not like the reckless way in which the Poles trampled on his principles and he remonstrated mildly with them, but Pilsudski, encouraged by the French, turned a deaf ear to these expostulations, and his defiance was triumphant. Both the French and Pilsudski understood the President's predilection and took full advantage of it. The cynicism of French diplomacy was never more apparent than in its dealings with Polish delinquencies. On the plea—which was not altogether a pretext—that the Poles were afraid of a Bolshevik invasion with German connivance, the French military urged the Allies to send arms and ammunition to Poland through Danzig. They also recommended that the divisions of the Polish legion formed out of the Polish prisoners captured in the War should be sent to Poland immediately to enable helpless Poland to resist the double menace to her young life.

The Supreme Council assented to these expedients. The Poles were armed and the Polish divisions, equipped with the necessary artillery, were despatched to Warsaw under a General Haller. The division was henceforth known as Haller's Army. Pilsudski out of these supplies of men and material created a formidable force. Haller's Army, which was ready for war when it arrived, was immediately marched into Galicia, ostensibly to drive off the Bolsheviks, but in reality to conquer the country and annex it to Poland. The Supreme Council sent a message to General Haller ordering his withdrawal. Of this command he did not take the slightest notice. Subsequently he pretended that he had never received the telegram in time to act upon the instructions it conveyed. Whether it was intercepted and held up by Pilsudski's orders—whether it had never been despatched from France—or whether they were all in a conspiracy to ignore it—we never discovered. President Wilson was not over-anxious to offend his Polish friends by pressing the enquiry too insistently. The result was that despite the appeals of the Galicians themselves to the Council of the Powers, their country was overrun and annexed to Poland. . . .

Decisions given by the Council that for the time being represented the federated nations of the world were flouted whenever they interfered with the ambitions of the nation against whom judgment was given. Most ominous of all was the fact that one of the Great Powers connived at the defiance of decisions in which it had taken part whenever it suited her policy that these decisions should not be carried out.[2]

Lloyd George's remarks make it very clear that the Poles had not managed to secure his sympathies, and, inasmuch as Wilson refused to commit himself to any territorial settlement until the Conference ratified the Covenant of the League, no action was taken on the Polish claims, and the matter was left in abeyance until the Committee on Polish Affairs could present its report. However, as soon as Wilson had sailed for the United States in mid-February, the French started their drive for immediate peace and pressed the demands for territorial adjustments in the east as well as in the west.

On February 23rd, Colonel House reported:

. . . On the East, Clemenceau thinks that Dantzig [*sic*] should go to Poland. Our experts also believe this to be the best solution and they are joined, I understand, in this belief by the British experts, but the British Government disagrees on this point. . . .[3]

Two days earlier House had received Wilson's cable saying that he "believed the Council of Ten would be going very much beyond its powers to attempt to settle anything beyond the military and naval terms of the treaty." However, Clemenceau and Lloyd George insisted on dealing with these matters, and the hard-pressed Colonel House went along with the two senior statesmen. By this time, House seems to have been firmly ensconced in the Franco-Polish camp, leaving only Lloyd George to fight for the Wilsonian concept of self-determination.

On March 7th Lloyd George had a discussion with Clemenceau.

I informed him that the British Government did not like Marshal Foch's proposal for placing the Polish frontier on a line drawn from Danzig to Thorn; that this would mean incorporating the whole of Eastern Prussia, which was overwhelmingly German, in the Republic of Poland, and that we did not want any more Alsace-Lorraines in Europe, whether in the East or the West. Clemenceau answered neither did he, he had had enough of them. Colonel House said that the American delegates had come to the conclusion that Danzig ought to be incorporated in Poland and he expected that ultimately the British delegates would also agree. We then went to look at the map and found that if Danzig were included in Poland Eastern Prussia presented a very serious geographical difficulty. Colonel House then said that Eastern Prussia might either be internationalised or converted into a separate republic. Clemenceau said that the more separate and independent republics were established in Germany the better he would be pleased. It was decided to await the Report of the Commission on this subject before continuing the discussion.[4]

The British Prime Minister held the fort until the President's return; and, on the 21st of March, Jules Cambon, chairman of the Committee on Polish Affairs, was ready to present his Committee's report. Lloyd George was not pleased.

When M. Cambon, the head of the Commission, produced the First Report, it was an indication of the almost insuperable difficulty of drawing a frontier line on a purely ethnological basis. It stated that:—

> . . . The Commission had followed as far as possible the ethnological principle, but it had been impossible to draw any lines which did not include alien populations on either side. Economic and strategic requirements had also been taken into account, in order that the new State thus delimited should have a fair chance of surviving. At all points, save one, the frontier adopted by the Commission gave the Poles less than they asked for. . . .
>
> In order to give Poland access to the sea, the Commission allotted a strip of territory enclosing the port of Danzig. There was another port further east, namely, Elbing, which had once been Polish, but which the Commission had decided to leave in East Prussia. Danzig had been Polish until the first partition of Poland, and its possession was a matter of life and death to that country. The discussions at present proceeding in regard to the transport of Polish troops to Poland through Danzig indicated the importance of that Port. Without access to the sea, Poland would be stifled. There were commercial and economic as well as military reasons to justify the attribution of Danzig to the Poles. Since its annexation by Germany Danzig had diminished in importance, and there was every reason to suppose that it would revive under

Polish rule. It was true that the townspeople themselves were mostly of German race, but the surrounding population was Polish. Danzig had communication with the interior by two railways, one leading to Thorn and the other to Mlawa. The Commission proposed to give both these lines to Poland.

East Prussia was doubtless the most Prussian part of Germany, and its capital, Koenigsberg, was a holy place of Prussianism. In the southern part of the province, notably in the district of Allenstein, the people were Polish, but the Poles here, unlike the majority of their countrymen, were Protestants, and had been very largely Germanised. They spoke German as much as Polish. The Commission therefore proposed that these people should be consulted concerning their future allegiance, and that a plebiscite should be held there.

The Report was the unanimous product of the Commission. It was signed by the British and American Commissioners as well as by the French and Italians. I was, however, seriously opposed to some of its recommendations and delimitations, on the ground that they proposed to transfer definitely German areas to Polish rule. When the Report came before the Conference, I therefore challenged some of its conclusions. This gave rise to one of the most significant and fundamental discussions of the whole Conference.

MR. LLOYD GEORGE said that the bulk of the recommendations of the Commission represented views which had secured general agreement. He would suggest that only controversial questions should be discussed, and that M. Cambon should be asked to give replies to any points raised on questions which might appear still open to discussion. He himself had one general question to put. He noted that the number of Germans to be included in the future Polish State, as marked out by the Commission, was not less than 2,132,000. This was a very large figure, and might spell serious trouble for Poland in the future. The Germans, moreover, might hesitate to sign any treaty containing such a provision. Any terms which no delegate or Government were likely to sign should make the Council hesitate. The present German Government had gained a temporary victory, but was not very strong. It was said that another rising was likely to take place in six weeks. The Government might not be able to withstand it. If the Allies should present a document requiring from Germany huge indemnities and the cession of a large German population to Poland, the German Government might collapse . . . He wished to ask whether the Commission could not restrict the Polish claims in such a way as to diminish the German population assigned to Poland. In the Danzig district alone 412,000 Germans were assigned to Poland. Was it necessary to assign so much German territory together with the port of Danzig? There was another district in which a German majority was being assigned to Poland, namely, that of Marienwerder. He asked whether this could not be avoided.

M. CAMBON said that in his general explanation he had pointed out that it was very difficult to make a frontier on purely ethnological lines. . . . Economic and strategic reasons therefore must be given weight. In the case of Marienwerder, for instance, if this place were left to Prussia, all the lines from Warsaw to the sea would pass through Prussian territory, and Poland would practically be cut off from the sea.

MR. LLOYD GEORGE agreed that it was hardly possible to draw any line which would not have Germans on both sides of it, but he thought it was very dangerous to assign 2,000,000 Germans to Poland. . . . To hand over millions of people to a distasteful allegiance merely because of a railway was, he thought, a mistake.

PRESIDENT WILSON drew attention to the very special effort made in late years by the German Government to colonise the very region to which Mr. Lloyd George had drawn attention. The Germans had sought to make a German cordon from Schneidemühl to Marienwerder in order to isolate Danzig from Poland. Hence, this was actually a region of political colonisation.

MR. LLOYD GEORGE said that he referred less to Marienwerder itself than to the country east of it, which was historically German.

M. CAMBON said that he regarded it as absolutely essential for Poland to have free access to the sea. This region afforded the best corridor from the inland districts to Danzig. He though that a large proportion of the German population which was of recent importation would quickly emigrate to other parts of Germany when the Polish State was constituted.

MR. LLOYD GEORGE said that he raised no objection in respect to the regions lately colonised by Germany, but he did not feel that he could assent to areas whose whole history was German being assigned to Poland.

PRESIDENT WILSON said that this would only be justified by

reciprocity. Many Poles in areas historically Polish were to be left within Germany.

MR. LLOYD GEORGE asked whether the Council proposed to define the frontiers of Germany finally on *ex parte* evidence alone. The other side had not been heard. It was not only a question of fairness to Germany but of establishing a lasting peace in Europe. It was neither fair nor prudent, because of a railway, to hand over large populations to a Government which they disliked.

M. CAMBON said that it was quite true the Commission had only heard the Poles, but he was not aware of any intention on the part of the Conference to listen to the Germans. The Commission had been asked to examine the means of setting up a Polish State with some prospect of continued life. The Commission had tried to approximate to the Polish State as it existed before the first partition. After thorough examination it had made recommendations of a far more modest character. . . . It was no use setting up a Poland deprived of access to the sea, as it would inevitably be the prey of Germany or of a reconstituted Russia. Poland must have not only a sea-board, but also full and free communication with Danzig. If he had to choose between protecting German populations, largely imported since the eighteenth century, and protecting the Poles, he unquestionably preferred the latter alternative. . . .

M. TARDIEU said that he wished to draw attention to two points. One was that the Committee set up to co-ordinate recommendations as to boundaries had unanimously approved the report of the Polish Commission. Secondly, the situation which Mr. Lloyd George wished to avoid was bound to recur everywhere. The Conference had undertaken to revive ancient States subjected for a number of years or centuries to an alien domination. It was inevitable that in every instance some of the dominating race would be found settled in these areas. With the best will in the world it would not be possible to settle frontiers on ethnological grounds alone. If the submerged nations were to be revived a mixed population must be included in them.

M. CAMBON added that the Polish Commission had also been unanimous in its conclusions.

MR. LLOYD GEORGE said that though the British delegates had accepted the conclusions, they had done so reluctantly. They regarded them as a departure from the principles of the Fourteen Points which had been adopted by the Allies. In some parts of the territory assigned to Poland the argument of political colonisation did not apply. We were told, moreover, that a region colonised with Germans as far back as the eighteenth century should be restored to Poland. Because fifty years ago some capitalists had built a railway which was convenient to the Poles the area surrounding it must be assigned to Poland, in spite of the undoubted German nationality of the population. M. Cambon had said that a corridor to the sea was necessary to Poland. He had nothing to say against this. The Vistula was a navigable river and must be made the principal artery for Polish commerce. There were, moreover, other railways. A railway could be removed, but a long settled population was not removed with the same ease. He thought that in accepting these proposals the Council would be abandoning its principles and making trouble not only for Poland, but for the world. Whenever it could be shown that the policy aimed at reversing the German policy of Polish expropriation the decision might be accepted by the Germans, but the areas which he had in mind would be represented as a "Germania Irredenta," and would be the seed of future war. Should the populations of these areas rise against the Poles, and should their fellow-countrymen wish to go to their assistance, would France, Great Britain, and the United States go to war to maintain Polish rule over them? He felt bound to make this protest against what he considered to be a most dangerous proposal.

President Wilson said that the discussion had brought out a difficulty which, it had been said, would be encountered in many cases, and he had not reached a definite conclusion in his own mind on the particular point under discussion. He hoped that the discussion would be carried far enough to bring out all its elements. Everywhere in Europe lots of foreign people would be found whose possession of the country could be justified by historical, commercial, and similar arguments. He acknowledged that the inclusion of 2,000,000 Germans in Poland was a violation of one principle, that Germany had been notified that free and safe access to the sea for Poland would be insisted on. The Allied and Associated Powers were therefore not open to the reproach that they were doing this merely because they had the power to do it. This was one of the things they had fought for. The difficulty was to arrive at a balance between conflicting considerations. . . . It must be realised that the Allies were creating a new and weak State, weak not only because historically it had failed to govern itself, but because it was sure in future to be divided into factions, more especially as religious differences were an element in the situation. It was therefore necessary to consider not only the economic but the strategic needs of this State, which would have to cope with Germany on both sides of it, the eastern fragment of Germany being one of a most aggressive character. There was bound to be a mixture of hostile populations included in either State. The Council would have to decide which mixture promised the best prospect of security. He was afraid himself of drawing the line as near the Danzig-Thorn railway line as Mr. Lloyd George suggested. He, however, felt the same anxieties as Mr. Lloyd George. The desire might arise among the Germans to rescue German populations from Polish rule, and this desire would be hard to resist. It was a question of balancing antagonistic considerations. He had wished to bring out the other elements in the problem. . . .

MR. LLOYD GEORGE . . . proposed that the report on the boundaries of Poland should be referred back to the Commission for reconsideration with a view to readjustment of the boundaries of East Prussia in such a manner as to exclude from the new Polish State territory historically as well as ethnologically Prussian, whilst ensuring to Poland secure access to the sea.

PRESIDENT WILSON suggested that the Commission should be merely asked to reconsider its recommendations in the light of the discussion.[5]

Obviously, Woodrow Wilson was not wholly convinced by Lloyd George's arguments, and he wavered between them and the advice he received from Professor Lord, his expert on Polish affairs. Although the British Prime Minister's cry "Do not let us create any more Alsace-Lorraines" rang out constantly all through the Conference, he on no other occasion put up as tenacious a fight for that idea as he did when he stood alone on the problem of Germany's eastern frontier.* The major importance the French attached to the Danzig problem became obvious the next day, when the whole metropolitan press launched a violent and concerted attack upon the British Prime Minister

* Going over the minutes of the Council the editor was unable to shake off an eerie feeling that somewhere behind the shaggy Welshman's chair there hovered druids whispering to him to beware lest 20 years later another generation of Englishmen should die for Danzig.

for the stand he had taken. The Council of Ten met in confidential sessions, therefore the French Foreign Office must have inspired these attacks.

Lloyd George himself says:

> My criticism of the Report of the Commission provoked a series of acrimonious attacks in the French Press. The Northcliffe Press joined in the onslaught. These animadversions gave all the appearance of being concerted, inspired and intimidatory. They appeared simultaneously the day after the discussion took place. There was nothing in the official communiqué issued at the end of our meeting which gave any information upon which these diatribes could have been based.[6]

Lloyd George, who claimed to be inured to public criticism, was infuriated by what he considered a French breach of faith; and, on his insistence, the Council of Ten broke up. Its place was taken by the Council of Four, composed solely of the four heads of government, and by the Council of Foreign Ministers, which, throughout the Conference, played only a secondary role. Although secrecy, even in the Council of Four, was never completely maintained, it became very much easier to pinpoint news leaks.

On March 22nd, the Committee on Polish Affairs reported to the Supreme Council that it had been unable to alter its conclusions; but Lloyd George did not surrender.

He says:

> Having regard to the composition of the Commission, this conclusion did not surprise me. Nor did it alter my view as to the essential injustice and imprudence of the suggested boundaries. I therefore persisted in my resistance. The French were obsessed with one idea, which poisoned and deflected their sense of justice in framing the Treaty. They were bent on taking the fullest advantage of this opportunity to reduce the potential strength of Germany. Any conceivable peace would leave that terrible foe with a substantially larger population than that of France. But every slice of territory cut off from the side of Germany meant a transfer of population and material resources from a secular enemy to a sound friend. . . . The possibility that Germany and France could ever become friends never entered into the calculation of any French statesmen I ever met. Nor was

the prospect that Poland and Yugoslavia might enter into amicable arrangements with Germany contemplated by the French delegation.

The American Polish experts were fanatical pro-Poles, and their judgment in any dispute in which Poland was concerned was vitiated by an invincible partisanship. . . .

I was as sincere an advocate of Polish independence as any member of the Commission, but I was convinced that to add to Poland populations which would be an alien and hostile element inside its boundaries would be a source of permanent weakness and danger and not of strength to this resurrected State. . . .

For that reason I renewed my pressure in the Conference to reject the recommendations which incorporated in Poland towns and territories which were overwhelmingly German by language, race and inclination.[7]

At this time, Lloyd George and a team of his experts retired to Fontainebleau to compose a policy paper, "Some Considerations on the Peace with Germany." This paper contained the following remarks on the Polish frontier:

I am . . . strongly averse to transferring more Germans from German rule to the rule of some other nation than can possibly be helped. I cannot conceive any greater cause of future war than that the German people, who have certainly proved themselves one of the most vigorous and powerful races in the world, should be surrounded by a number of small States, many of them consisting of people who have never previously set up a stable government for themselves, but each of them containing large masses of Germans clamouring for reunion with their native land. The proposal of the Polish Commission that we should place 2,100,000 Germans under the control of a people which is of a different religion and which has never proved its capacity for stable self-government throughout its history must, in my judgment, lead sooner or later to a new war in the East of Europe.[8]

Lloyd George's persistence at last began to make some impression on President Wilson, and he gradually came around to the Prime Minister's way of thinking. In his diary, David Hunter Miller records an interesting interview concerning the President's reasons for siding with Lloyd George on the question of Danzig.

Doctor Mezes came in in the afternoon and told me of the situation about the Polish report. Mezes had seen the President and it appears that Lloyd George was opposed to giving Danzig to the Poles, and the President agreed to this because he did not want Fiume to go to the Italians, and if Danzig went to the Poles he would have to consent to Fiume being Italian. So in his talk with Mezes he said that Danzig and the area around it was to be either free or international or independent. Mezes said all three words had been used, and when I asked Mezes specifically if it was to be connected with East Prussia, he said "no."[9]

Dr. Mezes was not one of the astutest diplomats on the American team, and his statements may be taken with a grain of salt; but, because the President's mind was, at that precise moment, greatly preoccupied with the Fiume problem, it is conceivable that he mentioned Fiume in connection with the Danzig problem, even though the two problems had very little in common. Whatever the reason was for the President's change of mind, he sided with Lloyd George from that moment on, as the minutes of the April 1st Council of Four meeting prove.

LLOYD GEORGE: I visualize Danzig as a free city with enough territory around it to give it breathing space. I would join that pygmy state to Poland by a customs union to prevent Germany from strangling Poland economically. The inhabitants of Danzig would know that their economic fate is linked to that of Poland, where all their commercial ties are, anyhow. By giving them independence we force them to identify economically with Poland, to which they will gradually become more and more attached. I feel sure that the same thing will happen in the Saar since that area will be economically attached to France while retaining its political independence. In fact, I would see to it that all the interests of Danzig's inhabitants are channeled toward Poland, while we let them keep whatever German laws and institutions they may wish to maintain. My primary interest is in seeing that too many Germans are not included in Poland. According to the Commission's report there are 420,000 Germans in the Marienwerder district alone. I would leave that district in East Prussia, and give Poland sovereign rights on the railway.

PRESIDENT WILSON: Couldn't the fate of these German-speaking areas be decided by plebiscite?

LLOYD GEORGE: If there are to be plebiscites, I shall accept the decisions of the populace.

PRESIDENT WILSON: The question is how the Poles are going to like our plans. I mentioned the idea of a free city for Danzig to Domski some time ago and he hit the ceiling. We shall have to give the Poles sovereign rights on the Vistula since they occupy the whole of the west bank. The river only skirts the German frontiers of East Prussia for a short stretch.

LLOYD GEORGE: The railway from Danzig to Thorn would remain in Polish territory. . . .

CLEMENCEAU: We cannot decide anything definite unless the Poles are present.

PRESIDENT WILSON: No, but we can agree among ourselves.

LLOYD GEORGE: It is vain to hope that we can ever satisfy the Poles.

PRESIDENT WILSON: They will have to accept whatever solution we consider reasonable.

CLEMENCEAU: They will not, without making a big fuss.

LLOYD GEORGE: If they will not accept it, let them do better by themselves. I believe we should work out a solution and then call in the Poles and present it to them.

PRESIDENT WILSON: Are we then agreed to create Danzig a Free State?

LLOYD GEORGE: Yes, under the sovereignty of the League of Nations.

PRESIDENT WILSON: How do you visualize that?

LLOYD GEORGE: I would like to see a High Commissioner representing the League of Nations in Danzig. That would keep the Germans from meddling in the affairs of the little state. The High Commissioner could have a position similar to that of our Governors General in Canada or Australia, whose presence in no way prevents the inhabitants from freely governing themselves.

PRESIDENT WILSON: We have to add that the district of Marienwerder may by means of a plebiscite join East Prussia, provided freedom of transit is guaranteed to the Poles. I would like to say that this is the solution which, on the whole, I have always favored.

LLOYD GEORGE: Our Foreign Office has always recommended this solution. After all, we do not owe the Poles a great deal. They fought against us as much as for us during the war. What we have to avoid is to make it difficult for the Germans to sign the treaty.

PRESIDENT WILSON (to Clemenceau): How do you feel about the latter point?

CLEMENCEAU: I am not at all sure that you will succeed in buttering up the Germans.

PRESIDENT WILSON: We should not permit ourselves to be guided by the Polish state of mind. I saw Domski and Paderewski in Washington and I asked them to outline to me the boundaries of Poland as they had them in mind, and they presented me with a map on which they claimed half the world.

LLOYD GEORGE: All I ask is that we do not put into the treaty any articles for which we, in the future, are not ready to go to war. France will go to war for Alsace-Lorraine, if her rights there are ever contested. But are we prepared to go to war for Danzig?

PRESIDENT WILSON: Furthermore, we may not violate the principles which we ourselves have laid down as a basis of peace. All we promised Poland was free and secure access to the sea and, at the same time, we have always declared that we will respect ethnographic frontiers as far as possible. If you agree, I shall have Professor Haskins re-examine the question. . . .

PRESIDENT WILSON: I believe that the question of the Polish frontiers has been solved.

CLEMENCEAU: I was not very much disposed to accept that kind of a solution. But having listened to you I am inclined to follow your lead. But I cannot help thinking that we must take utmost care not to create chaos in Poland.[10]

Finding himself deserted by Wilson, on April 3rd Clemenceau gave in with good grace and went along with his colleagues.

PRESIDENT WILSON: Professors Haskins and Headlam Morley have got together with M. Tardieu to examine the suggestions we made with regard to Danzig and they have come to an agreement.

LLOYD GEORGE: We were already agreed among ourselves, except for the reservations made by M. Clemenceau.

CLEMENCEAU: I have given the matter some thought and I am inclined to agree with you. It is essential to arrive at a solution which is acceptable to the Poles. I do not want to break with them and you know how difficult they can be.

PRESIDENT WILSON: To sum up: we propose to constitute a Free

State composed of the City of Danzig and the area immediately surrounding it which is inhabited by Germans. That Free State is to be joined to Poland by a customs union. In the Marienwerder district the regions inhabited by Germans will be consulted by plebiscite and may, if they so wish, be joined to East Prussia. In the latter case the river Vistula will come under the jurisdiction of the international river control, such as has been worked out by our special committee. The Germans may obtain the right to build, in times of peace, direct railroad communications with East Prussia and with Russia crossing the territory of the Free State of Danzig.

LLOYD GEORGE: We have to provide equal rights for Polish communications between Danzig and Warsaw, for the Mlawa line cuts across the Marienwerder district.

CLEMENCEAU: On the whole, I do not dislike the whole scheme.

LLOYD GEORGE: So, we are all agreed? What is your opinion, M. Orlando?

ORLANDO: I agree.

CLEMENCEAU: Have we decided on the remaining German-Polish frontiers?

PRESIDENT WILSON: We have accepted the recommendations of the Commission, reserving our right to re-examine them when we decide on the frontiers of Germany as a whole.

LLOYD GEORGE: I have no comments to make with regard the report of the Commission except on the subject of Danzig.*[11]

On April 9th, Mr. Paderewski was invited to state his case before the Council of Four. If Clemenceau had pinned his hopes on the great Polish musician-patriot, he was sorely disappointed. Paderewski proved a far more accomplished musician than diplomat. In fact, his presentation before the Council is worth detailed study as a classic example of how not to make a plea. In almost every sentence the great pianist sounds a wrong note.

LLOYD GEORGE: We now have the report of our special subcommittee dealing with the problem of the Polish frontiers. I notice that the Free State we propose to create around the city of Danzig will have 324,000 inhabitants of which only 16,000 are Poles. The

* It is interesting to note that the question of Upper Silesia was passed over by the Big Four, until the problem was brought up by the German delegation. (See Chapter IX, page 342.)

Marienwerder District—which will decide its fate by plebiscite and which can be incorporated in East Prussia if its population so desires —has a population of 164,000 with fewer than 26,000 Poles. These figures seem to me to justify the policy we have been advocating.

PRESIDENT WILSON: The report provides the necessary safeguards for Polish access to the sea.

LLOYD GEORGE: It also provides guarantees for free German communications between West and East Prussia as well as for Polish communications between Warsaw and Danzig.

ORLANDO: How many Germans will remain on Polish territory after the frontiers have been rectified according to the Commission's proposal?

PRESIDENT WILSON: More than two million.

ORLANDO: Let us say two million two hundred thousand. Deduct from that four hundred and fifty thousand inhabitants of Danzig and Marienwerder and you still have roughly one million eight hundred thousand Germans left in Poland.

PRESIDENT WILSON: It cannot be helped, since the German population is widely scattered and its presence on Polish soil is due to systematic colonization in the first place.

LLOYD GEORGE: It is inevitable. What we do not want is to sever from Germany territories which have always been part of East Prussia even at a time when Poland was an independent state. . . .

Mister Paderewski is introduced.

PRESIDENT WILSON: We are presently doing our best to settle Polish affairs in such a way as to avoid planting seeds of future dangers.

We are trying to draw the frontiers of Poland along ethnic lines and to assure Poland free access to the sea without incorporating in the Polish State any more Germans than is absolutely necessary. We intend to create a Poland which contains as few enemies as possible.

The plan we have worked out—and I can assure you that no other problem has been more conscientiously studied—can be summarized as follows:

Danzig with its surrounding territory will be severed from Germany and will be organized as a distinct autonomous political unit. It will be joined to Poland by a customs union and the conduct of its foreign relations will be in Polish hands.

We have provided for all the necessary guarantees for unhampered communications between Poland and Danzig. Poland will have sovereign rights on the Vistula and on the railroad which runs along the left bank of the river. Poland will be guaranteed unhampered use of the Danzig-Mlawa railroad while Germany will have the same facilities on the railroad which cuts across Danzig territory in its transit from East to West Prussia.

The solidly German settlements southeast of Danzig as well as the settlements in southern East Prussia shall decide their future political allegiances by plebiscites. It is our aim to eliminate the danger posed to Poland by a "Germania irredenta." Experience has proved that there are no more serious and no more lasting causes of international conflicts.

We shall now be glad to hear your opinions about the merits or demerits of our plan.

PADEREWSKI: Since I did not expect to be called upon today I have come to this discussion ill prepared. But I am authorized to express to you my country's sentiments:

The Polish Diet, probably the most democratic assembly in the world today, has asked me to convey to you its respects and to express to you its full confidence in you. It has requested me to express to you its most sincere wishes. It desires, first of all, a complete alliance with the Entente, and, secondly, the necessary territorial guarantees for our national existence. Unfortunately we know the Germans better than you do. We have been their neighbors for the past 700 years. Believe me, no matter how little you take from Germany there will always be a "Germania irredenta." The Germans are presently playing a shrewd diplomatic game and we Poles are likely to be their first victims. Danzig is indispensable to Poland which cannot breathe without this window to the sea.

Today, Polish patriotism alone enables the government to maintain order in our country. Poland is surrounded by areas of chaos and violence. It stands like a fortress of political order in Eastern Europe. But this condition depends entirely upon our confidence in you. If this confidence were lost, disappointment and despair would sweep the country opening the door to catastrophe like Bolshevism.

Poland must be strong and it cannot be strong without Danzig.

Looking at the districts inhabited by Germans along the Mlawa line we see that, according to statistics, the district of Stuhm, for instance, is 47 percent inhabited by Poles. But if we take a more honest figure—the number of Polish children attending schools—we arrive at 59 percent. In the Marienwerder District that figure is 47 percent.

LLOYD GEORGE: Is that not an argument in favor of a plebiscite?

PADEREWSKI: The population is still frightened; it does not feel that the Germans are yet beaten.

LLOYD GEORGE: There will be guarantees to insure a free vote. We will evacuate all military forces in the territory and establish a temporary Inter-Allied administration. If your figures are correct—and I have no intention of doubting them—the plebiscite will be in your favor.

PADEREWSKI: In the territory as a whole German soldiers and officials make up 11.45 percent of the population. In the most German District—that of Rosenberg [*sic*]—the Polish population is 17 percent of the total, but, on the other hand, German officials and soldiers amount to 19 percent.

If the city of Danzig were polled—not by German officials but under conditions which guarantee a free vote—I feel sure that it will vote for the annexation by Poland. That is where all its economic interests lie.

LLOYD GEORGE: If you are unable to annex Danzig will you accept a plebiscite instead?

PADEREWSKI: Our Diet, an assembly composed of workers and peasants with a sprinkling of middle-class representatives, is deeply democratic and has no desire for any conquests. But the Diet unanimously demands Danzig. That is the voice of the Polish people of which I am the servant. Poland's representatives make the incorporation of Danzig a "conditio sine qua non," the same as the incorporation of Upper Silesia and the reintegration of Lemberg. It also wants a federation with Lithuania.

LLOYD GEORGE: On that last point I do not think that we have received any reports.

PADEREWSKI: But the question of Danzig is a matter of life and death for us.

PRESIDENT WILSON: But we do intend to put Danzig entirely at Poland's disposal. We shall make it a free city such as they were in the Middle Ages, and it will be within the customs boundaries of Poland which, to all intents and purposes, would have the same economic rights as if it were sovereign.

LLOYD GEORGE: A kind of Home Rule for Danzig. You would

conduct the city's foreign relations and Danzig will be even less autonomous from you than Canada, for instance, is from England.

PADEREWSKI: But Danzig will remain in the hands of the German population, consequently in the hands of Germany to which it will ultimately return.

PRESIDENT WILSON: Did you not just tell us that the population's economic interests will induce the city to join Poland? Our own information leads us to the same conclusion.

PADEREWSKI: But you must take national sentiment into account. Germany is not beaten yet.

LLOYD GEORGE: Really?

PADEREWSKI: She is at this moment challenging your right to pass troops through Danzig and she uses revolutions and Bolshevism as means to her ends.

PRESIDENT WILSON: How long do you think Germany can afford to use means which must lead to her ruin?

PADEREWSKI: The German obedience-instinct is something unbelievable. They are capable of starting and stopping revolutions on command. In Eastern Poland we see retreating German troops actually prepare quarters for the advancing Bolsheviks.

Germany can dispense with Danzig. She has a number of great ports at her disposal: Emden, Bremen, Hamburg, Stettin, Koenigsberg. That is enough for sixty million inhabitants. And twenty-five million Poles are not to have a single port?

PRESIDENT WILSON: On the contrary, we are trying to assure you of the use of the port of Danzig by setting up the kind of government there which will give you the least amount of trouble in the future.

PADEREWSKI: We would treat the Germans well who live on Polish territory. We would not persecute them as they persecuted us.

CLEMENCEAU: Will you agree to a plebiscite?

PADEREWSKI: I shall consent to plebiscites wherever they serve to resolve differences between ourselves and our friends, with Bohemia or Lithuania. But not with our enemies.

Even so, our problem would not be solved—even if we had Danzig—unless you give us the territory which links the city with Poland. If you have to choose would it not be better to sacrifice three hundred thousand Germans rather than twenty-five million Poles?

LLOYD GEORGE: The easiest solution would be if Danzig elected to become Polish or—if she voluntarily joined up with you for fear of seeing another port growing up at her doorstep. But we do not want to create another Alsace-Lorraine in Danzig where Germany could pose as the victim.

PRESIDENT WILSON: Will you not be satisfied with special guarantees for the use of the railroad?

PADEREWSKI: We know the Germans too well to trust any guarantees to which they might agree. They have not changed since the tenth century. We have known their "scraps of paper" for a long time. I would like to remind you of the time when the Grand Master of the Teutonic Knights signed a treaty with some Pomeranian and Polish nobles and invited them to dinner where he had them all assassinated. Those are the kind of treaties we have made with Germans in the past. I ask you to consider what I have said and to let me know what conclusions you have reached.

PRESIDENT WILSON: We are grateful to you for having given us your opinions and I thank you for having responded to our call.[12]

Twice more the Council of Four took up the matter of Germany's eastern frontiers, before finally settling on the terms incorporated in the treaty which was handed to the German delegates. The first of these discussions took place on April 12th.

CLEMENCEAU: Before we convoke the Germans we should also clear up the question of Danzig.

LLOYD GEORGE: Haven't we all agreed to a solution?

CLEMENCEAU: Yes, but you have seen Paderewski's opposition. I believe that the Poles would agree to the independence of Danzig if the Marienwerder District were not left to Germany.

LLOYD GEORGE: It would be contrary to all our concepts to leave to Poland a territory so obviously German which has always been a part of ancient Prussia.

CLEMENCEAU: Paderewski's emotions were unimaginable. He even broke into tears.

PRESIDENT WILSON: You have to make allowances for his sensitivity; he is very highly strung.

LLOYD GEORGE: After all, the Poles have got their independence after a century and a half of servitude. If they do not think they are capable of survival just because we refuse to give them a territory containing a hundred and fifty thousand Germans . . .

President Wilson: I think we should send Paderewski a declaration over our joint signatures to explain our motives and to make the Poles understand that we have no desire to favor their enemies but, on the contrary, are acting solely to preserve them from future dangers.[13]

At the meeting on April 18th, President Wilson read the new text of the resolution on the question of Danzig and Marienwerder:

Danzig and its territory shall be constituted as a free Hanseatic city under guarantee of the League of Nations, which shall be represented by a High Commissioner.

The territory of Danzig shall be included in the Polish customs system. Poland shall direct the city's foreign relations and shall have possession of the railroads with free use of the port.

The populations of the districts of Stuhm, Riesenburg and Marienwerder shall be consulted by plebiscite as to their desire to become attached to Poland or East Prussia, after complete removal of all German troops. Polish sovereignty shall extend over the whole course of the Vistula River. Special transit rights shall be guaranteed to Germans on the railroad line which links East and West Prussia and to Poles on the Danzig-Mlawa line.

Lloyd George: Your text refers to Polish sovereignty on the Vistula. It must be made clear that this does not confer the right to interfere with the use of the river by the citizens of Danzig. . . .

Clemenceau: I admit I would prefer some other means to satisfy our Polish friends but, in all sincerity, I do not believe this is possible.

President Wilson: The text provides that the costs of the plebiscites over and above the amount which can be reasonably borne by the districts themselves shall be paid for by East Prussia.

Lloyd George: Would it not be better to say: "by the country the plebiscite has favored"?

M. Mantoux: M. Tardieu has asked me to remind you that the peace treaty with Germany must make mention of the German-Lithuanian frontier. The map prepared by the Commission on Polish Affairs shows a frontier line which would cut off Germany from the Baltic coast north of the Njemen and strip her of the port of Memel.

Lloyd George: On that question I shall have to refresh my

memory. (He withdraws and returns after consultation with his secretaries)

I see that, according to the Commission's report, the frontier has been drawn along the German-Lithuanian ethnic line and that, besides, Memel is the only possible outlet to the sea available to Lithuania. Under the circumstances I believe we can safely accept the recommendations of the Commission on Polish Affairs.

(The recommendations of the Commission on Polish Affairs are adopted.)[14]

Mention must here be made of Germany's southern frontiers with Czechoslovakia and Austria, although they remained virtually unchanged. In October and November of 1918 the Austro-Hungarian Empire had broken up into its component national parts. The republics of Czechoslovakia and Hungary had come into being and the territories of the Habsburg Monarchy which were inhabited by southern Slavs were incorporated in the Kingdom of Serbia, which assumed the somewhat unprepossessing name of "Kingdom of S.H.S." (Serbo-Croatian-Slovene Kingdom).

The German-speaking parts of the Habsburg Monarchy, on November 11, 1918, proclaimed the "German-Austrian Republic" (Deutsch-Oesterreichische Republik) and in the same declaration announced that the newborn state "was a part of the German Republic."

The proclamation, a document unique in the annals of history, reads in its entirety:

ARTICLE I.

German-Austria [Deutsch-Oesterreich] is a democratic Republic. All power emanates from the People.

ARTICLE II.

The German-Austrian Republic is an integral part of the German Republic.

Thus, the fathers of the young republic granted their progeny a life-span which extended only from the lecture of the first to the lecture of the second article of its "Declaration of Independence."

"Deutsch-Oesterreich" claimed sovereignty not only over the solidly German-speaking alpine regions of the Habsburg Monarchy (including Vienna), but also over the German-populated areas of northern and western Bohemia, which in the none-too-distant future were to become known as "the Sudetenland." By virtue of this declaration the population of the German Reich would have been increased by more than ten million. In view of the French phobia about the numerical superiority of Germans over Frenchmen, the Peace Conference naturally vetoed the proclamation. Deutsch-Oesterreich was commanded to stay independent and to change its name. It was to be known henceforth as the Republic of Austria.

Since the Czechoslovak Republic also claimed the German-settled parts of Bohemia and Moravia, the Peace Conference paid no heed to the claims of the Austrian Republic, and the frontiers between Germany and Czechoslovakia closely followed the old German/Austro-Hungarian frontier line.

The Treaty fixed the relationship between the German Reich and its Austrian neighbor in Section VI, Article 80:

> Germany acknowledges and will respect strictly the independence of Austria, within the frontiers which may be fixed in a Treaty between that State and the Principal Allied and Associated Powers; she agrees that this independence shall be inalienable, except with the consent of the Council of the League of Nations.

VII

Germany's Western Frontiers

The fiercest battles of the Paris Peace Conference were waged over the subject of Germany's western frontiers, as French aspirations clashed with American or, rather, Wilsonian principles. The memorandum Marshal Foch had presented to the British in London thoroughly alerted American and British statesmen to French plans and when the same proposals were put forth in Paris they met stubborn resistance from both President Wilson and Lloyd George.

The restoration of Alsace-Lorraine to France posed no problem in principle and the Conference wasted no time in discussing the matter. However, the details of restoring these provinces after nearly fifty years of German administration, colonization and industrial development did present a very serious problem, particularly inasmuch as France insisted that "restoration" include expropriating all German property, private as well as fiscal. In committee, André Tardieu, representing France, clashed violently with Maynard Keynes, Great Britain's economic expert. When Keynes refused to go along with France's unprecedented demands, Tardieu called him pro-German and finally drove him from the conference table. Tardieu himself gives an animated, though naturally somewhat biased, account of the arguments.

Once the Conference began, our rights [to Alsace-Lorraine] were never again challenged from any quarter. But when it came to its application, many difficulties arose, some of which were of a moral, others of a material order, but had the same origin.

Our Allies were willing in principle to entertain our demands. But it was their understanding that this should be subject to the same procedure and rules as applied to the other chapters of the Treaty of Peace. . . . We wished that by reason of its unique character this restitution should be accompanied both as regards persons and property by special conditions. And when we were told that what we wanted was contrary to the general principles of the Treaty, we replied: "All the more reason." . . .

I was . . . President of a Committee of three members, on which Mr. Charles H. Haskins represented the United States, and Mr. Headlam Morley, Great Britain. I had cause to congratulate myself upon the friendly understanding of both of my eminent colleagues. But the dozen experts, by whom each was accompanied, at times gave me great trouble. . . . Ten meetings lasting four hours each, in which Mr. Keynes poured out his pro-German views, taught me that with specialists feeling forfeits its rights. . . .

I asked first of all that the Allied Powers, and Germany with them, should recognize the moral grounds for the arrangements to be made. . . . Satisfaction was given us by the following paragraph:

> The High Contracting-Parties (thus including Germany) recognizing the moral obligation to redress the wrong done by Germany in 1871, both to the rights of France and to the wishes of the population of Alsace and Lorraine, which were separated from their country in spite of the solemn protest of their representative at the Assembly of Bordeaux, agree upon the following articles:

. . . According to a wording nowhere else used in the Treaty, the two provinces were "restored to French sovereignty." They were so restored contrary to what was done for other territorial transfers, not as from the date on which the Treaty of Peace was signed, but as from the date of the Armistice concluded on November 11, 1918. Their emanicipation *de facto,* in this particular case, sufficed to establish the right. The consequences were at once apparent in the section concerning nationality. . . .

In all other cases, the right of option in favour of the ceding Nation was admitted. We rejected and caused to be set aside this procedure. In Alsace-Lorraine, there is no right of option in favour of the Germans. On the contrary, the French Government alone has the right, under the Treaty and in the exercise of its restored sovereignty, to confer the title of "Frenchmen" to true Alsatians and Lorrainers which it recognizes as such. . . . Other clauses, relating also to persons, are based upon the same principle: fines inflicted by Germany to be refunded by her; judgments rendered by the civil or commercial courts, since August 3, 1914, between Alsatians and Lorrainers and Germans not to be executory until confirmed,—sentences for political offenses or misdemeanours after the same date to be quashed. . . .

Article 256 stipulated that Powers, to whom German territories were transferred, would acquire all property or real estate belonging to the Empire or to the States located within such territories and that the value thereof should be placed to Germany's credit by the Reparations Commission; I asked and obtained, despite this formal provision, despite the enormous increment of certain State properties—railways, for instance—since 1871 that France should have nothing to pay. Belgium alone obtained a like privilege in respect to the territories of Malmedy and Eupen. By certain no less legitimate, but no less exceptional enactments, we obtained recognition of our right to sequestrate and dispose of all property in Alsace-Lorraine belonging to Germans, as well as of the right to prohibit hereafter all German participation in private enterprises of public interest, such as mines, electric power stations, etc. . . . and lastly, of the right to annul all German interests in the exploitation of potash deposits. By this clear-cut and total suppression, the rights of France were wholly restored—a matter of no less importance to us than the material advantages assured by the foregoing clauses. What a conflict of arguments before reaching this point! When at last Mr. Keynes, who had led the attack, saw that he had lost, he left our conference room with an angry gesture. He has vented his spite in his notorious book. Mr. Keynes has his book. France has the Treaty. So all is well!

Some articles remained in abeyance in which the position of France was even more delicate. . . . We had asked and obtained the solemn and absolute severing of all bonds forged by might between Germany and Alsace-Lorraine. But, in some things, perfectly respectable interests made it necessary to maintain temporarily economic relations. . . . And again it was necessary in view of the ruins caused by the war, that the maintenance of such relations, indispensable to Alsace-Lorraine, should not entail to the benefit of Germany the reciprocity generally prescribed in like matters by the Treaty. . . . After what I have said of the state of mind of the Allies' experts, it can be guessed how easy this was. Despite the difficulty, France succeeded in obtaining both for herself and Alsace-Lorraine, all essential guarantees: the right for a period of five years to a special customs treatment without reciprocity for Germany; the guaranteed supply—for ten years and at the same rates as to Germans—of the electric current from the power stations on the left bank; the water power of the Rhine in its course through Alsace; the maintenance of private contracts with exclusive power to the French Government to cancel them—the maintenance in Germany and under German law of the industrial, literary and artistic rights of Alsatians and Lorrainers. Each of these derogations entailed hours of discussion. The final discussion lasted five days, it was over the port of Kehl. This port created by Germany just opposite Strassburg and splendidly equipped had been purposely used to the detriment of the Alsatian port. If . . . Kehl were to be free to compete in any way it chose, Strassburg would be finally throttled. So we asked that for a certain number of years . . . the two ports should . . . be placed under a single management. Objections rained upon us: Kehl is a German port: a German port cannot be placed under a French comptroller. . . . Our only reply was to ask the experts to make an investigation on the spot; as soon as they got back, our demand, contrary to precedent but in accordance with equity, was acceded to. . . .

France saw herself on the other hand obliged to comply with the ordinary rule on two other questions, which the Council of Four finally decided: . . . In Alsace-Lorraine as in our liberated regions and in Belgium, the national Government had redeemed from the inhabitants, at the rate of francs 1.25, the marks put in compulsory circulation by the German authorities during their occupation. It had consequently suffered the loss caused by the depreciation of that currency. France and Belgium demanded, not without reason, that this loss be borne by Germany. The Peace Conference decided otherwise, to avoid the contingent effect of such a principle in Central and Eastern Europe, where Germany had abused the compulsory circulation of her currency to an even greater extent. . . . A like solution prevailed as regards the damages sustained by Alsatians and Lorrainers, which were not placed to the debit of Germany. An injustice, at first sight; why make a distinction between the damage sustained at Baccarat in France, for which Germany has to pay, and the damage sustained at Thann, in Alsace, for which she does not have to pay? Here again the decision was dictated by prudence for although the destructions in Alsace-Lorraine were relatively of slight importance, other transferred territories, such as those which passed to Poland and

Roumania, would have been very difficult to verify. . . . The Conference thought it better not to run the risk.

Such as it is, the chapter of the Treaty dealing with Alsace-Lorraine presents a character of pure justice and draws from the war one of its grandest conclusions. Violated right restored to the full at the very point where violation had attained in modern times the maximum of its cynical brutality. To the full also is wiped out the wrong done both to these two provinces and to France and all proper steps are taken to prevent any of its consequences continuing in time of peace. . . .[1]

If some of the foregoing reads like double talk, there is a very good reason—it is. Tardieu is trying to justify the fact that the arrangements with regard to Alsace-Lorraine broke all international precedents. Unfortunately, they also set a precedent that has been followed in many cases since: making private rights and private property as "expropriable" as those of public bodies. Tardieu's argument basically amounts to this: Because a great deal of national sentiment was involved in the reacquisition of Alsace-Lorraine, France was justified in punishing all those who, in any way—no matter how innocently—had profited by the rape of these provinces during the intervening fifty years. Maynard Keynes happened to disagree.

The terms of the armistice had established Allied armies on the left bank of the Rhine and in four strategic bridgeheads on the right bank. The French had no intention of ever relinquishing these positions. When Marshal Foch's ideas received such a cool reception in London, he drew up another memorandum. This one differed from the first mainly in the language in which it was couched, language he obviously considered sufficiently "Wilsonian" to impress the President; it differed also in that it no longer insisted that German inhabitants of the Rhineland be drafted into the French army. The memorandum was presented to the Conference on January 10, 1919. It ran to more than 3,000 words,* but, fortunately, André Tardieu has provided us with a masterly condensation.

Marshal von Moltke placed the military frontier of Germany at the Rhine and at the end of one of his papers writes: "There can be no

* For full text see Baker: *Woodrow Wilson and World Settlement*, Vol. I, 228-237.

doubt about the ordinary strength of our theatre of operations on the Rhine. One thing only could endanger it—a premature offensive by us on the left bank with insufficient forces." And elsewhere he states: "The main line of defense of Prussia against France is the Rhine with its fortresses. This line is so strong that it is far from requiring all the forces of the monarchy."

Today this situation is reversed in favour of the coalition. The coalition cannot renounce its advantages, cannot relinquish its buckler of defense in that region—the Rhine—without seriously compromising its future. The "Wacht am Rhein" must be its slogan.

Henceforth the Rhine must be the Western frontier of the German peoples. Germany must be deprived of all access to or military utilization of it, that is to say, of all territorial sovereignty on the left bank of this River—in a word, of every facility to reach by sudden invasion, as in 1914, of Belgium and Luxemburg, the shores of the North Sea and threaten England; to move around France's natural defenses, the Rhine and the Meuse; to conquer her northern regions and approach that of Paris.

This is, for the present and the near future, a guarantee indispensable for the maintenance of peace, because:

1. Of Germany's material and moral situation.
2. Of her numerical superiority over the democratic countries of Western Europe.

The Rhine, a military frontier indispensable for the maintenance of peace, which is the aim of the coalition, offers no territorial advantage to any country. There is no question indeed of annexing the left bank of the Rhine, of increasing the territory of France or of Belgium but simply one of maintaining on the Rhine the common barrier of security essential to the society of democratic nations. There is no question of entrusting the guardianship of this common barrier to any one Power, but of assuring by the moral and material support of all the democratic powers the defense of their lives and futures by forbidding Germany, once for all, to carry war and her spirit of domination across the river.

Of course it will be the function of the Peace Treaty to fix the status of the inhabitants of the left bank of the Rhine not included within the French and Belgian frontiers.

But this arrangement, whatever it be, must take into consideration the military necessity set forth above and therefore,

1. Absolutely forbid to Germany all military access to, or political

propaganda in, the Rhenish territories of the left bank, perhaps even protecting this territory by a neutral zone on the right bank.

2. Assure the military occupation of the Rhenish territories of the left bank by Allied forces.

3. Guarantee to the Rhenish territories of the left bank the outlet necessary to their economic activities by bringing them into a customs union with the other Western States.

On these conditions, and in accordance with the universally accepted principle of the liberty of peoples, it is possible to conceive the establishment, on the left bank of the Rhine, of new autonomous States, governing themselves subject to the above reservations, an arrangement which with the aid of a strong natural frontier the Rhine will alone be capable of assuring Peace to Western Europe.[2]

Woodrow Wilson was determined not to get involved in problems of territorial claims, reparations, or any other matters of final peace settlement until his experts had had a chance to review every aspect of each problem and until he had his League of Nations organized and approved by the Conference. After that, he hoped, "everything would fall into place." Marshal Foch's memorandum therefore received neither the attention nor the prompt action the French had expected.

Among the delegates Foch's proposals furnished the subject of considerable discussion, but no action of any kind was taken before the President sailed for America. The way her Allies felt about the French attitude is clearly shown by the following entry in Colonel House's diary.

February 9, 1919: [Conference with Balfour] . . . We talked at great length of the French proposal of setting up a "Rhenish Republic" as a buffer state between Germany and France. The French have but one idea and that is military protection. They do not seem to know that to establish a Rhenish Republic against the will of the people would be contrary to the principle of self-determination, and that if we should establish it, the people could at any time become federated with the other German States. If we did such a thing, we would be treating Germany in one way and the balance of the world in another. . . . Yet we both have a profound sympathy for France and for the unhappy situation in which she finds herself—a situation which is serious because there are practically two Germans to one Frenchman.

The only hope France has for the future is the League of Nations and the spirit we hope to bring about through it. If after establishing the League, we are so stupid as to let Germany train and arm a large army and again become a menace to the world, we would deserve the fate which such folly would bring upon us.[3]

Before Woodrow Wilson sailed for America he deputized Colonel House to take his place while he was away. The minutes of the Supreme Council meeting of February 12th show how this delegation of authority came about: A special Committee set up to examine terms for the renewal of the armistice had suggested that "naval and military terms of peace should be drawn up immediately and imposed upon the enemy."

President Wilson . . . suggested the renewal of the Armistice on the present terms for a period which would be terminated on a few days' notice and that meanwhile the final military and naval terms of peace should be drawn up and presented separately to the Germans for acceptance on the understanding that nonacceptance of the whole of the terms would mean an immediate resumption of hostilities.

M. Clemenceau at first strongly protested and urged that the military terms could not be separated from the political, economic and financial terms. At the end of the morning meeting on February 12th, Mr. Balfour put President Wilson's idea into the form of resolutions. These were considered the same afternoon when President Wilson further developed his idea that the military terms of peace should be isolated from the other conditions of peace.

"He therefore thought it was possible to frame the terms of Germany's disarmament before settling the Terms of Peace. He was encouraged in this belief by the assurance that the Military Advisers could produce a plan in forty-eight hours. It might take more than forty-eight hours for the heads of Governments to agree to this plan."

M. Clemenceau demurred at some length at the idea of discussing a matter of such importance in the absence of the President who was about to return to America on a visit. To this, President Wilson replied that—

"In technical matters most of the brains he used were borrowed; the possessors of these brains were in Paris. He would, therefore, go away with an easy mind if he thought that his plan had been adopted in principle. He had complete confidence in the views of his Military

Advisers. . . . If his plan were agreed on in principle, he would be prepared to go away and leave it to his colleagues to decide whether the programme drafted by the technical advisers was the right one. He did not wish his absence to stop so important, essential and urgent a work as the preparation of a Preliminary Peace. He hoped to return by the 13th or 15th March, allowing himself only a week in America. But he did not wish that during his unavoidable absence, such questions as the territorial question and questions of compensation should be held up. He had asked Colonel House to take his place while he was away."

After some further discussion, the Supreme Council accepted part of Mr. Balfour's draft conclusions, which included the following:

"Detailed and final Naval, Military and Air Conditions of the Preliminaries of Peace shall be drawn up at once by a Committee to be presided over by Marshal Foch and submitted for approval to the Supreme War Council; these, when approved, will be presented for signature to the Germans, and the Germans shall be at once informed that this is the policy of the Associated Governments."[4]

As President Wilson boarded the SS *George Washington* on February 15th, he was quite confident that only military, naval and air questions would be decided in his absence, and that Edward House would not be called upon "to take his place" in making major policy decisions. But the French had other ideas. As soon as the President was safely out of the way, they started a sudden drive to get a preliminary peace concluded on French terms. Marshal Foch, instead of producing the "detailed and final naval, military and air conditions of the preliminaries of peace," which were to have been ready within forty-eight hours, channeled an urgent suggestion through the Chief of the British General Staff that preliminary peace be concluded with Germany immediately. House cabled the details of this proposal to the President.

PARIS, *February* 19, 1919

The following memorandum by the Chief of the British General Staff has just been sent me:

"I had an interesting interview with Marshal Foch this morning in which he expressed the following views: As the result of his recent discussions with the German representatives at Trèves, he is of opinion that under existing conditions we can dictate terms of peace to Germany. The German Government will agree to whatever terms we exact. But, he says, there is no time to lose. At present Germany has only one thought, and that is peace, the reasons being that her Government is insecure and wants peace in order to consolidate its position, and the people fear above all things a renewal of hostilities. Further fighting would take place on German soil, and the Germans are afraid of the devastation of their territory. In the opinion of the Marshal, Germany has at present no military forces with which she could hope to dispute the advance of the Allied armies.

"For these reasons Germany will agree to our terms if we are prompt, but no one can say how long the existing conditions will last. Delay is dangerous. The Marshal, therefore, strongly advocates the settling at once of the three principal conditions of the peace that the Allies intend to impose upon Germany; namely: 1. The strength of her armed forces; 2. Her frontiers; 3. The indemnity she is to pay. He considers that if these matters could be settled by the Peace Conference during the next few days, and if he could be entrusted with the mission of proceeding again to Trèves with the Allied terms, say this week, he would guarantee that the Germans would accept the terms on the following day. The world would then pass from a state of war to a state of peace for which it longs so ardently, and there would be universal rejoicing.

"As regards the three points mentioned above, Marshal Foch anticipates no difficulty in coming to an agreement during the next forty-eight hours as to the strength of Germany's peace army and navy. He is strongly in favour of saying to the Germans in this preliminary peace treaty that, whatever may be the fate of the Rhenish provinces and whatever form of government for these provinces the Allies may decide in favour of, under no circumstances will the German Empire extend beyond the Rhine. That in his opinion is essential for the security of France, and makes the settlement of the Western frontier a simple matter. He also considers that there should be no insuperable difficulties in settling a provisional frontier between Germany and Poland, which would be capable of modification in detail later. The Marshal would settle on a lump sum for Germany to pay, and suggested 100 *milliards* of francs. It is, he says, not his business to consider the actual sum, but he pleads forcibly for the principle of including a lump sum by way of indemnity in the terms to be presented to Germany the next time he goes to Trèves. If the conditions of a preliminary peace treaty can thus be imposed on Germany, the Allies can then turn their attention to the Russian problem, which must take time to solve. The Marshal thinks the Allies may lose the war if they fail to arrive at a satisfactory solution of the Russian question, either by Germany settling it in her own interests, or by the spread of anarchy. He favours the solution of helping all the anti-Bolshevik elements in Russia, and all the neighbours of Russia who are resisting Bolshevik encroachment. He would go so far as to accept German co-operation after the signing of his preliminary treaty of peace, and thinks it might be very valuable."

EDWARD HOUSE[5]

The President reacted swiftly and firmly to House's message, and cabled his reply the very next day.

. . . I have just read the memorandum given you by the Chief of the British General Staff on an interview with Marshal Foch. It seems to me like an attempt to use the good offices of the French [*sic*]* to hurry us into an acquiescence of their plans with regards to the western banks of the Rhine. . . . I know I can trust you and our colleagues to withstand such a programme immovably, except of course I am willing to have the strictly military and naval terms promptly decided and presented to the Germans. I am not willing to have anything beyond the military and naval terms [settled] and believe the Conference of Ten would be going very much beyond its powers to attempt anything of this sort. The determination of the geographic boundaries of Germany involves the fortunes and interests of the other peoples, and we should not risk being hurried into a solution arrived at solely from the French viewpoint. . . . Warm thanks for full information you are sending.[6]

But the Allies were relentlessly pressuring the Colonel into a solution. Lloyd George, just back from London, where he had gone to feel the pulse of his electorate and to consult with his cabinet colleagues, had one of his characteristic changes of mind. Although he had agreed with Wilson, before his departure, that nothing but strictly naval and military terms were to be settled in Wilson's absence, he now instructed Balfour to get an agree-

* Obviously should read: "British" instead of "French." (Ed.)

ment on the full peace terms at utmost speed. The temper of the British public had convinced him that speed in "getting the Tommies home" and "getting paid for the war" was essential to his political future. Accordingly, Balfour introduced a resolution at the Supreme Council meeting of February 22nd, after having discussed and cleared it with Pichon, the French Foreign Minister of the moment. (Clemenceau had been laid low by an assassin's bullet three days earlier, and was out of action.) The resolution stated:

(1) Without prejudice to the decision of the Supreme War Council to present Naval, Military and Air Conditions of Peace, to Germany at an early date, the Conference agrees that it is desirable to proceed without delay to the consideration of other preliminary Peace Terms with Germany and to press on the necessary investigations with all possible speed.

(2) The Preliminary Peace Terms, other than the Naval, Military and Air Conditions, shall cover the following points:

(a) The approximate future frontiers of Germany:
(b) The financial arrangements to be imposed on Germany:
(c) Our economic relations with Germany after the war:
(d) Responsibility for breaches of the Laws of War.

(3) In order that the Conference may have at its disposal with the least possible delay the result of the labours of the various Commissions which have been investigating these subjects it is requested that the various Commissions will send in their reports to the Secretary-General not later than Saturday, March 8th.* This will not apply to Commissions set up after February 15th which may be unable to render their final reports at so early a date, but it is requested that in these cases interim reports may be presented dealing with all matters affecting the preliminaries of Peace with Germany.[7]

Ray S. Baker comments on the resulting discussion in the Council of Ten:

Although this proposal had not even been mentioned before in the Council and there is no recorded discussion, it was instantly and enthusiastically accepted—save by Lord Milner (as will be shown later)

* A week before President Wilson could return.

and by Sonnino, who was not opposed to the principle but who did not want the German settlements made ahead of the Austrian. . . .

> M. PICHON agreed that Mr. Balfour had very correctly interpreted M. Clemenceau's views. M. Clemenceau held that the whole of the Preliminary Peace Terms should be pressed forward with as little delay as possible in order to take full advantage of the present situation in Germany. In this opinion M. Clemenceau was supported by Marshal Foch and his military advisers.
>
> Mr. HOUSE said he was very glad to see that the Conference intended to bring about as soon as possible a Preliminary Peace. . . . He had always felt that delay could only be favourable to Germany and the longer the signing of Peace were postponed, the more chance would there be of circumstances becoming less favourable to the Allies. In regard to the two proposals now before the Conference, very severe military terms would have to be imposed on the Germans. And he thought the Germans would be more inclined to accept those conditions if, at the same time, the whole Peace Terms were made known to them. . . .
>
> Mr. LANSING [said] . . . he would prefer to embody all the terms of a preliminary peace in one document . . . He thoroughly agreed with M. Clemenceau's viewpoint.

The only sincere support of Wilson's proposal was from Lord Milner, who had been present when it was accepted on February 12 (just as Lansing had been) and now proposed to stand upon the agreement made at that time. He thought it "more important than anything else for the Conference to devote its time to a consideration of the final naval and military terms with Germany. Once an agreement was reached on that subject, one compartment of the peace work would be finally dispensed with." At the following meeting Lord Milner returned again, more vigorously, to the argument, expressing almost exactly the idea of President Wilson and General Bliss. He said . . .

> Speaking for myself, personally, I still think that the final disarmament of Germany, I mean our bringing her down to that degree of strength for war purposes which we are willing to allow her permanently to maintain, is extremely urgent, that it is a step which we ought to take as soon as we possibly can, and that it is a step which, when taken, will greatly expedite the acceptance . . .

of all other conditions of peace. It is also an absolutely essential preliminary to our own demobilization.

But, of course, demobilization was exactly what the French did not want! And, as Pichon said, Clemenceau was in agreement with Foch; and Balfour, Lansing, and House were in agreement with Clemenceau. Colonel House indeed responded to Lord Milner's argument as follows:

> Mr. HOUSE persisted in his opinion that the Conference should go back to Mr. Balfour's original proposal as regards Germany.

With both French and Americans and Mr. Balfour, the leading British delegate, against him, it was useless for Lord Milner to pursue the argument.

One nation remained yet to be heard from, Japan. The Japanese delegates, Makino and Matsui, waited always, like their own stone Buddhas, in silence, until something arose that really concerned them. Then, in a low voice, in the fewest possible words, with an almost apologetic air, at the end of the meeting, they shot as straight as did their soldiers at Port Arthur.

> Baron MAKINO enquired whether the approximate future frontiers of Germany referred to in paragraph 2 (a) [of the Balfour resolution], included the German colonies.
>
> Mr. BALFOUR replied that it was intended to include the colonies. . . .
>
> M. MATSUI enquired, with reference to paragraph 2 (a) whether that would include all rights, such as rights over the railways and mines in China acquired by Germany.
>
> Mr. BALFOUR thought that the words "*inter alia*" would cover such questions.
>
> Mr. LANSING agreed, and remarked that the words "*inter alia*" would also cover the question of prisoners of war, which he had intended to raise separately.

Thus the Japanese, having inquired as to colonies, railroads, mines, Shantung, and been generously reassured by Mr. Balfour, relapsed again into silence. Here* was where the Shantung settlement, so bitterly attacked in America, was begun—while Wilson was away.

* See Chapter V.

By this simple process everyone had been assured of getting all the "practical details" into the preliminary treaty—boundaries, reparations, colonies, mines, railroads—without hindrance from the clogging idealism of Wilson's principles or reference to the League of Nations.[8]

It is difficult to understand what prompted Colonel House to give such unqualified support to a proposal that not only ran counter to the instructions he had received, but which–as he must surely have realized–also jeopardized his absent chief's whole Peace Conference strategy. He kept on discussing and negotiating matters President Wilson had felt sure were reserved for his return. On February 23rd House cabled Wilson:

At his request I had a conference yesterday with Clemenceau.

1. He is anxious to speed up and make an early peace with Germany. He . . . realizes the danger of delay.

2. He is insistent upon the creation of a Rhenish Republic. There will be about four million of Germans aggregated in this way. He desires that this Republic should be exempt from the payment of any indemnity; that they should have no armed force; that everything should be done to make them prosperous and contented so that they will not want to joint the German Federation and if they have such a desire they will not be permitted to do so.

3. On the east, Clemenceau thinks that Dantzig should go to Poland. Our experts also believe this to be the best solution and they are joined, I understand, in this belief by the British experts, but the British Government disagree on this point.

4. Clemenceau says that German Austria will not join the German Federation if they received an intimation from the Allies that they do not wish them to do so. He is insistent that this intimation be given them.

5. He thinks the entire terms should be given at once and that the military terms should not be made now [separately] as at first planned. There was afterwards common agreement on this point at our meeting at the Quai d'Orsay.

6. He thought he would be able to attend meetings in a few days. I doubt it. I feel he is by no means out of danger.

7. I assume that you are getting full reports of the meetings at the Quai d'Orsay.[9]

The next day he followed it up with another cable.

> . . . Our territorial experts are in substantial agreement with the British and French respecting boundaries of Germany. Tardieu, who since attack on Clemenceau, has become more prominent, said to me yesterday that France would be willing to have the Rhenish Republic set up only for a limited period of years, at the end of which the population would be permitted to decide for themselves what their future should be. He said that in that way a breathing space would be given to us all and France would secure protection until she recovered from the present war. The principle of self-determination would in this way be safeguarded. . . .[10]

Two days later a third cable announced the receipt of a memorandum from Tardieu.

> . . . Tardieu has submitted memorandum on French position respecting left bank of Rhine. I will cable you about this when I have had an opportunity of studying it. . . .[11]

Tardieu's lengthy memorandum of February 26th represented the second prong of the French attack on the American position at the Peace Conference.* It made the following points:

1. A common guarantee against recurrence of any sudden attack from Germany is necessary;
2. This guarantee cannot be assured either by the limitation or the suppression of Germany's military power, nor by the proposed clauses of the Covenant of the League of Nations;
3. This guarantee can only be found in fixing the Western Frontier of Germany at the Rhine, and in the occupation of the bridges by an inter-Allied force;

By these means:
- (a) the dangerous disproportion in strength between France and Germany would be eliminated;
- (b) one of the economic causes of German aggression would be disposed of (vulnerability of French industrial zones);
- (c) protection would be guaranteed to the smaller states whose safety the League seeks to secure;

* For full text see A. Tardieu: *The Truth About the Treaty,* 147 ff.

(d) the great historic road of invasion would be closed;
and

(e) a natural frontier equal for all would be created.[12]

The memorandum ended with the following plea:

Such is the principle that the French Government begs the Allied and Associated Governments to confirm and sanction by adopting the following decisions to be inserted in the provisions of the preliminaries of peace:

1. The Western frontier of Germany must be fixed at the Rhine;
2. The bridges of the Rhine must be occupied by an inter-Allied force;
3. The above measures to imply no annexation of territory to the benefit of any power.[13]

Two appendices accompanied the memorandum; the outline of a political system applicable to an independent Rhineland, and a study of the economic results of its independence, both on the left bank of the Rhine and in Germany itself.

The sole concession to the Anglo-American position in Tardieu's memorandum was the admission that the Rhenish Republic would not be forced to stay "independent" forever. Having made this concession, the French refused to budge another inch. In the Supreme Council, discussion continued on all the problems involved in making peace with Germany. On March 7th Colonel House cabled a lengthy report to the President concerning a meeting he had with Lloyd George and Clemenceau. The only mention of the French claims to the Rhineland was contained in one sentence: ". . . the left bank of the Rhine was discussed but no tentative agreement was reached. . . ."[14]

That same day Colonel House made a most revealing entry in his diary:

George and I had our conference with Clemenceau. . . . My cable to the President will tell the substance of the interview. We decided many other things that I did not put in my cable to the President because too much explanation would have been needed. . . . When the President is away I never hesitate to act and to take as much responsibility as either of the others.[15]

Lloyd George is somewhat more explicit about the discussion:

M. Clemenceau spoke strongly in favour of Tardieu's plan. Colonel House said he thought we might come to an agreement on these proposals provided the principle of self-determination was postponed until the whole of the terms of peace had been fulfilled. M. Clemenceau objected very strongly to this. He said that he did not believe in the principle of self-determination, which allowed a man to clutch at your throat the first time it was convenient to him, and he would not consent to any limitation of time being placed upon the enforced separation of the Rhenish Republic from the rest of Germany. I informed him that the British Government were really more alarmed about Foch's proposal for an Army of Occupation to hold the Rhine from the Dutch to the Swiss frontier for an indefinite period. When I said it would mean an army of at least 300,000 Clemenceau said he did not think it would take more than 100,000, and that they would only hold two or three bridgeheads. I then informed him that I did not believe Great Britain could make a permanent contribution to this army. Clemenceau replied that France might undertake that two-thirds of the army might be hers. I asked Colonel House whether America would contribute to a permanent Army of Occupation. He expressed great doubts but said he would put it to the President. I then said that Marshal Foch had not explained what his plan really meant. Clemenceau said there was a good reason why he had not explained it; it was because he did not understand it himself. He did not think he had thought it out and that as a matter of fact he was always changing his mind from day to day and that he never knew where he was. He promised to get Marshal Foch to submit the details of his proposal for our consideration.[16]

By now the President was seriously alarmed over the negotiations House was carrying on, and on March 10th he sent his deputy a somewhat exasperated cable.

. . . I hope you will not even provisionally consent to the separation of the Rhenish Province from Germany under any arrangement, but will reserve the whole matter until my arrival. . . .[17]

By the time the President's cable reached Paris it had become clear that, because of Lloyd George's opposition to the exaggerated French proposals, the Supreme Council would not be able to agree on any solution of the Rhineland problem prior to Wilson's return. Clemenceau, back in the driver's seat, put the brakes on the French drive for an immediate preliminary peace with Germany by asking for the creation of one more committee.

House noted in his diary:

March 10, 1919: [Conference with Lloyd George and Clemenceau] . . . We further agreed upon another committee to delineate the boundary lines of Germany. . . . Clemenceau named Tardieu, I named Mezes [his brother-in-law] and Lloyd George named Philip Kerr.[18]

Tardieu's account of the Committee's sessions is spirited, including references to his co-workers as both "friends" and "opponents."

We meet twice, on March 11 and 12, in Mr. Lloyd George's apartment at 23 rue Nitot. I explain . . . the proposals of my Memorandum of February 25. . . .

Mr. Mezes says little. These eight hours of discussion are a dialogue between Mr. Kerr and myself, and it is evident that through the voice of his Chief Secretary it is the British Prime Minister himself who—invisible but present—speaks with some reserve at the first meeting, more emphatically at the second. Is it possible, objects my opponent, to occupy a German territory, bridgeheads included, inhabited by seven million Germans? Is it possible, on the other hand, to separate these Germans from Germany without consulting them and thus to betray the very principles for which the Allies have fought? French tradition? But years have passed, and the historical argument has been too much used and abused by Germany against France, for France to be willing to make use of it against Germany. Besides, in her official declarations, both by her Government and her Parliament (December 30, 1916, January 10 and June 5 and 6, 1917, and November 4, 1918) France made no such demands. So it is impossible to participate in such an occupation. So, also, it would cause deep regret if France sought to undertake it alone; and Mr. Kerr sums up his objection as follows:

"In a word we quite agree with France as to the object to be attained. We are not sure we agree with her as to the method to be employed.

"We do not agree to military occupation. England is equally opposed both to a permanent Army, and to the use of British troops outside of English territory. Furthermore occupation tends to create a nationalistic irritation not only on the left bank of the Rhine but throughout all Germany. It may at the same time foster in Anglo-Saxon countries a propaganda unfavourable to the Allies, and especially to France. Besides, Germany being disarmed, is occupation necessary?

"Nor do we agree as to the creation of an independent State on the left bank of the Rhine. We see in it a source of complication and of weakness. If, after a longer or shorter period, this independent State asserts its will to reunite with Germany, what shall we do? If Press propaganda or public meetings with this end in view go on within its territory, are the troops of occupation to be used to prevent it? If local conflicts occur, whither will they lead? If war results from these conflicts, neither England nor her Dominions will have that deep feeling of solidarity with France which animated them in the last war.

"It is, therefore, impossible for us to accept the solution you propose."

I reply. I recall that the Rhinelanders are not Prussians. I show that the French proposal excluding annexation is the reverse of imperialistic; that the control of the League of Nations gives every facility for evolution; that France, after such unparalleled sufferings, has a right to insist upon the acceptance of the methods of her choice. Public opinion is hostile? Public opinion must be enlightened. It has already learned much during the war, and first of all this, that France is the sentinel of the Overseas Democracies. Besides in default of occupation, what guarantee is there that the treaty will be fulfilled? And I added:

"You say that England does not like English troops to be used away from home. It is a question of fact. England has always had troops in India and Egypt. Why? Because she knows that her frontier is not at Dover. But, the last war has taught her that her European frontier is on the Rhine and that the Rhine is more important to her than even the Suez Canal or the Himalayas.

"You say that the British public does not understand this question.

It is the duty of the British Government to make it understand. Neither did the English public understand in 1914 the necessity of conscription. War has taught it many things.

"You say that there is a danger of provoking nationalist irritation in Germany. The German defeat has already created this feeling. Wherefore, then, the need of protection against a risk which will exist in any case?

"You say that the Rhineland will revolt. Our answer is that fear of Bolshevism and dread of war-taxes dominate the Rhinelander, and that, moreover, we are not threatening them with annexation. We are offering them independence. Other peoples—the Germans of Bohemia, for instance—will, under the Treaty, have to accept a foreign sovereignty.

"If you object to a possible resistance of British opinion, we rely on the certain revolt of French opinion against a peace which would not include the occupation of the Rhine. England did not feel that the complete surrender of the entire German fleet permitted her to do away with her own. And France will not admit that the partial disarmament of Germany on land—partial, because, for twenty years, she will have at her disposal three million trained men—absolves France from the necessity of taking guarantees.

"To ask us to give up occupation, is like asking England and the United States to sink their fleet of battleships. We refuse.

"We want no annexation. But we want our security. We consider the question a vital one, and I do not even need to consult M. Clemenceau to declare, in his name, that we insist upon our demand."

Accordingly, I hand my friends a draft of seven articles and agree with them that, as no agreement has resulted from our conference, the question will have to be decided by the heads of Governments. The proposal I submitted was as follows:

March 12, 1919.

Western Frontier of Germany

1. In the general interest of peace and to assure the effective working of the constituent clause of the League of Nations, the Western frontier of Germany is fixed at the Rhine. Consequently Germany renounces all sovereignty over, as well as any customs union with the territories of the former German Empire on the left bank of the Rhine.

2. The line of the Rhine to be occupied under a mandate of the League of Nations by an inter-allied military force.

The extent and conditions of occupation in German territory of the bridgeheads of Kehl, Mannheim, Mayence, Coblenz, Cologne and Dusseldorf, necessary to the security of inter-allied forces to be fixed by the final Treaty of Peace. Until the signature of the said Treaty the conditions of occupation established by the Armistice of November 11, 1918, to remain in force.

In a zone of fifty kilometers east of her Western frontier Germany shall not maintain nor erect fortifications.

3. The territories of the left bank of the Rhine (except Alsace-Lorraine) to constitute one or several independent States under the protection of the League of Nations. Their Eastern and Southern frontiers to be fixed by the Peace Treaty. Germany undertakes to do nothing which could hinder the aforesaid State or States in the fulfillment of the duties or the exercise of the rights devolving upon them from the causes or the conditions of their creation.

4. Within one month after the signature of the present preliminaries of peace, the general conditions of evacuation of the higher German and Prussian civil officials at present on duty on the left bank of the Rhine, to be settled by a special agreement between the signatory Powers and the German Government.

5. Within two months from the signature of the present preliminaries of peace, a special agreement between the signatory Powers and the German Government to determine, under the guarantee of the League of Nations, the general conditions of liquidation of the German economic interests on the left bank of the Rhine.

6. The German Government undertakes to furnish every year to the independent State or States, which may be created on the left bank of the Rhine, the amount of coal necessary for their industries. This amount shall be credited to Germany in the general reparations account.[19]

As expected, the Committee merely confirmed the deadlock in the Supreme Council, and handed the hot potato back to the parent body. To assuage French feelings of insecurity and to break the impasse, if possible, Lloyd George came up with a new and startling idea. The Colonel, the most industrious recorder of events at Paris, notes in his diary:

March 12, 1919: . . . in the afternoon went to the Quai d'Orsay . . . Lloyd George asked to see me in the anteroom and we went out and talked for nearly a half-hour. He said he was seriously troubled concerning the French. In the first place he could not agree with them upon the question of the boundary of the Rhine and the creation of a Rhenish Republic upon the terms they had in mind. He was willing to give them protection in other directions. For instance, England would build a tunnel which would put English troops in France within 48 hours without having the vicissitudes of the sea to contend with. He would also be willing to say that in the event of an invasion, the British would come at once to the rescue, but he was not willing to maintain an army indefinitely at the bridgeheads of the Rhine and to do the other things the French desired which we both agree will eventually lead to another war.[20]

The next day, March 13th, the SS *George Washington,* with the President aboard, pulled in to Brest. Colonel House had rushed up from Paris to make his report. The President was deeply worried by what he heard. He complained to Mrs. Wilson:

House has given away everything I had won before we left Paris. He has compromised on every side, and so I shall have to start all over again and this time it will be harder, as he has given the impression that my delegates are not in sympathy with me. His own explanation for his compromises is that, with a hostile press in the United States expressing disapproval of the League of Nations as a part of the Treaty, he thought it best to yield some other points lest the Conference withdraw its approval altogether. So he has yielded until there is nothing left.[21]

As soon as Wilson arrived in Paris he met Lloyd George and together they went to see Clemenceau "under six eyes." The old Tiger was all set to do battle and started expounding France's demands. Woodrow Wilson took his breath away by saying: "There will be neither the establishment of an independent state on the left bank, nor occupation of the line of the Rhine, but America and England will sign with France a treaty by which they will engage themselves to support France with all their forces if Germany makes an unprovoked attack on

France." For once, Clemenceau was at a loss for words. He asked for time "to reflect and consult."

To give him a chance to catch up with the work that had accumulated during his absence, President Wilson requested that the Supreme Council meeting, scheduled for March 15th, be postponed. When the Council did meet on March 17th, the French were ready with their reply to the Anglo-American treaty proposal. André Tardieu again produced one of his masterly, if somewhat lengthy, memos in which the French accepted the joint British-American offer of a guarantee treaty in return for French renunciation of the "Rhenish Republic." But the French insisted on a thirty-year occupation of the left bank of the Rhine territory, and, in addition, laid claim to the Saar Valley Basin.*

The French counterproposals read:

III

POSSIBLE BASES OF AGREEMENT

Wishing to respond to the suggestion which has been made to it, the French Government thinks it its duty to set out in detail the general bases upon which agreement might be reached, these bases being the minimum guarantees indispensable to France.

It should be agreed, in the first place, that:

In case Germany, in violation of the peace conditions imposed upon her by the Allied and Associated Governments, should commit an act of aggression against France, Great Britain and the United States would bring to France the aid of their military forces.

Therefore:

(1) The date and the conditions of evacuation of the bridgeheads on the right bank, and of the territories on the left bank of the Rhine, to be fixed by the Peace Treaty (as one of the guarantees to be taken for the execution of the financial clauses).**

(2) Germany to maintain neither military force nor military organization on the left bank of the Rhine nor within fifty kilometers east of the river. The German Army to be forbidden to manoeuvre there. Recruiting to be forbidden there—even appeals for volunteers. Fortifi-

* For full text of memorandum see Tardieu: *The Truth About the Treaty*, 178-182.

** In other words an occupation for thirty years.

cations to be demolished there. No new fortifications to be erected there. No war material to be manufactured there. (Certain of these clauses already figure in the preliminary peace proposals: but in the present hypothesis it would be necessary to strengthen them.)

(3) Great Britain, the United States and France to have the right to satisfy themselves by means of a permanent Commission of Inspection that the conditions imposed upon Germany are complied with. (For without this right the preceding clause would be worthless.)

(4) Great Britain, the United States and France to agree to consider as an act of aggression any entry or attempted entry of all or any part of the German Army into the zone fixed in paragraph 2.

(5) Furthermore, Great Britain and France to recognize the right of France to occupy the line of the Rhine with five bridgeheads of a radius of twenty kilometers in case Germany, in the opinion of the Commission of Inspection, should violate the terms of paragraph 2 or any one of the military, aerial, and naval clauses of the peace preliminaries. (*In fact, if France gives up after thirty years' permanent occupation she must at least in case of danger of war resulting from Germany's violation of her pledges, be able to advance her troops to the only good defensive position, that is to the Rhine.*)

(6) Great Britain and the United States to recognize to France her frontier of 1814 and by way of reparation the right of occupation without annexation of that part of the coal basin of the Sarre not included within this frontier.

P. S. *It goes without saying that by act of aggression against France, the French Government also means any aggression against Belgium.*[22]

Wilson's proposal of a treaty guaranteeing France United States protection from aggression greatly disturbed the President's aides; they not only feared opposition to an "entangling alliance" in the States, but also felt that the President was laying the ax to one of the most fundamental tenets of the League of Nations: no separate alliances between member states. The minutes of the meetings of American Commissioners clearly show their misgivings.

March 20, 1919

Mr. White stated that he had had a conversation with Colonel House during which the latter had shown him a suggested text for an agreement between France, Great Britain and the United States which he thought would satisfy M. Clemenceau. The Commissioners discussed the drafting of this text, and felt that the wording could be much improved upon. They therefore drew up a substitute text. The Commissioners further requested Mr. Herter to submit this text to Colonel House with the statement to the effect that in their opinion the subject matter thereof was most prejudicial to the whole structure of the League of Nations and to the ideal for which the United States had entered the war and that they therefore would desire further time to consider it. They also wished it clearly understood that in re-drafting the text they were not expressing any opinion on the principle involved.

March 21, 1919

The Commissioners discussed the question of the suggested agreement between France, England and the United States which had been brought up at their meeting the previous day. They all expressed themselves very strongly against the principle involved in concluding such an agreement, and felt that the whole structure of the League of Nations would be most seriously compromised thereby. Mr. White was of the opinion that the time had come for a definite showdown with the French, and that unless an amicable agreement could be reached, we should sign a separate peace. The Commissioners felt that it was most essential that they should discuss the whole situation with the President in the very near future.[23]

The American Commissioners had no such misgivings, however, about surrendering the Saar Valley to French sovereignty. The "American Inquiry" had stated only five months earlier that "attachment of the Saar to France would be a clear violation of the President's principles," but the Commissioners now regarded the French proposals with favor. The fact that these proposals constituted a retreat from the original French demands for the establishment of a Rhenish Republic quite possibly influenced their judgment. Lloyd George also regarded

* David Hunter Miller has this to say on the subject: "Mr. White observed that through Colonel House he had learned that the President appeared to be in favor of giving to France the guarantee which she desired through a triple alliance. England was resolved to give this guarantee whether the United States did or not. Mr. White said that he told Colonel House that in the opinion of the other three Commissioners such an alliance would be extremely unfortunate, and absolutely fatal to the success of the League of Nations. Colonel House had replied that he would bring this view to the attention of the President."[24]

the French proposals as fully justified. Woodrow Wilson alone, even against the advice of his own Commissioners, fought stubbornly to prevent the annexation of the Saar by France.

From March 17th to April 22nd the battle of the Saar waged. It almost wrecked the Paris Peace Conference and finally ended in a compromise which saved the President's principle of self-determination and gave the French at least temporary control of the precious Saar coal mines.

The archives of Congress, and of Yale and Stanford Universities, contain reams of paper consisting of the minutes of the meetings of the Council of Four, the Council of Foreign Ministers and the various Commissions concerned, all of which give verbatim details of the ebb and flow of the battle.

No account, however, is quite as vivid as the report given by André Tardieu, who stood in the front line throughout the melee, and who told the story from the French point of view. His disarming candor reveals the innermost workings of French diplomacy, of which he was such a past master; and his close adherence to the facts, as they are recorded in the minutes, coupled with his lively, colorful style, gives his account the flavor of reportage by a first-rate war correspondent. The step-by-step retreat of the American representatives until the final "compromise" that gave France all she demanded except outright sovereignty over the Saar Basin is dramatically told. M. Tardieu is a highly enthusiastic Frenchman, and the editor will have to take the liberty of interrupting his account occasionally to mention some events of particular interest to American readers that Tardieu overlooks.

The problem of the Sarre Basin . . . is the only one that led to disagreement between the French and American representatives. It lasted ten days and at times assumed an aspect of conflict. . . .

A difficult problem, indeed, for it had two aspects: an economic aspect because of the coal mines, the ownership of which was essential—in equity and in fact—to a nation systematically ruined by Germany; and a moral and historic aspect because a large part of this territory was inhabited by people French by race, by tradition and by aspiration, which the Treaties of 1814 had left to France and which violence alone had torn from her in 1815. A difficult problem also because its two elements were geographically contradictory. . . . Our claim to the soil did not coincide with our claim to the sub-soil, and neither the one nor the other could be abandoned. . . . And nothing but the combination of these two solutions could satisfy the double claim which it was our duty to press.

This statement explains the difficulties encountered. These difficulties were not underestimated by the French delegations and they were met with frankness in a Memorandum which I myself drew up. . . .*

This memorandum offered a three-term solution imposed upon us by the circumstances: restoration to French sovereignty of the territories south of the frontier of 1814; a special political administration for the territories of the mineral and industrial basin north of this frontier; full ownership of the mines of these two zones. . . .

On the morning of March 28, M. Loucheur and I were summoned by the Council of the Four to President Wilson's residence. We were jointly entrusted with the verbal presentation of the French case. The moment we entered the meeting our impression was formed. Mr. Lloyd George did not attribute first rate importance to this matter. President Wilson on the contrary, wore a quizzical smile that foreshadowed objections.

I will not reproduce the statement made that day by M. Loucheur and myself, the whole substance of which was borrowed from the document I have just [mentioned]. The first interruptions showed us just where we stood. Mr. Lloyd George without hesitation expressed himself in favour of our contention so far as the ownership of the mines was concerned. He recognized that this ownership was due to us as a just compensation. With regard to the territories, he was less categorical. He admitted that an autonomous organization ought to be established for the entire coal basin; in other words that it should be detached from Germany. On the other hand, however, he did not admit our right to possess both the territories and the coal, and our claim for the frontier of 1814 alarmed him; he repeated the formula so often heard during the discussions: "Let us not renew the mistake committed by Germany in 1871 in the name of a fictitious historical right. Do not let us create a new Alsace-Lorraine."

Mr. Wilson, who at first had said nothing, then spoke. Mr. Lloyd George had accepted the greater part of our claims; the President, on the contrary, rejected them all. He admitted our right to take from the

* For full text of memorandum see Tardieu, *The Truth About the Treaty*, 251 ff.

Sarre Basin a quantity of coal equal to the deficit from our mines, due to the war. But he refused us the ownership of the mines, the frontier of 1814, and the autonomous organization suggested by Mr. Lloyd George. His point of view, presented in the most friendly, but most emphatic manner, was as follows:

"Never has France, in any public document, claimed the frontier of 1814. The bases of peace accepted by her speak of reparation for the wrong which she suffered in 1871—and not in 1815.

"Now these bases bind the Allies. The historical argument used by Germany against France to justify her theft of Alsace and Lorraine is a dangerous one. Let us avoid using it.

"The frontier of 1814 does not correspond to any economic reality. It would ruin the basin by cutting it in two, without assuring coal to France. A cession of territory, without an immediate plebiscite, would under these conditions be inadmissible.

"There is no Nation more intelligent than the French. If I thus frankly express my point of view I do not fear her judgment. I have so high an opinion of the intelligence of the French Nation that I believe she will always accept a principle based upon justice and applied fairly.

"I do not believe that this problem can be compared with that of Alsace-Lorraine. For half a century the world had its eyes turned towards Alsace-Lorraine. For half a century the world has never thought of those provinces as being German. The question of the frontier of 1814 has not quite the same character.

"I am ready to recognize that France should have the use of the mines for a period that shall be determined; but as there can be no question of depriving the local industries of coal the question of the ownership of the mines appears to me to be purely sentimental.

"I regret to make these objections and I apologize for it. It is painful to me to oppose France's wishes. But I could not act otherwise without failing in my duty."

The discussion from this time on went to the very roots of the problem. M. Clemenceau, who had allowed his colleagues to answer questions of fact and figures put by President Wilson, felt it necessary to intervene, and did so with rare elevation of thought.

"I have," he said, "a serious reservation to make. You eliminate sentiment and memory. The world is not guided by principles alone.

"You say you are ready to render us justice from the economic point of view, and I thank you for it. But economic interests are not everything. The history of the United States is glorious, but brief. One hundred and twenty years is a very long period for you; for us it is a short one. Our conception of history cannot be quite the same as yours.

"Our ordeals have created in us a profound sentiment of the reparation due us. The point at issue is not material reparation only; the need for moral reparation is no less great.

"I know all that you have done for victory but I believe that you will lose nothing by recognizing in this question a sentiment which is something different from your principles, but no less profound.

"When Lafayette and Rochambeau—two youths—went to the aid of America struggling for her independence, it was not cold reason or deeds of valour, common enough after all, which sowed the seed of affectionate gratitude which has sprung from their action; but an impression, a deep fellow-feeling that has linked our two nations forever.

"I am old. In a few months I shall have left politics forever. My disinterestedness is complete. I will defend before Parliament the conclusions that we shall reach here together; but if you do not listen to me today, you will lose an opportunity of riveting yet another link in the chain of affection binding France to America.

"There are, in this region, 150,000 Frenchmen. These men who in 1918 sent addresses to President Poincaré have also a right to justice. You wish to respect the rights of the Germans. So do I. But bear in mind the rights of these Frenchmen as you will have to bear in mind later the historic rights of Bohemia and of Poland.

"We shall soon resume this discussion. For the moment I merely ask you, when you are alone, to think over all I have just said to you and ask your conscience whether it does not contain a great deal of truth."

Thus, two principles confront each other. On one side, economic arguments which can be shown in figures; on the other side, moral arguments which can be weighed. On both sides a lively and honest desire for agreement, but the impossibility of reaching this agreement. Mr. Lloyd George favours a compromise. But the historical argument so dear to the French heart has no weight with any of our Allies. Our entire contention is disputed. We are far from the goal and the road is long and hard.

This dramatic meeting ended at twelve-thirty.[25]

Here M. Tardieu tactfully refrains from describing how dramatic that meeting really was; the dramatic highlight of the Conference, it was the meeting in which Clemenceau lost his temper, called President Wilson "pro-Boche," and stalked from the room, slamming the door behind him. Colonel House offers an excellent, secondhand account of the scene in his diary.

March 28, 1919: Lloyd George asked me to come to lunch with him for the purpose of discussing the Russian question. However, when I got there, he had just returned from the President's house and showed signs of considerable excitement. It seems that the long-expected row between either Clemenceau and the President, or Lloyd George and Clemenceau, had actually come. I am sorry it should have happened to the President rather than Lloyd George. They came near to calling one another names. The trouble arose over the question of the Western boundaries and of the Sarre Valley. The President told Clemenceau that the French were bringing up territorial questions that had nothing to do with the war aims of anybody, and that no one had heard of their intention to annex the Sarre Valley until after the armistice had been signed. Clemenceau grew angry at this and said that the President favored the Germans. The President replied that such a statement was untrue and that Clemenceau knew it was.

Clemenceau then stated that if they did not receive the Sarre Valley he would not sign the Treaty of Peace. To this the President replied: "Then if France does not get what she wishes, she will refuse to act with us. In that event do you wish me to return home?" Clemenceau answered: "I do not wish you to go home, but I intend to do so myself," and in a moment he left the house.[26]

Wilson himself referred to the incident on the following morning, saying to his advisers:

"Gentlemen, I am in trouble. . . . The matter is this: the French want the whole left bank of the Rhine. I told M. Clemenceau that I could not consent to such a solution of the problem. He became very excited . . . I do not know whether I shall see M. Clemenceau again. I do not know whether he will return to the meeting this afternoon. In fact, I do not know whether the Peace Conference will continue. M. Clemenceau called me a pro-German and abruptly left the room."[27]

But let us return to M. Tardieu's account of the French reaction to the dramatic meeting.

At two o'clock M. Clemenceau, M. Loucheur and I met again at the War Office and went over the situation which was not promising. Frontier of 1814—we were alone, therefore without hope of success. Ownership of the mines and creation of an autonomous state—we had Great Britain's support without, however, adequate guarantees either for the operation of the mines or above all for the liberation of the French inhabitants of the Sarre. Long experience had taught us that reasoning borrowed from the past had but little appeal for Mr. Wilson: there he feared to find the germ of new wars. The one point on which we felt a lesser resistance was the economic problem. Mr. Wilson contested our ownership of the mines: but already he recognized our right to work them. It was upon that point, therefore, that M. Clemenceau, M. Loucheur and I agreed unanimously to make our first effort. We would assert simultaneously two principles, distinct in their character but one in their consequence. The first was that operation of the mines required a special political organization of the territory. The second, that if our Allies believe there are too many Germans in the Sarre Basin to justify an immediate reunion with France, we on the other hand deem that there are in this same basin too many people of French origin and aspirations for France to consent to leave them under Prussian domination. The assertion of these three principles—ownership, complete guarantee of operation through a special political administration, safeguards for the rights of the inhabitants—became the bulwark of our defense. We dealt with them in three Notes, dated respectively March 29, and April 1 and 5.[28]

The main points of the French demands at that stage were:

1. full ownership of all the mines of the Sarre;
2. an economic regime which would permit development of the subsoil;
3. the Sarre region to be placed under League of Nations protection;

4. withdrawal of all German officials;
5. German residents to retain their nationality, but not permitted to participate in national elections or plebiscites;
6. all Germans desiring to leave the territory to be given all facilities to liquidate their possessions; and
7. France demands from the League of Nations the rights to
(a) occupy the territory militarily;
(b) issue visas (i.e. control travel in and out of the territory);
(c) veto local administrators, including schools; and
(d) appoint mayors and deputy mayors.

M. Tardieu continues his account:

The question of ownership is settled on March 31, when Mr. Wilson agrees to the transfer of the mines to France with certain guarantees of an economic order but on the condition that there should be no question either of displacing the frontier or of creating an independent State. His proposal which did not give us satisfaction . . . is as follows:

It is agreed in principle:

1. That full ownership of the coal mines of the Sarre Basin should pass to France to be credited on her claims against Germany for reparation.

2. That for the exploitation of these mines the fullest economic facilities shall be accorded to France, including particularly:

(a) Exemption from taxation on the part of Germany, including important export dues.

(b) Full mobility of labour, foreign and native.

(c) Freedom for the development of adequate means of communication by rail and water.

3. That the political and administrative arrangements necessary to secure the foregoing results be inquired into.

We are still far from the goal. Nevertheless on one important item, the points of view begin to harmonize. M. Clemenceau seizes the occasion. He takes the paper handed to him by the President. He reads and re-reads it—saying neither yes nor no. He states that before answering he must consult his advisers. So a committee of three is formed. I represent France, and I have the assistance of M. Louis Aubert, who for two years had most successfully directed the Press and Information Service of the French High Commission in America, and of M. Deflinne, Director of Mines. Professor Charles H. Haskins is the American delegate; Mr. Headlam Morley the British. France should remember the names of these two men; their uprightness and sympathetic understanding of our rights played a most important part in the results obtained. After ten meetings of several hours each, the demands of our engineers are accepted and on certain points completed. We agree on the technical conditions of the operation of the mines in German territory by the French State which was to own them. But that does not satisfy me. No technical clauses can avail if, on all sides, political and administrative pressure is to distort and warp them. I appeal to the good faith of my British and American colleagues with whom I was convinced in these circumstances, as in all others, I should not plead in vain and I obtain from them their signatures at the end of our report to the following declaration, the importance of which I need not emphasize:

> The undersigned are agreed in the opinion that if the above articles which appear to be necessary from the social and economic point of view were to be applied without the establishment of a special administrative and political régime, serious difficulties and conflicts would inevitably arise.
>
> (signed)
>
> André Tardieu
> Charles H. Haskins
> Headlam Morley.

Thus the second part of the problem rejected on March 31 by President Wilson and no less important for us than the first, is put forward by those who, up to that time, had not been entrusted with its discussion. From then on the negotiation is solidly established and if we finally have to give up our claim to the frontier of 1814, we shall at least obtain liberal and essential compensations; but not without another effort.[29]

At the President's request, Colonel House saw M. Tardieu on April 3rd and expressed the American stand as strongly as he could.

Tardieu [called]. I gave the talk which the President and I agreed upon last night. It had some effect upon him and I hope when it is repeated it will have some effect upon Clemenceau. I put our case as strongly as I could and took occasion to say as far as I could see, France had not reciprocated in any way. I disliked to recount our services to them but I thought it necessary. I disliked even more to tell him of our unselfish purposes. We were demanding nothing, and were merely trying to hold to the principles upon which the armistice had been made and to which all the belligerents had agreed.

The Sarre Valley was injected as an entirely new proposal . . . a proposal the Prime Minister himself agreed not to put forth if I thought it unreasonable. When this proposal was suggested, the only consideration brought forward was the value and the necessity of the coal which was to be given France in lieu of the destruction of the coal mines around Lens. The President had been in sympathy with this request and was willing to give France in fee simple the coal mines, but he was entirely unwilling to place under French sovereignty an absolutely German population. In our opinion it was not only inconsistent with the Fourteen Points, but it meant trouble for France. . . .

In reply to this, Tardieu brought attention to the fact that Foch had threatened to resign unless France insisted on the permanent occupation of the Rhine, although Clemenceau did not go that far. The upshot of the interview was that Tardieu is to see what practical arrangement can be worked out concerning the use of the mines by France. We will then take the next step, if indeed, there is to be a next.[30]

Tardieu continues:

On the morning of April 8, Mr. Lloyd George, after reading Mr. Headlam Morley's report, frankly sides with us. We offer either the establishment of an independent State linked to France by a Customs Union, or the sovereignty of the League of Nations with a mandate given to France, and a plebiscite at the end of fifteen years. Mr. Lloyd George presents at the same time two propositions similar to ours, and in a few words states his opinion:

"I would give the Sarre Basin its independence under the authority of the League of Nations.

"A Customs Union would attach it to France. There does not exist, it is true, any natural economic link between this region and Germany. All its relations are with Alsace and Lorraine.

"We must also not forget that this country was French in its greater part until the beginning of the nineteenth century; that it was taken away from France by force in spite of the opposition of English statesmen.

"We are opposed to all annexation. But we do not believe that it is possible for this region to live if we do not make it a political unit.

"I am convinced that, if in a few years a plebiscite takes place, this population will not ask to belong again to Germany."

Mr. House that day represented President Wilson who was ill. He admits that these solutions are "very interesting and worthy of close examination." It seems that a step forward has been made.

But on the same day, the eighth in the afternoon, President Wilson, who has returned to his place, again voices his hesitations. He approves our plan of economic clauses. On the other hand he approves neither change nor suspension of sovereignty. He also rejects the suggestion of a mandate and to meet the danger pointed out by us of incidents and conflicts, hands us a Note which merely proposes, instead of an independent political unit, the setting up of a Commission of Arbitration to settle the differences between the French mines and the German Government.

M. Clemenceau refuses. A short and lively debate ensues with a brisk volley of questions and answers. The President implores us not to make the peace of the world depend upon the question of the Sarre. M. Clemenceau replies that the peace of the world demands, first of all, that justice be established among the Allies. No conclusion is reached. The atmosphere is tense. Since March 27, the minor officials at the Hotel Crillon are nervous. The Chief of the Press Service, Mr. Ray Stannard Baker, is particularly active in spreading pessimistic reports. On April 6, he accuses M. Clemenceau of "claiming annexations." The following day, the seventh, the rumour spreads that the President, discouraged, has ordered the *George Washington* to Brest. The hour is critical.[31]

The hour was critical indeed, far more critical than Tardieu cares to admit. President Wilson, whose health had given way under the strain, had taken to his bed and, utterly disgusted with the intransigence of the French, had ordered the *George Washington* to be readied for his return to the United States. No doubt, Wilson's action was partly bluff. It was not as easy for him to "go home" as it had been for Clemenceau, who lived just "down the street." Once the President sailed for America the Peace Conference was over, his efforts a failure, and his dreams of a New World Safe for Democracy shattered. But bluff or no bluff, it worked, and the French proved slightly more inclined to compromise from then on.

Tardieu minimizes the French concessions in his account; but the French answer to the President's proposals of April 8th no longer mentions annexation, accepts a plebiscite after fifteen years, and only demands greater security of controls during those fifteen years. In Tardieu's words:

Once again, M. Clemenceau, M. Loucheur and I meet on April 8 at the War Office at seven o'clock in the evening. We weigh the consequence of an adverse decision. Nevertheless we decide not to yield. A Note, which I write during the night, states the reasons for our resistance. This Note distributed very early the next morning to the heads of Governments asserts both our spirit of conciliation and the impossibility of our making any further concessions.

April 9.

Answer to President Wilson's Note

V. Conclusion.

To sum up, the French Government, after having carefully studied President Wilson's Note of April 8, believes that this Note:

(1) Does not contain the administrative and political clauses which the experts' report of April 5 deems indispensable in order to avoid conflicts.

(2) Involves, by reason of this fact, great risk of stirring up local and general complications.

(3) Supplies Germany with a permanent means of obstructing French operation of the mines of the basin.

(4) Entirely re-opens the question at the expiration of fifteen years of France's right of ownership over the mines which was sanctioned by President Wilson's Note of March 31.

(5) Does not insure to the population in view of the proposed plebiscite the indispensable guarantees necessary after one hundred years of Prussian oppression.

The French Government wishes therefore to adhere to one of Mr. Lloyd George's proposals in harmony with those which it has itself formulated.

It is ready to complete them in conformity with President Wilson's suggestions:

(a) By a plebiscite after fifteen years;

(b) By a Court of Arbitration appointed to settle possible conflicts in the application of one or the other of these three solutions.

[signed] G. CLEMENCEAU

Henceforth the positions could hardly be modified or the solution much delayed. April 9 would in fact be decisive. At the morning meeting Mr. Lloyd George gave his full approval to our Note of the previous day and drew attention to the fact that the plebiscite at the end of fifteen years answered President Wilson's objections. The latter still holds out. But he and his counsellors waver under the force of our arguments.

The afternoon of the ninth he presents a new text which, without conferring the mandate upon France transformed into an administrative commission the Commission of Arbitration which he had suggested the previous day. I ask the President three essential questions:

1°—Will German sovereignty be suspended?

2°—Will the Commission have full rights, including that of dismissing officials?

3°—Will the elections to the Reichstag be suppressed?

President Wilson answers: "Yes."

On hearing this affirmative answer M. Clemenceau agrees to leave to the Committee, composed of Mr. Haskins, Mr. Morley and myself, the task of drafting a clause.

Working from five o'clock in the afternoon until three o'clock in the morning, our Committee, assisted by technical and legal experts, completes this task and on the morning of the tenth the draft is submitted to the Council of Four who accept it: it will become Section 4 of Part II of the Treaty. It sets forth in forty-six articles the principles which since March 28 France had defended before the Conference. The mines are yielded to us in full ownership with the most minute guarantees for their operation. In order to assure the rights and welfare of the population the Government is transferred for fifteen years to the League of Nations which delegates it to a Commission of five members. This Commission will have all the powers hitherto belonging to the German Empire, Prussia and Bavaria. A Customs Union will be established between France and the territory of the Sarre. At the end of fifteen years the population will vote by districts on the following questions: reunion with Germany: union with France: continuance of autonomy. If a mining district voted for Germany the latter would have the right to repurchase the mines of that district but with the obligation to supply France with the corresponding quantity of coal called for by her industrial and domestic needs. In all other cases the total ownership of the mines goes to France.

Such the solution furnished by the Treaty. Complex assuredly because the problem was complex—because France had to deal with Allies restrained by well-meaning hesitations and often incapable of grasping things from the same point of view as France, but just also because taking into account in this very complexity all the interests involved.[32]

Once the problem of the Saar Basin, the main stumbling block of the Conference, had been removed by "compromise," the problems of the western frontiers followed the same pattern. Fifteen years of occupation of the left bank of the Rhine and establishment of a 50-kilometer demilitarized zone on the right bank were speedily agreed upon, and, although Foch vigorously protested and kept on protesting to the very last, the French agreed to this watering down of their original "indispensable" security measures.

VIII

Reparations

Long before the Paris Peace Conference convened, it had become apparent to all observers that U. S. views on reparations differed widely from those of its "Associated Powers." While the peoples of England and France were being assured by their leaders that "the Germans will pay for everything," Woodrow Wilson was proclaiming "no annexations, no contributions, no punitive damages" as one of America's war aims.* The President's Fourteen Points spoke of "restoration of the occupied territories of Belgium, France, Roumania, Serbia and Montenegro," which the American delegation interpreted to mean solely reparation of damages suffered by the civilian populations. By filing their reservations to the Fourteen Points before accepting them as a basis for the peace treaty with Germany, the Associated Powers confirmed expressly that reparations were to apply to "damage done to civilan populations."

Farsightedly, the French slipped an escape clause into the actual Armistice terms ("XIX. With the reservation that any future claims of the Allies and the United States remain unaffected. . . .") which, in their opinion, relieved them of all restrictions of the Pre-Armistice Agreement. We have already noted the British-French attempt to slip "indemnities" into the peace negotiations** by setting up an Inter-Allied Committee on "reparations and indemnities," and how that effort was blocked by Colonel House.

* Speech on February 11, 1918.
** See Chapter I.

During Wilson's visit to London in December of 1918, Lloyd George sounded him out on the question of reparations. Wilson's response left a rather disappointed Prime Minister with the task of conveying the American viewpoint to the Imperial War Council.

With regard to indemnity, Mr. Lloyd George reported that he found the President, on the whole, stiffer than on any other question. The utmost concession he seemed inclined to make was that the claims for pure reparation should be tabled first, and that then other claims might possibly be considered afterwards. Mr. Lloyd George had pointed out that that practically ruled the British Empire out in spite of the enormous burdens it had borne, and that France and Belgium, who had borne a lesser burden, would practically get everything. He had pointed out also that as a matter of fact [Britain's] burden of over £6,000,000,000 to a population of 45,000,000 was much heavier than that of Germany with a similar debt distributed over 65,000,000 of people. Similarly, he had pointed out that Australia at this moment owed £75 for every man, woman, and child of her population, a loss which was just as real as any loss represented by destroyed houses. He had, however, failed to make any impression upon the President.

In answer to a question by Mr. Hughes, Mr. Lloyd George said that with regard to the question of economic barriers, raised in No. 3 of the President's Fourteen Points, the President had shown no inclination to raise the matter. His opinion was that President Wilson meant nothing in particular by that Article anyhow, and since he had brought it forward he had lost the election in the United States.[1]

If the British and French were apprehensive about Wilson's attitude, the American team felt equally uneasy about the demands the Allied Powers would make. Above all, they feared that they might attempt to link German reparations payments with the repayments of war loans. Colonel House revealed some of the American apprehension in his diary.

January 6, 1919: I suggested to my colleagues this morning that the finance and economic questions would meet us at every turn and that we might as well face them and have a show-down with our associates of the Allied Governments. . . .

If we go along the lines which the French, Belgian, and other Allied Governments are pursuing, Germany, I thought, could not sign a peace which left the amount of her obligations in doubt, to be determined as the future developed the amount of reparations to be paid. It would not be satisfactory to Germany and it would not be satisfactory to us. Germany could not put herself in a financial condition to pay an indefinite obligation. It therefore seemed the course of wisdom to ascertain how much Germany could pay within a reasonable time and then let the Allies settle between themselves what proportion of this sum each should receive. My colleagues were in agreement with me.

We have to meet the growing demand of the Allies that the United States not only cancel the sums which they owe us, but help them pay their own debts. I appreciate the seriousness of the situation and I am not averse to taking up the entire question and trying to help solve the distressing problems which this situation involves.

During the war the people were quite willing to pay excessive taxation. It was a matter of self-preservation. Then, too, the scale of remuneration was high. There is quite a different story to tell today, and if England, France, and Italy undertake to tax their people sufficiently to meet their national budgets, it will of course include the interest charges on their national debts. I am sure the devil will be to pay. I want to treat the matter sympathetically and generously, but I do not want to see the United States forced into an impossible and unsatisfactory position.[2]

David Hunter Miller explained the over-all American position on January 17, 1919.

. . . I lunched at the Majestic with Sir William Wiseman. . . . He asked what I thought about the indemnity question generally; that is, he said, substantially, "How are we going to get out of the statements made by Lloyd George during the campaign?" I told him that I thought the matter would be practically settled by the inquiry as to what Germany could pay, which would probably have to determine how it should be paid and when; and that any such question was not really a financial question of manner of payment, but a political and social question of how the people were really going to work to make the payment. . . .[3]

Alone among the major powers, the United States had no reparation claims to present and her interest in the matter was secondary, though by no means unselfish. On the SS *George Washington* Wilson had said that he "was not very interested in the economic part of the treaty" and he demonstrated this throughout the Conference. But he had brought along to Paris a brilliant team of economic and financial experts to give him his "guaranteed stand."

America's secondary interest in reparations arose from the fact that she had advanced large sums to the major Allied Powers during the war, and she had no intention of letting any of her creditors default on those war loans. She was therefore interested in seeing them get enough reparations from Germany to enable their depleted treasuries to meet their obligations. But another consideration also entered American thinking on the subject. If France and Great Britain were to be able to repay the war loans, the economy of Europe would have to return to normal as quickly as possible, and no purpose would be served by keeping Germany and the rest of Central Europe in a state of bankruptcy.

Once the Conference got under way it set up a Committee on the Reparation of Damages (CRD) whose terms of reference were: "to study and report on (a) how much the enemy countries ought to pay, (b) how much they could pay, (c) by what method, in what form, at what time and (on French insistence) under what guarantees payments could be made." Three subcommittees were set up to study each one of these problems.

The CRD was composed of a glittering array of personalities. The United States was represented by Vance McCormick, Chairman of the War Trade Board; Bernard Baruch, Chairman of the War Industries Board; Norman Davis, Commissioner of Finance; and by John Foster Dulles as legal adviser. Thomas A. Lamont, the Morgan partner who had negotiated Allied war loans, was alternate U. S. delegate. Great Britain's chief delegates on the Committee were William Hughes, the Australian Prime Minister; Lord Cunliffe, erstwhile Governor of the Bank of England; and Lord Sumner, an eminent British legal authority. The interests of France were entrusted to Louis-Lucien Klotz, Minister of Finance; Albert Lebrun, Minister for Liberated Areas, and future President of France; and Louis Loucheur, Minister for Reconstruction. In addition, Italy, Belgium, Greece, Poland, Portugal, Japan, Rumania, Serbia and Czechoslovakia were represented by their financial experts.

When, by mid-February, the CRD got to the heart of the subject, it soon became apparent that the differences between the American and Allied points of view were basic. On February 13th, John Foster Dulles addressed the Committee on behalf of the American Delegates.

Mr. President:

It was a matter of considerable chagrin to the American members of this commission when it developed, upon an analysis of the various memoranda on principles of reparation, that the memorandum of the United States appeared to be the least drastic in its terms. . . .

And if the character of our proposals is not attributable to a lack of severity in our condemnation of Germany, no more does it indicate that the Government and people of the United States are indifferent to the war costs with which they themselves are burdened. . . .

If then it is in accordance with our sentiment that the principles of reparation be severe, and in accord with our material interest that these principles be all inclusive, why, in defiance of these motives, have we proposed reparation in certain limited ways only? It is because, gentlemen, we do not regard ourselves as free. . . . We have before us a page . . . which is already filled with writing, and at the bottom are the signatures of Mr. Wilson, of Mr. Orlando, of Mr. Clemenceau, and of Mr. Lloyd George.

You are all aware, I am sure, of the writing to which I refer: It is the agreed basis of peace with Germany. It consists, so far as is relevant to our discussion here, of the Fourteen Points contained in an address of President Wilson of January 8, 1918, which, with certain qualifications, were accepted by the Allies, by the United States, and by Germany as the agreed basis of peace. On these terms, says the Allied memorandum, "they declare their willingness to make peace with the Government of Germany." This offer was accepted by the Government of Germany, and in reliance on the agreement resulting from such acceptance the enemy laid down his arms.

Among the terms of peace which were accepted by both sides we find provisions relative to reparation. What are these provisions?

The address of January 8th says:

> Belgium, the whole world will agree, must be evacuated and restored. . . . All French territory should be freed and the invaded portions restored. . . . Rumania, Serbia, and Montenegro should be evacuated; occupied territory restored.

The Allied qualification or enlargement of these provisions is contained in the following language:

> The President declared that invaded territories must be restored as well as evacuated and freed. The Allied Governments feel that no doubt ought to be allowed to exist as to what this provision implies. By it they understand that compensation will be made by Germany for all damage done to the civilian population of the Allies and their property by the aggression of Germany by land, by sea, and from the air.

The foregoing language thus constitutes, in so far as reparation is concerned, the terms upon which the United States and the Allies agreed to make peace with Germany and the terms upon which Germany accepted the armistice of November 11, 1918. . . .

Gentlemen, we have here an agreement. It is an agreement which cannot be ignored, and I am confident that no one here would propose to ignore it. I know that I have the full concurrence of all in the proposition that if this agreement constitutes a limitation upon our right to demand reparation of the enemy, that limitation will be respected.

And can there be any question that this agreement does constitute a limitation? . . .

We have thus agreed that we would give Germany peace if she would do certain specified things. Is it now open to us to say, "Yes; but before you get peace you must do other and further things"? We have said to Germany, "You may have peace if among other things you perform certain acts of reparation which will cost you, say, ten billion dollars." Are we not now clearly precluded from saying, "You can have peace provided you perform other acts of reparation which will bring your total liability to many times that which was originally stipulated." No; irrespective of the justice of the enemy making the latter reparation, it is now too late. Our bargain has been struck for better or for worse; it remains only to give it a fair construction and practical application.

The fundamental proposition, therefore, put forth by the American members of this commission is that we demand of Germany, as a condition of peace, all of that reparation, but only that, stipulated for by a fair construction of the agreement with Germany as to what the terms of peace should be.

We pass then to the construction and application of the agreed terms of peace. . . . Briefly, we take the view that the terms of peace proposed and accepted are not to be construed as waiving any clear right of reparation due under accepted principles of international law. We thus recognize that our agreement with Germany is not in derogation of those principles of jurisprudence upon which the French memorandum and upon which Mr. Hughes' address purport to base themselves. But we are also compelled to recognize that in so far as we base our claims, not upon contractional law but on the law of torts, we are restricted to damage arising from *illegal* acts. . . .

Accordingly it is the American proposition that where the enemy has committed an act clearly violative of international law as existing at the time of the commission of the act, he is liable to make reparation for the damage caused thereby. This involves the complete repayment to Belgium of the damage to her resulting from Germany's violation of her covenant not to make war upon Belgium. The illegality of this act and the duty of making reparation have already been formally admitted by Germany. It further means that the enemy is liable for damage resulting from such miscellaneous illegal acts as the deportation of civilians, attacks on undefended towns, sinkings of merchant vessels without warning, and other illegal acts too numerous to mention here.

In addition to this reparation due in accordance with recognized international law, there is the reparation which it was expressly agreed should become a part of the Treaty of Peace, and which reparation, to some extent, includes that due in accordance with international law, but which to a considerable extent goes beyond. This reparation expressly stipulated for involves a restoration of the invaded areas of Belgium, France, Rumania, Serbia, and Montenegro, and compensation for all damage done to the civilian population of the Allies and their property by the aggression of Germany by land, by sea, and from the air. . . .

I accordingly have the honor to propose, on behalf of the American members of this commission, that the commission accept as a fundamental principle that the reparation to be exacted from the enemy is that which is due in accordance with a fair construction of the written agreement of the Associated Governments with Germany as the terms of peace.

I further suggest, on behalf of the American members, that the commission next consider the most expeditious method of reaching an agreement as to the construction and application of the language of the agreement relative to reparation.[4]

The Prime Minister of Australia answered Mr. Dulles in a long, impassioned speech on February 14th. He himself summarized the main points of his discourse as follows:

(1) The Fourteen Points are not exhaustive as to reparation.

(2) It is admitted by the American memorandum that Belgium's full war costs must be paid, as Germany's attack on Belgium, whose neutrality she had guaranteed, was a violation of international law.

(3) Whatever rights Belgium has under international law, by reason of her neutralization, are clearly shared by those Powers who guaranteed her neutrality, and incurred fearful losses in enforcing it.

(4) The other Associated Powers (*e. g.*, United States and Italy), who helped to defend Belgian neutrality, can also claim their war costs.

(5) Therefore, even on the narrow basis of the American memorandum, reparation can be claimed for the whole war cost of the Associated Powers.

(6) But independently altogether of any question of violations of international law, full reparation is demanded by the principle of justice.

(7) The principle of justice, and the reign of law between states as between individuals, have been affirmed by President Wilson and incorporated in the terms and principles of peace accepted by the Associated Powers and by Germany, which clearly cover the demand of full reparation.

(8) Therefore, whether we apply the principles of the American memorandum, or whether we independently apply the principles formulated by President Wilson and accepted, of "the reign of law"

and a just peace in either case we reach the same conclusion, that we are entitled to reparation for the full costs of the war.[5]

France's Louis-Lucien Klotz denied the validity of the Pre-Armistice Agreement in a speech delivered the following day.

The American delegation declines to take up the discussion on the basis accepted by the memoranda of all the other delegations. They refuse to discuss whether the principles which we have formulated, that Germany shall repair in its entirety all the damage which she has caused, is or is not in conformity with justice and with right.

Perhaps, if I may be permitted to interpret certain words, certain silences of Mr. Dulles, the American delegation would be disposed to admit the justice of our argument concerning reimbursement of the cost of the war. But in their view it is too late for such claims. The case has been tried and decided. We are in the presence of a formal contract which becomes binding on the parties and from which they are not permitted to depart.

The American argument rests upon this assertion, that there exists a contract between the Allied and Associated Powers on the one hand, and Germany on the other hand, and that the terms of this contract are such as to deny to the Allied Powers the right to claim reimbursement for their war costs. If the American delegation cannot definitely support this assertion, its argument falls, and we find ourselves guided no longer by contractual law but by justice alone. . . .

Every contract implies reciprocal obligations and engagements. Where do we find these elements in the Allied contract? Have we, the Associated Powers, taken—impliedly let it not be forgotten—the undertaking not to demand from Germany reimbursement for the cost of the war? And what did Germany grant us in exchange? The engagement not to continue the war, to lay down their arms? It is thus in his argument that Mr. Dulles has defined the Allied contract.

We however assert, and assert in the most formal manner, that between the exchange of notes to which the American delegation refers, and where the American delegation would find the elements of a contract, and the surrender of Germany there is no relation of cause and effect. Germany surrendered on November 11th because she was conquered, and not because she found acceptable and equitable the conditions of President Wilson and of the Associated Powers. . . .

Between the German Government and the Associated Powers there exists but one document which has the form and the spirit of an agreement—to employ the English phrase—and which could reasonably be called such, that is the Armistice Convention of November 11, 1918.

If, then, on that date Germany had not consented at least to the minimum program of the Fourteen Points, if she had not agreed to deliver us as guarantees of safety considerable areas of territory and substantial quantities of material, the Associated Powers would without doubt have continued the war. But in the one, as in the other case, it was a question of minimum guarantees warranting the cessation of hostilities that Germany sought, that had become for her an imperative necessity. . . .

As in the case of the Rhineland, we are justified in formulating demands which are not perhaps expressly included in the Fourteen Points of President Wilson, but which are based, as we are ready to show, on justice and on right. And we will not have to support these claims on the basis of public international law as appealed to by the American delegation, which law unfortunately is derived but too often from precedents of force and violence, but on the "common law" of civilized nations, to which . . . President Wilson referred in the following terms:

> The things for which the Associated peoples of the world are fighting, and which must be conceded them before there is peace, are the following:
>
> The consent of all nations to be governed in their conduct toward each other by the same principles of honor and of respect for the common law of civilized society that govern the individual citizens of all modern states in their relations with one another; to the end that all promises and covenants may be sacredly observed, no private plots or conspiracies hatched, no selfish injuries wrought with impunity, and a mutual trust established upon a mutual respect for right. . . .

Today . . . the American delegation [would] have us admit—that we have impliedly renounced recourse to this common law. . . . And that our statesmen and generals meeting at Versailles have conceded without discussion and without debate that victorious France should be a ruined France, crushed for a century, perhaps forever? I cannot accept that unless it is proved.

I am in a position to give evidence on another point, having taken part in the work at Versailles on the 2d and 4th of last November.

If, in my opinion, there is no contract in accordance with which I have waived my rights to reimbursement for certain categories of expenses resulting from the war, on the other hand there does exist a contract by the terms of which I have expressly reserved these rights.

I have said that between the Allies and Germany there is but one written document which has up till now been signed, having the form and giving rise to the legal relations of a contract. This is the armistice convention of November 11, 1918, between the Allied and Associated Powers represented by Marshal Foch and Admiral Wemyss and the German delegation.

Now, as to the question which we are discussing, does this document contain any express reservation of our rights? Is it there specified that as concerns reparation of damages we have in advance tied our hands?

Let us open this agreement to the chapter entitled "Financial Clauses," the terms of which were by us carefully considered, weighed, and formulated. They were not hastily written. What are the first words? How is the first phrase drafted?

> XIX. Reserving all subsequent claims and demands on the part of the Allies and of the United States, reparation of damage.

Here is something clear.

Our rights are reserved as to all "subsequent claims and demands."

We have before us an express clause, which implies no limitation of our rights, which stipulates a full reservation of all our rights, particularly as concerns "reparation of damage." . . .

That which exists, that to which I hold, that to which I have a right to hold, is the fact that in a contract between the Allied Powers and Germany we have reserved our rights in reference to the financial clauses and the reparation of damage "as to all future claims and demands."

Therefore I have the honor to call on you to proclaim our right to integral reparation. You will see later how by agreement this right shall be applied. We will consider whether it is wise to exert our right to the full. We will settle the question of the priority of certain claims, a priority recognized I trust by all of the states represented here. We will then have settled the principles which will permit our sub-commissions to undertake a useful work.[6]

On February 19th Mr. Dulles again addressed the Committee.

Mr. President:

The very illuminating and instructive debate of recent days has brought forward certain arguments, which, unless they can be disposed of, seriously affect the validity of the principles proposed by the American delegation. . . .

This . . . leads me to a discussion of the point which Mr. Klotz developed and which, if I understand right, was to the effect that we have no agreement with Germany as to the terms of peace. To quote his words: "There exists only one document which has the form and the spirit of a contract, of an agreement, and which can legitimately be described as such. That document is the Armistice Covenant of November 11, 1918."

Gentlemen, this is a serious assertion, the consequences of which, if it be accepted, are momentous. It means that where we thought we had a chart, we have none. . . .

If you will refresh your recollection . . . you will see that Germany initiated the discussion by a request for an armistice, which request the German Government asked the President of the United States to transmit to his associates. The President of the United States refused to transmit such a request until all of the interested parties should be in complete agreement as to the basic terms of peace. The President even went so far as to refuse to consider an armistice on the understanding that a certain program should be "the basis for peace discussion." The President insisted on the withdrawal of this phrase and the substitution in lieu thereof of the phrase "terms of peace," as to which discussion would be limited to "the practical details of their application." The President transmitted this correspondence to the Allies, who replied that they were willing to make peace on the terms specified, with two qualifications, one of which was a clarification of the term specifying the compensation which should be made by Germany. This understanding was accepted by the President and communicated to Germany. Then—and then only—was the German Government advised that an armistice would be considered. You will thus see, gentlemen, that there were two series of negotiations—one as to the terms of peace, the other as to the terms of armistice—and that until there was agreement as to the terms of peace, consideration of an armistice was postponed. I cannot believe that Mr. Klotz now seriously contends that no agreement came into being when the Allies, after carefully considering this correspondence which had passed between the United States and Germany, stated: "They declare their willingness to make peace with the German Government on the terms of peace laid down by the President's address to Congress of January, 1918, and the principles of settlement enunciated in his subsequent address." I assert that there is in that declaration the spirit —nay, more, the form and substance of an agreement. We find every element legally necessary to constitute a binding contract. We have a proposal by one party, a negotiation leading to a change of terms, and a final acceptance by all, in reliance on which all of the parties, not only Germany, but the United States and others, have changed their position.

But I do not, I am sure, have to resort to a textbook of law and prove the existence of a legal agreement. This is not a transaction between petty merchants. When great France, in that critical hour and with issues of world-wide importance at stake, solemnly and in conjunction with her Allies, said to the United States for its guidance and for transmission to Germany: "We will make peace on specific terms," I know that the United States, that the world, can count upon France making peace on these terms.

So I cannot believe that I have understood Mr. Klotz aright in this matter and that France regards itself as free to propose terms other than those adopted by her on November 4, 1918. I feel that it must rather be the thought of Mr. Klotz that the armistice agreement, occurring after the agreement as to the terms of peace, in some way modified this binding engagement which she had assumed. . . .

It appears clearly throughout the correspondence . . . that it was understood that the armistice was peculiarly a matter for military advisers. The terms of peace were first settled by the highest political authorities of the Associated Governments. Had Marshal Foch and Admiral Wemyss, great as were their positions, power to amend and overrule by the armistice which they signed terms of peace which had previously been agreed to by President Wilson, Mr. Orlando, Mr. Lloyd George and Mr. Clemenceau? Obviously not. The armistice was, as the diplomatic correspondence shows it was to be, a military instrument framed by military advisers. But did Marshal Foch and Admiral Wemyss miscontrue their authority; did they purport to introduce into the armistice provisions which would modify the terms of peace to which their superiors had previously agreed? Such action, if they took it, could not be binding. But it is clear that they did not take it.

The armistice says that, reserving all rights as to future claims and demands, certain gold and securities are to be delivered up. Why was this reservation made? Obviously not to modify or affect the terms of peace, but to insure that, as a military and interim measure, further deliveries could be demanded. The right so reserved has been exercised subsequently in renewals of the armistice which require additional surrenders of property by Germany. If, therefore, we are here sitting as an armistice commission, I fully agree that we could consider the desirability of requiring further deliveries of goods by Germany, and exercise the rights reserved in the armistice of November 11th; but we are not the armistice commission. We are the peace commission. It is not our duty to construe and to apply the terms of the military armistice, but the peace terms. . . .

We accordingly turn back to those terms of peace, and I appeal to Mr. Klotz to reaffirm the solemn declaration of his Government, made on November 4, 1918, that France is willing to make peace with Germany on the terms then specified. If he does reaffirm that declaration, he must then be prepared to consider with me, not the terms of armistice, but the "terms of peace." . . .

There is left now for consideration the third proposition, that enunciated by the Hon. Mr. Hughes, to the effect that independently of any agreement as to the terms of peace, the Associated Governments are entitled to recover war costs through the operation of the principle that rights which arose by operation of law, upon the doing of an illegal act, are not waived and can be enforced. . . .

In the case of what countries can there be claimed to be a causal relationship between the violation of Belgium and general war costs? Great Britain based its declaration of war on the violation of Belgian neutrality, and I accordingly concede that it is arguable that the war costs of the British Empire are attributable to this act. But this cannot be said of the war costs of France. War came to France as a result of the declaration of war against her by Germany. The invasion of Belgium was but an incident to the prosecution of this war against France which had previously been determined upon. The war costs of Italy cannot be alleged to bear any relationship to the invasion of Belgium. The same is true of Serbia, of Greece, of Rumania, of Czechoslovakia, of Poland, of Russia, of Japan, of the United States.

Only in the case of Belgium and of Great Britain is it even arguable that there is a causal relationship between war costs as a whole and the invasion of Belgium. Having thus clarified the scope and application of the doctrine enunciated by Mr. Hughes, let us consider its validity even in this limited sphere.

Now, gentlemen, the question of the proper construction and the legal effect of the Treaty of London of 1839 is one which we could discuss for many months and then possibly not find ourselves in agreement. I do not wish to involve the commission in these difficult questions of construction. I will merely suggest to you one of several reasons why, in my opinion, the argument of Mr. Hughes is not sound. The Treaty of 1839 is in form a treaty for the benefit of Belgium. Mr. Hughes treats it as such. Historically, it had its birth in that understanding. Belgium desired to secure certain frontiers which would be strategically sound. The then five great Powers were unwilling to grant her those frontiers, but in exchange for the acceptance by Belgium of restricted frontiers, agreed to insure Belgian neutrality. The treaty thus constitutes what, in the common law, is known as a beneficiary contract, or contract for the benefit of a third party. This means then that when Great Britain, France, Russia, Austria, and Prussia agreed to disenable themselves from making war on Belgium, the benefit of that agreement ran in favor of Belgium alone. Accordingly, when Germany made war upon Belgium that was an illegal act—illegal, that is, in respect to Belgium, who was the beneficiary of the contract that war would not be made. Any special position, therefore, that results from a violation by Germany of its covenant made to the benefit of Belgium redounds to the benefit of Belgium, and not to the benefit of the other contracting powers.

That Great Britain may have been under a duty, moral or legal, to come to the aid of Belgium does not modify in any degree our conclusion that the benefits of the treaty ran in favor of Belgium. If Great Britain, in 1839, assumed an obligation, she did so in pursuance of what she then regarded as adequate consideration, and the performance of that duty could not give rise to a special right. Mr. Hughes stated, "Great Britain and France may be compared to the policeman whose sworn task is to prevent a breach of the law." Precisely—but does the policeman receive his hire from the wrongdoer when he arrests? No; in making the arrest the policeman has but performed his duty—nobly, gallantly, at great sacrifice, if you will, but still his duty. And the reparation made by the wrongdoer is made to the victim—not to the guardian of the law. . . .

If the argument which I make is sound, it leads to the conclusion that Belgium stands in a special position by reason of Germany's breach of her covenant not to make war on Belgium. That is a conclusion which has been accepted by the whole world, even including Germany, which formally admitted the illegality of its action in respect of Belgium and the duty of making full reparation therefor. If the argument of Mr. Hughes is sound, it leads to the conclusion that Great Britain, and Great Britain alone, shares the special position of Belgium. This is a conclusion so extraordinary that the Hon. Mr. Hughes, with that common sense and bigness of heart for which he is noted, was compelled to repudiate it. What form did his repudiation take? Did he say: My conclusion is unsound, therefore I must have reached it by unsound processes of thought? No; he said: My conclusion is absurd; therefore, I will multiply it by ten and the absurdity will disappear. After adopting reasoning which if sound led to the establishment of a special privilege for Great Britain in respect of war costs, he illogically but with a generosity which we can but admire invited us all to come and share it.

Gentlemen, if we hold to the domain of reason, we cannot adopt such methods. It is clear that under no principle of international law has Germany become our debtor for the general costs of the war. Any such right, if it is to exist, can be created only by agreement. So we are forced back again, inevitably, irresistibly, to the proceedings of November 4th, and the statement of the Associated Governments that they were willing to make peace with Germany on certain terms. There is our agreement. It provides, and the Allies took special steps to specify it: "Compensation will be made by Germany for all damage done to all civilian population of the Allies and their property by the aggression of Germany by land, by sea, and from the air." That is our agreement. It is not a basis of discussion—it is a term of peace. It does not provide for the expense to Governments of maintaining military establishments. . . .

It is not agreeable for me to stand here as proponent of an argument which seems, even in principle, to be in the interest of Germany. I say "even in principle" because I believe that the propositions enunciated by the American delegation are, practically, those which will secure the maximum of reparation and its most equitable distribution. To demand the gigantic total of war costs would, I agree with Mr.

Van Den Heuvel, be to jeopardize securing that specific reparation as to which Germany must clearly recognize her liability, and the satisfaction of which will tax her resources to the limit. But even so, the American delegation would not be participating actively in this debate did we not feel that vital principles were involved. . . .

Whatever we do here is, in any event, subject to review and I seriously question whether a decision on such important questions of principle as have been discussed here is within the competence of this commission. If you will refer to the resolution creating this commission, you will find nothing empowering us to determine basic principles. This commission was created "to examine and report on the question of the amount for reparation which the enemy countries should pay, and are capable of paying, as well as the form in which payment should be made." And I think it was added, "to recommend measures to guarantee payment." It was thus evidently assumed by the commission, as, in fact, they had reason to assume, that the terms of peace were settled and that all we had to do was to "determine the practical details of their application." . . . I therefore propose that we should cease discussion here and refer back to the Supreme War Council the question of whether, in their opinion, war costs are properly to be included in the bill for reparation to be presented to the enemy.[7]

In the absence of both President Wilson and Lloyd George, the Supreme Council did not feel competent to rule on the matter of inclusion of war costs, and the American Commissioners cabled the President for his decision.

Outside of the Committee, another problem occupied the minds of the various delegates: How were the Allies to divide reparation payments among themselves? What Tardieu called "the game of percentages" was avidly played—and the game was to continue to the end of the Conference. Every Allied delegation jealously watched its counterparts, fearful that they might "put something over" which would increase their share and diminish its own. Because no accurate figures on damages were available, the game was played with constantly changing estimates, which added great zest to the sport.

As the deadlock on war costs developed in committee, Bernard Baruch presented a comparative table of estimates to his fellow Committee members:

DISTRIBUTION OF REPARATION PAYMENTS AMONG THE ALLIES, ON THE BASIS OF DAMAGES SUFFERED:[8]

	excluding war costs	*including war costs*
FRANCE	43%	24%
GREAT BRITAIN	19%	40%
BELGIUM	24% *	1.7%
ITALY	6%	6%
SERBIA	4%	1.3%
UNITED STATES	——	25%
SCATTERING	4%	2%

* Belgium's war costs were included, since she represented a special case, having been "illegally invaded."

If reparations were calculated on the sole basis of damages suffered by civilian populations, countries whose territories had been occupied and fought over would naturally get the lion's share. Great Britain would get only a very small percentage of the loot. But Bernard Baruch's table proved that, unless it were possible to wring truly astronomical amounts from Germany, Belgium and France would get more actual cash if war costs were *not* included in reparations.

The Belgians, who had most to lose, very quickly got the point and, from then on, took a determined stand against inclusion of war costs in reparations. Feeling assured that their own war costs would be covered, they could easily afford to take that position. The case was somewhat different for the French, who had one thing in common with the British: they could not justify accepting "reparations for actual damages suffered" after having consistently assured their people that "the Germans would pay for everything." According to Tardieu, however, the French delegation was greatly impressed by Baruch's argument, and, throughout March, urged the exclusion of war costs upon the heads of the governments. Tardieu states that "this was the solution decided upon by the end of the month."

This solution was greatly facilitated by President Wilson's reply to his delegation's cable. From the high seas came this message:

I feel we are bound in honor to decline to agree to the inclusion of war costs in the reparations demanded. The time to think of this was before the conditions of peace were communicated to the enemy originally. We should dissent and dissent publicly if necessary not on the ground of intrinsic injustice of it but on the ground that it is clearly inconsistent with what we deliberately led the enemy to expect and cannot honorably now alter simply because we have the power.

WOODROW WILSON[9]

When this cable was communicated to the Allies even the British gave up, and war costs, as such, were never again mentioned. As Bernard Baruch puts it:

Fortified by this vigorous support from the President, the American delegates, in informal conference, were able shortly to secure the acquiescence of Mr. Lloyd George, Mr. Clemenceau and Mr. Orlando to the fundamental principle originally enunciated by the American delegation. This was that Germany's reparation obligations were to be determined in accordance with a fair construction of the Allies' pre-armistice declaration and that such construction excluded imposing upon Germany the "costs of the war," but was limited to what may be called actual damage.[10]

Wilson's veto put Lloyd George in a very bad spot. His recent visit to England had convinced the Prime Minister that the British public was getting restive; the press, and in particular Lord Northcliffe's influential section of it, was accusing him of "letting Wilson bully him to forgo British interests on Reparations to satisfy the President's sterile idealism";[11] and discontent with his handling of affairs in Paris was building up in Parliament. If war costs could not be included in "reparations," he would have to find some other way to increase Great Britain's share in the spoils.

American and British concepts of the sums that might be wrung from Germany were very far apart. The British had been led to think in terms of Lord Cunliffe's estimates of 120 billion dollars (480 milliard gold marks); the Americans considered even one third of that sum "perfectly absurd," as Colonel House noted after meeting with two of his fellow Commissioners on February 28th.

Davis and Lamont were pre-luncheon callers to report on the question of reparations. They came later this afternoon to again report and I advised them to agree to the sum of forty billion dollars (160 milliard gold marks), but to hedge it around with safeguards, as far as the United States was concerned, so that in no event would we be either legally or morally bound to help enforce its collection. That amount seems perfectly absurd, and the French and the British are as well aware of this as we are, but in order to meet public opinion which they have misled in their several countries, they intend to insist upon an amount that they know they cannot collect.[12]

But Lloyd George's whole political life hung in the balance and he was getting desperate. Finally, the Prime Minister's fertile brain hit on a scheme that might get him off the hook, and he got in touch with Colonel House about it.

March 6, 1919: . . . lunch with Lloyd George alone at his apartment. . . . He was especially interested in the question of reparations and said if I would help him out in this direction, he would be extremely grateful. By helping him out, he meant to give a plausible reason to his people for having fooled them about the question of war costs, reparations and what not. He admitted that he knew Germany could not pay anything like the indemnity which the French and the British demanded. He said my ideas and his were not different as to the actual sum she should pay, but he wanted the amount named to be large, even if Germany would never pay it, or even if it had to be reduced later. He said it was a political matter in which the English were greatly interested and he did not want to let the Conservatives "throw him" on a question of such popular concern.[13]

Apparently the Prime Minister's proposal left the Colonel at a loss for words. At least, he does not record his reply. A few days later this conversation was to have an even more breathtaking sequel.

Lloyd George kept busy working every side of the street. In the Council of Four, where House substituted for the absent President, the Prime Minister tried at least to increase Britain's percentage of the gross. He says:

I placed before M. Clemenceau and Colonel House the position in respect to indemnity; that we could not agree to any proposal that postponed payment in respect of indemnity until the reparation claims had been completely discharged; that it was more than possible that Germany might not be able to do more than pay the reparation claims, in which case Britain would be left out altogether. I further suggested that the instalments should be divided in the proportion of three to two—three being allocated to reparation, and two to indemnity, in proportion to the claims allowed for each country under each head. M. Clemenceau said that of course he could not be expected to answer without further consideration, but that he would let me know soon. He then asked Colonel House what he thought of the plan, and Colonel House replied that he thought that it was a very fair plan and he afterwards repeated this observation. This seemed to make an impression on Clemenceau.[14]

Even if Clemenceau were to accept Lloyd George's proposal, that would only improve Britain's quota in the reparation payments by a few percentage points. The Prime Minister had to work another angle.

The Reparation Subcommittee was unable to arrive at any definite and concrete suggestions as to how much Germany ought to pay and how much she could pay. The Big Four therefore decided to set up a Special Secret Committee that would produce some definite figures they could work with. Colonel House has an account of, and some caustic comments on, that meeting.

March 10, 1919: The two most important events of the day were the conference between Clemenceau, Lloyd George and myself at the Ministry of War at 10:30, and the meeting in the afternoon at the Quai d'Orsay.

Lloyd George asked Clemenceau if he had thought over his proposal concerning the division of the sum which, it will be remembered, was three parts for reparation and two parts to go for the cost of the war, to be called, however, something else. . . . Clemenceau claimed that he had not reached a conclusion. We then discussed the general financial question, especially as to reparations, and agreed to appoint representatives to meet at 10 o'clock tomorrow morning to discuss the question and to report back to us. Clemenceau named Loucheur, I named Norman Davis and Lloyd George . . . named Montagu, Secretary of State for India. . . .

Both Clemenceau and Lloyd George said they hoped a large sum would be agreed upon because of the political situations in England and France. I was amused and struck by the cynical way in which they discussed their people. Both of them practically confessed that they knew Germany could not pay anything like the sum they had in mind to suggest, and that it was merely done to meet the expectations and desires of their constituents. Lloyd George declared that he had not purposely misled the English people but that some how [*sic*], during the recent election, there was a perfect groundswell for the Germans to pay the cost of the war, and while he knew it was an impossibility to realize such expectations, he followed and was one of the most vociferous of the lot in demanding that the cost of the war should be paid by Germany.[15]

Though Lloyd George and Clemenceau were unanimous in demanding that an impossible sum be written into the Treaty, their motives were very different. Lloyd George needed that sum purely to quiet his constituents, and he was quite willing to permit the Germans to default on it and pay a far smaller, "reasonable" amount. Clemenceau, on the other hand, wanted a large sum, one that Germany could not possibly pay, because French occupation of the Rhineland was to be linked with reparation payments in the Treaty and evacuation would be made a *quid pro quo* of full payment of reparations. If the sum written into the Treaty could be made large enough so that Germany could never pay it, then France would have the Rhineland, no matter what other sections of the Treaty provided.

However, the Special Secret Committee did not come up to the expectations of the Big Four. Instead of producing the "political sum" Lloyd George and Clemenceau needed, the experts, all reasonable men, including M. Loucheur who was gambling with his political life, had worked out a "maximum realizable sum," roughly thirty billion dollars (120 milliard gold marks). Messrs. Davis, Montagu and Loucheur reported:

In endeavoring to arrive at what Germany can pay and how she can pay it, it is necessary to take into consideration the following questions:

(a) The future labor and political situation of Germany and the length of time necessary for her to return to her pre-war efficiency;

(b) Whether or not she can be made to work for the next 30 years practically on a war basis, by restricting her imports to absolute necessities and, in addition, be given freedom of the markets of the world for the sale of her products;

(c) To what extent such a plan will throw the burden of reparation on England and France by closing Germany as a market for their export products and making these countries, together with other countries of the world, a dumping ground for Germany's surplus products, to the detriment of the trade of the countries concerned;

(d) Just what amount Germany would be willing to undertake to pay without breaking off negotiations and forcing military occupation or other similar action upon the Allies.

Before the war Germany's exports were less than her imports. In 1913 (the best year in her history), Germany's imports exceeded her exports by 300 million dollars. Against this unfavorable balance, her receipts from mercantile freights, profits of German enterprises and investments abroad, insurance and remittances from Germans living abroad, amounted to approximately 700 to 800 million dollars. This covered the trade deficit and left a surplus of approximately 400 to 500 million dollars. If her ships and her foreign investments are taken from her, this source of income will be withdrawn, and according to pre-war figures Germany would not be able to make any payment abroad. However, Germany spent approximately 400 million dollars per annum on her Army and Navy, and if the amount of labor and material thus consumed were turned into the production of essentials, Germany could have produced an exportable surplus, approximately sufficient to cover her trade deficit and leave a balance of 100 million dollars—assuming that a market could have been found for such exportable surplus.

On the other hand, there was apparently, in 1913, no unfilled demand for any further products, and if Germany had exported such additional amount, it would have been through a corresponding decrease in the exports of other countries.

The question therefore resolves itself entirely into how much can be saved by Germany confining her imports to essentials, and how much can the consumptive power of the world be increased.

On a liberal basis, we estimate that Germany might possibly pay from 10 to 20 billion dollars over a period of 20 to 30 years.

As nearly as we can judge from the present estimates, the damage done by Germany for which she is liable under the strictest interpretation of the exchange of notes between President Wilson and the German Government, as modified by the Allies on November 4 and accepted by President Wilson, might amount to approximately 25 billion dollars. It is felt that Germany should, if possible, be forced to pay at least this amount, and that, if the demands are confined to this interpretation, which the Germans have accepted, the moral opinion of the world would force Germany to pay this amount if she can do so, no matter how many years it may take to do so. On the other hand, it is felt that if Germany should even reluctantly obligate herself to pay more than that, she might, within a few years, repudiate the entire obligation as having been an imposition, and the moral opinion of the world might support her in this. We believe, however, that this will not arise, because Germany would prefer an occupation rather than agree to any greater amount [than 30 billion dollars].

As to the estimates which have been given by some eminent bankers, to the effect that Germany would be able, over a period of 30 years, to pay 3 or 4 billion dollars per annum, we can say only that we are satisfied that such a performance on the part of Germany is utterly impossible, because in the first place she would never agree to such an undertaking, and in the second place, even if she were able to do so, which is improbable, it could only be done by absolutely destroying the trade of England and France and other countries of the world, and in order to do so Germany would have to develop a state of efficiency such as has never been known in the history of the world, and if she can do this, there is nothing we can do which would prevent Germany from overrunning the world thereafter.

We therefore recommend that a demand be made upon Germany to pay a capital sum of 30 billion dollars, one-half of which shall be paid in dollars or sterling or gold marks at the standard of weight and fineness at the beginning of the war, and that the other half should be payable in German currency, at par of exchange.

Of the 15 billion dollars to be paid in foreign currency, we think that approximately 4 or 5 billion dollars might be paid by Germany within the next two or three years, through the liquidation of her foreign properties abroad, including the amount credited to her for her merchant fleet and German properties in ceded territories. The balance of this amount, say 10 or 11 billion dollars, we think should be paid, beginning in 5 years, and amortized within 30 years.

We are recommending that half of the 30 billion dollars be paid in German currency, because we are satisfied it cannot be paid in any other way. The German currency received in this way could be reinvested to a certain extent in Germany and could probably be withdrawn in the next 30 to 60 years.

At the beginning of the war, the total national wealth of Germany was estimated at 75 billion dollars, of which 15 billion dollars was invested in industrial enterprises. Even if all of the German industries were purchased by foreign capital, it would therefore be impossible to invest more than 15 billion dollars now in such a way—which is absolute proof of the impossibility of investing German marks to the extent reckoned by the parties who have made such high estimates as to Germany's ability to pay.

(We subsequently found Germany did not have 4 or 5 billion in foreign countries and all idea of this dropped.)[16]

The Big Four, of course, turned down their Special Committee's report. Neither Lloyd George nor Clemenceau could afford to think in terms as small as those presented by Davis, Montagu and Loucheur.

Having failed again to attain the desired end by circumventing the CRD and its subcommittees, Lloyd George had one more try at enlisting the help of his American friends. His first approach to Colonel House had been purely tentative and he had received no reply of any kind. He now sent Bonar Law into the breach with a very definite proposal, one that required an answer. As usual, Colonel House diligently records the British *démarche.*

March 16, 1919: Bonar Law, Davis tells me, made an open proposal to him today that we should agree to ask fifty billion dollars indemnity from Germany but to take it in marks, and to even let the Germans know privately that we did not expect her to pay the full amount, and after five years or some such period, she would not be expected to pay anything further. Davis very rightly replied that he did not think the United States would wish to be a party to such transaction. The purpose, of course, is to fool the British public.

Davis and I feel, and I so expressed myself to Balfour, that the wise thing to do would be to tell the British public that Germany is bankrupt and that the British financial experts and statesmen were mistaken in believing she could pay the enormous sums they and their public at one time had in mind. That, if it were possible to get such an amount out of Germany, it would only be possible in the event the British would consent to lend the Germans an enormous sum in order to revive their commerce. If they did this, Germany would then become not only a competitor for British trade throughout the world, but would probably come near monopolizing it. It would be better therefore to accept Germany as a bankrupt and to take what she could actually pay, or what was in sight rather than create another British debt in order to place Germany in a condition to be a commercial rival. Balfour agreed with this conclusion and will pass it on to both George and Law.[17]

The American Commissioners were deeply shocked by the Prime Minister's suggestion that they connive with the British and the enemy, with whom they were, after all, still at war, to pull the wool over the eyes of the British public and, incidentally, deceive their common ally, France. Colonel House, who understood the Prime Minister's quandary, took pity on him and submitted a plan of his own. He notes in his diary on March 17th:

Wiseman . . . said George was worried about the question of reparation, both as to amount and as to how he was to satisfy the British public. I wrote out a plan which I told Wiseman to submit to him and which I thought might cover the case. The feature of my suggestion was that the sum of thirty billion dollars could be set as a maximum figure, and that a commission should meet once a year to determine how much Germany could pay the following year and also to determine whether the amount of thirty billion was excessive for reparation demands. In this way the French and English could let Germany evade an impossible payment.[18]

No doubt, the Colonel meant well, but he apparently did not realize that Lloyd George's proposals were his only way of saying that he would like to join the Americans in their "sensible" reparation policy, but could neither offend his electorate nor officially line up against France. Besides, Colonel House's thirty billions were only three-fifths of the fifty billions Lloyd George had set his heart on. In addition, even if he himself had accepted the Colonel's suggestions, there was not the slightest chance that Clemenceau would go along. The House plan would not give

France an excuse to remain on the left bank of the Rhine, which was at all times her foremost war aim.

By their refusal to permit the inclusion of "war costs" in "reparations" the Americans had produced the dilemma in which the British and the French found themselves. Lloyd George's efforts to enlist the help of his American friends had generated the idea of "theoretical liability" as opposed to "actual liability." Looking for a formula to soften the effects of American intransigence and, incidentally, to accommodate Lloyd George, John Foster Dulles produced what became known as the "war guilt" clauses of the Treaty.

Philip M. Burnett, the United States reparation expert, writes:

> The second force in the resolution of the war costs issue, that of the American concession on theoretical responsibility, was introduced, . . . by Dulles, outside the formal discussion. On February 21, Dulles drafted an unofficial text reflecting the thought of the members of the American delegation. According to this, Germany should be made liable for war costs, *only in theory*. "Certain of the governments at war with Germany," Dulles wrote, "believing that it is just and within the contemplation of the principles agreed to . . . that the German Government shall . . . make reparation for the entire cost of the war . . . the Government of Germany recognizes its liability in the premises." He added: "It is agreed, however, that the ability of the German Government . . . to make reparation is limited . . . and accordingly the governments at war with Germany renounce the right to insist upon reparation other than is expressly specified for herein." This concept of a high theoretical liability (that is, for integral reparation) with a lower actual liability, reworded by Dulles in successive drafts, was ultimately embodied . . . in the text of the so-called "war guilt" clauses of the Treaties. Its purpose . . . was to enable Allied statesmen to fulfill at least in words the expectations of their constituents. As a concession from the Americans to their Allies, it became the mitigating element in the final Allied surrender on the war costs issue.[19]

The "war guilt" clauses, Articles 231 and 232 of the Treaty of Versailles, which introduce Part VIII, the section on Reparations, read:

Section I.

GENERAL PROVISIONS.

Article 231.

The Allied and Associated Governments affirm, and Germany accepts, the responsibility of Germany and her Allies for causing all the loss and damage to which the Allied and Associated Governments and their nationals have been subjected as a consequence of a war imposed upon them by the aggression of Germany and her Allies.

Article 232.

The Allied and Associated Governments recognize that the resources of Germany are not adequate, after taking into account permanent diminutions of such resources which will result from other provisions of the present Treaty, to make complete reparation for all such loss and damage.
The Allied and Associated Governments, however, require, and Germany undertakes, that she will make compensation for all damage done to the civilian population of the Allied and Associated Powers and to their property during the period of the belligerency of each as an Allied or Associated Power against Germany by such aggression by land, by sea and from the air, and in general all damage as defined in Annex I. hereto. . . .[20]

These clauses proved the main target of German popular anger and indignation, and very largely contributed to the world's opinion that the Treaty of Versailles was based upon injustice. They were the rallying point of German nationalist sentiment in the 1920's and '30's, and world opinion, which by then had swung away from blaming Germany and her Allies for causing the war, and had generally accepted the theory that the war had been brought on by economic causes, saw in the articles proof of the Treaty's inherent injustice.

John Foster Dulles, writing in 1938, when the consequences of Article 231 were already fully apparent, explains the almost accidental way this fatal clause was born.

Analysis of the documents shows that the participants suffered from "blind spots." Of these the most important is that illustrated by the "war guilt" provision (Article 231). In the light of subsequent developments it may be that this article was the most important single article in the Treaty. Thereby, in German eyes, Germany was branded with moral guilt for the World War, and the German people, under threat of wholesale starvation and military devastation, were compelled to accept this verdict as true. It was the revulsion of the German people from this article of the Treaty which, above all else, laid the foundation for the Germany which we see today. There was thus created a sense of injustice and a reaction against the imputed moral inferiority which was so intense as easily to lend itself to capitalization by leaders who were adept at arousing and directing human emotion. The significance of Article 231 was not adequately perceived by the reparation delegates or apparently by their Chiefs of State. The article emerged as an attempted compromise of the American viewpoint and that of the Allied Powers with respect to Germany's liability for "war costs." The Allies had, as we have noted, reluctantly acquiesced in the stand of President Wilson and the American delegation that Germany's contractual liability for reparation should be deemed limited by the Pre-Armistice Agreement and that this did not contemplate liability for "war costs." But while the Allies were prepared to concede that the Treaty should embody the *consequences* of such acquiescence on their part, they were not willing, doubtless for political reasons, that the Treaty should record the fact that by the Pre-Armistice Agreement they had waived that right to "integral" reparation which their people demanded. The British and French were thus insistent that the Treaty should consecrate their right to full reparation and excuse the exaction of only a part thereof on the ground of Germany's limited capacity to pay. In view of the extreme difficulty encountered in securing Allied acceptance of any limitation flowing from the Pre-Armistice Agreement, the American delegates were disposed to accept a compromise in form and Article 231 was the expression of that compromise.

So intent were the American, British, and French delegates upon finding words that would compromise their own differences, so swayed were they by emotion against Germany, that the permanent effect upon Germany was not adequately perceived or considered. The reparation delegates had never been charged with the problem of war responsibility, which had been entrusted to another section of the Conference. They had no thought of consciously trespassing upon the work of the "Penalties" section. In their own minds they were merely finding a formula for solving different opinions as to Germany's theoretical liability for reparation. It came therefore as a surprise when German observations on the Conditions of Peace showed that this section could plausibly be, and in fact was, considered to be a historical judgment of "war guilt." The Treaty terms had by then become so generally known that modification of Article 231 was politically impossible and the reply of the Allied and Associated Powers to the German observations may have completed the metamorphosis of Article 231 from that which had originally been in the minds of the draughtsmen. It can thus be said that the profound significance of this article of the Treaty came about through accident, rather than design.[21]

But Dulles' efforts provided neither the British nor the French with any greater reparation amounts, and Lloyd George desperately cast about to find some heading under which Britain's share of Germany's payments might possibly be increased. He finally hit upon "Pensions and Allowances." If pensions paid to veterans and allowances paid to the disabled and the widows and orphans of the war were to be included in the claims against Germany, Great Britain's share in the sums obtained would skyrocket and Lloyd George would be able to "point with pride" instead of having to "deeply regret." He therefore had Lord Sumner draw up a lengthy memorandum in which were set forth all the legal arguments for including pensions in the reparation claims against Germany. When that document was presented to Wilson, the President angrily brushed it aside as an attempt to circumvent his expressed determination to stick to "what we deliberately led the enemy to expect and cannot honorably alter simply because we have the power."

But Lloyd George, refusing to accept defeat, enlisted the aid of General Smuts, with whom Wilson was on the very best of terms. Smuts produced a short and powerful paper setting forth in human terms what Sumner had attempted to formulate in legal phraseology. The purpose was the same: inclusion of pensions and allowances in reparations.

March 31, 1919

The extent to which reparation can be claimed from Germany depends in the main on the meaning of the last reservation made by the Allies in their Note to President Wilson of — November, 1918. That reservation was agreed to by President Wilson and accepted by the German Government in the Armistice negotiations, and was in the following terms:

> "Further, in the conditions of peace laid down in his address to Congress on January 8th, 1918, the President declared that invaded territories must be restored, as well as evacuated and made free. The Allied Governments feel that no doubt ought to be allowed to exist as to what this provision implies. By it they understand that compensation will be made by Germany for all damage done to the civilian population of the Allies and to their property by the aggression of Germany by land, by sea, and from the air."

In this reservation a careful distinction must be made between the quotation from the President, which refers to the evacuation and restoration of the invaded territories, and the implication which the Allies find in that quotation and which they proceed to enunciate as a principle of general applicability. The Allies found in the President's provision for restoration of the invaded territories a general principle implied of far-reaching scope. This principle is that of compensation for all damage to the civilian population of the Allies in their persons or property, which resulted from the German aggression, and whether done on land or sea or from the air. By accepting this comprehensive principle (as the German Government did) they acknowledged their liability to compensation for all damage to the civilian population or their property wherever and however arising, so long as it was the result of German aggression. The President's limitation to restoration of the invaded territories only of some of the Allies was clearly abandoned.

The next question is how to understand the phrase "civilian population" in the above reservation, and it can be most conveniently answered by an illustration. A shop keeper in a village in northern France lost his shop through enemy bombardment, and was himself badly wounded. He would be entitled as one of the civilian population to compensation for the loss of his property and for his personal disablement. He subsequently recovered completely, was called up for military service, and after being badly wounded and spending some time in the hospitals was discharged as permanently unfit. The expense he was to the French Government during this period as a soldier (his pay and maintenance, his uniform, rifle, ammunition, his keep in hospital, etc.) was not damage to a civilian, but military loss to his Government, and it is therefore arguable that the French Government cannot recover compensation for such expense under the above reservation. His wife, however, was during this period deprived of her bread-winner, and she therefore suffered damage as a member of the civilian population, for which she would be entitled to compensation. In other words the separation allowances paid to her and her children during this period by the French Government would have to be made good by the German Government, as the compensation which the allowances represent was their liability. After the soldier's discharge as unfit, he rejoins the civilian population, and as for the future he cannot (in whole or in part) earn his own livelihood, he is suffering damage as a member of the civilian population, for which the German Government are again liable to make compensation. In other words the pension for disablement which he draws from the French Government is really a liability of the German Government, which they must under the above reservation make good to the French Government. It could not be argued that as he was disabled while a soldier he does not suffer damage as a civilian after his discharge if he is unfit to do his ordinary work. He does literally suffer as [a] civilian after his discharge, and his pension is intended to make good this damage, and is therefore a liability of the German Government. If he had been killed on active service, his wife as a civilian would have been totally deprived of her bread-winner, and would be entitled to compensation. In other words the pension she would draw from the French Government would really be a liability of the German Government under the above reservation, and would have to be made good by them to the French Government.

The plain, commonsense construction of the reservation, therefore, leads to the conclusion that, while direct war expenditure (such as the pay and equipment of soldiers, the cost of rifles, guns and ordnance and all similar expenditure) could perhaps not be recovered from the Germans, yet disablement pensions to discharged soldiers, or pensions to widows and orphans or separation allowances paid to their wives and children during the period of their military service are all items representing compensation to members of the civilian population for damage sustained by them, for which the German Government are liable. What was spent by the Allied Governments on the soldier himself, or on the mechanical appliances of war, might perhaps not be recoverable from the German Government under the reservation, as not being in any plain and direct sense damage to the civilian population. But what was or is spent on the citizen before he became a soldier, or after he has ceased to be a soldier, or at any time on his family, represents compensation for damage done to civilians and must be made good by the German Government under any fair interpretation of the above reservation. This includes all war pensions and separation allowances; which the German Government are liable to make good, in addition to reparation or compensation for all damage done to property of the Allied peoples.[22]

Woodrow Wilson was unable to withstand the heartrending arguments of his South African friend. Much to the dismay of his advisers he decided to permit inclusion of "pensions and allowances" in the reparation claims Germany was to be billed for. The immediate reaction of the American Commissioners was set down in a memorandum by Dulles.

There were present President Wilson, and Messrs Baruch, Davis, Lamont, McCormick & Dulles. The President was first shown the reparation plan which had been agreed to the previous day with Messrs Montagu and Keynes and which provided for a determination by a commission of the amount of damage for which the enemy should make reparation and which further provided for a reference to arbitral decision of the question of the inclusion of any category of damage as to which any member of the commission entertained doubt and provided the capacity of the enemy to pay was not exhausted without the inclusion of such item. It was explained to the President that this was a scheme to avoid a present decision by the American Commissioners on the propriety of including pensions and separation allowances. It was further stated to the President that Mr. Lloyd George had refused to accept this plan and had insisted unqualifiedly for the inclusion of the items mentioned. This compelled a decision by the U. S. The President stated that he had been very much impressed by a memorandum by Smuts in favor of pensions and separation allowances and was clearly disposed to feel that the deprivation of the civilian population of the services and earning capacity of persons who were called to the colors and then perhaps killed or wounded was "damage to the civilian population" in the sense of the Allied declaration of Nov. 4th. Mr. McCormick pointed out that the legal advisors of the Commission, and including Mr. John W. Davis felt that such damage was not within the meaning of such Allied declaration when this declaration was subjected to construction and in the light of the surrounding circumstances. The President stated in substance that he did not regard this as a matter for decision in accordance with strict legal principles; that it was probable that the question of pensions was not specifically considered in November and that the statement then made was in a very general way a loose terminology. He was, however, continuously finding new meanings and the necessity of broad application of principles previously enunciated even though imperfectly, and that he felt that justice would be done by compelling the enemy to make good, if they were able, damage of this category. Mr. Dulles pointed out that it was very difficult to draw any logical distinction between a family which had been damaged by having their breadwinner drafted and another family which had been damaged to an equivalent extent by having to pay for the equipment of that soldier and that there was danger that to accept pensions would involve admitting against the enemy all war costs, including the cost of maintaining military organizations. The President stated that he did not feel bound by considerations of logic and that where in fact the state had made payments to the civilian population to save them from loss to which they would otherwise have been subjected it was a proper subject of reparation under the agreed terms of peace. It was thereupon agreed that pensions, including those in the form of separation allowances would be allowed. The President proposed that the French scale should be adopted.

[*signed*] JOHN FOSTER DULLES
April 1, 1919[23]

Another participant, Lamont, afterwards wrote:

. . . I well remember the day upon which President Wilson determined to support the inclusion of pensions in the reparation bill. Some of us were gathered in his library in the Place des États-Unis, having been summoned by him to discuss this particular question of pensions. We explained to him that we couldn't find a single lawyer in the American delegation that would give an opinion in favor of including pensions. All the logic was against it. "Logic! Logic!" exclaimed the President, "I don't give a damn for logic. I am going to include pensions!" Now Mr. Wilson was, least of all men, lacking in logic. For logicians who may stand aghast at his offhand utterance, I hasten to explain that it was not a contempt of logic, but simply an impatience of technicality; a determination to brush aside verbiage and get at the root of things. There was not one of us in the room whose heart did not beat with a like feeling. . . .[24]

In a letter to Philip Burnett, dated May 24, 1937:

Mr. Lamont stated that the last sentence of the passage . . . ("There was not one of us in the room whose heart did not beat with a like feeling") has been found sometimes to give a wrong impression. He continued: "In this sentence I meant to indicate clearly my sympathy and the sympathy of the rest of us present with the general feeling expressed by President Wilson that in some occasions a strong sentiment is a matter worthy of applause rather than adverse criticism. I find, however, that casual readers of this sentence are inclined to think that I meant at the end that we sympathized with President Wilson in his attitude *to include pensions*. That was by no means the case. Our opinions were absolutely unchanged, as all the preceding paragraphs show. It was only in the matter of the President's showing of a very generous human feeling that we showed sympathy. . . ."[25]

Inclusion of "pensions and allowances" in the amount Germany might be legitimately billed for almost doubled the sum the Allies could demand from the enemy. For all practical purposes, however, the inclusion only had the effect of increasing the percentage Great Britain would receive and reducing the French share in proportion. Bernard Baruch clearly demonstated the reasons.

The inclusion of these items was vigorously urged by all the Allies, particularly Great Britain and France. With the abandonment of general war costs, these items afforded the only remaining basis for a large financial compensation from Germany for the tremendous sacrifices in blood and treasure which had been made by the British Empire. The French were insistent in view of the demands of their people that Germany should pay and thus relieve this sorely tried people, who have suffered more than the world probably will ever realize.

Unless the French delegates were firmly convinced of Germany's ability to pay considerably in excess of a capital sum of $15,000,-

000,000, it is difficult to understand their acceptance of the inclusion of pensions and separation allowances in the categories which Germany had to pay. It was forcibly brought to their attention that probably Germany could not pay much more than a capital sum of $15,000,000,000. Hence, if pensions and separation allowances were included in the bill *pari-passu* with the other categories, France would not receive so large an amount as if these items were left out.

Without pensions and separation allowances, the bill against Germany was estimated to be approximately $15,000,000,000, which it was generally thought she could pay. France would have received full payment for her devastated areas. With the inclusion of pensions and separation allowances without a priority for the devastated areas, France would have a larger bill to present, but would receive a less sum of money than if she had excluded these items. On the other hand, England and her dominions would get more.

Sooner or later, if the amount of Germany's indebtedness is fixed at about a capital sum of $15,000,000,000, France must insist either upon a priority for her devastated areas or a larger percentage than her claims under the categories would entitle her to; otherwise she will lose out.

There was a division among the American delegation which made it frankly hesitant between maintaining on the one hand its original strict and possibly legalistic construction of the pre-armistice declaration (which would have excluded pensions and separation allowances), and supporting on the other hand a liberal construction which would admit the right of compensation for damage to the homes and families behind the front as well as damage to the houses at the front.

Some advanced the principle that financial loss resulting from the absence of a wage earner did not cause any more "damage to the civilian population" than did an equal financial loss involved in the payment of taxes to provide military equipment and like war costs. On the other hand, it would not be easy to meet the contention that Germany should be liable for compensation not merely for damage to the buildings upon which civilians depended for housing, but also for injury or loss of life of those upon whom the civilians depended for support. Payment for a destroyed chimney was not to be placed above compensation for a lost life or a pension for a blinded or wounded soldier.

In addition, it was argued that the inclusion of these terms would not increase the amount which Germany would pay. Her debit without them would amount to all that she could pay as a capital sum. It was urged that it merely changed the proportion of the distribution of collections among the Allies on what seemed to them to be a more equitable and satisfactory basis.[26]

At last the British Prime Minister's tortuous labors had been crowned with success. Jan Smuts' formula assured Great Britain and the Dominions the main share of whatever sum of money might be squeezed from the lemon. The French attitude is understandable in light of the primary French objective: to force upon the Germans a sum far in excess of their ability to pay. Only secondarily were the French interested in laying their hands on actual cash, despite their official protestations. All that remained for the Conference to do now was to agree on the total amount of damage suffered by the occupied territories, calculate the amount of "pensions and allowances" the belligerents would have to shoulder, ascertain how much Germany could be made to pay and how long it would take her to pay it, and then write the sum total into the Peace Treaty.

However, the Peace Conference never solved any one of those problems. Neither of the reparation subcommittees charged with determining how much Germany could and should pay were able to come up with any concrete sums, or even reasonable estimates. By the end of March, all hope of writing a fixed sum into the Treaty had faded. The reasons for this have been summarized by Bernard Baruch.

. . . The first thought, and a perfectly proper one, that occurs is, Why was not a fixed sum determined and settled in the Treaty of Peace? The American contingent contended all the way through for a fixed and reasonable sum. Their reasons were that it was better for all concerned to have a definite amount. It was well for the Allies so that they would know exactly what they could depend upon to aid in the rehabilitation of their own financial and economic life, and it was well for Germany and the other debtor nations to know what they had to pay, so that they could set about paying it. While all might have agreed that a fixed sum should be determined within the limit of Germany's ability to pay, many difficulties appeared.

No one knew how much Germany owed. . . . No one knew how much Germany could pay. . . . There was a wide divergence among the Allied experts as to what Germany could pay. The amounts discussed varied from $8,000,000,000 to $120,000,000,000, both extremes, singularly, being of English origin. One of the difficulties in the situation was that a certain great English financial expert asserted with confidence that Germany could pay the latter figure. The amount of damages under the treaty categories was estimated by various delegates at from $25,000,000,000 to several times that sum.

Another obstacle in the way of fixing a definite sum was the unwillingness of the various delegations to present official estimates of the amount of their damage. During meeting after meeting of the first sub-committee of the Commission on Reparation, the American delegates urged and pleaded for figures of damages. They recognized that no precisely accurate figures could then, if ever, be given. There were, however, methods of computation available which could be trusted to give approximately accurate results. The American delegates themselves had such estimates not only for the United States, but for other nations. The figures were based on the field examinations and studies made by American experts. But while each nation sought access to these American estimates as a guide to the damage suffered by other nations, no nation was willing to accept the American estimate as applicable to itself.

The British delegation was disposed to support the American delegation in its efforts to secure definite figures and itself finally filed a provisional estimate of British losses. The French remained obdurate to the end and refused to make any estimate of their losses, on the ground that at that time such estimates would be only guess-work, and that the least conscientious guesser would be the greatest gainer.

Finally, the American delegation took the position that it could not consent to demanding any fixed sum from Germany unless satisfied of damage to at least that amount.

The refusal of most of the Allies to introduce any evidence of their own on this point or to accept the American estimates was, therefore, one of the compelling reasons leading to the postponement of fixing the amount of the German indemnity to a time when the amount of damage could be more scientifically estimated. The American delegates could with difficulty resist giving opportunity for scientific and careful estimation and checking of each nation's claims. It was fairly obvious that such claims would exceed Germany's ability to pay, yet the precise accuracy of each claim was none the less of great practical moment. This was the more true, since these claims were then expected to constitute the basis upon which each nation was to share in the payments that Germany makes.

The situation was further complicated by the attitude of the peoples of the nations involved. They demanded the uttermost farthing from Germany under the categories, on the theory that their burdens should not be made heavier to themselves and lighter to Germany. Germany in 1870 had been enabled to extract from France $1,000,000,000, an amount then not dreamed possible of payment. Germany had, in a short period of time, grasped such a large share of the world's trade as to create a perhaps exaggerated impression of her commercial and financial powers and recuperative ability. These facts made even the most conservative pause in determining the amount within her ability to pay. Indeed, there was divergence of opinion even among delegations as to the amount that Germany could pay.

Many doubted the wisdom of collecting too large an amount because of the adverse effect it might have upon the creditor nations, and argued along the following line:

> Obviously only a relatively small portion of Germany's debt could be paid out of her then existing resources. The limit of her resources was agreed upon to be not more than $5,000,000,000, including ships, credits, etc. From this amount was to be subtracted the payment for the armies of occupation and amounts necessary for food and raw materials for Germany's rehabilitation. Further payments would have to be earned by the performance of services for the rest of the world in the form primarily of exports.
>
> The amount of reparation thus becomes the measure of service which the world is willing that Germany should render to it. Large reparations could be paid only under conditions whereby the world affords Germany every encouragement to render to the balance of the world more service than the balance of the world renders to Germany. It further implies that the Allied and Associated Powers will force the German people to surpass their own in modesty of living, in industry, and in productive energy. Qualities which every Allied Government would desire to inculcate into their own people would be adopted by the German people, thanks to the external coercion which the Allied and Associated Powers would be threatening.
>
> Germany would become the workshop of the world. Not only

would the world's market be opened to the goods made in Germany, but the economic life of the world would necessarily adjust itself to the dependence upon German service. Once the reparation period were passed, it would be impossible for the economic fabric of the world at once to be readjusted to independence of that service upon which it had long become dependent. Trade would continue to move in its accustomed channels. Now, however, Germany's excess of service to the world would be at a price, with the result that the value of service rendered by Germany as reparation during the next generation would, in large part, be recovered by Germany in succeeding generations, and Germany would dominate the economic movement of the world.

In the unanimous report of the reparations section of the Peace Conference, it is stated that large reparation payments will require that Germany "turn herself into a nation of exporters organized for the purpose of paying the reparation claims of the Associated Governments, . . . The development by the enemy countries of such a policy as just described may lead to the creation, especially in Germany, of an organization so highly developed and so skillful as to be calculated in the future to have considerable and perhaps unfavorable influence upon the markets of the world."

While the force of the foregoing observations appealed in principle to some, it was natural that the various Allied and Associated Powers should have different practical reactions. France, burdened with debts, with great industrial areas blasted, with man power shattered, was concerned primarily with securing relief during the next generation. In the face of immediate financial and economic problems of extreme gravity, the specter of German economic supremacy thirty years hence did not appear alarming, particularly as France herself had never been a dominant factor in international trade.

This attitude of France was largely shared by Italy and Serbia. Belgium, however, was apparently more apprehensive of the danger of forcing Germany to organize into a great industrial machine. Great Britain should logically have been even more apprehensive, as being less dependent upon relief from Germany and as desirous herself to play the principal role of manufacturer and broker for the world. The English were, however, reluctant frankly to adopt a policy of moderate reparation, which, however much in the real interest of

Great Britain, would have involved a direct repudiation of election pledges.

The United States, while directly involved to a relatively small amount, was interested from the standpoint of stabilizing world conditions. If it is to be a recipient of German reparation payments, it will be only to a comparatively small extent. *But unquestionably the industrial and financial development of the whole world for a long time to come will be largely influenced by the reparation settlement.*

The Americans continually brought forward the necessity of fixing a definite sum. They urged the necessity of doing so because of the needs of the Allies themselves. They urged that money given now and expended would be of greater value than a larger sum received later. They urged the crying need of all the Allied peoples for rehabilitation and readjustment, and the necessity for this purpose of a new basis of credit. What they had in mind was the preservation of the economic structure and the saving of Europe from bankruptcy.

The President and his financial advisers passed days and weeks vainly endeavoring to convince their colleagues in the Allied and Associated Governments that it was impossible for Germany to pay anything like the sums required under the categories. They further submitted that even if this were possible, the Allied Governments could not afford, and would in time recognize that it was not to their advantage, to exact payments that could be made only at the expense of their own trade. *Therefore, in the American view it was to the interest of the Allied and Associated Governments to fix a reasonable, definite amount that Germany could pay and that they could afford to have her pay. . . .*

To expect that these problems could receive any wise final solution at the Peace Conference itself discloses a visionary confidence that ignores the complexity of the questions and the difficulty of the conditions under which the peace negotiators had to labor.

The world demanded and was entitled to expect a prompt formulation of conditions of peace. Final solution of the reparation clauses necessarily had to be deferred. The difficulties were accentuated by the need of securing acceptance of the reparation solution by the affected nations that were to be signatories to the treaty. All of these nations were interested in reparations from varying points of view.

Furthermore, reparations had become a leading popular and political issue among the European allies. The white heat of war had not yet had time to cool. Reparation was popularly regarded as a measure of moral retribution rather than as an index of future trade movements. This popular feeling could not but influence the peace delegates.

One must be either ignorant, vicious, or an impractical idealist to contend that in the foregoing circumstances it was humanly possible to have found at the Peace Conference a sound, definitive solution of the German reparation problem which would have met with ratification. No one man or group of men is responsible for the conditions which created this situation; they inhered in the character of the war itself and in the war's aftermath.

The American delegates realized at last the insurmountable obstacles to fixing at that time a reasonable amount of reparation. Thus they came to the conclusion that they should not assume the responsibility of objecting to an effort by the Allies to collect from Germany what she owed them, provided they would agree to certain safeguards against the dangers of such a course.

The United States, relatively speaking, had no great direct interest in what Germany was to pay, but she had a sincere desire for all nations concerned that the world should not be thrown into disorder and its commerce deranged by an attempt to create and collect a debt which could not be paid.

Because of misrepresentations and misconceptions as to the amount that Germany could pay and as to the amounts which she owed, it was impossible to agree upon an amount to be exacted from her. What she *could* pay was in any event less than the amount that she *should* pay. . . .

The Peace Conference accordingly adopted a provisional solution of the question of the amounts to be paid by Germany in succeeding years. The experts of the Allied and Associated Powers were in substantial agreement that the quick, realizable surplus assets of Germany amounted to about $5,000,000,000. This figure was accordingly adopted to measure the values which Germany must surrender by May 1, 1921.

The value of reparation in kind—namely, ships, coal, reconstruction material, etc.,—made prior to this date, is accounted as a credit toward the sum.[27]

Once the idea of arriving at a fixed sum had been given up, the Conference could do no more than agree on categories of damages for which Germany could be held financially responsible. After innumerable conferences, the list of categories was finally narrowed down to the following ten:

(1) Damage to injured persons and to surviving dependents by personal injury to or death of civilians caused by acts of war, including bombardments or other attacks on land, on sea, or from the air, and all the direct consequences thereof, and of all operations of war by the two groups of belligerents wherever arising.

(2) Damage caused by Germany or her allies to civilian victims of acts of cruelty, violence or maltreatment (including injuries to life or health as a consequence of imprisonment, deportation, internment or evacuation, of exposure at sea or of being forced to labour), wherever arising, and to the surviving dependents of such victims.

(3) Damage caused by Germany or her allies in their own territory or in occupied or invaded territory to civilian victims of all acts injurious to health or capacity to work, or to honour, as well as to the surviving dependents of such victims.

(4) Damage caused by any kind of maltreatment of prisoners of war.

(5) As damage caused to the people of the Allied and Associated Powers, all pensions and compensations in the nature of pensions to naval and military victims of war (including members of the air force), whether mutilated, wounded, sick or invalided, and to the dependents of such victims, the amount due to the Allied and Associated Governments being calculated for each of them as being the capitalized cost of such pensions and compensation at the date of the coming into force of the present Treaty on the basis of the scales in force in France at such date.

(6) The cost of assistance by the Government of the Allied and Associated Powers to prisoners of war and to their families and dependents.

(7) Allowances by the Governments of the Allied and Associated Powers to the families and dependents of mobilised person or persons serving with the forces, the amount due to them for each calendar year in which hostilities occurred being calculated for each Government on the basis of the average scale for such payments in force in France during that year.

(8) Damage caused to civilians by being forced by Germany or her allies to labour without just remuneration.

(9) Damage in respect of all property wherever situated belonging to any of the Allied or Associated States or their nationals, with the exception of naval and military works or materials, which has been carried off, seized, injured or destroyed by the acts of Germany, or her allies on land, on sea or from the air, or damage directly in consequence of hostilities or of any operations of war.

(10) Damage in the form of levies, fines and other similar exactions imposed by Germany or her allies upon the civilian population.[28]

With no concrete figures to go on, the reparations discussions drifted into an Alice-in-Wonderland world in which both the CRD and the Council of Four discussed the problems with no fixed points of reference. A few excerpts from the minutes of the CRD and the Big Four meetings will suffice to demonstrate the manner in which the best financial and political brains of the times were forced to negotiate.

April 2, 1919

MR. CRESPI: I propose we name the States who are to participate in the indemnity, namely, England, France, Italy, Belgium and Serbia, and that we provide for a commission to determine the method of distribution.

MR. LAMONT: It is essential that we agree to a method of distribution before the treaty is signed.

MR. CRESPI: If we cannot agree, shall we not arbitrate?

MR. LAMONT: We all agree that we must decide in one way or another before the treaty is signed.

MR. CRESPI: But if we cannot?

MR. LAMONT: If we cannot, then we can consider the Italian proposal. . . .

MR. DAVIS: The American Delegation must propose an amendment to article two by substituting the words "to the extent of their utmost capacity" for "at whatever cost to themselves."

MR. LOUCHEUR: We cannot accept this together with the thirty-year clause. This might mean France would get nothing.

MR. DAVIS: Both Mr. Wilson and Mr. Lloyd George say that enslavement for one generation is enough.

MR. LOUCHEUR: I do not think that the matter could have been put up to them properly.

MR. DAVIS: You are unduly pessimistic in saying France may get nothing.

MR. LOUCHEUR: I do not know. After France, in 1871, paid the five milliards she was exhausted and could do nothing for twenty years thereafter.

MR. DAVIS: The situation we are in may lead us to fix the amount payable by Germany.

MR. CHIESA: We think we should fix the sum to be paid within thirty years.

MR. LOUCHEUR: I agree in principle, but we cannot, in fact, agree with either Great Britain or the United States as to figures.

MR. LAMONT: The discussion is getting out of order. I think that each of us could advantageously get more precise instructions from his respective chief of state: Word has just come to me which indicates that the four heads have been discussing these matters and may have reached conclusions of which we are ignorant.

MR. KLOTZ: I cannot continue in any case with this discussion. The plan as at present presented has no merit. Nothing is definite and no government has anything on which to base a financial policy. The Americans have withdrawn one after another of the clauses that mean anything, e.g., "at whatever cost," etc.

MR. LAMONT: Is the substitution "to the extent of their utmost capacity" agreed to by the British?

MR. MONTAGU: I accept because I understand Mr. Lloyd George has agreed that the thirty-year is best, and if so, it is inconsistent to say "at whatever cost."

MR. LOUCHEUR: I foresee we must submit two texts—one French and the other United States and England. We should like, however, to have an opportunity to confer with Mr. Clemenceau.

MR. KLOTZ: Are you willing to specify thirty years, but provide that if the sum due cannot be paid in that time, the Commission may extend it?

MR. MONTAGU: A hard and fixed limitation is dangerous. Could not the Commission even extend payments at Germany's request?

MR. CRESPI: Fixing a thirty-year period involves great uncertainty as to what Germany can pay. She may refuse to work during this period. We must fix a sum.

MR. LOUCHEUR: France does not oppose a fixed sum in principle, but we cannot fix the amount of damage. . . .

MR. LAMONT: I understand that the French desire to change the period of payments from thirty to forty years.

MR. DAVIS: I suggest we tentatively put it at thirty-five and see if President Wilson will accede. I am sure he will not agree to forty. . . .

MR. DAVIS: Is it necessary to make such a list of categories an integral part of the treaty; would it not be better to agree among ourselves, and only show to Germany if she demands it?

LORD SUMNER: It should be an integral part of the treaty, otherwise the Germans will contend it has not the same validity as the treaty clause itself.

MR. DAVIS: I think it is weakness to indicate the necessity of an interpretation.

MR. LAMONT: I think, however, that the United States can accept Mr. Montagu's proposal, subject to agreement as to the "interpretation clause" to be annexed. Let us now pass on to paragraph three. The French have suggested forty years in lieu of thirty, and Mr. Davis has suggested thirty-five, subject to the President's approval.

MR. KLOTZ: I cannot accept in principle the idea of this paragraph. It is inconsistent with our assertion that Germany must pay at whatever cost to herself. There should be no limit of years.

MR. DAVIS: We cannot collect over one hundred years, for example. We are bound to be limited by Germany's capacity. The Commission within two years will decide how much Germany is to pay, but these payments cannot extend beyond the length of time fixed.

MR. KLOTZ: The Commission should fix the amount of the respective annual payments but not for how long they should run. Can the time be extended under the provisions of paragraph four?

MR. LAMONT: No.

MR. MONTAGU: Could not the Commission be authorized to fix the annuities in relation to Germany's capacity to pay and also be left free to fix the period over which payments should run. . . .

MR. CRESPI: I think it dangerous to let Germany know, as paragraph four seems to, that she can secure modifications in the terms fixed by the Commission. . . .

MR. DAVIS: It is our view that all we should demand is Germany's utmost capacity for thirty years. The sum due under the categories, including pensions, will unquestionably exceed this. We cannot require, however, that Germany pay such a sum as $100,000,000,000 capital amount.

MR. KEYNES: Are we precluded from taking fifty-year bonds?

MR. DAVIS: Yes.

MR. KEYNES: Then I regard the clauses as objectionable. Is the

United States prepared to cancel Allied debts to the United States not paid in thirty years?

LORD SUMNER: Can we adopt the principle that if Germany puts off payments long enough, she will be excused entirely?

MR. KLOTZ: Let us adjourn until 9:30 P.M., so we can confer now with Mr. Clemenceau.

MR. LOUCHEUR: Let me first be clear: Mr. Montagu seems to suggest the postponement of Germany's *debt*, while Mr. Davis contemplates the possible postponement of what the Commission thinks Germany *can pay* in thirty years.

MR. CHIESA: Germany will never sign unless told how much she must pay.

. . . .

MR. KLOTZ: I have now talked with Mr. Clemenceau and must state definitely that the French cannot accept the American change from "whatever cost" to "utmost capacity" if "utmost capacity" is to be qualified by a thirty-year or similar period.

MR. LAMONT: Then there will have to be two texts submitted to the Council of Four.

MR. MONTAGU: I earnestly urge that we compromise by agreeing to the thirty years in principle but give the Commission power to postpone payments. If this is done, I am not sure that the change in paragraph two as proposed by the United States is necessary.

MR. DAVIS: We must change paragraph two, even if the thirty-year period is made elastic.

MR. MONTAGU: What is the United States' position—that nothing is to be paid after thirty years? If so, everything is uncertain.

MR. DAVIS: Is it your idea that after the Commission finds how much Germany owes, it must require this entire amount of Germany within the thirty-year period, even if the amount were, say £20,000,000,000? This obviously cannot be paid in thirty years, and under the power of postponement it means that Germany will practically be enslaved for several generations.

MR. MONTAGU: I propose categories which will make it certain that the amount will be less than this.

MR. LOUCHEUR: Since when is it enslavement to compel payment of a debt? I appeal to President Wilson's seventh and eighth points, which require, without reservation, that Belgium and France be restored. Does the American Delegation still accept these points?

MR. DAVIS: Of course we accept the President's points. As to slavery, it is a long time since people have been imprisoned for debt.

MR. LOUCHEUR: We are not talking about imprisonment. France will have to bear her burden for more than thirty years.

MR. MONTAGU: I wish to state that while the British Delegation here personally prefers Article Two as it originally was drafted, we are willing to accept the American amendment, provided that power is given the Commission to extend payments, if necessary, beyond thirty years, or to accept bonds maturing subsequently.

MR. DAVIS: Is it your idea that the Commission is to fix as the amount to be paid in thirty years, the total bill or what the Commission thinks Germany can reasonably be expected to pay in a thirty-year period?

MR. MONTAGU: It is my idea that the Commission would make the entire bill payable, spreading it over thirty years in the manner in which it deemed to be most equitable.

MR. LAMONT: The American plan is that the Commission shall only fix the amount which it considers Germany can reasonably be expected to pay in thirty years. If, for instance, they found that the debt in accordance with the categories was $40,000,000,000, and Germany's reasonable ability to pay in thirty years was but $30,000,000,000, they would fix the latter amount as Germany's obligation.

MR. LOUCHEUR: Then the only significant figure is that of Germany's capacity. Why should time and energy be wasted in figuring up claims? I again appeal to President Wilson's seventh and eighth points, which say nothing about the obligation to restore being limited by a thirty-year capacity.

. . . .

MR. LAMONT: Has Mr. Keynes had an opportunity to study this new proposal?

MR. KEYNES: I have no information to indicate whether the $500,000,000 reserved for food and raw materials is adequate. The fact that the Council of Ten decided that it would require £125,000,000 to furnish Germany food up to September indicates that the present French amendment does not make adequate provisions for foodstuffs and raw materials for two years. I have prepared an alternative amendment which I propose.

(Mr. Keynes' proposed amendment is read.)

MR. KLOTZ: This is subject to the same objections which I have exposed before. At the rate we are figuring the expenses of the Army of Occupation, say 600 millions of Francs per month, and food supplies at the present rate, say 23 milliards of Francs, until 1921, will exhaust the $5,000,000,000 payment entirely.

MR. BARUCH: What is your solution?

MR. LOUCHEUR: Let Germany pay $5,000,000,000 for reparation and set aside a small amount for food and make Germany work to pay for the rest.

MR. KEYNES: Our estimate of $5,000,000,000 was based on the assumption that Germany would work and make exports. This item is already taken account of. I further think Mr. Klotz is too pessimistic in his estimates as to German food requirements. He does not take account of the new harvest. Mr. Klotz previously referred to Mr. Lloyd George having decided the matter in accordance with Mr. Klotz's views. I have seen Mr. Lloyd George and he states that he was under a misapprehension, thinking that the $5,000,000,000 was exclusive of German exports. I further point out that under my amendment Germany can only get food and raw materials out of the initial payment, if the Allies at the time approve, and such approval could be withheld if Germany is not working.

MR. LOUCHEUR: Germany is continuously opposing us even today. The delegates who went to get dyestuffs returned with nothing. We must be firm. France cannot accept Mr. Keynes' proposal.

MR. CHIESA: I accept the French text.

MR. LAMONT: The United States accepts Mr. Keynes' amendment, which leaves decision as to Germany getting raw materials to the decision of the Allied Governments.

MR. MONTAGU: Shall we not now discuss categories?

MR. KLOTZ: We are not through with the text.

MR. CHIESA: I understand the Council of Four have decided to divide the indemnity between Great Britain, France, Italy, Belgium and Serbia. Should not this be inserted in paragraph six?

MR. LOUCHEUR: I think this was only a casual consideration of the Council of Four and not a formal decision. Let us leave the matter to them.

MR. KLOTZ: It is useless to discuss categories unless the French plan is adopted. If the thirty-year period is retained, categories are unimportant. I suggest the appointment of a drafting committee to prepare a precise statement of the result of our deliberations, for submission to the Council of Four. We can meet tomorrow at three and approve the work of the drafting committee.

. . . .

MR. DAVIS: We are only in favor of getting from Germany all that can be gotten in thirty-five years.

MR. KLOTZ: How can we now say how long it will take Germany to meet her debt when we do not yet know the latter?

MR. MONTAGU: I propose that it be left to the Commission to decide throughout how long a period Germany shall pay.[29]

April 3, 1919

MR. DAVIS: I understand that the first matter before the Conference is the adoption of categories of damage pursuant to Article 2 of the text under consideration.

MR. MCCORMICK: I present herewith the United States' proposal as to categories. . . .

MR. JOUASSET: I understand it was the original intention to use the report of the First Sub-Committee as a list of categories, but this was abandoned as being too complicated; nevertheless, I think we should regard the present list as based on such report and consider the extent to which the categories in the report of the First Sub-Committee are included.

MR. KLOTZ: May I ask why we abandoned the careful work of the First Sub-Committee, under the able direction of Lord Sumner? As Chairman of the Reparations Commission I feel a responsibility in the matter.

LORD SUMNER: We do not intend to be disrespectful of the work of the Reparations Commission, but the utility of its work is affected by the new decisions of the four chiefs of State. The British delegation understands that they have decided that the only categories to be admitted are, broadly, injuries to person and damage to property. The report of the First Sub-Committee is too exhaustive to be useful under these abbreviated instructions.

MR. DAVIS: Mr. Klotz should know that the change relative to categories results from a proposal which he himself presented to the Council of Four. We shall nevertheless bear in mind Annex 15 (Report of First Sub-Committee) as we proceed. Is there any objection to paragraph 1 of the American proposal? . . .

MR. CRESPI: Should not the categories be attached as an integral part of the Treaty?

MR. DAVIS: It may be regarded as wise strategy to withhold the categories unless and until the Germans demand them.

MR. KLOTZ: It is essential that they be presented to and accepted by the enemy.

MR. MCCORMICK: Let us leave this to the chiefs of government as a question of strategy as to how the categories can be presented in the most effective way.

MR. CHIESA: The note at the end of the categories seems to imply that individuals can present their claims directly to the enemy.

MR. DULLES: I do not think the note is open to that construction. It is, of course, understood that each State will present the claims of itself and its subjects. The note merely means that in some cases the State will present claims on behalf of its subjects, and in other cases on account of damage which has been suffered by the State itself through relieving the damage of individuals and being subrogated to their rights.

MR. MONTAGU: I agree with Mr. Klotz that the categories must be in the Treaty.

MR. DAVIS: I think we all agree; but it is a matter of procedure as to whether the categories should, in the first instance, be presented as part of the Treaty.

MR. KLOTZ: Let us, in reporting to the Council of Four, state that the British, French and Italians regard it as essential that the categories be a part of the preliminaries of peace.

MR. DAVIS: This is agreeable. . . .

MR. KLOTZ: It may not be considered as good policy to use Article 1 and the first half of Article 2. It may make an unfortunate impression to recite the inability of the enemy to pay. Also this portion is merely in the nature of a preamble and might, perhaps, better form a part of the general preamble clauses of the Treaty.

MR. MONTAGU: I understand that the political chiefs of the British Government regard it as wise to have in the treaty a clause indicating that we are taking from the enemy everything we can, but, unfortunately, the enemy cannot pay for all the loss and damage which the Allies have suffered.

MR. MCCORMICK: I think the preamble is useful. We are adopting an unusual method in not fixing a definite sum. The preamble tends to explain this, and, further, prepares the public mind for disappointment as to what actually can be secured. Of course, the Council of Four will place this in any part of the Treaty which they think wise.

LORD SUMNER: I suggest the word "immediate" instead of "complete" in Article 2.

MR. DAVIS: The United States cannot accept this, as this might impliedly leave the enemy liable for further amounts than the last sentence of paragraph 2 contemplates. Is not Mr. Klotz satisfied with Mr. McCormick's explanation relative to Articles 1 and 2?

MR. KLOTZ: Yes. I wish further to suggest, however, that it seems to me to be absurd to state that the enemy's "resources are not unlimited." It makes us absurd to assert solemnly this axiomatic fact.

MR. LOUCHEUR: Since last night I have been carefully studying Articles 2 and 3, in the hope that it might be possible for us to agree to them. I am now clear, however, that the French cannot accept them. We insist on actually having Germany pay to the "utmost capacity" as Article 2 provides, and not nullifying this by the limitations of Article 3.

MR. MONTAGU: Could you not put all of her capacity into a 30-year payment and then postpone?

MR. LOUCHEUR: I had not understood that this was possible under the language of Article 3.

MR. DAVIS: Nor is that the United States' understanding.

MR. LOUCHEUR: May I give a concrete illustration? Let us assume that the claims under present categories are $50,000,000,000 (which, in fact, I think they will be approximately) and that the Commission estimates Germany's capacity to pay in 30 years at $30,000,000,000. Such $30,000,000,000, I understand, becomes Germany's obligation. If the Commission then finds they have made a mistake and Germany in the 30 years can only pay $10,000,000,000, is Germany's debt cancelled at the end of 30 years to the extent of the unpaid $20,000,000,000?

MR. DAVIS: No; Germany will have defaulted and must make good. I think, however, that the Commission will probably operate under a maximum and minimum scheme, which will render the contingency you indicate remote. The Commission will further have latitude by permitting certain percentages to be paid in marks.

MR. LOUCHEUR: Your answer to my inquiry relieves me considerably.

MR. DAVIS: I do not see that the clause is open to the construction you first indicated.

MR. LOUCHEUR: In the French translation it certainly is not clear. Having cleared up this point, may I now say that the French regard it as essential that the Treaty itself specify that Germany must pay *all* of her claims, and that the Commission has not power to name any obligation less than this, but merely to make percentages of it payable in marks or internal bonds.

MR. McCORMICK: At present we leave this to the discretion of the Commission.

MR. DAVIS: The Commission, if it so decides, can do this.

MR. LOUCHEUR: We have agreed to the abandonment of many categories of damage, at considerable sacrifice to France. The balance must be paid in one way or another.

MR. DAVIS: In this discussion we are assuming the functions of the Commission which we propose to set up.

MR. LOUCHEUR: We cannot admit in the treaty a form which admits the possibility that Germany will not pay at all. It would be preposterous to be having Germany paying interest on her domestic obligations and defaulting in her debt to the Allies, if the latter were willing to accept payment in German internal obligations or marks.

MR. DAVIS: Other committees are dealing with Germany's internal debts, and it may likely be provided that the Allies have a lien on German income ahead of any German internal obligations.

MR. LOUCHEUR: Germany's capacity to pay, if we accept payment in marks or bonds, is unlimited, and we accordingly cannot admit the possibility of payment of less than all that is due us.

MR. DAVIS: I cannot admit that Germany's capacity, even in this form, is unlimited. A country can be destroyed by being compelled to issue almost unlimited amounts of currency.

MR. KLOTZ: Shall it be France or Germany that is to be destroyed?

MR. MONTAGU: The Commission must be given precise instructions relative to this matter, and I think Mr. Loucheur's point can be considered in preparing such instructions.

MR. LOUCHEUR: This will be useful, but the instructions will be secret, and unless we have it in the treaty, Germany will deny that it was contemplated that the Commission should have such broad powers. France cannot let the fate of her people rest on the majority vote of any commission.

MR. DAVIS: The very reason we set up the Commission and gave it two years in which to work is because such questions as Mr. Loucheur brings up cannot be settled in a few hours or even a few days. I do not feel that we can usefully continue this discussion and propose that we adjourn with the understanding that each delegation will report back to its Chief of State the text under consideration with the reservations and comments which have been made.

(The meeting adjourned.)[30]

April 5, 1919, 11 A.M.

MR. CLEMENCEAU: What is the status of the reparation matter?

MR. KLOTZ: As a result of numerous conferences there has been drawn up a so-called "Anglo-American Project," upon which the French delegation has made certain reserves.

The first article is of a political character. Should this appear in the financial clauses, or should it not preferably appear in the general preamble clauses?

MR. LLOYD GEORGE: I sympathize with Mr. Klotz's point of view. This first article is hardly adequate to meet the political situation, either British or French. The British House of Commons has not been satisfied with the declarations made the other day by Mr. Bonar Law. British public opinion demands that Germany pay all the loss that they have caused. We agree, however, that Germany cannot pay more than what is stipulated for by this text.

MR. CLEMENCEAU: I am not sure that I agree as to that, but in any case Germany cannot pay all that she owes.

MR. LLOYD GEORGE: The important thing is to have it clearly appear that if the reparation demanded by us is limited, it is because we recognize the material impossibility of getting complete payment.

COLONEL HOUSE: I think we can agree on this.

MR. DAVIS: The American delegation has no special interest in the first article. In drafting it we have attempted to meet the views of Great Britain and France.

MR. CLEMENCEAU: Then it must state that Germany recognizes all the loss she has caused. It is not sufficient to state that we affirm it.

MR. LLOYD GEORGE: We must say that the Allies assert their claim and that Germany recognizes her obligation for all the costs of the war.

MR. HOUSE: This would be contrary to the terms of the armistice and the note you addressed to the American Government. The text must be drafted so as not to constitute a violation of our engagements.

MR. DAVIS: It can be said that Germany is morally responsible for the war and all the consequences thereof, and legally that she is responsible in accordance with the formula adopted for damage to property and to persons.

MR. CLEMENCEAU: This is a question of drafting. I think we can reach an accord.

MR. KLOTZ: It was originally proposed to require Germany to make reparation for damage caused to life and property "at whatever cost to herself." This is now changed to reparation limited to the capacity of Germany during thirty years.

MR. LLOYD GEORGE: I do not understand that to be the meaning of the text under consideration.

MR. KLOTZ: I venture to disagree. If the Commission decides that Germany owes $50,000,000,000, but thinks that Germany in thirty years can only pay $30,000,000,000 or $40,000,000,000, the difference—that is to say, $20,000,000,000 or $10,000,000,000 will be cancelled.

MR. LLOYD GEORGE: Lord Sumner thinks that Germany should be obligated to pay in thirty years, but if she cannot carry out her obligations in this period the Commission will be authorized to prolong the period of payment.

MR. LOUCHEUR: We are in entire agreement, but the British delegation in our previous conferences did not support this point of view.

LORD SUMNER: I think there is a misunderstanding as to the language. Mr. Montagu accepted the thirty-year limit because he understood Mr. Lloyd George desired it. The French ask whether if in thirty years, all is not paid, the balance will be abandoned. I say "No." That is the reason why the Commission is given power to extend the period, and, if necessary, to accept payment in German internal bonds.

MR. LOUCHEUR: If you had previously expressed yourself this way, this discussion would never have arisen. However, the American delegation clearly expressed the contrary view.

MR. DAVIS: It is my understanding that the Commission will determine how much they think Germany can pay in thirty years, and this will become Germany's obligation, even though it is less than the amount of the debt. Once, however, the sum is fixed, Germany must pay it, even though it takes more than thirty years.

MR. LLOYD GEORGE: I am in agreement with the French delegation. If you say to the Commission: Limit yourself to fixing Germany's capacity for thirty years, you impose a limit.

MR. LOUCHEUR: You seem to admit that the Commission can limit the payment in accordance with Germany's capacity.

MR. CLEMENCEAU: I cannot agree to the Commission exercising such power without previous approval of the interested governments.

MR. DAVIS: There is little practical difference between a period of thirty years and a period of forty years, because the interest eats up the principal. We are trying to get up something which Germany can be brought to accept.

MR. KLOTZ: Yes, but also it must be acceptable to the French. I recognize that it is highly desirable that Germany pay in thirty years, but if she cannot it should be Germany and not France which is to suffer.

The Commission should have power to grant extensions. It is humanly impossible to determine Germany's capacity for thirty years in 1921.

COLONEL HOUSE: All our experts seem to agree that we should take a basis of thirty years.

MR. LOUCHEUR: There is an ambiguity. The Commission meets. What will it do? According to the American delegation it will fix Germany's capacity for thirty years.

MR. LLOYD GEORGE: Is that what Colonel House thinks?

COLONEL HOUSE: Yes.

MR. CLEMENCEAU: Is the Commission to determine how much Germany can pay in thirty years?

MR. DAVIS: Yes.

MR. LOUCHEUR: Then the difference between that sum and the amount of damage is lost?

MR. DAVIS: The Commission is simply given two years to do what we have tried to do here, namely, determine how much Germany can pay and consequently how much she shall be obligated to pay.

MR. CLEMENCEAU: I cannot accept this plan.

MR. ORLANDO: The text seems to me to provide that Germany must pay up to the limit of its capacity. We cannot really fix any limit to the capacity in view of the uncertainties of the future, and it would be dangerous to adopt a limit which would be an incentive to bad faith and refusal to work.

MR. LAMONT: I think our discussion is theoretical rather than practical. These are matters which we are leaving to the Commission.

MR. LLOYD GEORGE: I propose to modify the text so that it will provide that the Commission will determine how much Germany should pay and then taking into account Germany's estimated capacity, shall require this payment in thirty years and have power to prolong the period if it turns out that all cannot be paid in this period.

MR. KLOTZ: I understand (1) the Commission determines the

amount of the debt, (2) considers Germany's capacity and apportions the sum over a thirty-year period, (3) if payment is not made in thirty years, extends the period.

MR. DAVIS: I think thirty years should remain the limit.

MR. LLOYD GEORGE: There is a strong argument against this. We shall all be badly off for many years and it will take Germany ten years to get on her feet. We really cannot tell what the capacity of Germany will be. We do not know what Germany can pay in the next thirty years. Mr. Davis may say Germany must know what her obligation is, but the Germans know very well what they have destroyed and they know the condition of the devastated regions for they have been there for a long time. They know of the boats they have sunk and of the pensions we shall have to pay. They will, therefore, have an approximate idea of what they owe. If they offer to reconstruct, themselves, the destroyed houses, that will eliminate at least one of the uncertain elements.

COLONEL HOUSE: In this case, why name a Commission? Why not simply draw up a list of categories?

MR. LLOYD GEORGE: The Commission will have to study compensation for lives lost and the restitution of stolen and damaged articles.

COLONEL HOUSE: As Mr. Davis said, if the period is too long interest charges will make complete payment impossible.

MR. LLOYD GEORGE: I recognize the force of this observation. It might very well be that there is no gain in prolonging payments for 100 years, rather than 50 years, but there is a big difference between 30 years and 50 years.

COLONEL HOUSE: Have not the estimates of German capacity been based on Germany as she existed in 1914?

MR. LLOYD GEORGE: No, in Lord Cunliffe's report account is taken of loss of Alsace-Lorraine, merchant fleet, etc.

COLONEL HOUSE: I thought a few minutes ago that we were almost in agreement.

MR. LLOYD GEORGE: We almost were, but I do not know that we are now.

COLONEL HOUSE: President Wilson has always understood that our estimates were based on a thirty-year period.

MR. DAVIS: In conceding pensions we did so on the theory that this would not increase materially the actual amount that Germany would have to pay, but would rather affect the method of distribution, because we regarded Germany's capacity as being agreed to as within the thirty-year limit.

MR. LLOYD GEORGE: I have opposed those who insist that Germany pay all the costs of the war. I am not willing that she should pay less than to her full capacity.

COLONEL HOUSE: Possibly it would be better not to fix a time limit.

MR. LLOYD GEORGE: I propose a text on the following lines: The Commission shall determine Germany's capacity to pay in the future and concurrently shall prepare a plan of annuities within the limits of the total sum due, fixing what in its opinion Germany should pay in thirty years. Believe me, Germany will not object as much as it is thought about payment. She knows what she owes and is ready to meet the situation.

COLONEL HOUSE: Why in this case not simply say that Germany recognizes its obligation to pay for the reparation of damage caused to property and to persons, without enumerating all the categories which have been suggested and without stipulating for a thirty-year limit? We could draft this in three lines.

MR. KLOTZ: We can go back to the first Anglo-American text. Let us adjourn and meet later to consider a text along the lines proposed by Mr. Lloyd George.

(The meeting adjourned.)[31]

April 5, 1919, 4 P.M.

(A proposed interpretation of Article 2, constituting categories of damage, is read.)

MR. LLOYD GEORGE: I note that the American text refers to damage resulting from acts in violation of formal engagements and of recognized principles of international law. I assume that Belgium is primarily contemplated but I should make clear that if that language is used, Great Britain will claim for all damage resulting from the consequences of submarine warfare, and as a party of the treaty guaranteeing the neutrality of Belgium, will claim for all war costs.

MR. DULLES: This category was proposed with the construction which has been developed by the American delegation before the Plenary Commission on Reparations.

COLONEL HOUSE: We can eliminate this Article if Belgium is otherwise adequately protected.

MR. LLOYD GEORGE: I do not think that any special clause is

necessary to protect Belgium. Yesterday the King of Belgium presented Belgium's demands for reparation. I think everything he spoke of is included in the British list of categories. I do not see how Belgium can be distinguished from France, for instance.

MR. MCCORMICK: Belgium alone as the beneficiary of the treaty in accordance with the principles as argued and declarations made, has a right to reimbursement for costs of the war.

MR. LLOYD GEORGE: It is England and France who have actually paid Belgium's war costs.

COLONEL HOUSE: We will accept the British project as a base if Belgium is protected.

MR. KLOTZ: Two texts have been presented—one American and the other British. The American text was adopted by France under reserve of two additions and by Italy under reserve of one addition. The American text has been carefully studied. If we now revert to the British text, we will have to make a new study. Therefore, I propose we continue with the American text as the basis of discussion.

COLONEL HOUSE: I understand that both texts were drawn up at the same time and have been studied, and I am ready to discuss the British text.

MR. LLOYD GEORGE: Does Mr. Klotz accept the interpretation of the American category 6, given by Mr. McCormick, which will place Belgium in a different position from France? I think the British system of going more into detail is better from a political point of view.

MR. LOUCHEUR: We have no objection to discussing the British text.

MR. CLEMENCEAU: I propose that we take up the proposal of Mr. Lloyd George made at the close of this morning's meeting. I cannot confer upon any Commission the power of fixing Germany's capacity of payment. I would say this: Germany owes "X" for damage caused to life and property. This sum "X" the Governments can reduce in the future, if they see fit, but I am not prepared at present to consent to any reduction. We shall see what is possible and what is not. We will take into account conflicting interests; we will leave the door open for a liberal solution, but in the name of the French Government, and after having consulted my colleagues, I insist that the treaty of peace fix what Germany owes us, at least to the extent of indicating the character of damage for which reparation is due. We shall reserve the right to reduce this amount. Let us fix a period of thirty years, in accordance with the desire which has been expressed by the majority, and require the Commission to demand payment within thirty years of all that Germany owes. If this is demonstrated to be impossible, the Commission will have the right to postpone beyond thirty years.

The proposal of Mr. Lloyd George seems to authorize the Commission to fix a figure less than that which is due. This I cannot accept.

MR. LLOYD GEORGE: Will Mr. Klotz read his proposal?

MR. KLOTZ: I reply to the question of Colonel House of this morning: "Why not simply declare that Germany should make compensation for damage to life and property without fixing a period of payment." If the capacity of Germany requires that payments be deferred for fifty years, we are ready to accord fifty years. If the Commission decides that Germany's total debt is 60,000,000,000 sterling, it will decide whether this can be paid in thirty or forty years.

MR. CLEMENCEAU: That is not very clearly expressed.

MR. KLOTZ: I mean that consideration must be given to the capacity payment in order to fix the number of annuities.

MR. HOUSE: It seems to me that Mr. Clemenceau's conclusion is very close to the American proposal.

MR. LOUCHEUR: Mr. Clemenceau says: What is due is due. The Commission cannot let Germany pay less. The Governments themselves, however, reserve the power to reduce the amount. The Commission will only have power to extend the period of payment. We indicate a period of thirty years as a guide, conditioned however, upon the possibility of the sum being paid within this time.

MR. MCCORMICK: In other words, everything must be paid however long it takes.

MR. DAVIS: This is a complete departure from the principles upon which we have been working for three months. We have been working on the theory that Germany must pay all that she can for thirty years or thirty-five at the most. Beyond this date the interest charges are so heavy that payment of principal becomes impossible.

With respect to capacity, we have made studies and those of the American delegation are between twenty-five and thirty-five billion dollars. These figures were reached without consideration of the amount due. Finally, we decided that it was better not to attempt to fix any figure, but in working on this new basis we tend to abandon our principle that Germany should pay measured by her capacity.

MR. LLOYD GEORGE: What we had been doing was to endeavor to find out how much Germany could pay, irrespective of the categories of damage. We were trying in that way to conform to the principles of President Wilson. We were unable to reach a conclusion along those lines; that is the reason we now adopt another method but Mr. Davis wishes to impose the limits of both methods.

I do not think that the difficulties which Mr. Davis fears are real. If we allow Germany to pay in goods, to reconstruct herself destroyed areas, machines, etc., a great part of the problem is solved. Germany's difficulty is not to find money, but money which is available for foreign payments. By permitting payment in kind the exchange problem is substantially solved.

MR. KLOTZ: With respect to Article 5, it is better politics to separate reparation payments and sums to be employed for the benefit of Germany. If the Army of Occupation is maintained on its present basis for two years, its expenses will amount to 14 milliards of francs. If the supply of Germany is added to this, practically nothing will remain for our devastated regions; so that what will appear to us and the enemy as a reparation payment will in reality be employed quite otherwise.

MR. LLOYD GEORGE: Your estimate of the expense of the Army of Occupation is exaggerated because the army can shortly be very substantially reduced.

MR. LOUCHEUR: It is better to fix definitely the amount for food and raw materials, say 5 milliards of francs.

MR. LAMONT: We have already discussed this point and you will observe that the present text, drafted by the British delegation, provides for disbursements for food and raw materials only if the Allied and Associated Powers judge this to be necessary.

MR. LOUCHEUR: Yes, but I recall the recent discussions as to supplying Germany. These should not be perpetuated, and we should now fix a definite amount.

MR. LAMONT: It will be to Germany's interest not to waste this money.

MR. LLOYD GEORGE: If you fix a definite sum, Germany will only spend it and then come for more.

MR. KLOTZ: I reassert the danger of making the reparation payment seem so much larger than it really will be. I would rather reduce the figure to 20 milliards of francs and really make it all reparation, except for the expense of the Army of Occupation. That would be least apt to deceive our people.

MR. LLOYD GEORGE: I prefer a system which gives us continuous control. This is better than turning over a specific sum to Germany, particularly as we have no idea as to what kind of a Government Germany will have.

MR. KLOTZ: There is one other question: We should fix guarantees. This is always done in private transactions, and should surely be done here. Can we not have a charge on the income of the railroads, ports and customs?

MR. LLOYD GEORGE: I do not see any gain in this. What would we get if we took the customs? We must look at this simply from the point of view of how Germany is to be compelled to observe the treaty as a whole. Of course, the detailed question of the form of payments, bonds, etc., will be left to the financial experts.

I am surprised that nothing has been proposed in regard to direct and immediate reconstruction.

MR. BARUCH: If Germany formally undertakes to pay a definite sum, I do not see how guarantees, such as Mr. Klotz suggests, will add anything.

MR. DAVIS: The furthest we could go, I think, would be to maintain a partial occupation until the first payment was completed.

MR. CLEMENCEAU: As Mr. Lloyd George suggests, I think the restoration of buildings should be expressly mentioned.

MR. LOUCHEUR: This is particularly important for France, Belgium and Italy. It constitutes really a method of payment. We must be able to get not only the reconstruction of houses but also certain supplies, such as coal. Even if France gets the benefit of the Sarre mines, its deficit will be 18 million tons after taking normal amounts from Great Britain. We must have a right to get this from Germany, otherwise she can withdraw it or grant it only at fantastic prices. This question of coal has equal importance for Italy. The treaty should say definitely that we have the right to choose modes of payment, so as to insure the reconstruction of destroyed towns and materials necessary for industries.

[MR.] CLEMENCEAU: I suggest that a definite text be proposed by Mr. Loucheur.[32]

Colonel House gives vent to his exasperation in his diary.

April 5, 1919: I sat both morning and afternoon in the Council of Four. (Pres. Wilson lay ill in bed in the next room.) The only subject discussed was Reparations which, instead of being called by that name, might well be termed the question of "loot." . . . The sitting of the Council of Four yesterday discussing the amount which Germany was to be forced to pay reminded me of a lot of children telling one another what they intended to do when they "grew up."

April 7, 1919: [Today's meeting] was the most footless of many footless meetings. We had agreed absolutely upon the terms of reparations. Loucheur, after a draft of the terms had been prepared, told Davis that Clemenceau had read and approved it *in toto.* This was in response to my endeavor to have the draft approved without the crossing of a *t* or the dotting of an *i.* . . . Loucheur told me time and again after we had accepted and voted over a few verbal and unimportant changes, that it was the last, and yet, when the very next sentence was ready, suggestions for changes would be made. . . . At six o'clock I left.

I crossed the street* to tell the President about the meeting and he thoroughly approved what I had done. We wasted the entire afternoon, accomplished nothing, for the text when finished was practically what it was when we went into the meeting. Any drafting committee could have done it better. This is what makes me so impatient at the whole procedure of the Conference. Instead of drawing the picture with big lines, they are drawing it like an etching. If the world was not aflame, this would be permissible, but it is almost suicidal in times like these to try to write a treaty of peace, embracing so many varied and intricate subjects, with such methods. . . .

The President and I were thoroughly discouraged when we talked the matter over and we wondered what the outcome was to be.

April 8, 1919: The President met with the three Prime Ministers in the afternoon and, much to my delight, they came to a tentative settlement of the question of reparations. The President yielded more than I thought he would, but no more I think than the occasion required. We had a long talk over the telephone about it tonight.[33]

In the end the CRD simply shifted all its problems onto the shoulders of the Reparations Commission which, endowed with almost sovereign powers, was charged with fixing the amounts and modes of Germany's payments. The only concrete figure written into the Treaty was the sum of 20,000,000,000 gold marks ($5,000,000,000) which Germany was to pay before May 1, 1921, "pending the full determination of the claims of the Allied and

* The meeting was being held in Lloyd George's apartment in the rue Nitot, opposite the President's house. [*Note by Seymour.*]

Associated Powers." The Reparations Commission would have two years in which to solve the problems that had stymied the CRD.

Article 233.

The amount of the above damage for which compensation is to be made by Germany shall be determined by an Inter-Allied Commission, to be called the Reparations Commission, and constituted in the form and with the powers set forth hereunder and in the Annexes II to VII inclusive hereto.

The Commission shall consider the claims and give to the German Government a just opportunity to be heard.

The findings of the Commission as to the amount of damage defined as above shall be concluded and notified to the German Government on or before May 1, 1921, as representing the extent of that Government's obligations.

The Commission shall concurrently draw up a schedule of payments prescribing the time and manner for securing and discharging the entire obligation within a period of thirty years from May 1, 1921. If, however, within the period mentioned, Germany fails to discharge her obligations, any balance remaining unpaid may, within the discretion of the Commission, be postponed for settlement in subsequent years, or may be handled otherwise in such manner as the Allied and Associated Governments, acting in accordance with the procedure laid down in this part of the present Treaty, shall determine.[34]

From the American point of view, there was a decided advantage to these arrangements. It had become obvious that in the atmosphere then prevailing at the Paris Conference no "sensible arrangement" could be arrived at. "Reparations" had become an emotional rather than an economic or financial issue, and the American Commissioners felt that only when the passions of the postwar era had been given time to cool could a settlement conforming to economic reality be reached. The United States representative on the Reparations Commission would be in a very strong position, because all belligerents were heavily in debt to the U. S. A. It was felt that he could more readily make economic reason prevail at Commission meetings than in the passion-laden atmosphere of the Paris Peace Conference. Unfortunately, it did not quite work out that way.

IX

Negotiations With the Germans

The Germans were summoned to appear in Paris on April 17th. When they arrived they were escorted to the Hotel des Reservoirs at Versailles where they were quartered behind barbed wire, for their "protection." This measure may have been intended as a deliberate insult, but it proved wholly necessary because the Parisians took to pelting the German delegates with assorted vegetables, fruits and occasional rocks. Two German delegates were injured by thrown rocks and had to be repatriated for hospitalization.

For three weeks the German delegation waited at their quarters, because the Peace Treaty was not ready. In fact, the Peace Conference was almost at the point of breaking up completely. The Italians had walked out of the Conference in anger over the question of Fiume, the Belgians, dissatisfied with their share of reparations, threatened to boycott the Conference, and, depending upon how the Conference was to decide the Shantung question, either the Japanese or the Chinese were likely to refuse to sign the Treaty. The Big Four (now reduced to Three, without Italy) labored frantically to straighten out matters, and the various commissions were busy tying up loose ends and putting final touches on the Treaty's articles.

By the beginning of May, 1919, matters began to sort themselves out. The Italians, having sacrified Orlando on the altar of *sacro egoismo*, somewhat shamefacedly returned to Paris under the leadership of Signor Tittoni; the Belgians, deciding that a middle-sized loaf was better than no loaf at all, became willing to cooperate; and the Chinese left the Conference as soon as the

Shantung question was solved in favor of Japan, "leaving judgment of the decision to history." Finally the Treaty was ready to go to press. When the Allied statesmen saw the result of their labors they were shocked. Herbert Hoover recalls:

I was awakened at four o'clock on the morning of the 7th of May, 1919, by a troubled servant who explained that there was a messenger waiting with a very important document which he would give to no one else than myself. It was the printed draft of the Peace Treaty which was to be handed to the Germans that day. I at once read it. While I had known many of the ideas, agreed upon by committees, I had not before envisaged it as a whole. I was greatly disturbed. In it hate and revenge ran through the political and economic passages. Many provisions had been settled without consideration of how they affected other parts. Conditions were set up upon which Europe could never be rebuilt or peace come to mankind. It seemed to me the economic consequences alone would pull down all Europe and thus injure the United States. I arose and went for a walk in the deserted streets at early daylight. In a few blocks I met General Smuts and John Maynard Keynes. If ever there was something telepathic it was in that meeting. It flashed in all our minds why the others were walking about at that time of day. In comparing notes, I found Smuts and Keynes especially interested in the political pattern, while I had given more thought to the economic side. We agreed that it was terrible and we would do what we could among our own nationals to make the dangers clear.

Keynes at that time was a young economist connected with the British delegation. Lloyd George did not like him, referring to him as the "Puck of Economics." He had a brilliant mind, powerful in analysis and expression. Like most modern intellectuals, he was constantly groping for new shapes and forms for the world rather than for wisdom in what to do next. That sort of mind has a high place in the world, although it sometimes gets on the nerves of the fellow who has to keep the machinery of civilization operating in the meantime. However, Keynes and I agreed fully on the economic consequences of the treaty.[1]

The 80,000-word Treaty of Versailles was handed to the German representatives at the Trianon Palace Hotel, and Clemenceau, as President of the Conference, opened the proceedings with a few crisp words.

GENTLEMEN, PLENIPOTENTIARIES OF THE GERMAN EMPIRE,

This is neither the time nor the place for superfluous words. You have before you the accredited plenipotentiaries of the great and lesser Powers, both Allied and Associated, that for four years have carried on without respite the merciless war which has been imposed upon them. The time has now come for a heavy reckoning of accounts. You have asked for peace. We are prepared to offer you peace.

The volume that will be handed to you by the Secretary General of the Conference will give you to know the conditions we have agreed upon. To study these conditions, you will, needless to say, be given every facility, to say nothing of those courtesies customary among all civilized peoples.

To make known to you something else that is in my mind, I must of necessity add that this second Peace of Versailles which is now to be the subject of our discussions has been too dearly bought by the nations who are represented here for us not to be unanimously resolved to use all the means in our power to obtain every satisfaction due us.

I shall have the honor of acquainting the plenipotentiaries with the order of discussion that has been adopted. If, thereafter, anyone has any observations to offer, an opportunity for this will of course be given.

There will be no verbal discussion, and observations must be submitted in writing. The plenipotentiaries of Germany will be given fifteen days in which to put into French and English their written observations on the entire Treaty. . . .[2]

Count Ulrich von Brockdorff-Rantzau, the German Republic's Minister of Foreign Affairs who headed the German peace delegation, caused a sensation by remaining seated while delivering his country's formal reply.

Gentlemen, we are deeply impressed with the great mission that has brought us here to give to the world forthwith a lasting peace. We are under no illusions as to the extent of our defeat and the degree of our powerlessness. We know that the strength of the German arms is broken. We know the intensity of the hatred which meets us, and we have heard the victor's passionate demand that as the vanquished we shall be made to pay, and as the guilty we shall be punished.

The demand is made that we shall acknowledge that we alone are guilty of having caused the war. Such a confession in my mouth would be a lie. We are far from seeking to escape from any responsibility for this World War, and for its having been waged as it has. The attitude of the former German government at the Hague Peace Conferences, its actions and its omissions in the tragic twelve days of July may have contributed to the catastrophe, but we with all emphasis deny that the people of Germany, who were convinced that they were waging a war of defense, should be burdened with the sole guilt of that war.

Nobody would wish to contend that the catastrophe goes back merely to the fateful moment when the successor to the throne of Austria-Hungary fell a victim to murderous hands. In the past fifty years the imperialism of all European states has constantly poisoned the international situation. The policy of retaliation, the policy of expansion, and a disregard of the right of national self-determination have played their part in that illness of Europe which came to its crisis in the World War. The Russian mobilization made it impossible for statesmen to find a remedy, and threw the final decision into the hands of military power.

Public opinion in every enemy country is echoing the crimes Germany is said to have committed in the war. Here, too, we are ready to admit that unjust things have been done. We have not come here to diminish the responsibility of the men who have waged the war politically and economically, and to deny that breaches of the law of nations have been committed. We repeat the declaration which was made in the German Reichstag at the beginning of the war: injustice has been done to Belgium and we shall make reparations.

But in the manner of waging war, Germany was not the only one that erred. Every European nation knows of deeds and of individuals which the best of their people remember only with regret. I do not want to reply to reproaches with reproaches, but, if we alone are asked to do penance, one should remember the Armistice. Six weeks went by before we obtained an armistice, and six months before we came to know your conditions of peace. Crimes in war may not be excusable, but they are committed in the struggle for victory, when we think only of maintaining our national existence, and are in such passion as makes the conscience of peoples blunt. The hundreds of thousands of noncombatants who have perished since November 11, because of the blockade, were destroyed coolly and deliberately after our opponents had won a certain and assured victory. Remember that, when you speak of guilt and atonement.

The measure of guilt of all those who have taken part can be established only by an impartial inquiry, a neutral commission before which all the principals in the tragedy are allowed to speak, and to which all archives are open. We have asked for such an inquiry and we ask for it once more.

At this conference, where we alone and without our allies are facing our many opponents, we are not without protection. You yourself have brought us an ally: that justice which was guaranteed us in the agreement as to what should be the principles governing the treaty of peace. In the days between October 5 and November 5, 1918, the Allied and Associated governments swore that there would be no peace of violence, and inscribed on their knightly banners a peace of justice. On October 5 the German government proposed that the basis of peace should be the principles set forth by the President of the United States of America, and on November 5 their Secretary of State, Mr. Lansing, declared that the Allied and Associated Powers had accepted this basis, with two definite reservations. The principles of President Wilson thus became binding for both parties to the war, for you as well as for us, and also for our former allies.

Certain of the foregoing principles call upon us to make heavy national and economic sacrifices. But by such a treaty, the sacred and fundamental rights of all peoples would be protected. The conscience of the world would be behind it, and no nation that violated it would go unpunished.

Upon that basis you will find us ready to examine the preliminary peace which you have submitted to us, with the firm intention of joining with you in rebuilding that which has been destroyed, in making good whatever wrong has been committed, above all the injustice to Belgium, and in showing mankind new goals of political and social progress. Considering the confusing number of problems which arise, we ought, as soon as possible, to have the principal problems examined by special commissions of experts, on the basis of the treaty which you have submitted to us. Our principal problem will be to restore the broken strength of all the nations which took part in the war, and do it by providing international protection for the welfare, health, and freedom of the working classes.

I believe we should then proceed to restore those parts of Belgium and Northern France which have been occupied by us and which have been destroyed by the war. We have taken upon ourselves the solemn obligation to do so, and we are resolved to execute it to the extent which has been agreed upon between us. In this we are dependent upon the co-operation of our former opponents. We cannot accomplish it without the technical and financial participation of the victor nations, and they could accomplish it only with our co-operation. Impoverished Europe must desire to bring about this reconstruction as successfully, but at the same time at as little cost as possible. Such a project could be carried through only by means of a clear and businesslike understanding as to the best methods to be employed. To continue to have this done by German prisoners of war would be the worst of methods. Unquestionably such work can be done cheaply. But it would cost the world dear if hatred and despair should overcome the German people, forced to think of their sons, brothers, and fathers still held prisoners, and languishing as if in penal servitude. We cannot arrive at a lasting peace without an immediate solution of this problem, a problem which has already been postponed too long.

Experts on both sides will have to give thought as to how the German people can best meet the financial obligations called for by such reparations, without collapsing under the weight of their burden. A financial breakdown would take from those who have a right to reparations the advantages which are theirs by right, and would throw into irreparable disorder the whole European economic system. The victors as well as the vanquished must guard themselves against this menacing danger and its incalculable consequences. There is only one means of removing it: belief without reservation in the economic and social solidarity of all nations, and in a free and all-comprising League of Nations.

Gentlemen, the sublime idea of deriving from the most terrible catastrophe in history the greatest of forward movements in the development of mankind, by means of the League of Nations, has been put forth and will make its way. But only by opening the gates of the League of Nations to all who are of good will can the goal be attained, and only by doing so will it be that those who have died in this war shall not have died in vain.

In their hearts, the German people will resign themselves to their hard lot if the bases of the peace, as mutually agreed upon, are not destroyed. A peace which cannot be defended before the world as a peace of justice would always evoke new resistance. No one could sign it with a clear conscience, for it could not be carried out. No one could venture to guarantee its execution, though this obligation is implied in the signing of the treaty.

We shall, with every good intention, study the document submitted to us, in the hope that our meeting may finally result in something that can be signed by all of us.[3]

Many Allied participants, among them Colonel House, Harold Nicolson and Lloyd George, have given classic descriptions of the scene at the Trianon Palace. A lesser known, but equally fascinating description comes from the pen of Dr. Walter Simons, the legal adviser to the German Delegation. It is interesting to see how that historic event looked from the other side of the green table, as he described it in a letter to his wife.

. . . The six delegates, five secretaries—Haniel, Stockhammern, Lersner, Rödiger, and I—and some German journalists were driven through the park to the Hotel Trianon, at the entrance of which a number of camera men were waiting for us. The French liaison officer, Colonel Henry, and a number of civilian and military functionaries received us and accompanied us to the hall of the session between solid ranks of representatives of all the states that were at war with us. It was interesting to me to observe the varying expressions on the faces of our "conquerors." The French showed either exaggerated hatred or marked, but possibly assumed, spirit of chivalry, the British haughty withdrawal. One Japanese evinced an intense, I might almost say a scientific curiosity. The hall of the session was arranged so that a great rectangle of tables stood in the center. When we entered we were facing Clemenceau, the President of the Conference. To his right sat Wilson and Lansing, to his left were Lloyd George and Bonar Law. On our left the nearest of our opponents were the French and the Italians, and on our right the Japanese. The table at which sat the six German delegates formed one of the two small ends of the rectangle, opposite Clemenceau. In the center the interpreters were seated; and behind the table of the delegates were the secretaries, in seats somewhat higher. Since my place was in the middle of the German secretaries, I was directly opposite Clemenceau, and had a good view of the whole assembly. Clemenceau, who has perhaps lived the most extraordinary life that fate could give to any mortal, makes a strangely bourgeois impression, in spite of his untamable expression.

He wore grey gloves over his short, thick hands, and he did not remove them during the session. When we had taken our seats, he rose and spoke his introductory words in short staccato sentences which he threw out as if in a concentrated anger and disdain, and which from the very outset, for the Germans, made any reply quite futile. When Count Brockdorff-Rantzau remained seated while he gave his answer, this caused a general sensation. But he had told me beforehand that he would remain seated. In a diagram of the hall of the session which appeared in the French newspapers, the German table had already been designed as "banc des accusés." The Count therefore had heard, in spirit, the words, "the prisoner will stand up," and it was for that reason he kept his seat. He spoke with a voice that was remarkably calm, precise, and curt; he had our interpreters translate every sentence in turn into both French and English, the French proving to be not very good, and the English excellent. One must give Clemenceau credit for curbing his temper sufficiently to keep him from interrupting Rantzau's speech; but his face became red with anger. Wilson listened attentively, and the English translation, spoken with great passion, obviously made its impression upon him, although not a favorable one. The British feigned boredom and indifference. Lloyd George laughed and Bonar Law yawned. Most of the other delegates paid close attention, which can perhaps be attributed to the fact that they had difficulty in understanding one of the three languages spoken. After a brief half-hour Clemenceau closed the session just as laconically and sharply as he had opened it. Again, on the way to the door, we had to run the gauntlet. Rantzau lighted a cigarette, which caused a sensation. Meanwhile twice as many camera men had gathered at the door as before, and the moving picture cameras were still clicking as we drove away.

I cannot very well tell you what went on in me in that half hour; the predominant feeling was that of a great unreality. Outside of the big window at my right there was a wonderful cherry tree in bloom, and it seemed to me the only reality when compared with the performance in the hall. This cherry tree and its kind will still be blooming, when the states whose representatives gathered here exist no longer.

The treaty which our enemies have laid before us is, in so far as the French dictated it, a monument of pathological fear and pathological hatred; and in so far as the Anglo-Saxons dictated it, it is the work of a capitalistic policy of the cleverest and most brutal kind. Its shamelessness does not lie in treading down a brave opponent, but in the fact that from beginning to end all these humiliating conditions are made to look like a just punishment, while in truth there is in them neither shame, nor any respect for the conception of justice. . . .

We are all of one opinion here, that this treaty cannot be accepted in its present form. Nevertheless, my counsel is not to give vent to our just indignation, but to do everything that will make negotiations possible. Every week that we gain will weaken the position of our opponents. The better this treaty becomes known, the more impossible will it be to put into effect. We must avoid the sudden breaking off of negotiations, which would give our opponents the desired opportunity to gain honors and the spoils of victory by a last military drive, which would once more whip up the dying military instincts of their people, the kind of result that was brought about by our astounding attack in the East after Trotsky had broken off the negotiations at Brest-Litovsk. You can imagine how strange one thing is for me. We are here playing the same role as that in which I often saw the collaborators of Trotsky at Brest-Litovsk. We are even subjected to the same outward restrictions. It is useful, however, to recall what the Russians did and what they omitted to do.[4]

In Brockdorff-Rantzau the young German Republic had picked the worst possible representative. Though he undoubtedly was an able man, he was the very image of the Prussian Junker as depicted in *Punch*. Ramrod straight, abrupt in speech and manner, stern and, at the moment, overflowing with hatred and frustration, his very presence seemed to link the German Republic with the authoritarian Imperial Reich the Allies had been fighting. No amount of German diplomacy could probably have reversed the verdict of the "Preliminary Peace Conference of Paris," even if the German Republic had had a Talleyrand or a Metternich at its disposal in 1919. But the German Republic might have projected a more sympathetic image to the world if it had chosen a more humble representative of the people to speak for it at Versailles.

The bulging briefcases of the German delegates contained definite and detailed instructions from the German Foreign Office. These are now available and are worth reading, for they give an idea of what the Germans expected to encounter at the Peace Conference.

I. General Principles

In all probability the Allies will submit a final draft of a treaty, with the explanation that it can only be accepted or rejected. It is not advisable to present a comprehensive counter-draft treaty. It can only be a question of presenting single counterproposals.

The general basis for the evaluation of the Allied terms is the Wilson program, which is binding upon both Germany and her opponents. Questions which are not explicitly mentioned in this program, but which will be negotiated at the Peace Conference, are to be solved in the spirit of this program. In this realm belongs, in addition to the question of the freedom of the seas which is to be decided in accordance with Wilson's original point of view, the question of Northern Schleswig and that of the Anschluss of German Austria. The latter question is to be discussed only if the Allies explicitly put their ban on the Anschluss of German Austria.

II. Territorial Questions

1. ALSACE-LORRAINE

Wilson's Points demand that "the wrong done to France by Prussia in 1871 . . . should be righted." On principle, a demand should be made that the people of Alsace-Lorraine be granted the right of self-determination, which right is to be exercised by means of a free plebiscite.

The plebiscite is to apply in the whole of Alsace-Lorraine, or at least to the regions which are linguistically and ethnologically German. The method of voting shall be as follows: In bilingual sections, according to communities or parishes, and otherwise, according to counties. All persons over twenty years of age who were living in Alsace-Lorraine on August 1, 1914, shall have the right to vote. Before the plebiscite takes place the French army of occupation will be replaced by local militia or neutral police troops, and French administrative authorities will be replaced by nationals of Alsace-Lorraine or by neutrals or by commissions evenly divided.

In case of the ceding of the entire territory, we should demand the frontier of 1871, i.e., in the east, the valley of the Rhine, and in the north, the present northern boundary of Alsace-Lorraine.

Again in the case of the ceding of Alsace-Lorraine, our economic interests in that region should be safeguarded by suitable economic agreement. Special emphasis is to be laid upon the utilization of the potash deposits, and upon our obtaining phosphorus iron ore (Minette) from Alsace-Lorraine. Agreements should be sought in the matter of making the Rhine navigable down to Basle and also of navigation in general and the right to share in the water-power.

2. THE SAAR

The separation of this territory from Germany, its being placed under a special international administration, and the demand for a future plebiscite are unacceptable. If possible, Allied control of its coal production is to be avoided. The claims of France in this respect, which are based upon the destruction of the mines in Northern France, can be satisfied by an exchange of coal and coke for phosphorus iron ore. Agreements of that kind should be concluded for a few years only.

3. THE RHINELAND, THE RHENISH PALATINATE, AND RHENISH HESSE

To sever these regions from Germany would be the beginning of dismemberment and is therefore to be rejected on principle. We should also decline to accept all terms which would offer an occasion for the gradual isolation and the subsequent separation of these areas from the Reich. Above all, we should insist on having the customs frontier follow the frontier of the Reich.

A different position may be taken in the case of Malmédy and Montjoie. If the Allies point out that the population of these areas demand union with Belgium, a plebiscite should be conceded.

4. POLAND

The Wilson program provides for an independent Polish state, which should include the territories inhabited by indisputably Polish population, which should be assured a free and secure access to the sea, and whose political and economic independence and territorial integrity should be guaranteed by international covenant.

Disputes as to which territory is to be considered Polish, according to these principles, can be settled only by a nonpartisan tribunal, whose decisions must be governed by a popular plebiscite. The plebiscite is to be limited to the province of Posen, beyond the line of demarcation,* because it is only there that an area which linguistically is almost solidly Polish can be found. We should endeavor, if possible,

* Provisional boundary between Germany and Poland before the delimitation of the definitive frontier by the Peace Conference. [L.]

to push the line of demarcation farther back. It would be unjustifiable to include West Prussia and Upper Silesia, because in that case East Prussia would be severed from the Reich, and because the possession of Upper Silesia, which produces 22 percent of Germany's coal, is indispensable to the life of Germany; and furthermore, union with Poland would not be in the interest of the population of Upper Silesia.

A plebiscite should be held after the conclusion of peace, and after the Polish troops have been replaced by neutral gendarmerie. As to the method of voting: voting will be by communities or parishes, and changes will be made only if favored by two-thirds of those voting. The right to vote shall be the same as that prevailing under the law which regulates elections to the National Assembly, with this exception: The right to vote shall also be shared by German residents who fled from the province, on condition that those voting had been German citizens and had lived in the province for one year. After the plebiscite, racial enclaves should possibly be exchanged.

Free access to the sea must not be created by a Polish corridor to Danzig, which would separate East Prussia and parts of West Prussia from the Reich. Polish interests are rather to be safeguarded by economic measures: the establishment of free zones in one or several Baltic ports, the facilitation of through traffic, reciprocal arrangements governing railroad service, the improvement of the navigation of the Vistula and the Bug rivers, and agreements concerning shipping on these rivers.

In the economic sphere, we should seek to secure the import of agricultural produce from the province of Posen. The opportunity for negotiations should be so used as to bring about general commercial agreements with Poland, especially with reference to through traffic.

5. THE CLAIMS OF CZECHOSLOVAKIA AND LITHUANIA

None of the disputed territories is inhabited by an indisputably Czech or Lithuanian population. These peoples have not made any demands for separation. A plebiscite in these areas must therefore be refused.

6. NORTHERN SCHLESWIG

Regarding the right of self-determination in the bilingual parts of Northern Schleswig, the same procedure will be used for voting in all areas, i.e., voting by communities or parishes. In other respects, the same procedure is to be used as that for Poland. In case a plebiscite *en bloc* should be imposed upon us, we should demand that the southern boundary of the plebiscite area should be a line running north of the Lister Tief, south of Emmerleff, north of Hoyer, north of Dahler, northwest of Abel, north of Söllstedt, north of Königsberg, north of Wester-Hoist, north of Aösleben, west of Graul, then along the county border of Apenrade to Flensburger Föhrde, along the northern bank of the Flensburger Föhrde to the Baltic Sea. For the determination of the frontier so-called Kugelungsverfahren; in case the withdrawal of German troops and officials is demanded, mixed commissions under neutral chairmanships should be appointed.

7. THE GENERAL CONSEQUENCES OF TERRITORIAL CESSIONS

(*a*) The Financial Statement. In the matter of the public utilities which must be ceded by the Reich and by the Prussian state, the debts of the Reich and of Prussia should be assumed, proportionate to population, by the ceded territories.

(*b*) The inhabitants of the territories to be ceded should have the right to choose between applying for citizenship and leaving the area in question with their possessions.

(*c*) The continuance of all pensions and annuities, whether federal, state, or municipal, should be guaranteed.

(*d*) In the case of governments which acquire territory formerly German, there should be adjustments of all questions of social insurance due.

(*e*) Concerning the effect of territorial cessions on church parishes, primarily we should strive to gain guarantees for the Protestant churches, in the sense that one's creed should not be affected by a change of frontier. So far as the Catholics are concerned, nothing should prevent a subsequent regulation of this question with the Holy See. Should the Allies demand that the matter be brought to a settlement in the treaty, Germany should demand that parish boundaries be made identical with the new national frontiers.

8. GERMAN TERRITORIES UNDER OCCUPATION

A demand should be made for the immediate evacuation of German territories under occupation at the time of the conclusion of peace. If need be, additional guarantees should be offered for the payment of our obligations.

Whenever the occupation of territory continues, the powers of the army of occupation and its numbers should be precisely defined.

Above all, there should be an agreement that the local authorities may communicate freely with the central authorities; that all officials are to be appointed and dismissed solely by the appropriate German authority; that the army of occupation shall not interfere with political, economic, and commercial conditions existent in the country; and that the German customs frontier should *de facto* still be the actual frontier of the Reich, and that the German customs shall be supervised solely by the German authorities. In addition, colored troops should not be made a part of the army of occupation.

III. The Protection of National Minorities

Germany is, in principle, in favor of the protection of national minorities. This protection could best be regulated within the framework of the League. In the treaty we should demand certain guarantees for those German minorities, which, after the ceding of territories, will be under foreign sovereignty. These minorities should be allowed to preserve their German culture; they should be granted the right to maintain and to attend German schools and churches, and to publish German newspapers. If possible, we should try to effect further cultural autonomy on the basis of records in national registry offices.

IV. Reparations

The basis [for reparations claims] is to be the Lansing Note of November 5, 1918, according to which Germany has to make reparations for all damages caused to the civilian population in Allied countries and to their property. We should start from the premise that the note refers only to the occupied territories and that Germany has to make reparations only for the damage caused by German troops in the occupied territories. (Kind of reparations: reconstruction by German entrepreneurs or contractors.)

Therefore, reparations for damages to Allied state property and for damages outside of the occupied territories should be refused on principle. On the other hand, as a consequence of our taking this point of view, we must refrain from making claims for reparations of any kind.

If, however, we are forced to relinquish the above point of view, we should maintain the right to make counter-claims in proportion to the Allied claims. In reference to submarine warfare, we should maintain the point of view that it was a defense measure justifiable against the English hunger blockade, the blockade having been contrary to international law. In any case, we should refuse to pay damages caused by submarine-cruiser warfare, or for damages to armed ships traveling in convoy or without lights. Insofar as violations of international law may form a basis for reparation claims, this should be decided by courts of arbitration.

Reparations to Italy and Rumania are to be refused for the reason that the aggressions of both countries came as a result of their breach of allied faith with us. Possible reparations to be paid to Serbia and Montenegro are to be paid by the states created from the former Austro-Hungarian monarchy and by Bulgaria.

The Allies must present detailed statements for the sums demanded. Restitution already made on the basis of the Armistice agreement, that is, German rolling stock, war materials, and the like, already handed over, must be reckoned in the account as reparations. Where there are cases in dispute, the sum of the claims shall be fixed by an international court of arbitration. Reparations for damages should be in the form of reparations in kind, as far as possible. We should make an attempt to gain the right to make reparations in long-term payments.

V. General Economic-Political Conditions

A. Relations between Germany and foreign countries must be resumed in full and at once.

Above all, the following should be regarded as essential: (*a*) The repeal of the extraordinary laws discriminating against Germans abroad; (*b*) The right of Germans to live and work freely abroad; (*c*) The ending of the blockade. Exact knowledge must be obtained as to whether and to what degree we are still subject to certain restrictions on exports and on imports of raw materials. Black and grey lists must be abolished; (*d*) The blockade barring free communications and the movements of individuals ought to be ended simultaneously with the blockade of goods. Otherwise, a return to normal international relations is impossible; (*e*) It is especially important that Germans and the interests of German firms abroad should be restored to their previous status. Everything should be done to obtain payment of their just claims in the currency of the country in question. These matters, as well as those of the restoration of private law, above all in the field of commercial patent rights, copyrights, and the like—as also the order in which obligations must be met—come within the domain of law; (*f*) We must seek in every way to regain control by September 1, 1919, over our merchant fleet, so that it may move as freely as before the war.

B. Insofar as the future regulation of general economic relations is concerned, we shall assist in putting into practice that Wilsonian principle which provides that international relations shall be free, equal, and without barriers. First of all, however, we must obtain Germany's immediate admittance to membership in the League of Nations.

Furthermore, we must be granted full freedom in our domestic policies, in order to arrange our economy along the lines of our new political order, based on principles of socialized economics.

In order to provide Germany with an opportunity to accelerate her productivity as soon as possible and her exports to the highest possible degree, an effort should be made to obtain: (*a*) The recognition in principle of free competition in the acquisition of raw materials, or at least the assurance of a sufficient quota, in case raw materials are allotted internationally; (*b*) An open door for exports to all colonies, protectorates, spheres of influence, and other territories in Asia and Africa; (*c*) The preservation of the German cables and the possibility of establishing airplane and wireless stations in Germany and abroad (this latter question appears to be of the greatest importance for our future exports; if our rights in this respect should be threatened, we might propose the internationalization of all cable connections); (*d*) Guarantees that German commerce will be allowed to compete in eastern and southeastern Europe; also guarantees of the right of bonded transit for goods (in reference to Poland as a country representing both a market and a transit problem, this is a matter which shall be settled definitely in connection with the ceding of portions of the province of Posen and the creation of the Vistula waterway); (*e*) Full freedom to regulate our economic relations with third countries by means of special treaties, if necessary; (*f*) As far as possible, the restoration of the legal bases of the economic relations to conditions which existed before the war, with the right to short-term cancellation of fixed terms and tariffs contained therein. Insofar as this cannot be attained, or if such agreements are canceled, most-favored-nation clauses should be agreed upon, together with a precise agreement on their extent.

In addition, desiderata to be made a part of the treaty if practicable, are: (*aa*) The possibility of prohibiting imports and exports, for the transition period; (*bb*) Equal rights with the nationals of other countries; (*cc*) Freedom of transit; (*dd*) Equality or most-favored-nation treatment for shipping; (*ee*) These agreements to be applicable to the colonies also; (*ff*) Freedom to control relations with individual countries by means of special economic treaties corresponding to the requirements of these countries.

VI. Financial Questions

1. Owing to the long duration of the Armistice and the increasingly severe conditions of the renewals of the Armistice, Germany's present situation, as compared to that at the time of the acceptance of the Fourteen Points, has become considerably more difficult; nevertheless, Germany is prepared to carry the burdens assumed at that time.

2. Germany must be in a position to pay her debts in neutral countries, and to assume the obligations incurred by private guarantors. She must also be enabled to maintain her internal debt service, for in case of nonfulfillment her economic system would no longer be effective, as a result of the collapse of her credit institutions, especially the savings banks and the social-insurance system. In order to achieve this, Germany is willing to tax herself to the utmost. To do this, however, it must be assumed that she will, of course, be afforded the possibility of economic recovery.

3. By openly setting forth the extent of our domestic obligations and the balance of payment due to foreign countries, we must show that Germany cannot go beyond fulfilling the obligations incurred under the Fourteen Points.

4. Since Germany cannot raise the required sums in foreign currency, she must be allowed to make reparations in kind, as far as possible. For the rest, the privileges of a secured loan should be granted to her. The possibility may also be considered of Germany's ceding her war claims on her allies.

5. Sources of income such as customs duties, taxes on tobacco, liquor, and so forth, might be pledged to guarantee payment of the interest on loans and the repayment of the principal, as also reparations payments and the payments for the necessary raw materials. But no interference with the German administration of the above taxes is to be conceded, so long as we meet our obligations. No public debt.

6. Allied control of our system of payment (as in the agreement of Trier) must not be conceded.

7. Since the maintenance costs of war prisoners are approximately

the same on both sides, we should try to come to an agreement by which the costs will be considered as canceled.

VII. General Legal Questions

1. The resumption of diplomatic and consular relations;

2. Agreements that have not been annulled by the Treaty of Versailles are to be renewed, with the reservation that within a year either party may ask for new terms, as being justified by obsolete conditions;

3. The immediate return of all German prisoners of war and interned civilians. Repatriation should begin immediately after the concluding of the preliminaries of peace, and must be carried out in the shortest time possible under the circumstances. All attempts to compel prisoners to restore devastated areas are to be unconditionally rejected. Participation in the work of restoration by freely chosen workers of all nationalities might be proposed;

4. Detailed agreements for the protection of laborers, labor legislation, and labor insurance, based on the draft published by the Ministry of Labor;

5. The restoration of private rights:

(1) War laws contravening private rights shall be declared null and void, above all those forbidding payments to, or commerce with the enemy, and decrees governing the custody, sequestration, and liquidation of enemy property;

(2) The settlement of the consequences of these war laws on the basis of complete reciprocity;

(3) Permission to obtain immediate information concerning property in enemy countries which has been taken under government supervision or administration;

(4) Arbitrated decisions on disputed claims which originated during or before the war;

6. Mutual and reciprocal understandings on the embargo, on prize ships, and also on their cargoes;

7. Liberal amnesty for prisoners of war and interned civilians, as also for inhabitants of occupied territories. Permission to retry enemy aliens who were sentenced but who had put themselves in a state of contumacy during the war;

8. The restitution of property rights possessed by the German missionary societies, as also permission for them to resume their work in their former areas.

VIII. Colonies

Settlements based on the Wilson program shall be sought as follows:

1. Territorial questions.

a) German equality with other Powers, in the right to own colonies. Accordingly, also, the demand should be made that on principle the German colonies be returned.

b) Germany is prepared to negotiate with the Allies in the matter of the ceding of individual colonies, but shall negotiate as their rightful owner.

c) Germany is ready to pledge her colonies wholly or in part as guarantees of her obligations. This pledge, however, must not include occupation. The income from the colonies should be relinquished to the Allies only in the event that we do not punctually meet our obligations.

2. There shall be a new international settlement of sovereign rights in the colonies.

a) Germany is prepared to accept the principle that international regulations shall be established for all colonies. Matters to be dealt with in particular are:

aa) The protection of the natives from slavery, alcohol, epidemics, and the traffic in arms;

bb) An assurance of free economic and cultural activity for all nations;

cc) Guarantees of peace by means of neutralization and demilitarization.

b) If need be, Germany is willing on principle to have her former sovereign rights transformed into those of a mandatory of the League of Nations, provided this new rule is applied equally to all tropical colonies. Germany should be given proportionate consideration in the distribution of mandates.

3. The indemnification for German firms in the colonies which have suffered losses during enemy occupation.

IX. Disarmament

A one-sided obligation upon Germany to disarm must be rejected. Germany is prepared, however, in line with the Wilson program, to give guarantees for the future that these armaments will be reduced to the minimum required for security, provided that other countries, especially former opponents and neighboring states, are willing to give equal guarantees. On this basis Germany proposes:

1) Extensive disarmament on land with a reciprocal and simultaneous abolition of compulsory military service;

2) The razing of fortifications on the left bank of the Rhine may be conceded, but not the withdrawal of all troops. Readiness to evacuate the left bank of the Rhine only if France and Belgium establish a corresponding demilitarized zone;

3) The demand for destruction of German railroads on account of their strategic importance must be refused, because all railroads are economically necessary;

4) The creation of international marine police, in which all seafaring nations shall have a proportional part; this is to be accompanied by an international prohibition of armed ships at sea except for the said marine police. Armaments necessary for coastal defense may be maintained;

5) Apart from the question of the creation of a League of Nations, the principle of a far-reaching freedom of the seas outside of territorial waters ought to be acknowledged, as also freedom of commerce and news service in peace as well as in war;

The precise formulation of this principle, as also rules, prohibitions, and agreements resulting therefrom, should be reserved for a special treaty.

X. THE LEAGUE OF NATIONS

Germany is emphatically in favor of a League of Nations, which is conceived in terms of the equality of nations, whether great or small.

International disputes should be settled by a court of arbitration, insofar as they cannot be settled by diplomatic negotiation, or by the mediation of a third power, or by the findings of special commissions. Such court of arbitration should in case of necessity be enforced by all the members of the League.

The Paris draft of the Covenant already published should be opposed, insofar as it departs from these basic principles and the original Wilson program.

This has special reference to the following points:

1. The Covenant provides that the five great enemy Powers shall enjoy a predominant position. If any differentiation is to be made between the Great Powers and other powers, then Germany should be granted the same rights as the other Great Powers;

2. The method of arbitration in the case of questions of special interests is not satisfactorily worded; it should be left to a nonpartisan tribunal;

3. In spite of the exclusive character of the League, non-members are expected to assume the obligations of members, in the event of a dispute;

4. The decisions arrived at in the matter of the German colonies are completely one-sided and unjust.

XI. The Question of War Guilt

According to information received, the Allies will seek to justify the severity of the conditions imposed upon us by claiming that Germany was responsible for the outbreak of the war. This assertion must be opposed by the delegation at Versailles. Emphasis must be laid upon the fact that the events which led to the outbreak of the war are not yet sufficiently known, since, in the case of all the governments concerned, what they have made public contains only a part of the truth; that, moreover, the events of the final weeks cannot be judged alone. They must be viewed in relation to the development of European politics since 1871, to permit of a verdict which can say how far the policies of individual European states have contributed to the war.

It is in vain that Germany has proposed that the question of war guilt should be investigated by a neutral commission; this has met with downright refusal, since the guilt of Germany has supposedly been proved. We refuse to accept this enemy decision. No one can be at the same time prosecutor and judge. The German government has itself initiated an investigation of the causes of the war and its prolongation. We expect the Allied governments to do the same, and we must refuse to discuss the question of guilt until the investigation has been concluded.

The bases on which Germany agreed to make peace with her opponents in November, 1918, in accordance with the principles laid down by the President of the United States of America, determine those obligations for which Germany has agreed to make reparations. The meeting of these obligations is a matter independent of any further settlement of the question of war guilt. We can therefore enter upon peace negotiations with the question of war guilt left aside.[5]

Clemenceau's remarks at the Trianon Palace had shattered any hopes the Germans might have entertained of discussing peace terms with the representatives of the Allied and Associated Powers. As soon as they had digested the contents of the Treaty, which shocked them far more than they had expected, they filed what amounted to a blanket rejection of the Treaty with the President of the Conference (Clemenceau) who curtly brushed it aside.

May 9, 1919

SIR,

The German Peace Delegation has concluded its first survey of the Conditions of Peace. It has been forced to realize that the basis of the peace of justice mutually agreed upon has been abandoned; the promise expressly made to the German people and to the whole of mankind is a thing that the delegation was not prepared to see rendered illusory in this manner.

The draft treaty includes demands which are intolerable for any nation. Furthermore, in the opinion of our experts, many of these demands cannot be met. The German delegation will make good this contention point by point and will in due course submit its observations and the supporting details to the Allied and Associated governments.

Accept, Sir, the assurance of my highest esteem.

[Signed] BROCKDORFF-RANTZAU[6]

The Germans then settled down to the laborious task of protesting the Treaty article by article. They first concentrated their attacks on Article 231, the "war guilt" clause. Besides resentment at having "the judgment of history passed upon the German people by four vengeful men" the Germans had other, far more materialistic, reasons for attacking this clause. The way Part III of the Treaty was formulated, all reparation claims seemed based upon Germany's admission that she was "responsible for the war," and if the Germans succeeded in knocking out that provision the whole case for reparations would collapse.

May 13, 1919

MR. PRESIDENT:

In the draft of a Peace Treaty submitted to the German Delegates, Part VIII, concerning reparation, begins with Article 231, which reads as follows:

The Allied and Associated Governments affirm and Germany accepts the responsibility of Germany and her Allies for causing all the loss and damage to which the Allied and Associated Governments and their nationals have been subjected as a consequence of the war imposed upon them by the aggression of Germany and her Allies.

Now the obligation to make reparation has been accepted by Germany by virtue of the note from Secretary of State Lansing of November 5, 1918, independently of the question of responsibility for the war. The German Delegation cannot admit that there could arise, out of a responsibility incurred by the former German Government in regard to the origin of the world war, any right for the Allied and Associated Powers to be indemnified by Germany for losses suffered during the war. The representatives of the Allied and Associated States have moreover declared several times that the German people should not be held responsible for the faults committed by their Government.

The German people did not will the war and would never have undertaken a war of aggression. They have always remained convinced that this war was for them a defensive war.

The German Delegates also do not share the views of the Allied and Associated Governments in regard to the origin of the war. They cannot consider the former German Government as the party which was solely or chiefly to blame for this war. The draft Treaty of Peace transmitted (by you) contains no facts in support of this view; no proof on the subject is furnished therein. The German Delegates therefore beg (you) to be so good as to communicate to them the report of the Commission set up by the Allied and Associated Governments for the purpose of establishing the responsibility of the authors of the war.

Pray accept, Mr. President, the assurances of my high consideration,

BROCKDORFF-RANTZAU[7]

On May 20th Clemenceau answered the Germans.

MR. PRESIDENT:

In your note of May 13th you state that Germany, while "accepting" in November, 1918, "the obligation to make reparation" did not understand such an acceptance to mean that her responsibility was involved either for the war or for the acts of the former German Government.

It is only possible to conceive of such an obligation if its origin and cause is the responsibility of the author of the damage.

You add that the German people would never have undertaken a war of aggression. Yet, in the note from Secretary of State Lansing of November 5th, 1918, which you approve of and adduce in favor of your contention, it is stated that the obligation to make reparation arises out of "Germany's aggression by land, sea and air."

As the German Government did not at the time make any protest against this allegation, it thereby recognized it as well-founded.

Therefore Germany recognized in 1918 implicitly but clearly, both the aggression and her responsibility.

It is too late to seek to deny them today. It would be impossible, you state further, that the German people should be regarded as the accomplices of the faults committed by the "former German Government." However, Germany has never claimed, and such a declaration would have been contrary to all principles of international law, that a modification of its political regime or a change in the governing personalities would be sufficient to extinguish an obligation already undertaken by any nation.

She did not act upon the principle she now contends for either in 1871 as regards France, after the proclamation of the Republic, nor in 1917, in regard to Russia after the revolution which abolished the Tzarist regime.

Finally, you ask that the report of the Commission on Responsibility may be communicated to you. In reply we beg to say that the Allied and Associated Powers consider the reports of the Commissions set up by the Peace Conference as documents of an internal character which cannot be transmitted to you.

Accept, Mr. President, etc.

G. CLEMENCEAU[8]

Brockdorff-Rantzau replied four days later.

SIR,

The contents of Your Excellency's note of 20th inst., concerning the question of Germany's responsibility for the consequences of the war, have shown the German Peace Delegation that the Allied and Associated Governments have completely misunderstood the sense in which the German Government and the German nation tacitly gave their assent to the note of Secretary of State Lansing of November 5th,

1918. In order to clear up this misunderstanding the German Delegation find themselves compelled to call back to the memory of the Allied and Associated Governments the events which preceded that note.

The President of the United States of America had several times solemnly declared that the World War should be terminated not by a Peace of Might, but by a Peace of Right, and that America had entered the war solely for this Peace of Right. For this war-aim the formula was established: "No annexations, no contributions, no punitive damages."

On the other hand, however, the President demanded the unconditional restitution of the violated Right. The positive side of this demand found expression in the fourteen points which were laid down by President Wilson in his message of January 8th, 1918. This message contains two principal claims against the German nation: Firstly, the surrender of important parts of German territory in the West and in the East on the basis of national self-determination; secondly, the promise to restore the occupied territories of Belgium and the North of France. Both demands could be acceded to by the German Government and the German nation, as the principle of self-determination was concordant with the new democratic constitution of Germany, and as the territories to be restored had been aggressed by Germany with the terrors of war through an act contrary to the Law of Nations, namely by the violation of Belgium's neutrality.

The right of self-determination of the Polish nation had, as a matter of fact, already been acknowledged by the former German Government, just the same as the wrong done to Belgium.

When, therefore, in the note the Entente transmitted by Secretary of State Lansing on November 5, 1918, to the German Government a more detailed interpretation was given of what was meant by restoration of the occupied territories, it appeared from the German point of view to be a matter of course that the duty to make compensation, established in this interpretation, could not relate to other territories than those the damaging of which had to be admitted as contrary to Right and the restoration of which had been proclaimed as war-aim by leading enemy statesmen. Thus President Wilson in his message of January 8, 1918, expressly termed the reparation of the wrong done to Belgium as the healing act without which the whole structure and validity of international law would be forever impaired. In a like manner the English Prime Minister, Mr. Lloyd George, in his speech made in the House of Commons on October 22, 1917, proclaimed:

> The first requirement always put forward by the British Government and their Allies has been the complete restoration, political, territorial and economic of the independence of Belgium and such reparation as can be made for the devastation of its towns and provinces. This is no demand for war indemnity, such as that imposed on France by Germany in 1871. It is not an attempt to shift the cost of warlike operations from one belligerent to another.

What is here said of Belgium, Germany had to acknowledge also with regard to the North of France, as the German armies had only reached the French territories by the violation of Belgium's neutrality.

It was for this aggression that the German Government admitted Germany to be responsible, it did not admit Germany's alleged responsibility for the origin of the war or for the merely incidental fact that the formal declaration of war had emanated from Germany. The importance of State Secretary Lansing's note for Germany rather lay in the fact of the duty to make reparation not being limited to the restoration of material value, but being extended to every kind of damage suffered by the civilian population in the occupied territory, in person or in property, during the continuance of warfare, be it by land, by sea or from the air.

The German nation was certainly conscious of the one-sidedness lying in their being charged with the restoration of Belgium and Northern France, but being denied compensation for the territories in the East of Germany which had been invaded and devastated by the troops of the Russian Tzarism, acting on a long premeditated plan. They have, however, acknowledged that the Russian aggression must, according to the formal provisions of the Law of Nations, be differently stated than the invasion of Belgium and have therefore desisted from demanding compensation on their part.

If the Allied and Associated Governments should now maintain the view that compensation is due for every act contrary to the Law of Nations which has been committed during the war, the German Delegation does not dispute the correctness in principle of this standpoint; they beg, however, to point out that in such case Germany also has a considerable damage-account to set up and that the duty to compensate incumbent on her adversaries, particularly as against the German civilian population, which has suffered immeasurable injury by the blockade of Starvation, a measure opposed to the Law of Nations, is not limited to the time when actual warfare was still being carried on from both sides, but arises in special pregnancy with regard to the time when only a one-sided war was waged by the Allied and Associated Powers against a Germany which had voluntarily laid down arms. This view of the Allied and Associated Governments, at any rate, departs from the agreement which Germany had entered into before the Armistice was concluded. It raises an endless series of controversial questions on the horizon of the Peace negotiations and can only be brought to a practical solution through a system of impartial international arbitration, an arbitration as provided for in Article 13, Part 2, of the Draft of the Conditions of Peace. This clause prescribes:

> Disputes as to the interpretation of a treaty, as to any question of international law, as to the existence of any fact which if established would constitute a breach of any international obligation, or as to the extent and nature of the reparation to be made for any such breach, are declared to be among those which are generally suitable for submission to arbitration.

Your Excellency has further pointed out in your note of 20th inst., that according to the principles of international law no nation could through any alteration of its political form of government or through a change in the persons of its leaders, cause to be extinguished an obligation once incurred by its government. The German Peace Delegation is far from contesting the correctness of this principle; they also do not protest against the execution of the agreement introduced by the former government's proposal of October 5th, 1918, but they do take objection to the punishment, provided for by the Draft of the Peace Treaty, for the alleged offences of the former political and military leaders of Germany. The President of the United States of America on December 4th, 1917, declared that the war should not end in vindictive action of any kind, that no nation or people should be robbed or punished because the irresponsible rulers of the country had themselves done deep and abominable wrong. The German Delegation does not plead these or other promises to avoid any obligation incumbent on Germany by the Law of Nations, but they feel entitled to call them to memory if the German nation is to be held responsible for the origin of the war and made liable for its damages.

Whilst the public negotiations immediately preceding the conclusion of the Armistice were still going on, the German nation was promised that Germany's lot would be fundamentally altered if it were severed from the fate of its rulers. The German Delegation would not like to take your Excellency's words to mean that the promise made by the Allied and Associated Governments at that time was merely a ruse of war employed to paralyze the resistance of the German nation, and that this promise is now to be withdrawn.

Your Excellency has finally contended that the Allied and Associated Governments had the right to treat Germany after the same methods as had been adopted by her in the Peace Treaties of Frankfort and Brest-Litovsk. The German Delegation for the present refrains from examining in what respects these two acts of peace differ from the present Peace Draft, for it is now too late for the Allied and Associated Governments to found a claim of right on these precedents. The moment for so doing had come when they were put before the alternative of accepting the fourteen points of the President of the United States of America as a basis of Peace or rejecting them. In these fourteen points the reparation of the wrong done in 1870–1871 was expressly demanded and the Peace of Brest-Litovsk was spoken of as a deterrent example. The Allied and Associated Governments at that time declined to take a peace of violence of the past as a model.

The German nation never having assumed the responsibility for the origin of the war, has a right to demand that it be informed by its opponents from what reasons and on what evidence the conditions of Peace are based on Germany's being to blame for all damages and all sufferings of this war. It cannot therefore consent to be put off with the remark that the data on the question of the responsibility collected by the Allied and Associated Governments through a special Commission are documents of an internal nature of these Governments. This, a question of life or death for the German nation, must be discussed in all publicity; methods of secret diplomacy are here out of place. The German Government reserve for themselves the liberty of coming back on the subject.

Accept, Sir, the assurance of my high esteem.

BROCKDORFF-RANTZAU*[9]

* Both the Germans and the Allies filed extensive memoranda with the Conference on the subject of war responsibility. These documents, of great historical interest, run to such length that they have been left out of this book. The reader is referred to Documents 51 and 52 in Luckau's *The German Delegation at the Paris Peace Conference.* (Ed.)

After having protested almost every single article of the Treaty in a succession of notes, the Germans, on May 29th, filed their counterproposal. This document, of roughly 25,000 words, suggested plebiscites in every area that Germany was to cede (including Alsace-Lorraine), requested immediate admission of Germany to the League of Nations, and offered payment of reparations not exceeding 100,000,000,000 gold marks ($25,000,-000,000). President Wilson called a meeting of his Commissioners to discuss what lines American policy should take.

THE PRESIDENT: Gentlemen, we have come together in order that we may hear from you on the question of the German counter-proposals. We all have moving recollections of the struggles through which we have gone in framing the treaty, and the efforts we made that were successful, and the efforts we made that were unsuccessful to make the terms different from what they are, and I have come here not to express an opinion but hear opinions, and I think perhaps the best course to follow will be to get a general impression from each other as to which parts of the German counter-arguments have made the greatest impression upon us.

Just as a guide, I find that the parts that have made the greatest impression on our British colleagues are the arguments with regard to the eastern frontier with Poland, the parts with regard to reparations, the parts about the period of occupation, together with the point about the League of Nations, their impression being that the Germans might very well be given reasonably to expect that the period of their probation would not be long in the matter of admission into the League. Those are the four points, the four subjects upon which the German counter-proposals have made the deepest impressions upon them. That might be the start.

The reparation is the biggest point. That involves left-overs of the financial clauses. I would be glad to hear from anyone of our financial group who would like to express himself on that point.

MR. NORMAN H. DAVIS: We feel that the Germans have really given us a basis for getting together properly on reparation, by coming back with a fixed sum. . . . There is a considerable possibility of getting together there, if we can get the French to agree upon a fixed sum. . . . We have always insisted on the necessity of having a fixed sum, because by leaving it indefinite we had to give considerable powers to the Reparations Commission, and that is what seems to worry the Germans more than anything else. . . .

THE PRESIDENT: May I ask that what I say by way of reference to our British colleagues be not repeated outside of this room, because I am at liberty to use it only for the purposes of this conference. But here are the alternative methods of reparation which were suggested: first, that the Germans should undertake as a contract the whole task of restoration, that is to say, the physical restoration of the ravaged parts of northern France, and that a sum should be fixed in the treaty of peace, under several items in the category of damages, the principle being that inasmuch as it was impossible now to estimate what the actual restoration would cost, that they should be put under contract to restore northern France within a definite period, and that, since the rest of the categories would perhaps hold them, a definite sum ought to be arrived at in regard to that.

The alternative plan was—and it is a rather vague one—that the Germans should sign the reparation clauses as they stand, but that three months should be given them to effect an arrangement for fixing a definite sum in cash as a compensation of all claims. That the reparation clauses were to stand, giving them three years for proposals as to the definite sum.

MR. BARUCH: We discussed those two alternatives that you speak of, Mr. President, yesterday, but we still feel that the best solution would be to come to a fixed sum now, to start with. . . .

MR. LAMONT: . . . whichever way one looks at it, from the Allied point of view or from the German point of view, it is better to make it definite. Germany cannot start her economic and industrial life, cannot gain any credit, as long as it remains open. . . .

MR. DAVIS: We are convinced, Mr. President, that on account of Europe's financial situation today it is a most important thing to fix an amount, and an amount which Germany and the world itself have some hope of her being able to pay, and carrying out, which can be used as a basis for France and Italy and the other countries getting on their feet and meeting their requirements.

Under the present arrangements, as the Germans very properly state, if they are not prosperous and cannot get back to work they will pay nothing, but on the other hand, if they buckle down to work and work hard and save, the harder they work and the more they save, the more they will pay. And that is a rather poor incentive for the Germans to buckle down and work hard. But if there is a fixed amount which will let them see a chance of getting from under some day, I believe that would be a better incentive for them.

THE PRESIDENT: How about the other side of it: a fixed sum will form a basis of credit for the other nations, but what will form a basis for Germany's credit?

COLONEL HOUSE: It was practically a fixed sum.

THE PRESIDENT: Yes, there would be that definiteness in it, but where would her assets be?

MR. DAVIS: We must insist upon her being left with sufficient assets as a working capital.

THE PRESIDENT: As a matter of fact the Reparations Commission can do that.

MR. DAVIS: They are permitted to leave her with certain assets, except the ships. We feel that some arrangement certainly must be made whereby Germany can at least have a sufficient number of those ships, either retaining them or making some arrangement for getting them back, so that she will have enough for her own trade, and which I understand amounts to about one-third of the ships which she has turned over.

SECRETARY LANSING: Now Germany offers a fixed sum, does she?

MR. DAVIS: Yes.

SECRETARY LANSING: It is 100 milliards of marks?

MR. DAVIS: Yes. Of course they make quite a large amount of deductions. They say that they will pay the first sum of 20 milliards of marks in the first seven years, but that you must deduct from that the war materials they have turned over and everything else they have turned over and will turn over under the treaty, and also the proportionate share of the pre-war and the war debt of Alsace-Lorraine and of that part of the territory that Poland gets, which they estimate roughly would amount to about three million dollars.

MR. LAMONT: Still, Mr. Secretary, it is very striking that they have made two definite offers: the offer of 20 milliards, and the further offer to devote to reparations a sum annually amounting approximately to the total net peace budget of the German Empire, between $750,000,000 and one billion dollars.

SECRETARY LANSING: As I recall it, they offer to pay 20 milliards of marks on or before May 1st, 1926, and then they offer to pay one milliard a year after that. But they will increase it, on the basis that their people shall not be taxed more than the greatest amount paid by any injured country.

MR. DAVIS: They say that as a result they will be compelled, according to that, to tax that heavily; but at least 20 milliards they offer to pay within seven years, and without interest. That is not a capital sum. If you reduce that to a capital sum that will amount to 12½ or 15 milliards. We feel, from a practical standpoint, that it is better to have it interest bearing. Of course you have to give them a few years before they can afford to pay interest, because otherwise it would run so fast against them that they could not catch up.

SECRETARY LANSING: It does not come so very far from the 15 billions of dollars talked about.

MR. LAMONT: It is a little bit less. After you take away deductions it would amount to the capital sum of 10 billion dollars.

THE PRESIDENT: Do you understand that the French this morning were not willing to consider an alteration or change of that sort? . . .

MR. VANCE MCCORMICK: He [Tardieu] said that every modification proposed by the British was against the French. The British never mentioned any concession regarding ships or the colonies, and Mr. Tardieu called Mr. Lloyd George's attention to that fact. Mr. Tardieu's position was that they should not agree to a change in the present treaty; that during these five months the experts have discussed these questions pro and con, and having finally come to a decision, it would be fatal to change any principle whatever. The question of machinery of execution, as you stated in your note, might be considered; that was the position the French took. And as he went out of the room he intimated to Mr. Lamont that he might consider such questions as the question of the reparation clauses, along the line we have just been discussing, provided it was not opening the door to concessions along the other lines. France could not afford to concede anything further.

THE PRESIDENT: Would he regard fixing a capital sum as a modification of principle, or a method?

MR. MCCORMICK: A method. Didn't you gather that? (Addressing Mr. Lamont.)

MR. LAMONT: Yes. Mr. Loucheur, of course, has more to say about that than Mr. Tardieu has. If it had not been for the British "Heavenly Twins"* we could have gotten together with Loucheur months ago.

MR. DAVIS: Now he is a little bit worried about that political aspect of it, but if there are some changes made which would affect the

* Lords Sumner and Cunliffe. [Ed.]

British I think it would have a certain influence on the French, but, as Tardieu says, the only changes that are proposed are practically those that affect the French.

COLONEL HOUSE: Premier Clemenceau told me last night that he was willing to discuss Silesia. He was not willing to discuss the period of occupation, and he was not willing to discuss any of the other things that Lloyd George wanted.

THE PRESIDENT: Did he say that he would not discuss reparation?

COLONEL HOUSE: No, and I gathered that he would. I think we could get him to discuss reparation. And I also think—much to my surprise—that he would about the League of Nations. He said he would not consider for a moment letting the Germans in now, and I said: "Well, your attitude about that I think is the worst attitude for France, and I cannot understand it. It seems to me that you can see that the sooner the League of Nations gets its grip on Germany the better it would be for France." He said: "I concede that; that is all right; but not for the moment. Presently." So I don't think he is going to be very bad on that. I think the Germans could be told privately that Germany will come in very shortly. I think we could get him to consent to that.

THE PRESIDENT: Well, if you gentlemen of the reparation group had a free hand—if only we ourselves were concerned—what would you propose with regard to the reparation?

MR. DAVIS: Well, we have not definitely agreed among ourselves as to just what we would propose, but we certainly are in accord with this, that we would propose and insist upon a fixed sum, and that that fixed sum would be as high as we really could get Germany to agree to without having a bayonet at her throat, because, after all, the important thing, as stated before, is to get something which can be used as a basis for France and Italy to get more credit, and which will not be so burdensome as will prevent Germany from going ahead with restoring her industrial life, because, after all, what they need to do more than anything is to get people to work, and they have pretty nearly all exhausted their credit. Loucheur is worried about that now, and the important thing is not so much what Germany can pay now, really just now, as fixing a reasonable amount which the German people are willing to buckle down to attempting to pay, and which the investors of the world think she will pay,—and they are rather apt to believe that Germany will pay what she undertakes to pay.

THE PRESIDENT: The aspect of the subject which interests me is the world aspect of it. Unless these securities that Germany is going to give are known to be worth something they cannot be used as a basis for credit, and somebody else will have to supply the credit. Now they cannot be made worth anything unless Germany has the means of going to work and producing. Which is the result of saying that they cannot be made worth anything unless she has assets to begin with to establish her own credit. And therefore the thing has two sides to it; not only the aspect of Germany and France and Italy —but the world aspect; working out a method by which this sum would be made not only definite but worth something, by having means for Germany to get to work.

MR. DAVIS: Yes, we think so.

THE PRESIDENT: Now it seems to me that we could have made it evident to the Germans, by explaining to them, that the real functions of the Reparations Commission, are, as I understand them to be, to help them in carrying out their obligations. The only trouble is, that it is one thing to say that this is the way the Reparations Commission is going to work, and another thing to find it in the treaty. Because we, of the present group of persons, are putting a certain interpretation on the treaty, but there will be others following us who may not put the same interpretation upon it.

MR. DAVIS: We probably have not got in there as clear a picture of what our idea was as to the policy that would be followed by the Reparations Commission as we should have, and it would be well, and it would undoubtedly affect the Germans, if they could be told.

THE PRESIDENT: Why not write—I don't know what the language would be—an accompanying memorandum, agreed to by all the powers, as to the method of administration by the Reparations Commission?

MR. BARUCH: Of course if we fixed a sum the Reparations Commission would die. If we fixed a definite sum, and Germany agreed to it, and she delivered, the Reparations Commission, as we have got it set up, would die, and another would be set up to receive the funds and bonds.

MR. DAVIS: The Reparations Commission was set up principally because they were leaving this matter indefinite, and because we were imposing a burden upon Germany concerning which there was some doubt as to her capacity to meet. But as it was clearly understood that they must follow a constructive policy, and that Germany could not pay anything unless she was given facilities and working capital it was absolutely necessary to set up this commission, with the idea of getting all they could out of Germany, but doing this in a broad way. But that is not the picture that is really conveyed in there (i.e., in the Treaty). The powers of the Reparations Commission are, in a sense, destructive as far as Germany is concerned—they could be—but it ought to be explained to the Germans that no intelligent people could perform its destructive powers unless Germany wilfully failed to comply.

There is no limitation on what the Reparations Commission can do, and since the armistice the agreements with the Germans have been outrageously violated by the French, as for instance, the Luxembourg protocol, etc., and the Germans have had an experience of what the giving of this power has meant, and they complained of it, to which I responded and asked them if they did not think they were entitled to it. They have got evidence to show that the commissions have thus far been outrageously unfair.

THE PRESIDENT: You think that difficulty would be met then by a fixed sum?

MR. SUMMERS: Unquestionably. We have always rewarded, by pensions and in similar ways, deeds of heroism, and each nation has chosen to reward its heroes as it saw fit, and to place that on the Germans on the basis that the French have awarded theirs is unprecedented in the history of the world. And if we had stood for actual reparation we might get some place within a rational sum, which Germany could pay, and we would have a basis for understanding upon that amount.

MR. LAMONT: Mr. President, I believe our difficulties with Germany would fade away if you and Mr. Clemenceau and Mr. Lloyd George would instruct your technical committees to arrive at a definite sum within twenty-four hours instead of two years, and at the same time to reach an agreement as to how much working capital should be left in Germany's hands.

THE PRESIDENT: We instructed them once to find a definite sum. And then we got Klotz on the brain.

MR. LAMONT: Mr. Lloyd George kicked over the traces, but now he has come back to the fold.

MR. DAVIS: You remember they used to change commissions such as this, in times gone by, every time they decided against the wishes of the heads of the states.

COLONEL HOUSE: Do you remember how we always knew, when

the individual members would come into a meeting just what the trend of the meeting was going to be that day?

THE PRESIDENT: Now the joke of it is that Lord Sumner was one of those who contributed to the unanimous counsel of the British the other day, and he takes a different position now.

MR. LAMONT: I believe we could get together on this point.

MR. DAVIS: Of course on those constructions you should make the necessary consequential changes in the Reparations Commission, and if possible do something to get away with it. I am afraid you will have to have a reparations commission for a while.

But it is necessary to have a commission, really, to receive the funds and the bonds, and open the trust for the proper distribution at the proper time.

THE PRESIDENT: The other most prominent subject is the subject of the occupation of the Rhenish Provinces for five, ten and fifteen years. And I say in the same confidential way that I indicated a moment ago, that Mr. Lloyd George represented his military advisers and his cabinet as all together a unit that the period of occupation should extend over a period of only two years, with a possibility of extending it further in case the Germans refused to carry out the terms of the treaty, or in any deliberate way failed to carry out the terms. That creates a very serious impasse between the British and French opinion.

If I may just say a word of explanation, the French military opinion, as it has been interpreted to me, does not believe that the fifteen-year occupation is in any way satisfying. As I understand it, Marshal Foch wanted to occupy the Rhenish provinces for thirty years, the probable period of payment of reparation, and it was a compromise, I infer, which reduced it to fifteen years. And they have made an arrangement under which this interesting comment has been made, that the areas of occupation, one for five, one for ten and one for fifteen years,—all abutting on the Rhine, of course—extend in a line northwest and southeast, not east and west, and the reason given me for that was that extending that way they would always protect the direct route from Germany to Paris. But the direct route is not the route that is at all likely to be taken.

The route that has usually been taken, and that was taken this time, is the northern route, across which lies the area which is to be first evacuated, and the territory next most likely to be used, from a military point of view, is to be evacuated in ten years, and the territory which would certainly not be used is to be evacuated in fifteen years.

And the intimation was that the real object was the control of the navigation of the Rhine. That is the last area, and all this occupation touches, of course, Lorraine and the commercial interests of France that center on the Rhine.

So that the question of occupation has this drawback to it: it is not strictly speaking a military question, apparently. It is a means of quieting public opinion during the period that Germany is certainly not going to be able to do anything in a military line, and withdrawing their forces just at about the time when she is likely to recuperate, which is not, if I am stating it correctly, a military proposition at all.

And another very serious drawback to it—at least from the point of view of several of the powers, on reparations—is that Germany is to pay for this Army of Occupation, and it would cost several hundreds of millions to maintain it, and those millions would come out of the reparations, and if you have a fixed sum—not otherwise—it would be that much in addition to the French portion of the reparations, because everyone contends that the Army of Occupation will be French. They would not expect Great Britain and ourselves to furnish more than some small number that would be sufficient to keep the colours afloat and justify the name of an inter-allied force.

So I do not know who it calls for to discuss it, if I am right that it is not strictly a military question, and if it is a civil question it is a question involving many embarrassments, chiefly embarrassments of French public opinion.

But I would be very glad if the military people would fire away at it if they have anything to say. . . .

General Bliss: Mr. President, I would like to say one word on that subject. I think as you just stated, it is almost entirely a political question rather than a military one, because no essential military objects will be accomplished by the military occupation of the territories proposed to be occupied under the proposed conditions. And I have never been in favour of the prolonged military occupation and I base my views on two considerations: the first is the matter of good sound policy, and the other sound business.

As a matter of policy I have always—and a good many other military men agree with me on that—looked with apprehension on the possibilities of a military occupation of a territory, the people of which we will be officially at peace with for a long time. It is so likely to result in incidents that will bring about the very thing that we want, of course, to avoid, and that is a resumption of war. It has always seemed to me that it is almost a slap in the face of the League of Nations, in which we are all so interested, to assume that the execution of this treaty, extending over a long term of years, can only be accomplished by a military force instead of by this League of Nations, which presumably at an early date will be in operation.

Then you have yourself pointed out the reason why it is not sound business.

Mr. Ribot in the speech that he made in the French Senate the other day used figures which I have no doubt are exaggerated, but they still, after making a due allowance for exaggeration, indicate a wasteful amount of money that would be simply eaten up in the collection of the remainder, and he estimated that out of the first 25 milliards of francs that would come from Germany, partly to the French and partly to the Belgians, at least 15 milliards of it would be eaten up in the expense of the army of occupation. I think that figure is exaggerated, and he probably assumes a continuance of an army of occupation approximating the present force there, which now numbers a million men—a grossly exaggerated and unnecessary number for any purpose that it is agreed it may be called upon to accomplish.

The Marshal's demand is that after the signature of peace there be maintained an army of thirty infantry divisions, and not to exceed five cavalry divisions, which, together with all the attached services, would amount to somewhere in the neighbourhood of 600,000 men. It is not enough for war, on the supposition that Germany could resume the war—which she cannot do—and it is entirely unnecessary on the assumption that she cannot resume the war. He proposes to keep that army there during the period of disarmament in Germany. Now no one knows how long that will be. The Germans in their reply have said that it is technically impossible to execute the clauses of the treaty on which time limit was imposed, within the time limits imposed; that the time limits should be prolonged, and they say the matter should be subject of negotiations. And in the Marshal's office yesterday afternoon in the conference which we had, it was agreed by all that it was absolutely impossible to comply with the terms, so far as the time limits are concerned.

The President: Did the French agree to that?

General Bliss: Oh, yes. Now how long that will continue, nobody knows. But during its continuance, during all this period, military control of commissions will be kept in operation, which will also be contributing to the diminution of the available funds that they get out of Germany for reparations and otherwise.

Now those who have read the German counter-proposals on the subject of military, naval and air terms, know that they accept everything in principle subject to their admission into the League of Nations, and in regard to this term of occupation—whatever it be—if Germany is at any time to be admitted into the League of Nations, certainly that occupation in Germany must cease the moment she is so admitted. It would be intolerable, and there is no provision in any part of the Covenant for the occupation of territory of a nation which has been accepted into membership in the League of Nations, which acceptance is only done after you are satisfied that she has given every guarantee to comply with the League's obligations.

I understand that there has been some consideration given to a very material reduction in the period of occupation, and I hope that it can be carried through, and that whatever that time will be—

THE PRESIDENT: (Interrupting) By whom, General?

GENERAL BLISS: Based on the German proposals, there has been more or less consideration given—

THE PRESIDENT: By the French?

GENERAL BLISS: Well, it has been discussed. I don't think the French are willing to consider it now, but to take not to exceed four months to consider that. It might be prolonged long after that and still come within the limits proposed in the treaty, and I take it if any change is made at all, or if the present figures are kept to five, ten or fifteen years, occupation should cease the moment Germany becomes a member of the League of Nations.

Personally I hope very much that the term of occupation made by common agreement will be very materially reduced.

THE PRESIDENT: The only door for consideration which Mr. Clemenceau said he was willing to leave open yesterday, was the cost. I was interested to know just what he would consider, and he said at first that he would not consider the reduction of the term of occupation at all, that was impossible for him, and then he subsequently said he would consider it from the point of view of the cost. Now just what and how much that meant I do not know; we did not go into it. But of course that is a very serious side. If they agree to a fixed sum of reparation, then every dollar of what has been spent on occupation is a reduction of that sum.

MR. DAVIS: It goes to support their army.

THE PRESIDENT: It goes to support their army, yes, but they would not otherwise be paid to support so large an army. I don't know how large an army they would otherwise have. Can you tell us, General?

GENERAL BLISS: Under their organic law they would have 800,000 men, and I have not seen nor heard any word from any source nor have I heard of any proposition being before their legislature to modify that.

COLONEL HOUSE: Don't you suppose it would be possible upon these disputed questions, that is, not upon all the German questions, but upon some of them, to appoint committees of the experts and see what modifications, if any, could be made and agreed upon?

THE PRESIDENT: Well, the plan I had in mind was to have our own conference, as we were advised that Mr. Orlando was having his this morning, and Mr. Clemenceau is having his,—in order that we might, without having any of the usual round-about expressions of international intercourse, learn each others' minds, real minds, and then my idea was that each one of our groups would either retire, and they, or some representatives whom they would select, would meet the corresponding groups of the other countries and have an exchange of views.

COLONEL HOUSE: That was what I had in mind.

THE PRESIDENT: Have a clearing house.

COLONEL HOUSE: Wouldn't it modify the general selection if we knew what the commission that Mr. Davis is on is doing?

THE PRESIDENT: John W. Davis?

COLONEL HOUSE: Yes.

MR. JOHN W. DAVIS: I don't know that that commission has any more to do than to recommend the size of the army. All they have to do is to draw up a scheme of the organization of the army and the size.

THE PRESIDENT: That might soften the blow to them.

MR. JOHN W. DAVIS: Yes, make it a little bit less Draconian.

SECRETARY LANSING: Is it possible to fix the time when Germany can be admitted into the League of Nations?

THE PRESIDENT: I don't honestly think it is. I think it is necessary that we should know that the change in government and the governmental method in Germany is genuine and permanent. We don't know either of them yet.

SECRETARY LANSING: When are we going to know? When are you going to get consent from all these countries, from France or the Executive Council?

THE PRESIDENT: I think that France would be one of the first.

MR. DAVIS: Do you think it would if it were conditioned upon withdrawing the Army of Occupation? That is mentioned as a condition upon Germany coming into the League of Nations.

THE PRESIDENT: Except as to Germany paying for the army. I think she would be sick of the Army of Occupation.

MR. DAVIS: She wants to control this from an economic standpoint too.

THE PRESIDENT: But I don't see how they can do that without a proper convention.

MR. DAVIS: We have a convention now, you know, with them, and they are all the time springing the Economic Council, and they do not stand by the convention.

THE PRESIDENT: Convention of what?

MR. DAVIS: Among the Allied and Associated Powers.

THE PRESIDENT: But the convention I am speaking of is the permanent convention, the fifteen-year convention under which there would be no interference with the economic or industrial life of the country whatever.

MR. DAVIS: But now I see there is a convention between the Allied and Associated Powers that there would not be an interference, and the French are not living up to it.

THE PRESIDENT: My only hope is that when we sign peace those things will be settled.

. . . .

THE PRESIDENT: Now what about the eastern borders of Germany?

DR. R. H. LORD: . . . the general tenor of the German argument about the cession to be made to Poland struck me as a rather weak attempt to escape from the principle laid down in the fourteen points with regard to the united Polish state, containing all Polish territories, and a secure access to the sea. . . .

The point which the Germans lay most stress on, perhaps, is the question of Upper Silesia, and perhaps that is a question on which it is better—

COLONEL HOUSE: (Interrupting) They ask for a plebiscite there, and following that plebiscite, what in your opinion would be the result?

DR. LORD: My opinion is that it would result favorably to Poland

—I have very little doubt about that—if it could be arranged under conditions that would ensure a fair expression of the popular will. . . .

Under present conditions it is impossible to have a fair plebiscite. You would have to occupy the country with Allied troops, and I wonder whether the Allied and Associated Governments are prepared to do that. . . .

Upper Silesia is a country where a very great part of the land and a great part of the industries of the country are in the hands of a very small group of great magnates. There is such a concentration of property in the hands of a few great families as you find almost nowhere else in Germany. They are in the hands of such families as the Hohenlohe, von Pless, and half a dozen others. And then the great industries of the country are also controlled by German capital. It means that the Polish population is economically, without a doubt, in great dependence upon German land owners and capitalists. . . . I can think of few countries where the countryman finds it so dangerous to express his opinion at the polls.

As for the other general fact about the Upper Silesian situation, the part of Upper Silesia which the treaty proposes to give to Poland . . . comes as near to being indisputably Polish territory as any part of eastern Europe.

The chief value of that territory to Germany, of course, lies in its immense mineral wealth, which is undoubtedly the fact, as their response says that Upper Silesia produces 23 percent of the total coal output of the German Empire, and I think it is something like four-fifths of the production of zinc, and a large part of the production of iron. . . .

If Upper Silesia contains about one-quarter of Germany's coal output, it contains about three-quarters of the coal output of the territories of Polish nationality, so the loss to Germany on the one hand would also mean that it would be a serious blow and a loss to Poland on the other. Three-quarters of her coal would be a far more decisive thing.

MR. LAMONT: I don't see how that could be a loss to Poland, because she never had it.

THE PRESIDENT: But it is theoretically Polish.

COLONEL HOUSE: That was never a part of Poland, was it?

THE PRESIDENT: Creating a state out of Polish population in some places like Upper Silesia which never constituted a part of ancient Poland, isn't that right, Dr. Lord?

DR. LORD: Not entirely, Mr. President. The German memorandum is an extremely fallacious article in its historical data. It states repeatedly that Upper Silesia belonged to Germany for 750 years, which is not at all true. Upper Silesia was Polish from the beginning; was Polish for several centuries.

THE PRESIDENT: You mean it was part of the Polish state, or only Polish in population?

DR. LORD: Part of the Polish state, and it resulted in there being there a Polish population. It passed from Poland to Bohemia some time in 1500; from Bohemia it passed to Austria in 1600, and it passed to the Germans in 1700; so it belonged to the German state, to the Germans, about 200 years.

MR. LAMONT: It has not belonged to Poland for 400 years.

SECRETARY LANSING: Isn't the real point the question where the coal is used after it is mined? Is it used mainly in Poland today?

DR. LORD: No. There was a considerable export to Poland, but in the main the coal was used in eastern Germany, in the region east of Berlin. Now they point out that a great part of that territory which is wholly dependent on Silesia is going to Poland. Poland and West Prussia do consume a great part of it. A great part of it went to Austria-Hungary also.

SECRETARY LANSING: Where did what is now new Poland get her coal if she did not get it from Silesia?

DR. LORD: Russian Poland got about six million tons a year in the Dombrowka district. There is a coal mining region in Russian Poland and also a smaller coal mining region in Galicia.

SECRETARY LANSING: And German Poland got how much of its coal from this region?

DR. LORD: All of it.

SECRETARY LANSING: How much did they use?

DR. LORD: I cannot give you the exact figures.

SECRETARY LANSING: Approximately?

DR. LORD: I know that in Poland this winter they were practically without coal.

SECRETARY LANSING: Then Poland will get a good deal more coal than she had before, if she gets this area?

DR. LORD: It depends on what you mean by "Poland."

SECRETARY LANSING: I am speaking of this territory that is now embraced in the new boundaries.

DR. LORD: Yes.

SECRETARY LANSING: She would get a good deal more coal?

DR. LORD: Yes.

THE PRESIDENT: After all that is probably susceptible of solution in a different way; by guarantees obtained as to the supply of coal, that is, putting no restrictions on the supplying of coal to Germany.

MR. BARUCH: It is true that the coal and the iron is more or less locked up in the mines of Germany, and, as suggested by you, in the division of this territory it should be guaranteed that the coal and iron should go, anyhow for a number of years until there is a chance for readjustment, to the places it had gone before.

THE PRESIDENT: That no restrictions should be placed on it.

MR. DAVIS: Where it goes naturally. To do that, under the present treaty Poland has a right to take over all this property, the privately owned property, after the war, which is a rather unusual procedure; while the Germans have developed this, the Polish government can come and purchase all this property and turn it over to Polish citizens.

THE PRESIDENT: They have to pay for it.

MR. DAVIS: That is true, but Germany has to pay for it.

THE PRESIDENT: How do you mean?

MR. SUMMERS: Germany agrees to reimburse her nationals.

THE PRESIDENT: You mean the property can be expropriated?

MR. DAVIS: Not for public use but for private use. In other words, the German government has to pay its citizens for the property which the Polish government wants to take from them.

MR. TAUSSIG: The Polish government may take it from the people who now own it, and the valuation is fixed by the Polish government, without any control or supervision of any kind. I think that is one of the worst provisions of the treaty.

MR. PALMER: That is one of the unexpected results of the application of the general clauses to a case with which we have not been concerned at all. The general committee on Alien Enemy Property hadn't anything to do with Alsace-Lorraine or Poland, which we understood were to be covered by different clauses entirely—as took place in the case of Alsace-Lorraine. It is astonishing to me that there should exist in Silesia any such effect as has been outlined, and I think Silesia ought to be treated by itself. A large territory like that should have its own special clauses covering it, because this particular language which we have adopted for application under totally different circumstances, has an unexpected effect.

THE PRESIDENT: That had escaped my notice.

MR. PALMER: I am not sure that it has that result, Mr. President, but if it has, it should be provided for.

MR. BARUCH: The economic feature of the Silesian question should be taken up and have special treatment as regards the distribution of the assets, and also the questions of private property and other matters of that kind, and I think that it does require and is entitled to special treatment.

MR. DAVIS: It is not supposed that the Polish government should take that—

THE PRESIDENT: That is not in the Polish part of the treaty.

MR. DAVIS: It is not in the Polish part, Mr. President. Poland has been construed in this treaty as one of the Allied Governments. It is in the economic clauses.

MR. TAUSSIG: Poland figures as one of the Allied and Associated Powers, and in drafting those provisions of the Allied and Associated Powers, I don't believe that it was expected that it would be a constituted state, figuring in every respect as a duly constituted Allied and Associated Power, but they had it in the treaty draft. I do not think, Mr. President, there would be any serious difficulty in disposing of that problem. I think the disposition of the German property, after it came under Polish jurisdiction, would not be difficult. I think it is more a matter of sentiment. The sentimental features of it are more important,—the fact of depriving the Germans of property which has been German for many centuries presents a more serious difficulty; there is a sentimental difficulty on both sides.

THE PRESIDENT: Now is there not in Paris some Polish representative with whom you could discuss these economic aspects of the matter at once so as to see if there is not some arrangement that would not be so objectionable in regard to raw materials, and this matter of expropriation?

MR. BARUCH: This might affect reparations, Mr. President. This property that is taken over by the Polish government, that is not to be held under the economic clauses.

SECRETARY LANSING: I want to ask another thing in connection with the Polish coal supply. Northeast of Teschen there is a large area which I understand is coal bearing and undeveloped which will come to Poland. Is that correct?

DR. LORD: In the northeastern part of Teschen?

THE PRESIDENT: No.

SECRETARY LANSING: Northeast of Teschen.

THE PRESIDENT: It does not mean the Teschen coal basin. As they show the area on the map I should think it is about one-fifth of a large coal area that extended northeastward into Poland. Is that well established that there is a large coal bearing region there in Poland that is undeveloped?

DR. LORD: There is a considerable area, in Galicia especially, where I think they expect a large development. In general this coal area comes just at the intersection of the old frontiers of Austria, Russia and Prussia. The basin is divided between the three powers, most of it being on the Prussian side, all of it being in Polish territory with very slight exceptions, and the undeveloped parts are mainly towards the east, in Austria, and, to a very slight extent, in what was formerly Russian territory.

SECRETARY LANSING: About one-twelfth of that area is developed. I do not mean to say one-twelfth of the wealth, but one-twelfth of the area.

. . . .

MR. LAMONT: Shall we hear further from you, or go to the Allied groups directly?

THE PRESIDENT: I think it would be better if you would take the initiative and seek a conference.

MR. MCCORMICK: Express a fixed sum?

THE PRESIDENT: Find out if you can get a common agreement. As I was pointing out in the beginning, they (the British) have taken the American position at last, and that is a pretty good position.

MR. HOOVER: Did Mr. Dresel say what points the Germans are most insistent upon the modification of? If we take their reply, they contend as vigorously for things of no moment as for things of great moment.

MR. DRESEL: When I was in Germany more than a month ago the thing that struck me most was the Saar Basin, but that may be because that had come out and the others had not yet come out. They did not know about the eastern Silesian coal mines at that time, but the Saar Basin was the one point on which they laid the most stress. They said they would give up the coal, but did not want to give up the control to France entirely.

MR. HOOVER: I had a consultation, and there are three or four points which they raised most insistently: the fixed indemnity at some sum; the modification of the Saar Basin terms; the period of occupation, and the Silesian coal mines. They seemed to be more insistent upon that than Danzig. . . .

THE PRESIDENT: We have been bearing on this point of the Saar Basin, and we have gotten concessions on other points. Are there any points that anybody would like to raise? . . .

GENERAL BLISS: They will not accept the military points unless they are admitted into the League. If they are admitted they will accept, and they undertake to go ahead of the terms in one or two cases.

MR. TAUSSIG: There runs through the German proposals a criticism or complaint that in matters of execution of the treaty there is no consultation at all with the Germans. It lays down that the amount should be fixed by the Allied and Associated governments; that the details should be regulated by the Allied and Associated governments. And they, in a succession of clauses, complain that that was put in with deliberate intent to keep the Germans from giving their views. As the treaty is framed, in a succession of clauses that does appear, and does look as if it is a deliberate attempt to keep Germany from having anything to say upon questions of execution. They complain about the way the quota or amount of shipping that Germany shall have is to be arrived at; the Kiel harbour shall be commanded by the Rhine Commission, having a larger representation of Frenchmen than Germans.

THE PRESIDENT: Those things, I think, will all work themselves out in operation. But it is necessary to consult the army with regard to them. . . .

Mr. Lansing was asking me if I did not think it would be a good idea to ask each of our groups to prepare a memorandum of what might be conceded, and while I do not want to be illiberal in the matter, I should hesitate to say "yes" to that question. The question that lies in my mind is: "Where have they made good in their points?" "Where have they shown that the arrangements of the treaty are essentially unjust?" Not "Where have they shown merely that they are hard?", for they are hard—but the Germans earned that. And I think it is profitable that a nation should learn once and for all what an unjust war means in itself.

I have no desire to soften the treaty, but I have a very sincere desire to alter those portions of it that are shown to be unjust, or which are shown to be contrary to the principles which we ourselves have laid down.

Take the Silesian question, for example: we said in so many words in the documents which were the basis of the peace, that we would make a free Poland out of the districts with Polish population. Now where it can be shown that the populations included in Poland are not indisputably Polish, then we must resort to something like a plebiscite. I agree with Dr. Lord that in the territory like northern Silesia the sincerity of the plebiscite might be questioned—in fact it might be very difficult to have a plebiscite that was a real expression of opinion, and therefore we would have to go by what we believed was the preponderance of the wishes of the population.

But I believe that where we have included Germans unnecessarily, the border ought to be rectified. Or where we have been shown to have departed from our principles, then we must consider what adjustments are necessary to conform to those principles.

Take Poland's access to the sea. For strategic reasons our Polish experts—the group of Allied experts—recommended a corridor running up to Danzig and it included some very solid groups of German populations. We determined in that case to leave the Dantzig district to the Germans and to establish a plebiscite.

Where the railway track from Danzig to Warsaw runs, notwithstanding the capital strategic importance of that railway to Poland, that railway is to remain German if its population votes to remain German.

I think that we have been more successful than I supposed we could possibly be in drawing ethnographic lines. . . .

Similarly, if the reparations clauses are unjust because they won't work—not because they are putting the heavy burden of payment upon Germany (because that is just)—but because we are putting it on them in such a way that they cannot pay, then I think we ought to rectify that.

I put it this way: We ought to examine our consciences to see where we can make modifications that correspond with the principles that we are putting forth.

SECRETARY LANSING: That is what I say, Mr. President, but I should not confine it to "injustice"; where we have made a mistake I should not say it was an injustice. I should say that where it is something that is contrary to good policy that I do not think that is unjust; I simply think that we made an error, and we ought to correct it. That was my idea of what modifications should be suggested; not that we would adopt them, but to say whether it was wise to adopt them, so that we would have something in writing, something to work with. It is all in the air now.

THE PRESIDENT: The great problem of the moment is the problem of agreement, because the most fatal thing that could happen, I should say, in the world, would be that sharp lines of division should be drawn among the Allied and Associated Powers. They ought to be held together, if it can reasonably be done, and that makes a problem like the problem of occupation look almost insoluble, because the British are at one extreme, and the French refusal to move is at the opposite extreme.

Personally I think the thing will solve itself upon the admission of Germany to the League of Nations. I think that all the powers feel that the right thing to do is to withdraw the army. But we cannot arrange that in the treaty because you cannot fix the date at which Germany is to be admitted into the League. It would be an indefinite one.

SECRETARY LANSING: Would that be done only by unanimous consent?

MR. HOOVER: The document provides that on two-thirds vote of the Council she should be admitted.

SECRETARY LANSING: But France, being on the Council, would have the decision.

COLONEL HOUSE: I agree with the President: let Germany in, and when she gets in, the other follows.

SECRETARY LANSING: And the army is to be paid for by Germany, because the French nation would not consent to making it so long if they had to pay for it.

COLONEL HOUSE: In a way she has to pay for it. They are going to make Germany pay all she can pay. Every dollar that is taken out for the army is taken away from French indemnities.

THE PRESIDENT: Every man in the French army is taken away from French industries too.

What is necessary is to get out of this atmosphere of war, get out of the present exaggerated feelings and exaggerated appearances, and I believe that if we can once get out of them into the calmer airs it would be easier to come to satisfactory solutions.

MR. DAVIS: You assume, Mr. President, that the other chiefs of state are instructing their other technical delegations to get together with us in the same way?

THE PRESIDENT: I am assuming it without any right; I am taking it for granted.

COLONEL HOUSE: I don't think it will make any difference. You are doing it anyway.

THE PRESIDENT: Now I hope anybody else who has been convinced by the German arguments will speak up.

MR. HOOVER: Apart from all questions of justice, how far does the question of expediency come in?

THE PRESIDENT: In order to get them to sign, do you mean?

MR. HOOVER: In order to get them to sign. It strikes me that that is a more important thing than the question of justice or injustice, because the weighing of justice and injustice in these times is pretty difficult.

THE PRESIDENT: Yes, nobody can be sure that they have made a just decision. But don't you think that if we regard the treaty as just, the argument of expediency ought not to govern, because after all we must not give up what we fought for. We might have to fight for it again.

MR. HOOVER: But we look at expediency in many lights. It may be necessary to change the terms of the reparation in view of getting something, rather than to lose all. And it is not a question of justice; justice would require, as I see it, that they pay everything they have got or hope to get. But in order to obtain something it may be expedient to do this, that and the other. Much the same might apply to the Saar and the Silesian coal basins.

THE PRESIDENT: I admit the argument that it might be expedient to do certain things in order to get what you are after. But what you mean is the question of expediency in order to obtain the signature?

MR. HOOVER: I would go even further than the point I mention,—that if it was necessary to alter the Saar and the Silesian terms, that such alteration would not contravene the principles of justice.

THE PRESIDENT: I do not see any essential injustice in the Saar Basin terms.

DR. HASKINS: I believe that everyone feels that the League of Nations has something very real and very important to do. The Saar Basin is something for the League of Nations to do.

THE PRESIDENT: We have removed the only serious element of injustice in that arrangement as it stood. Germany had to pay a certain sum in gold at the end of the period for the mines, or else the plebiscite was of no practical result. France obtained sovereignty over the region. We have altered that.

MR. WHITE: There is still the question of the vote.

DR. HASKINS: There are two or three minor modifications in the clauses that are necessary in the matter of clarity,—Mr. White has raised one of them—where the language did not seem perfectly clear.

THE PRESIDENT: In order to obtain what we intended?

DR. HASKINS: Yes.

MR. DAVIS: It is necessary to get peace as soon as possible. If Europe does not get together, the situation is going to be awful. Our appropriations have run out, practically; in about another month we won't have any money at all.

THE PRESIDENT: We won't have any appropriated money, you mean?

MR. DAVIS: We won't have any money appropriated for that purpose. When real war is not being conducted it is much more difficult to get money. The way people now feel about bonds, it would be difficult to get money. And the sooner they can get something and issue some obligations which these countries can use as a basis of credit, the better off we will be.

MR. WHITE: If we make certain modifications in the financial and economic clauses, would that not be enough, don't you think?

MR. DAVIS: We feel it would, if we can get together on that. Now whether these other questions are such that Germany will not agree to sign, we don't know. But I mean their reply makes us feel rather hopeful that we can certainly get together on reparations.

THE PRESIDENT: Well, I don't want to seem to be unreasonable, but my feeling is this: that we ought not, with the object of getting it signed, make changes in the treaty, if we think that it embodies what we were contending for; that the time to consider all these questions was when we were writing the treaty, and it makes me a little tired for people to come and say now that they are afraid the Germans won't sign, and their fear is based upon things that they insisted upon at the time of the writing of the treaty; that makes me very sick.

And that is the thing that happened. These people that over-rode our judgment and wrote things into the treaty that are now the stumbling blocks, are falling over themselves to remove these stumbling blocks. Now, if they ought not to have been there I say, remove them, but I say do not remove them merely for the fact of having the treaty signed.

MR. WHITE: Do the French remind you of that?

THE PRESIDENT: Not so much as the British. Here is a British group made up of every kind of British opinion, from Winston Churchill to Fisher. From the unreasonable to the reasonable, all the way around, they are all unanimous, if you please, in their funk. Now that makes me very tired. They ought to have been rational to begin with and then they would not have needed to have funked at the end. They ought to have done the rational things, I admit, and it is not very gracious for me to remind them—though I have done so with as much grace as I could command.

MR. DAVIS: They say that they do not quite understand why you permitted them to do that.

COLONEL HOUSE: So they say you are responsible for their doing it.

THE PRESIDENT: I would be perfectly willing to take the responsibility if the result is good. But though we did not keep them from putting irrational things in the treaty, we got very serious modifications out of them. If we had written the treaty the way they wanted it the Germans would have gone home the minute they read it.

Well, the Lord be with us.

Thereupon, at 1:15 P.M., the meeting adjourned.[10]

General Tasker H. Bliss submitted a "brief analysis of the German Counter-Proposals on the military terms of the draft Treaty" which, because of its statesmanlike approach, is worth reading.

June 6, 1919

DEAR MR. PRESIDENT:

The following is a brief analysis of the German Counter-Proposals on the military terms of the draft Treaty.

1. Germany accepts the fundamental principles of the military, naval and air terms, subject to the condition that, on the conclusion of Peace, she be admitted with equal rights into the League of Nations.

2. If admitted to the League, she voluntarily waives her equality of rights in the following regards;—she agrees to disarm *at once* and to abolish universal military service provided the other States of the League undertake, within *two years* from the conclusion of Peace, to also disarm and abolish universal military service.

3. In agreeing to reduce her armed forces to the number required by the Treaty, she asks that a transition period be granted to her, to be arranged by a Special Convention and, if necessary, confirmed by the League of Nations, during which period she may maintain such armed forces as may be shown to be necessary and are agreed upon in order to preserve internal order "which," she says, "is at present seriously shaken."

4. In the League, she demands the right conceded to every other member to organize and arm such forces as the League permits her to have according to her judgment.

5. On condition of admission to the League, she agrees to the provision for dismantlement of certain fortresses and the establishment of the zone which is to remain unoccupied by military forces.

6. With reservation as to necessary financial measures, Germany agrees to surrender not only the force specifically required by Article 185 of the Treaty, "but also all ships of the line."

7. She says that the time-limits imposed for the execution of certain clauses are technically impossible of observance and their necessary prolongation must be the subject of negotiation. This also applies to the conversion of war material released from the army and navy to peaceful, and especially to economic, objects.

8. As regards aerial navigation, she accepts any limitations to which all members of the League are subjected and will grant equal and reciprocal rights to these members as regards flight over and landing upon German territory.

9. In regard to many unmentioned details connected with the foregoing she proposes immediate verbal negotiations.

COMMENTS.

Paragraph 1 above.

It seems to be the general opinion that Germany will be far less a menace to the peace of the world if she is inside rather than outside of the League. If the question of the future status of Germany with respect to the League were a matter for present decision by the Council of the Powers, I should venture to suggest the following for consideration.

It seems to me to be good policy to avoid, as far as possible, anything which continues the status of Germany as that of a *probable* enemy for an indefinite time after the signature of peace. Therefore, while it is proper to deny her admission into the League of Nations until she has indicated her good faith, it might be wise to tell her the conditions under which we shall decide whether or not she is showing good faith.

The terms of the Treaty may, broadly, be divided into two general classes. The first class includes those terms the object of which is to put Germany in such a position of military weakness as will enable us to enforce (if she should secretly intend not to act in good faith) the other class of terms. If Germany faithfully executes this first class of terms, it seems to me that it is reasonable evidence of her good faith in complying with all the other terms.

It might, therefore, not be unwise to say to Germany that on the complete execution of all the military, naval and air terms, she will be admitted into the League.

Paragraph 2 above.

If this proposal could be agreed to, it would bring the world at once into near sight of assured and continued peace.

Paragraph 3 above.

This proposition has a better basis of sound sense than the one to fix an arbitrary figure to last an indefinite time although we should feel sure that this figure is too small at present and too large for the future. The maintenance of the peace of Europe depends upon the establishment and continuance of a stable and orderly government in Germany. While the present forces of disruption are at work, it is the general opinion that the military force proposed in the Treaty to be left to Germany is too small for the present. Yet, if we fix in the Treaty a military force for Germany, it can only be modified subsequently by having the Treaty provide for a subsequent convention to pass upon the question. This is, in reality, the substance of the German proposition. Of course it all depends upon whether the Powers will agree to take into consideration at the end of two years the proposition for their own disarmament and abolition of universal military service. If they refuse to do this while Germany, on the other hand, proposes to immediately disarm and abolish military service, I am afraid that it puts Germany in a better light as regards her intention to abolish militarism than it does the Powers.

In short, if there could only be some satisfactory agreement as to a definite time for the admission of Germany into the League, on the fulfillment of such conditions as will establish her good faith, there should be no difficulty about the military, naval and air terms. If it be a fact that there is a considerable element in Germany now looking towards and striving for better things, their hands will be strengthened by liberality of treatment on this subject,—a liberality which will not in the slightest degree prejudice the fulfillment of the other clauses of the Treaty and which, on the other hand, will probably assure their more exact fulfillment.

Cordially yours,
TASKER H. BLISS[11]

The Allied reply to the German counterproposals rejected all of the German suggestions except one: the plebiscite in Upper Silesia. David Lloyd George, who had been greatly impressed with the German arguments regarding the Upper Silesian territory, made himself the advocate of the plebiscite solution, which he pushed through in the face of French and Polish opposition and American indifference. He himself relates:

On the question of Upper Silesia the President was obdurate. When the provisional Treaty was submitted to the Germans, their reply made such a powerful case on the question of Upper Silesia that the British Imperial Delegation resolved to demand a reconsideration of this question. . . .

It was agreed to amend the Draft Treaty by providing that the apportionment of Upper Silesia should be subject to the wishes of the inhabitants, to be ascertained by a plebiscite conducted under the auspices of the Great Allied Powers.

Before finally deciding this issue, the Council of Four invited M. Paderewski to appear before them to present the Polish case against the proposed modifications in the Treaty.

In the course of his statement he challenged the justice of the plebiscite and he also entered into an elaborate defence of Polish aggressiveness in Galicia. Here the Polish Army was taking steps to annex by force the whole of this province against the obvious wishes of the majority of the inhabitants, who resisted the advance of the Poles by every means at their disposal. By race, language and religion the people were Ukrainian. M. Paderewski explained to me that the action of the Polish Army was not "an offensive but a defensive advance."

Here is a more detailed description of this "defensive" operation with which this charming artist beguiled the Council of Four:—

[M. PADEREWSKI:] However decisive were our efforts, we could not keep back those boys of twenty years of age. They went on. They simply marched like a storm. They made thirty-five, forty kilometres a day without any opposition, and they took back that territory, and if you are interested in the fact that there should be no bloodshed in the country, I am able to tell you that the whole offensive in Galicia has not cost us a hundred people in killed and wounded. There were no battles. In many places, the population, stimulated by the news of Polish troops advancing, took the matter in hand themselves. The Polish population is very numerous there, —about a third of the inhabitants being Poles,—about 37 per cent.

MR. LLOYD GEORGE: Does Poland claim the whole of Galicia?

M. PADEREWSKI: Historically, yes.

MR. LLOYD GEORGE: Do they claim that the whole of Galicia should be annexed to them?

M. PADEREWSKI: We have given autonomy to this country. We claim the whole of Galicia. We claim it for the simple reason that it is absolutely impossible to define ethnographically this country, because curiously enough, and we should be rather proud of the fact, in the centre of Galicia there is more of a Ukrainian population than on the border. The farthest districts of Galicia are more Polish than the immediate surroundings of Lemberg. There isn't a neighbourhood of Lemberg which contains 80 per cent.

PRESIDENT WILSON: The main point, I take it, is not so much the slight redrawing of the boundary so as to leave as many Germans outside of Poland as possible, but the question of Upper Silesia. My own judgment is that, notwithstanding the fact that they admit that it has an overwhelming Polish population, the very great mineral riches of Silesia are of great concern to them. We have been considering a plebiscite under international supervision and under such rules as an international commission should set up, to get the German troops out and any German officials who might be interfering with it, and it was on that general series of subjects that we were anxious to have your views.

M. PADEREWSKI: . . . The Upper Silesian territory is divided into two sections, one of which, the eastern, is mining—industrial —and the other, the western part, is agricultural. The western part of the Silesian territory is under the influence of the Catholic clergy. That Catholic clergy has been brought up in a very strong German spirit by the Archbishop of Breslau, and the influence of that clergy is most dangerous for us, because those people rule absolutely our people, and in the case of a plebiscite, they would, even in spite of our majorities, amounting in many districts to 90 per cent and more, they would decidedly follow the orders of that German clergy. From that point of view a plebiscite is absolutely impossible. In the eastern district the people, of course, are free from that influence; they are more conscious of their nationality and of their political aspirations, and they would, of course, declare themselves for Poland.

M. CLEMENCEAU: In what district is it that the Catholic clergy is so strong?

M. PADEREWSKI: In the western part of Silesia. In the eastern part the labour population—the workers, the miners—with them it is different. We are not afraid of that. The vote would be decidedly in our favour, but there would be some inconvenience in having that district alone assigned to us, because it would put the whole mining industry, the whole of those industrial plants, on the frontier. Consequently, they would be quite accessible to any invasion, accessible to the destruction of any gunshot. It is positively on the border. We could not really, if we were asked, agree to a plebiscite. . . .

THE PRESIDENT: Then your expectation would be that the agricultural communes would go to Germany?

M. PADEREWSKI: Yes.

THE PRESIDENT: Then your frontier would probably be the Oder?

M. PADEREWSKI: Yes.

MR. LLOYD GEORGE: If you took the opinion of Silesia, as a whole, it would be German?

M. PADEREWSKI: Yes, as a whole it would be German.

If there is any essential change in that which has been already granted to Poland, I should immediately resign, because I could not return to my country if there is any such change as a plebiscite here, or any essential change in the disposition of the territory which has been already made public as granted to my country. If there are such changes, I couldn't have anything more to do with politics, because it would be absolutely impossible to rule my country. You know that revolutions begin when people lose faith in their leadership. These people have belief in me now, because they were told by me, and most emphatically, that these things promised to them would be given to them. Well now, if something is taken away from them, they will lose all faith in my leadership. They will lose faith in your leadership of humanity; and there will be revolution in my country.

MR. LLOYD GEORGE: No promises were made. We made certain proposals to the Germans. Nobody ever suggested that those were an ultimatum, and that the Germans must accept them, every line without alteration. . . .

Here is Poland that five years ago was torn to pieces, under the heel of three great powers, with no human prospect of recovering its liberty; certainly without the slightest chance of recovering it by its own exertions. Why, during the four or five years of the War Poles were actually fighting against their own freedom in so far as they were fighting at all. We were capturing Poles on the Western front, and capturing them on the Italian front. That was the condition of things. Now, you have got at the very least, even if you took every one of these disputed parts away,—you have got twenty millions of Poles free, you have got an absolutely united Poland. It is a thing which no Pole could have conceived as possible five years ago; and in addition to that, they are claiming even populations which are not their own. They are claiming three millions and a half of Galicians, and the only claim put forward is that in a readjustment you should not absorb into Poland populations which are not Polish and which do not wish to become Polish. That is the only question in dispute. The Poles had not the slightest hope of getting freedom, and have only got their freedom because there are a million and a half of Frenchmen dead, very nearly a million British, half a million Italians, and I forget how many Americans. That has given the Poles their freedom, and they say they will lose faith in the leadership which has given them that, at the expense of millions of men of other races who have died for their freedom. If that is what Poles are like, then I must say it is a very different Poland to any Poland I ever heard of. She has won her freedom, not by her own exertions, but by the blood of others; and not only has she no gratitude, but she says she loses faith in the people who have won her freedom.

M. PADEREWSKI: I am very sorry I gave you that impression. Perhaps I did not express myself precisely enough. If I say that I would not be able to lead these people any more because they may lose faith in my leadership, I don't mean to imply that they are losing faith in your leadership.

MR. LLOYD GEORGE: I was only referring to what you said. We won freedom for nations that had not the slightest hope of it,—Czechoslovakia, Poland, and others. Nations that have won their freedom at the expense of the blood of Italians and Frenchmen and Englishmen and Americans. And we have the greatest trouble in the world to keep them from annexing the territory of other nations and imposing upon other nations the very tyranny which they have themselves endured for centuries. You know, I belong to a small nation, and therefore I have great sympathy with all oppressed nationalities, and it fills me with despair the way in which I have seen small nations, before they have hardly leaped into the light of freedom, beginning to oppress other races than their own. They are more imperialist, believe me, than either England and France, than certainly the United States. It fills me with despair as a man who has fought all his life for little nations.

M. Paderewski protested vehemently against the imputation that the Poles were animated by imperialistic ambitions. I replied:—

". . . What I mean by imperialism is the annexation of peoples of a different race against their will, or even a people of the same race against their will. I consider the annexation of Alsace, though the race was German, as culpable as the annexation of Lorraine, when the people were French. It is the annexation of people against their will."

Subsequently both M. Paderewski and M. Dmowski came before the Council of Four to enter a final protest against the alterations made in the Draft Treaty. M. Paderewski spoke with an emotional fervour which from a man of his genuine and unselfish patriotism was moving:—

He said that he could not conceal the fact that this decision was a very serious blow to Poland. First it would affect the people of Poland sentimentally. They believed President Wilson's principles like the Gospel. The second reason was that it would cause bitter disappointment. If the plebiscite did not bring the result he hoped for it would be their poor neighbours of Polish race who would be the first to suffer. For centuries they had been treated like slaves. They had been driven out of their country and sent to Westphalia and compelled to forced labour in Berlin and elsewhere. They had hoped in future to live decent lives on their ancestral soil. If the plebiscite did not come up to expectations it would cause terrible disappointment. Thirdly, the country, owing to the plebiscite, would be in a chaotic condition and he hoped, therefore, that it would be taken within three or six months of the Peace, in order to quieten things down. It would increase the excitement in Poland. The plebiscite was not like an election, since it was to decide the destiny of the country perhaps for centuries. The people would become demoralised. All sorts of impossible and unreasonable promises would be made. This was why the people of Poland did not accept the idea.

He ended by saying that the Polish Delegation could only accept the decision "with profound respect but with deep sorrow."[12]

The Big Four decided to hold a plebiscite in Upper Silesia. This plebiscite, held by districts, awarded the eastern part of the territory, including the main mining areas, to Poland, while the western districts voted for Germany.

The Allied reply to the German proposals also contained a lengthy exposition of the Conference's view of German responsibility for the war. It reaffirmed the contention that Germany was indeed guilty of having caused the war and insisted that the German Government acknowledge the fact by its signature. Thus, articles 231/232, innocently conceived to accommodate the exaggerated British and French reparation demands, became one of the most important and most controversial parts of the Treaty.

The Allied reply furthermore contained these sentences:

In conclusion the Allied and Associated Powers must make it clear that this letter and the memorandum attached constitute their last word.

They have examined the German observations and counter-proposals with earnest attention and care. They have, in consequence, made important practical concessions, but in its principles, they stand by the treaty.

They believe that it is not only a just settlement of the great war, but that it provides the basis upon which the peoples of Europe can live together in friendship and equality. At the same time it creates the machinery for the peaceful adjustment of all international problems by discussion and consent, whereby the settlement of 1919 itself can be modified from time to time to suit new facts and new conditions as they arise.

It is frankly not based upon a general condonation of the events of 1914–1918. It would not be a peace of justice if it were. But it represents a sincere and deliberate attempt to establish "that reign of law, based upon the consent of the governed, and sustained by the organized opinion of mankind" which was the agreed basis of the peace.

As such the treaty in its present form must be accepted or rejected.

The Allied and Associated Powers therefore require a declaration from the German Delegation within five days from the date of this communication that they are prepared to sign the treaty as it stands today.

If they declare within this period that they are prepared to sign the treaty as it stands, arrangements will be made for the immediate signature of the peace at Versailles.

In default of such a declaration, this communication constitutes the notification provided for in Article II of the Convention of February 16, 1919, prolonging the armistice which was signed on November 11, 1918, and has already been prolonged by the agreement on December 13, 1918, and January 16, 1919. The said armistice will then terminate, and the Allied and Associated Powers will take such steps as they think needful to enforce their terms.

French text signed: CLEMENCEAU[13]

Faced with this ultimatum, the German Government attempted to get away with conditional acceptance of the Treaty. It balked at accepting the "war criminal" and "war guilt" clauses. A lengthy note handed to the Conference on June 22nd culminated in this declaration:

The Government of the German Republic accordingly gives the declaration of its consent, as required by the Note of June 16, 1919, in the following form:

"The Government of the German Republic is ready to sign the Treaty of Peace without, however, recognizing thereby that the German people was the author of the war, and without undertaking any responsibility for delivering persons in accordance with Articles 227 to 230, of the Treaty of Peace."

Weimar, June 21, 1919

BAUER,
President of the Reichs-Ministry.

Accept, Mr. President, the expression of my distinguished consideration.

VON HANIEL[14]

Clemenceau promptly killed the German attempt to accept the Treaty conditionally.

June 22nd, 1919

The Allied and Associated Powers have considered the note of the German delegation of even date and in view of the short time still remaining feel it their duty to reply at once. Of the time within which the German Government must make its final decision as to the signature of the Treaty less than twenty-four hours remain. . . . The Allied and Associated Powers therefore feel constrained to say that the time for discussion has passed . . . and must require of the German representatives an unequivocal decision as to their purpose to sign and accept as a whole, or not to sign and accept the Treaty as finally formulated. . . .[15]

Rather than sign, Brockdorff-Rantzau resigned and brought down the German government. Just three hours before Allied armies were to begin marching across the Rhine on the way to Berlin and Weimar, a reorganized German government received the Reichstag's consent to sign the Treaty "under duress."

SIR,

The Minister of Foreign Affairs has requested me to submit the following note to your Excellency:

"The Government of the German Republic is overwhelmed to learn from the last communication of the Allied and Associated Powers that the Allies are resolved to enforce, with all the power at their command, the acceptance even of those provisions of the Treaty which, without having any material significance, are designed to deprive the German people of their honor. The honor of the German people cannot be injured by an act of violence. The German people, after their terrible sufferings during these last years, are wholly without the means of defending their honor against the outside world. Yielding to overpowering might, the Government of the German Republic declares itself ready to accept and to sign the Peace Treaty imposed by the Allied and Associated Governments. But, in so doing, the Government of the German Republic in no wise abandons its conviction that these conditions of peace represent injustice without parallel.

(*signed*) VON HANIEL

June 22nd, 1919[16]

Accordingly the new German Foreign Minister, Dr. Mueller and his assistant Dr. Bell, fitted out with the necessary credentials, were dispatched to Paris to accomplish the shameful task of "signing away the honor of the German People." On June 28th, the fifth anniversary of the shots that rang out in Sarajevo, ushering in the war, the Treaty of Versailles was signed in the same Hall of Mirrors where Bismarck, forty-eight years earlier, had proclaimed the "German Empire."

Harold Nicolson devotes a couple of pages of his Paris diary to the ceremony.

June 28, *Saturday*

La journée de Versailles. Lunch early and leave the Majestic in a car with Headlam Morley. He is a historian, yet he dislikes historical occasions. Apart from that he is a sensitive person and does not rejoice in seeing great nations humbled. I, having none of such acquirements or decencies, am just excited.

There is no crowd at all until we reach Ville d'Avray. But there are poilus at every crossroad waving red flags and stopping all other traffic. When we reach Versailles the crowd thickens. The avenue up to the Chateau is lined with cavalry in steel-blue helmets. The pennants of their lances flutter red and white in the sun. In the Cour d'Honneur, from which the captured German cannon have tactfully been removed, are further troops. There are Generals, Pétain, Gouraud, Mangin. There are St. Cyriens. Very military and orderly. Headlam Morley and I creep out of our car hurriedly. Feeling civilian and grubby. And wholly unimportant. We hurry through the door.

Magnificent upon the staircase stand the Gardes Républicains—two caryatides on every step—their sabres at the salute. This is a great ordeal, but there are other people climbing the stairs with us. Headlam and I have an eye-meet. His thin cigaretted fingers make a gesture of dismissal. He is not a militarist.

We enter the Galerie des Glaces. It is divided into three sections. At the far end are the Press already thickly installed. In the middle there is a horseshoe table for the plenipotentiaries. In front of that, like a guillotine, is the table for the signatures. It is supposed to be raised on a dais but, if so, the dais can be but a few inches high. In the nearer distance are rows and rows of tabourets for the distinguished guests, the deputies, the senators and the members of the delegations. There must be seats for over a thousand persons. This robs the ceremony of all privilege and therefore of all dignity. It is like the Aeolian Hall.

Clemenceau is already seated under the heavy ceiling as we arrive. "Le roi," runs the scroll above him, "gouverne par lui-même." He looks small and yellow. A crunched homunculus.

Conversation clatters out among the mixed groups around us. It is, as always on such occasions, like water running into a tin bath. . . .

People step over the Aubusson benches and escabeaux to talk to friends. Meanwhile the delegates arrive in little bunches and push up the central aisle slowly. Wilson and Lloyd George are among the last. They take their seats at the central table. The table is at last full. Clemenceau glances to right and left. People sit down upon their escabeaux but continue chattering. Clemenceau makes a sign to the ushers. They say "Ssh! Ssh! Ssh!" People cease chattering and there is only the sound of occasional coughing and the dry rustle of programmes. The officials of the protocol of the Foreign Office move up the aisle and say "Ssh! Ssh!" again. There is then an absolute hush, followed by a sharp military order. The Gardes Républicains at the doorway flash their swords into their scabbards with a loud click. "Faites entrer les Allemands," says Clemenceau in the ensuing silence. His voice is distant but harshly penetrating. A hush follows.

Through the door at the end appear two huissiers with silver chains. They march in single file. After them come four officers of France, Great Britain, America and Italy. And then, isolated and pitiable, the two German delegates: Dr. Müller and Dr. Bell. The silence is terrifying. Their feet upon a strip of parquet between the savonnerie carpets echo hollow and duplicate. They keep their eyes fixed away from those two thousand staring eyes, fixed upon the ceiling. They are deathly pale. They do not appear as representatives of a brutal militarism. The one is thin and pink-eyelidded: the second fiddle in a Brunswick orchestra. The other is moon-faced and suffering: a privat-dozent. It is all most painful.

They are conducted to their chairs. Clemenceau at once breaks the silence. "Messieurs," he rasps, "la séance est ouverte." He adds a few ill-chosen words. "We are here to sign a Treaty of Peace." The Germans leap up anxiously when he has finished since they know that they are the first to sign. William Martin, as if he were theatre manager, motions them petulantly to sit down again. Mantoux translates Clemenceau's words into English. Then St. Quentin advances towards the Germans and with the utmost dignity leads them to the little table on which the treaty is expanded. There is general tension. They sign. There is general relaxation. Conversation hums again in an undertone. The delegates stand up one by one and pass onward to the queue which waits by the signature table. Meanwhile people buzz round the main table getting autographs. The single file of plenipotentiaries waiting to approach the table gets thicker. It goes quickly. The officials of the Quai d'Orsay stand around, indicating places to sign, indicating procedure, blotting with neat little pads.

Suddenly from the outside comes the crash of guns thundering a salute. It announces to Paris that the second Versailles treaty has been signed by Drs. Müller and Bell. Through the few open windows comes the sound of a distant crowd cheering hoarsely. And still the signature goes on.

We had been warned it might last three hours. Yet almost at once it seemed that the queue was getting thin. Only three, then two, and then one delegate remained to sign. His name had hardly been blotted before the huissiers began again their "Ssh! Ssh!" cutting suddenly short the wide murmur which had again begun. There was a final hush. "La séance est levée" rasped Clemenceau. Not a word more or less.

We kept our seats while the Germans were conducted like prisoners from the dock, their eyes still fixed upon some distant point of the horizon.

We still kept our seats to allow the Big Five to pass down the aisle. Wilson, Lloyd George, the Dominions, others. Finally, Clemenceau, with his rolling satirical gait. Painlevé, who was sitting one off me, rose to greet him. He stretched out both his hands and grasped Clemenceau's right glove. He congratulated him. "Oui," says Clemenceau, "c'est une belle journée." There were tears in his bleary eyes.

Marie Murat was near me and had overheard. "En êtes-vous sûre?" I ask her. "Pas du tout," she answers, being a woman of intelligence.

Slowly the crowd in the room clears, the Press through the Rotonde, and the rest through the Salle d'Honneur. I walk across the room, pushing past empty tabourets, to a wide-open window which gives out upon the terrace and the famous Versailles view. The fountains spurt vociferously. I look out over the tapis vert towards a tranquil sweep of open country. The clouds, white on blue, race across the sky and a squadron of aeroplanes races after them. Clemenceau emerges through the door below me. He is joined by Wilson and Lloyd George. The crowds upon the terrace burst through the cordon of troops. The top-hats of the Big Four and the uniforms of the accompanying Generals are lost in a sea of gesticulation. Fortunately it was only a privileged crowd. A platoon arrives at the double and rescues the big four. I find Headlam Morley standing miserably in the littered immensity of the Galerie des Glaces. We say nothing to each other. It has all been horrible.

And so through crowds cheering "Vive l'Angleterre" (for our car carries the Union Jack) and back to the comparative refinement of the Majestic. . . .

Celebrations in the hotel afterwards. We are given free champagne at the expense of the tax-payer. It is very bad champagne. Go out on to the boulevards afterwards.

To bed, sick of life.[17]

Herbert Hoover, who observed the ceremony from the benches of the American delegation, carried away a similar impression.

On Saturday, June 28, we all went to the Hall of Mirrors at Versailles to witness the signing by thirty-two nations. General Smuts signed the Treaty as a British delegate and at the same time issued a press statement denouncing it and demanding revision.

I took satisfaction in the great spiritual lift the ceremony gave to the French people, as it was in this same Hall nearly fifty years before where they had been ruthlessly humiliated by the Germans. But I had difficulty in keeping my mind on the ceremony. It was constantly traveling over the fearful consequences of many of the paragraphs which these men were signing with such pomp, and then going back to the high hopes with which I had landed in Europe eight months before. I did not come away exultant.[18]

X

United States Refusal to Ratify the Treaty

As soon as the Treaty with Germany was signed, the Big Four broke up. Wilson left Paris on the very day of the signing, and Lloyd George returned to England shortly after. Clemenceau alone of the Quadrumvirate remained to guide the lower echelon personnel of the Foreign Offices of 32 nations as they labored over the treaties of Saint-Germain, Trianon, Neuilly and Sèvres, which ended the war with Austria, Hungary, Bulgaria and Turkey respectively.

Woodrow Wilson hurriedly returned to Washington to get the Senate's approval of the Treaty. On his arrival in the United States in the first days of July, Wilson encountered a sympathetic public and a critical, though not yet hostile, Congress. By getting all the Senate's amendments written into the Treaty, Wilson had taken most of the wind out of the sails of the anti-Treaty forces. Both the nation's press and American public opinion seemed strongly in favor of the results of the President's Paris labors. Woodrow Wilson felt quite confident that the Senate would not deny him the necessary two-thirds majority, in spite of the fact that he now faced a Republican-dominated body.

The newly organized Senate had made Henry Cabot Lodge, Wilson's archfoe, Chairman of its Committee on Foreign Relations, and had packed the Committee with "irreconcilables." Though the "irreconcilables," unswerving opponents of the League, were only a minority within the Republican Party, most of the Republican members of the Committee were of that group. Lodge himself was a "moderate," opposed to the League as it stood, but apparently willing to accept it if the Covenant were altered to meet his demands.

Ex-President Taft voiced the majority Republican opinion regarding the packing of the Committee on Foreign Relations.

The leaders of the Republican Party have proved their purpose by fixing the Committee on Foreign Relations so they should have Republicans enough to give them a majority without the vote of Mr. McCumber, known to be favorable to the treaty and by a careful selection of Republicans for that majority whose opposition to the treaty has been pronounced. Senator Kellogg naturally would have been taken before Senator Moses, a new Senator and one whose term expires in two years. Senator Kellogg however ventured to make a speech in favor of the League of Nations even before the covenant was agreed upon and declined to sign the "round robin."[1]

Almost immediately upon his arrival in Washington, Woodrow Wilson submitted the Treaty of Versailles to the Senate (July 10, 1919). He accompanied it with an ardent plea for acceptance of the Treaty and the Covenant it encompassed.

It was our duty to do everything that it was within our power to do to make the triumph of freedom and of right a lasting triumph in the assurance of which men might everywhere live without fear.

Old entanglements of every kind stood in the way,—promises which Governments had made to one another in the days when might and right were confused and the power of the victor was without restraint. Engagements which contemplated any dispositions of territory, any extensions of sovereignty that might seem to be to the interest of those who had the power to insist upon them, had been entered into without thought of what the peoples concerned might wish or profit by; and these could not always be honorably brushed aside. It was not easy to graft the new order of ideas on the old, and some of the fruits of the grafting may, I fear, for a time be bitter. But with very few exceptions, the men who sat with us at the peace table desired as sincerely as we did to get away from the bad influences, the illegitimate purposes, the demoralizing ambitions, the international counsels and expedients out of which the sinister designs of Germany had sprung as a natural growth. . . .

The atmosphere in which the Conference worked seemed created, not by the ambitions of strong governments, but by the hopes and aspirations of small nations and of peoples, hitherto under bondage to the power that victory had shattered and destroyed. . . .

And out of the execution of these great enterprises of liberty sprang opportunities to attempt what statesmen had never found the way before to do; an opportunity to throw safeguards about the rights of racial, national and religious minorities by solemn international covenant; an opportunity to limit and regulate military establishments where they were most likely to be mischievous; an opportunity to effect a complete and systematic internationalization of waterways and railways which were necessary to the free economic life of more than one nation and to clear many of the normal channels of commerce of unfair obstructions of law or of privilege; and the very welcome opportunity to secure for labor the concerted protection of definite international pledges of principle and practice. . . .

The promises governments were making to one another about the way in which labor was to be dealt with, by law not only but in fact as well, would remain a mere humane thesis if there was to be no common tribunal of opinion and judgment to which liberal statesmen could resort for the influences which alone might secure their redemption. A league of free nations had become a practical necessity. . . .

And so the most practical, the most skeptical among them turned more and more to the League as the authority through which international action was to be secured, the authority without which, as they had come to see it, it would be difficult to give assured effect either to this treaty or to any other international understanding upon which they were to depend for the maintenance of peace. . . .

War had lain at the very heart of every arrangement of the Europe,—of every arrangement of the world—that preceded the war. Restive peoples had been told that fleets and armies, which they toiled to sustain, meant peace; and they now knew that they had been lied to: that fleets and armies had been maintained to promote national ambitions and meant war. They knew that no old policy meant anything else but force, force,—always force. And they knew that it was intolerable. Every true heart in the world, and every enlightened judgment demanded that, at whatever cost of independent action, every government that took thought for its people or for justice or for ordered freedom should lend itself to a new purpose and utterly destroy the old order of international politics. Statesmen might see difficulties, but the people could see none and would brook no denial. A war in which they had been bled white to beat the terror that lay concealed in every Balance of Power must not end in a mere victory of arms and a new balance. . . .[2]

Separately, and almost three weeks later, the President submitted the United States guarantee pact with France (July 29, 1919). There can be little doubt that the Treaty would have been ratified, probably even without any reservations, if the Senate had been able to vote during those summer months. Public opinion, the nation's press and a Democratic–Moderate Republican majority of the Senate supported ratification. Senator Moses, some years later, was quoted as follows: "If the rules of the Senate had permitted a quick decision the Versailles Treaty would have been ratified without reservations."[3]

Lodge and his colleagues on the Committee were, of course, aware of the situation, and they played for time. Two weeks were consumed by having the Treaty read aloud, paragraph by paragraph, while six weeks were devoted to public hearings. Participants at the Paris Conference, among them Robert Lansing and David Hunter Miller, were subjected to merciless cross-examinations in the hope of getting them to testify against one or another provision of the Treaty. In the case of the Secretary of State, that hope was gratified; he could not resist disavowing his chief on the Shantung question and other crucial points. On top of such legitimate testimony the Committee also heard from many self-appointed representatives of American minority groups, all of whom had some fault to find with the outcome of the Paris negotiations. Thirteen hundred pages of testimony were taken from representatives or purported representatives of Albanian, Chinese, Czechoslovakian, Egyptian, Estonian, Hungarian, Indian, Irish, Italian, Latvian, Lithuanian, Persian, Swedish, Ukrainian and Yugoslavian groups.

The President, who, of course, could not be called upon to testify, requested the privilege of addressing the Committee, and did so on August 19th.

. . . Nothing, I am led to believe, stands in the way of ratification of the treaty except certain doubts with regard to the meaning and implication of certain articles of the Covenant of the League of Nations; and I must frankly say that I am unable to understand why such doubts should be entertained. You will recall that when I had the pleasure of a conference with your committee and with the committee of the House of Representatives on Foreign Affairs at the White House in March last, the questions now most frequently asked about the League of Nations were all canvassed with a view to their immediate clarification. The Covenant of the League was then in its first draft and subject to revision. It was pointed out that no express recognition was given to the Monroe Doctrine; that it was not expressly provided that the League should have no authority to act or to express judgment on matters of domestic policy; that the right to withdraw from the League was not expressly recognized; and that the constitutional right of the Congress to determine all questions of peace and war was not sufficiently safeguarded. On my return to Paris all these matters were taken up by the Commission on the League of Nations and every suggestion of the United States was accepted.

The views of the United States with regard to the questions I have mentioned had, in fact, already been accepted by the Commission and there was supposed to be nothing inconsistent with them in the draft of the Covenant first adopted—the draft which was the subject of our discussion in March—but no objection was made to saying explicitly in the text what all had supposed to be implicit in it. There was absolutely no doubt as to the meaning of any one of the resulting provisions of the Covenant in the minds of those who participated in drafting them, and I respectfully submit that there is nothing vague or doubtful in their wording.

The Monroe Doctrine is expressly mentioned as an understanding which is in no way to be impaired or interfered with by anything contained in the covenant, and the expression "regional understandings like the Monroe Doctrine" was used, not because any one of the conferees thought there was any comparable agreement anywhere else in existence or in contemplation, but only because it was thought best to avoid the appearance of dealing in such a document with the policy of a single nation. Absolutely nothing is concealed in the phrase.

With regard to domestic questions, Article 16 of the Covenant expressly provides that, if in case of any dispute arising between members of the League the matter involved is claimed by one of the parties "and is found by the council to arise out of a matter which by international law is solely within the domestic jurisdiction of that party, the council shall so report, and shall make no recommendation as to its settlement." The United States was by no means the only Government interested in the explicit adoption of this provision, and there is no doubt in the mind of any authoritative student of international law that such matters as immigration, tariffs, and naturalization are incontestably domestic questions with which no international body could deal without express authority to do so. No enumeration of domestic questions was undertaken because to undertake it, even by sample, would have involved the danger of seeming to exclude those not mentioned.

The right of any sovereign State to withdraw had been taken for granted, but no objection was made to making it explicit. Indeed, so soon as the views expressed at the White House conference were laid before the commission it was at once conceded that it was best not to leave the answer to so important a question to inference. No proposal was made to set up any tribunal to pass judgment upon the question whether a withdrawing Nation had in fact fulfilled "all its international obligations and all its obligations under the covenant." It was recognized that that question must be left to be resolved by the conscience of the Nation proposing to withdraw; and I must say that it did not seem to me worth while to propose that the article be made more explicit, because I knew that the United States would never itself propose to withdraw from the League if its conscience was not entirely clear as to the fulfillment of all its international obligations. It has never failed to fulfill them and never will.

Article 10 is in no respect of doubtful meaning when read in the light of the covenant as a whole. The council of the League can only "advise upon" the means by which the obligations of that great article are to be given effect to. Unless the United States is a party to the policy or action in question, her own affirmative vote in the council is necessary before any advice can be given, for a unanimous vote of the council is required. If she is a party, the trouble is hers anyhow. And the unanimous vote of the council is only advice in any case. Each Government is free to reject it if it pleases. Nothing could have been made more clear to the conference than the right of our Congress under our Constitution to exercise its independent judgment in all matters of peace and war. No attempt was made to question or limit that right.

The United States will, indeed, undertake under Article 10 to "respect and preserve as against external aggression the territorial integrity and existing political independence of all members of the League," and that engagement constitutes a very grave and solemn moral obligation. But it is a moral, not a legal, obligation, and leaves our Congress absolutely free to put its own interpretation upon it in all cases that call for action. It is binding in conscience only, not in law.

Article 10 seems to me to constitute the very backbone of the whole covenant. Without it the League would be hardly more than an influential debating society.

It has several times been suggested, in public debate and in private conference, that interpretations of the sense in which the United States accepts the engagements of the covenant should be embodied in the instrument of ratification. There can be no reasonable objection to such interpretations accompanying the act of ratification provided they do not form a part of the formal ratification itself. . . .[4]

The President's plea, however, did not sway the Committee. When its majority report reached the Senate floor on September 10th it contained forty-five amendments and four reservations, and it was clear that the opposition was determined to kill or cripple the Treaty with amendments. Noting that the tide was running against him in Congress, the President had decided to appeal to the voters directly, and had gone on a speaking tour to rally his supporters. Covering more than 8,000 miles and making 37 speeches in 29 cities in the course of 22 days, Woodrow Wilson drove himself to the utmost limit of his physical capacity. On September 25th he spoke in Pueblo, Colorado.

When you come to the heart of the covenant, my fellow citizens, you will find it in article 10. . . . Article 10 provides that every member of the League covenants to respect and preserve the territorial integrity and existing political independence of every other member of the League as against external aggression. Not against internal disturbance. There was not a man at that table who did not admit the sacredness of the right of self-determination, the sacredness of the right of any body of people to say that they would not continue to live under the government they were then living under, and under article 11 of the covenant they are given a place to say whether they will live under it or not. . . .

Yet article 10 strikes at the taproot of war. Article 10 is a statement that the very things that have always been sought in imperialistic wars are henceforth foregone by every ambitious nation in the world. I would have felt very lonely, my fellow countrymen, and I would have felt very much disturbed if, sitting at the peace table in Paris, I had supposed that I was expounding my own ideas. . . . I proposed nothing whatever at the peace table at Paris that I had not sufficiently certain knowledge embodied the moral judgment of the citizens of the United States. I had gone over there with, so to say, explicit instructions. Don't you remember that we laid down fourteen points which should contain the principles of the settlement? They were not my points. In every one of them I was conscientiously trying to read the thought of the people of the United States, and after I uttered those points I had every assurance given me that could be given me that they did speak the moral judgment of the United States and not my single judgment. Then when it came to that critical period just a little less than a year ago, when it was evident that the war was coming to its critical end, all the nations engaged in the war accepted those fourteen principles explicitly as the basis of the armistice and the basis of the peace. In those circumstances I crossed the ocean under bond to my own people and to the other governments with which I was dealing. The whole specification of the method of settlement was written down and accepted beforehand, and we were architects building on those specifications.[5]

This was the last plea the President was able to make. That same evening the President collapsed and was rushed back to Washington, where he suffered a stroke on October 2nd. He remained incapacitated for nearly eight months and the pro-Treaty forces were left leaderless during the most crucial weeks of the session.

The Senate, meanwhile, had pared down the reservations to fourteen,* and Senator Lodge presented them to his colleagues.

1. The United States so understands and construes article 1 that in case of notice of withdrawal from the League of Nations . . . the United States shall be the sole judge as to whether all its international obligations and all its obligations under the said covenant have been fulfilled. . . .

* The fifteenth reservation was added before the final vote in March of 1920.

2. The United States assumes no obligation to preserve the territorial integrity or political independence of any other country by the employment of its military or naval forces, its resources, or any form of economic discrimination, or to interfere in any way in controversies between nations . . . under the provisions of article 10 or to employ the military or naval forces of the United States, under any article of the treaty for any purpose, unless in any particular case the Congress . . . so provide.

3. No mandate shall be accepted by the United States . . . except by action of the Congress of the United States.

4. The United States reserves to itself exclusively the right to decide what questions are within its domestic jurisdiction and declares that all domestic and political questions relating wholly or in part to its internal affairs, including immigration, labor, coastwise traffic, the tariff, commerce, the supression of traffic in women and children and in opium and other dangerous drugs, and all other domestic questions, are solely within the jurisdiction of the United States and are not under this treaty to be submitted in any way either to arbitration or to the consideration of the council or of the assembly of the League of Nations, or any agency thereof, or to the decision or recommendation of any other power.

5. The United States will not submit to arbitration or to inquiry by the assembly or by the council of the League of Nations, provided for in said treaty of peace, any questions which in the judgment of the United States depend upon or relate to its long-established policy, commonly known as the Monroe doctrine; said doctrine is to be interpreted by the United States alone and is hereby declared to be wholly outside the jurisdiction of said League of Nations and entirely unaffected by any provision contained in the said treaty of peace with Germany. . . .

8. The United States understands that the reparation commission will regulate or interfere with exports from the United States to Germany, or from Germany to the United States, only when the United States by act or joint resolution of Congress approves such regulation or interference.

9. The United States shall not be obligated to contribute to any expenses of the League of Nations . . . or for the purpose of carrying out the treaty provisions, unless and until an appropriation of funds available for such expenses shall have been made by the Congress of the United States. . . .

10. No plan for the limitation of armaments proposed by the council of the League of Nations under the provision of article 8 shall be held as binding the United States until the same shall have been accepted by Congress, and the United States reserves the right to increase its armament without the consent of the council whenever the United States is threatened with invasion or engaged in war.

11. The United States reserves the right to permit, in its discretion, the nationals of a covenant-breaking State, as defined in article 16 of the covenant of the League of Nations, residing within the United States or in countries other than such covenant-breaking State, to continue their commercial, financial, and personal relations with the nationals of the United States. . . .

14. Until Part I, being the covenant of the League of Nations, shall be so amended as to provide that the United States shall be entitled to cast a number of votes equal to that which any member of the League and its self-governing dominions, colonies, or parts of empire, in the aggregate shall be entitled to cast, the United States assumes no obligation to be bound, except in cases where Congress has previously given its consent, by any election, decision, report, or finding of the council or assembly in which any member of the league and its self-governing dominions, colonies, or parts of empire, in the aggregate have cast more than one vote.

The United States assumes no obligation to be bound by any decision, report, or finding of the council or assembly arising out of any dispute between the United States and any member of the league if such member, or any self-governing dominion, colony, empire, or part of empire united with it politically has voted.

15. In consenting to the ratification of the treaty with Germany the United States adheres to the principle of self-determination and to the resolution of sympathy with the aspirations of the Irish people for a government of their own choice adopted by the Senate June 6, 1919, and declares that when such government is attained by Ireland, a consummation it is hoped is at hand, it should promptly be admitted as a member of the League of Nations.[6]

As the debate continued, it became obvious that the Treaty would only be ratified if some, at least, of the reservations were accepted. But from his sickbed, the President entreated the Democratic Senators to vote against ratification of a Treaty with reservations. The Lodge resolution, he said, "does not provide for ratification but, rather, for the nullification of the Treaty."

On the day of actual voting (November 19th), Senator Borah, one of the most persuasive and vociferous leaders of the "irreconcilables," delivered a speech in which he brilliantly stated the case for his point of view.

When the league shall have been formed, we shall be a member of what is known as the council of the league. Our accredited representative will sit in judgment with the accredited representatives of the other members of the league to pass upon the concerns not only of our country but of all Europe and all Asia and the entire world. Our accredited representatives will be members of the assembly. They will sit there to represent the judgment of these 110,000,000 people—more than—just as we are accredited here to represent our constituencies. We cannot send our representatives to sit in council with the representatives of the other great nations of the world with mental reservations as to what we shall do in case their judgment shall not be satisfactory to us. If we go to the council or the assembly with any other purpose than that of complying in good faith and in absolute integrity with all upon which the council or the assembly may pass, we shall soon return to our country with our self-respect forfeited and the public opinion of the world condemnatory.

Why need you gentlemen across the aisle worry about a reservation here or there when we are sitting in the council and in the assembly and bound by every obligation in morals, which the President said was supreme above that of law, to comply with the judgment that our representative and the other representatives finally form? Shall we go there, Mr. President, to sit in judgment, and in case that judgment works for peace join with our allies, but in case it works for war withdraw our cooperation? How long would we stand as we now stand, a great Republic commanding the respect and holding the leadership of the world, if we should adopt any such course? . . .

We have said, Mr. President, that we would not send our troops abroad without the consent of Congress. Pass by now for a moment the legal proposition. If we create executive functions, the Executive will perform those functions without the authority of Congress. Pass that question by and go to the other question. Our members of the council are there. Our members of the assembly are there. Article 11 is complete, and it authorizes the league, a member of which is our representative, to deal with matters of peace and war, and the league through its council and its assembly deals with the matter, and our accredited representative joins with the others in deciding upon a certain course, which involves a question of sending troops. What will the Congress of the United States do? What right will it have left, except the bare technical right to refuse, which as a moral proposition it will not dare to exercise? Have we not been told day by day for the last nine months that the Senate of the United States, a coordinate part of the treaty-making power, should accept this league as it was written because the wise men sitting at Versailles had so written it, and has not every possible influence and every source of power in public opinion been organized and directed against the Senate to compel it to do that thing? How much stronger will be the moral compulsion upon the Congress of the United States when we ourselves have indorsed the proposition of sending our accredited representatives there to vote for us?

Ah, but you say that there must be unanimous consent, and that there is vast protection in unanimous consent.

I do not wish to speak disparagingly; but has not every division and dismemberment of every nation which has suffered dismemberment taken place by unanimous consent for the last 300 years? Did not Prussia and Austria and Russia by unanimous consent divide Poland? Did not the United States and Great Britain and Japan and Italy and France divide China and give Shantung to Japan? Was that not a unanimous decision? Close the doors upon the diplomats of Europe, let them sit in secret, give them the material to trade on, and there always will be unanimous consent. . . .

Mr. President, if you have enough territory, if you have enough material, if you have enough subject peoples to trade upon and divide, there will be no difficulty about unanimous consent.

Do our Democratic friends ever expect any man to sit as a member of the council or as a member of the assembly equal in intellectual power and in standing before the world with that of our representative at Versailles? Do you expect a man to sit in the council who will have made more pledges, and I shall assume made them in sincerity, for self-determination and for the rights of small peoples, than had been made by our accredited representative? And yet, what became of it? The unanimous consent was obtained nevertheless.

But take another view of it. We are sending to the council one man. That one man represents 110,000,000 people.

Here, sitting in the Senate, we have two from every State in the Union, and over in the other House we have Representatives in accordance with population, and the responsibility is spread out in accordance with our obligations to our constituency. But now we are transferring to one man the stupendous power of representing the sentiment and convictions of 110,000,000 people in tremendous questions which may involve the peace or may involve the war of the world. . . .

What is the result of all this? We are in the midst of all of the affairs of Europe. We have entangled ourselves with all European concerns. We have joined in alliance with all the European nations which have thus far joined the league, and all nations which may be admitted to the league. We are sitting there dabbling in their affairs and intermeddling in their concerns. In other words, Mr. President—and this comes to the question which is fundamental with me—we have forfeited and surrendered, once and for all, the great policy of "no entangling alliances" upon which the strength of this Republic has been founded for 150 years.

My friends of reservations, tell me, where is the reservation in these articles which protects us against entangling alliances with Europe?

Those who are differing over reservations, tell me, what one of them protects the doctrine laid down by the Father of his Country? That fundamental proposition is surrendered, and we are a part of the European turmoils and conflicts from the time we enter this league. . . .

Lloyd George is reported to have said just a few days before the conference met at Versailles [*sic*] that Great Britain could give up much, and would be willing to sacrifice much, to have America withdraw from that policy. That was one of the great objects of the entire conference at Versailles [*sic*], so far as the foreign representatives were concerned. Clemenceau and Lloyd George and others like them were willing to make any reasonable sacrifice which would draw America away from her isolation and into the internal affairs and concerns of Europe. This league of nations, with or without reservations, whatever else it does or does not do, does surrender and sacrifice that policy; and once having surrendered and become a part of the European concerns, where, my friends, are you going to stop?

You have put in here a reservation on the Monroe doctrine. I think that, in so far as language could protect the Monroe doctrine, it has been protected. But as a practical proposition, as a working proposition, tell me candidly, as men familiar with the history of our country and of other countries, do you think that you can intermeddle in European affairs and never permit Europe to intervene in our affairs?

We can not protect the Monroe doctrine unless we protect the basic principle upon which it rests, and that is the Washington policy. I do not care how earnestly you may endeavor to do so, as a practical working proposition your league will never come to the United States. . . .

Mr. President, there is another and even more commanding reason why I shall record my vote against this treaty. It imperils what I conceive to be the underlying, the very first principles of this Republic. It is in conflict with the right of our people to govern themselves free from all restraint, legal or moral, of foreign powers. . . .

Sir, since the debate opened months ago those of us who have stood against this proposition have been taunted many times with being little Americans. Leave us the word American, keep that in your presumptuous impeachment, and no taunt can disturb us, no gibe discompose our purposes. Call us little Americans if you will but leave us the consolation and the pride which the term American, however modified, still imparts. . . .

We have sought nothing but the tranquillity of our own people and the honor and independence of our own Republic. No foreign flattery, no possible world glory and power have disturbed our poise or come between us and our devotion to the traditions which have made us a Nation, unselfish and commanding. If we have erred we have erred out of too much love for those things which from childhood you and we together have been taught to revere—yes, to defend even at the cost of limb and life. If we have erred it is because we have placed too high an estimate upon the wisdom of Washington and Jefferson, too exalted an opinion upon the patriotism of the sainted Lincoln. . . .

Senators, even in an hour so big with expectancy we should not close our eyes to the fact that democracy is something more, vastly more, than a mere form of government by which society is restrained into free and orderly life. It is a moral entity, a spiritual force as well. And these are things which live only and alone in the atmosphere of liberty. The foundation upon which democracy rests is faith in the moral instincts of the people. Its ballot boxes, the franchise, its laws, and constitutions are but the outward manifestations of the deeper and more essential thing—a continuing trust in the moral purposes of the average man and woman. When this is lost or forfeited your outward forms, however democratic in terms, are a mockery. Force may find expression through institutions democratic in structure equal with the simple and more direct processes of a single supreme ruler. These distinguishing virtues of a real republic you can not commingle with the discordant and destructive forces of the Old World and still preserve them. You can not yoke a government whose first law is that of force and still hope to preserve the former. These things are in eternal war, and one must ultimately destroy the other. You may still keep for a time the outward form, you may still delude yourself, as others have done in the past, with appearances and symbols, but when you shall have committed this Republic to a scheme of world control based upon force, upon the combined military force of the four great nations of the world, you will have soon destroyed the atmosphere of freedom, of confidence in the self-governing capacity of the masses, in which alone a democracy may thrive. We may become one of the four dictators of the world, but we shall no longer be master of our own spirit. And what shall it profit us as a Nation if we shall go forth to the domination of the earth and share with others the glory of world control and lose that fine sense of confidence in the people, the soul of democracy?

Look upon the scene as it is now presented. Behold the task we are to assume, and then contemplate the method by which we are to deal with this task. Is the method such as to address itself to a Government "conceived in liberty and dedicated to the proposition that all men are created equal"? When this league, this combination, is formed four equal powers representing the dominant people will rule one-half of the inhabitants of the globe as subject peoples—rule by force, and we shall be a party to the rule of force. There is no other way by which you can keep people in subjection. You must either give them independence, recognize their rights as nations to live their own life and to set up their own form of government, or you must deny them these things by force. That is the scheme, the method proposed by the league. It proposes no other. We will in time become inured to its inhuman precepts and its soulless methods, strange as this doctrine now seems to a free people. If we stay with our contract we will come in time to declare with our associates that force—force, the creed of the Prussian military oligarchy—is after all the true foundation upon which must rest all stable government. Korea, despoiled and bleeding at every pore; India, sweltering in ignorance and burdened with inhuman taxes after more than one hundred years of dominant rule; Egypt, trapped and robbed of her birthright; Ireland, with 700 years of sacrifice for independence—this is the task, this is the atmosphere, and this is the creed in and under which we are to keep alive our belief in the moral purposes and self-governing capacity of the people, a belief without which the Republic must disintegrate and die. The maxim of liberty will soon give way to the rule of blood and iron. We have been pleading here for our Constitution. Conform this league, it has been said, to the technical terms of our charter, and all will be well. But I declare to you that we must go further and conform to those sentiments and passions for justice and freedom which are essential to the existence of democracy. . . .

Sir, we are told that this treaty means peace. Even so, I would not pay the price. Would you purchase peace at the cost of any part of our independence? We could have had peace in 1776—the price was high, but we could have had it. James Otis, Sam Adams, Hancock, and Warren were surrounded by those who urged peace and British rule. All through that long and trying struggle, particularly when the clouds of adversity lowered upon the cause, there was a cry of peace —let us have peace. We could have had peace in 1860; Lincoln was counseled by men of great influence and accredited wisdom to let our brothers—and, thank Heaven, they are brothers—depart in peace. But the tender, loving Lincoln, bending under the fearful weight of impending civil war, an apostle of peace, refused to pay the price, and a reunited country will praise his name forevermore—bless it because he refused peace at the price of national honor and national integrity. Peace upon any other basis than national independence, peace purchased at the cost of any part of our national integrity, is fit only for slaves, and even when purchased at such a price it is a delusion, for it can not last.

But your treaty does not mean peace—far, very far, from it. If we are to judge the future by the past it means war. Is there any guaranty of peace other than the guaranty which comes of the control of the war-making power by the people? Yet what great rule of democracy does the treaty leave unassailed? The people in whose keeping alone you can safely lodge the power of peace or war nowhere, at no time and in no place, have any voice in this scheme for world peace. Autocracy which has bathed the world in blood for centuries reigns supreme. Democracy is everywhere excluded. This, you say, means peace.

Can you hope for peace when love of country is disregarded in your scheme, when the spirit of nationality is rejected, even scoffed at? Yet what law of that moving and mysterious force does your treaty not deny? With a ruthlessness unparalleled your treaty in a dozen instances runs counter to the divine law of nationality. Peoples who speak the same language, kneel at the same ancestral tombs, moved by the same traditions, animated by a common hope, are torn asunder, broken in pieces, divided, and parceled out to antagonistic nations. And this you call justice. This, you cry, means peace. Peoples who have dreamed of independence, struggled and been patient, sacrificed and been hopeful, peoples who were told that through this peace conference they should realize the aspirations of centuries, have again had their hopes dashed to earth. One of the most striking and commanding figures in this war, soldier and statesman, turned away from the peace table at Versailles declaring to the world, "The promise of the new life, the victory of the great humane ideals for which the peoples have shed their blood and their treasure without stint, the fulfillment of their aspirations toward a new international order and a fairer and better world, are not written into the treaty." No; your treaty means injustice. It means slavery. It means war. And to all this you ask this Republic to become a party. You ask it to abandon the creed under which it has grown to power and accept the creed of autocracy, the creed of repression and force.[7]

Other remarks delivered that same day are noteworthy, though not for their content; the speaker, Senator Harding of Ohio, would be, a year later, the newly elected President of the United States.

I have not liked this treaty; I think, as originally negotiated, it is a colossal blunder of all time, but, recognizing the aspirations of our own people and the people of the world to do something toward international cooperation for the promotion and preservation of peace and a more intimate and better understanding between nations, I have wished to make it possible to accept this covenant. I could, however, no more vote to ratify this treaty without reservations which make sure America's independence of action, which make sure the preservation of American traditions, which make sure and certain our freedom in choosing our course of action, than I could participate in a knowing betrayal of this Republic. . . .

The trouble with the whole league covenant is that it was hastily negotiated to be made the foundation of a treaty of peace, when there ought to have been a treaty of peace negotiated with a league of nations created in the deliberate aftermath. . . .

I know, Mr. President, that in this covenant we have originally bartered American independence in order to create a league. We have traded away America's freedom of action in order to establish a supergovernment of the world, and it was never intended to be any less. I speak for one who is old-fashioned enough to believe that the Government of the United States of America is good enough for me. In speaking my reverence for the Government of the United States of America, Senators, I want the preservation of those coordinate branches of government which were conceived and instituted by the fathers, and if there is nothing else significant in the action of this day, you can tell to the people of the United States of America and to the world that the Senate of the United States has once more reasserted its authority, and representative government abides.[8]

When the Senate proceeded to vote, a combination of Wilsonian Democrats, moderates and irreconcilables defeated the resolution, signaling America's rejection of the Treaty and the League by a vote of 39 yeas and 55 nays. If the Wilsonian Democrats had voted for Lodge's resolution the Treaty would have been carried 81 to 13.

The reasons for the Senate's rejection were not as simple as they may appear from the foregoing presentation. Partisan considerations, honest objections to some provisions of the Treaty, particularly to Article 10 of the Covenant, and a general desire by the Senate to reassert its power after the President's authoritarian regime during the war, all contributed to the result. One historian has summarized the situation as follows:

A wave of isolation and disgust with Europe spread over the country; and this feeling together with some rational criticism of the terms, and a good deal of party politics, caused the Senate to repudiate Wilson's work.[9]

The result of the vote shocked the country. It seemed like a flat rejection of America's war effort to turn down the new order which would "make the world safe for Democracy." After mature deliberation the Senate reconsidered its November 19th vote and sent the Treaty back to Committee on February 9th. It re-emerged from there on the 10th and a month later (March 19th) the final vote was cast. Once again, Wilson refused all compromise and, as far as the United States was concerned, the Treaty of Versailles was buried by a vote of 49 to 35—just seven votes short of passing.

In March, 1920, the United States of America was the only power still at war with Germany. On May 15th, Congress passed a joint resolution ending the war, but President Wilson refused to append his signature.

. . . I have not felt at liberty to sign this resolution because I cannot bring myself to become party to an action which would place ineffaceable stain upon the gallantry and honour of the United States.

The resolution seeks to establish peace with the German Empire without exacting from the German government any action by way of setting right the infinite wrongs which it did to the peoples whom it attacked, and whom we professed it our purpose to assist when we entered the war. . . .

A treaty of peace was signed at Versailles on the twenty-eighth of June last which did seek to accomplish the objects which we had declared to be in our minds, because all the great governments and peoples which united against Germany had adopted our declarations of purpose as their own, and had in solemn form embodied them in communications to the German government preliminary to the armistice of November 11, 1918. But the treaty as signed at Versailles has been rejected by the Senate of the United States, though it has been ratified by Germany. By that rejection and by its methods we had in effect declared that we wish to draw apart and pursue objects and interests of our own, unhampered by any connexions of interest or of purpose with other governments and peoples. . . .

Such a peace with Germany—a peace in which none of the essential interests which we had at heart when we entered the war is safeguarded—is, or ought to be, inconceivable, is inconsistent with the dignity of the United States, with the rights and liberties of her citizens, and with the very fundamental conditions of civilization.

I hope that in these statements I have sufficiently set forth the reasons why I have felt it incumbent upon me to withhold my signature.

WOODROW WILSON

The White House
May 27, 1920[10]

It was not until October 18, 1921, under the Presidency of Warren G. Harding, that a separate peace with Germany was finally signed and ratified.

A JOINT resolution of July 2, 1921, terminating the war between the United States and the Governments of Germany and Austria-Hungary, set forth, in Section 2, "that in making this declaration, and as a part of it, there are expressly reserved to the United States of America and its nationals any and all rights, privileges, indemnities, reparations, or advantages, together with the right to enforce the same, to which it or they have become entitled under the terms of the armistice signed November 11, 1918, or any extensions or modifications thereof; or which were acquired by or are in the possession of the United States of America by reason of its participation in the war or to which its nationals have thereby become rightfully entitled; or which, under the treaty of Versailles, have been stipulated for its or their benefit; or to which it is entitled as one of the principal allied and associated powers; or to which it is entitled by virtue of any Act or Acts of Congress; or otherwise." Section 5 further provided that "all property of the Imperial German Government, or its successor or successors, and of all German nationals which was, on April 6, 1917, in or has since that date come into the possession or under control of, or has been the subject of a demand by the United States of America or of any of its officers, agents, or employees, from any source or by any agency whatsoever . . . [and all similar property of the Imperial and Royal Austro-Hungarian Government or its nationals, as of December 7, 1917] . . . shall be retained by the United States of America and no disposition thereof made, except as shall have been heretofore or specifically hereafter shall be provided by law until such time as the Imperial German Government and the Imperial and Royal Austro-Hungarian Government, or their successor or successors, shall have respectively made suitable provision for the satisfaction of all claims against said Governments respectively, of all persons, wheresoever domiciled, who owe permanent allegiance to the United States of

America and who have suffered, through the acts of the Imperial German Government, or its agents, or the Imperial and Royal Austro-Hungarian Government, or its agents, since July 31, 1914, loss, damage, or injury to their persons or property, directly or indirectly, whether through the ownership of shares of stock in German, Austro-Hungarian, American or other corporations, or in consequence of hostilities or of any operations of war, or otherwise, and also shall have granted to persons owing permanent allegiance to the United States of America most-favored-nation treatment, whether the same be national or otherwise, in all matters affecting residence, business, profession, trade, navigation, commerce and industrial property rights, and until the Imperial German Government and the Imperial and Royal Austro-Hungarian Government, or their successor or successors, shall have respectively confirmed to the United States of America all fines, forfeitures, penalties, and seizures imposed or made by the United States of America during the war, whether in respect to the property of the Imperial German Government or German nationals or the Imperial and Royal Austro-Hungarian Government or Austro-Hungarian nationals, and shall have waived any and all pecuniary claims against the United States of America."

ARTICLE I.

Germany undertakes to accord to the United States, and the United States shall have and enjoy, all the rights, privileges, indemnities, reparations or advantages specified in the aforesaid Joint Resolution . . . [of July 2, 1921] . . . including all the rights and advantages stipulated for the benefit of the United States in the Treaty of Versailles which the United States shall fully enjoy notwithstanding the fact that such Treaty has not been ratified by the United States.

ARTICLE II.

(1) [The rights and advantages stipulated in the Treaty of Versailles] for the benefit of the United States, which it is intended the United States shall have and enjoy, are those defined in Section 1, of Part IV, and Parts V, VI, VIII, IX, X, XI, XII, XIV, and XV.

The United States in availing itself of the rights and advantages stipulated in the provisions of that Treaty mentioned in this paragraph will do so in a manner consistent with the rights accorded to Germany under such provisions.

(2) That the United States shall not be bound by the provisions of

Part I of that Treaty, nor by any provisions of that Treaty including those mentioned in Paragraph (1) of this Article, which relate to the Covenant of the League of Nations, nor shall the United States be bound by any action taken by the League of Nations, or by the Council or by the Assembly thereof, unless the United States shall expressly give its assent to such action.

(3) That the United States assumes no obligations under or with respect to the provisions of Part II, Part III, Sections 2 to 8 inclusive of Part IV, and Part XIII of that Treaty.

(4) That, while the United States is privileged to participate in the Reparation Commission, according to the terms of Part VIII of that Treaty, and in any other Commission established under the Treaty or under any agreement supplemental thereto, the United States is not bound to participate in any such commission unless it shall elect to do so.

(5) That the periods of time to which reference is made in Article 440 of the Treaty of Versailles shall run, with respect to any act or election on the part of the United States, from the date of the coming into force of the present Treaty.

[Seal.] Ellis Loring Dresel
[Seal.] Rosen

The treaty with Germany, signed at Berlin on August 25, was ratified by the Senate on October 18 with the understanding "that the United States shall not be represented or participate in any body, agency or commission, nor shall any person represent the United States as a member of any body, agency or commission in which the United States is authorized to participate by this Treaty, unless and until an Act of the Congress of the United States shall provide for such representation or participation"; and "that the rights and advantages which the United States is entitled to have and enjoy under this Treaty embrace the rights and advantages of nationals of the United States specified in the Joint Resolution or in the provisions of the Treaty of Versailles to which this Treaty refers." The treaty was ratified by the German Government on November 2, and on November 14, following the exchange of ratifications at Berlin on the 11th, the treaty was proclaimed.[11]

By bowing out of the peace settlement America fundamentally changed the pattern of the postwar world the Peace Conference had envisaged. Deprived of American participation, the League of Nations lost a great deal of prestige and power; the world's money market, already operating in a vacuum due to the uncertainty of war loan and reparation payments, was further disrupted as debtor and creditor nations started traveling in opposite directions; and public opinion the world over seriously began questioning the soundness of the Paris peace structure now that its main architect had quit the project.

Europe's immediate reaction to America's defection was one of shock and incredulity. Few people had imagined that the United States Senate would disavow the President so completely. But, as time went on, Europe accepted the fact and the various nations adjusted to the inevitable in accordance with the stakes they had in the peace settlement.

In Britain the shock of America's refusal to underwrite the Treaty her President had been so instrumental in shaping was somewhat cushioned by the relief Downing Street felt at being released from the guarantee to France that Lloyd George had so rashly initiated in one of the Conference's most critical moments. Britain was in the process of readjusting her foreign policy to the new continental balance of power created by the Treaty, and any close commitment to France might prove highly embarrassing. Britain was, in fact, rapidly pulling away from its wartime alliances, as Clemenceau was to discover when he visited Lloyd George in 1921. He writes: ". . . as I was passing through London on my way to Oxford to receive an honorary degree, Mr. Lloyd George asked me to come and see him in the House of Commons. His first words were to ask me if I had anything to say to him. 'Yes, indeed,' I replied. 'I have to tell you that from the very day of the armistice I found you an enemy of France.' 'Well,' he rejoined, 'was that not always our traditional policy?' "[12] . . . The Prime Minister's bluntness might possibly have been meant to deflect an attack by a quip, but the statement contained a great deal of truth. Although enmity to France by no means prompted Britain's actions, she was rapidly and determinedly withdrawing from the Continent and was quite prepared to let France adjust to the new circumstances as best she could.

The writings of Maynard Keynes and Harold Nicolson among others had alerted the British public to the pitfalls of the Treaty and, as the great letdown swept the country in the wake of the sacrifices, the heroics and the hysteria of the war, the English reverted to their traditional isolation which they found "splendid," took America's default in their stride and, like their overseas cousins, strained to get "back to normalcy."

To France, however, the U. S. Senate's refusal to ratify the Treaty and to even discuss the guarantee pact was an almost mortal blow. At the Paris Conference France had surrendered what she considered her minimum security program in exchange for the Anglo-American guarantee pact and the supposed protection of a League of Nations, backed by the might of the United States. Suddenly she found herself without the Anglo-American guarantee, without the powerful backing of the League, and without her own security program.

Georges Clemenceau fell victim to America's withdrawal. Violently attacked for having bartered France's security for worthless American promises, the old Tiger was forced to resign on January 20, 1920, just two months after the U. S. Senate had rejected the Treaty. Clemenceau's political career was shattered and his lifelong ambition to become President of the Republic was thwarted. He followed Orlando and Wilson into the political doghouse, whence he growled out his resentment to the very end of his days (1929). He was succeeded by Raymond Poincaré, his bitterest enemy and a diehard *revanchist*, compared with whom Clemenceau had indeed been a moderate.

The defection of the United States had thrown France back on her own resources and compelled her to try to revive her original security program. The time to rewrite the Treaty had passed, but France was determined to "correct the mistakes of the Conference" and, in one way or another, to achieve her prime objective: the emasculation of Germany. The fact that that policy found no support in either Great Britain or Italy only made the French feel all the more insecure and isolated.

The Senate's repudiation of Woodrow Wilson's promises was a deeply traumatic experience to France. The French felt betrayed and humiliated and saw their hard-won victory turn sour. Nor has France gotten over that trauma to this day, nearly half a century later. When Charles de Gaulle, in 1963, insists on providing France her own private *force de frappe*, because, as he argues, no American President can commit the United States to any future action, no matter how sincere his promises and assurances might be, the reactions of the French chief of state are, at least partly, conditioned by the French trauma of Versailles.

The German reactions to America's withdrawal from the Treaty were twofold: on the one hand it represented a welcome breakup of the enemy's wartime alliance, much sooner than the Germans could possibly have hoped for, but, on the other hand, it meant that American influence to mitigate the enforcement of the Treaty's conditions, which the Germans had heavily counted upon, would now be lacking. Treaty enforcement would now be largely in the merciless hands of the French.

By the time the United States ratified its Peace Treaty with Germany, the Weimar Republic had become a going concern. By 1921 the German government had eliminated the various "Bolshevik" pockets that had formed throughout the country, had extinguished the civil wars which flickered up here and there, had put down a serious attempt of the military to re-establish itself in power (Kapp *Putsch,* 1920), had adopted a model constitution, and had, in all but spirit, become a true, if somewhat precariously balanced, democracy.

The German people never accepted what they came to call "the Versailles Dictate." Germans felt no guilt about having fought or supported a war which they honestly believed to have been a war of self-defense against "a world of foes." The unanimous determination of all segments of the German people to resist the Versailles Dictate and to reverse its rulings as soon as possible, forced every political party in Germany, from the far right through the "democratic" center to the far left, to write "Treaty Revision" on its banners, and since German governments depended on parliamentary majorities for their survival they were all inevitably committed to the same goal.

XI
Conclusion

The fate that befell the Versailles Treaty is too well known to need retelling; to go into the details of its demise would mean writing the history of Europe during the twenty-year period between the two World Wars. For a long time to come, historians will debate whether the Treaty's failure was due to its provisions or to the way it was executed. Today there seems to be little left of the labors of the Paris Peace Conference and the resulting treaties. All they seem to be good for these days is to take the blame for the turbulence of the inter-war era and even for World War II itself.

From where we sit today it is very easy for us to see mistakes that were made at Paris; it is easy to criticize the peacemakers of 1919 for their greed, for their shortsightedness, for their soaring idealism, and for the compromises they made with each other and with their own consciences. It is as easy as it is unfair. The peacemakers of Paris faced the desperate urgency of putting the world back into a semblance of order after the unprecedented cataclysm that had swept over it. Because the world was still afire, because Bolshevism threatened to engulf it if order were not speedily restored, they could not wait until the tempers of the war had had time to cool, until the forces which the war had unleashed had had time to sort themselves out, until cold reason and common sense could take over from violent emotion. Maybe it was their most fatal mistake, but nobody thought so at the time when all the world was crying for a speedy settlement.

The preceding chapters of this book have all been documentary presentations of events with an absolute minimum of editorial comment. I would like to close this book with some very personal thoughts of my own. They may seem out of place in a documentary survey of historical developments; I can only let the reader be the judge.

We know by now that the results of the Paris Peace Conference were neither perfect nor lasting. The elaborate peace structure of the French châteaux was a long series of compromises between two incompatible and uncompromisable conceptions of the postwar world. A thick layer of hypocrisy was used to hold together the compromises between Wilsonian idealism and the concrete, materialistic war aims of the Allies. Harold Nicolson has reviewed the reasons for the Treaty's built-in hypocrisy in some honest, soul-searching passages.

> We came to Paris confident that the new order was about to be established; we left it convinced that the new order had merely fouled the old. We arrived as fervent apprentices in the school of President Wilson: we left as renegades. I wish to suggest that this unhappy diminution of standard was very largely the fault . . . of democratic diplomacy. We arrived determined that a Peace of justice and wisdom should be negotiated: we left it, conscious that the Treaties imposed upon our enemies were neither just nor wise. To those who desire to measure for themselves the width of the gulf which sundered intention from practice I should recommend the perusal of the several notes addressed to the Supreme Council by the German delegation at Versailles. . . . It is impossible to read the German criticism without deriving the impression that the Paris Peace Conference was guilty of disguising an Imperialistic peace under the surplice of Wilsonism, that seldom in the history of man has such vindictiveness cloaked itself in such unctuous sophistry. Hypocrisy was the predominant and unescapable result. Yet was this hypocrisy wholly conscious, wholly deliberate? I do not think so. I certainly agree that the sanctimonious pharisaism of the Treaties is their gravest fault. Yet was there any conscious dissimulation? In some cases (such as the article forbidding Austria to join Germany) a deliberately evasive form of words was consciously employed. Yet in most cases, hypocrisy *just happened*. How did it happen? The fact that, as the Conference progressed, we were scarcely conscious of our own falsity, may indicate that some deterioration of moral awareness

had taken place. We did not realise what we were doing. We did not realise how far we were drifting from our original basis. We were exhausted and overworked. We kept on mumbling our old formulas in the hope that they still bore some relation to our actions. There were few moments when we said to ourselves "This is unjust": there were many moments when we said to ourselves "Better a bad treaty today, than a good treaty four months hence." In the dust of controversy, in the rattle of time-pressure, we lost all contact with our guiding stars. In interludes the dust would settle, the machine would stop, and we would observe, with tired regret, that these stars were themselves fading pale against the sky. "*Il faut aboutir*" they shouted at us: and we returned to the din and dimness of our compromises. We still desired ardently to maintain our principles intact: it was only in the after-vacancy that we realised that they remained for us only in the form of empty words: it was then, and then only, that we faced the fact that the falsity of our position had led us into being false. It was by then far too late.

The above is not written in any desire to defend our state of mind. I am examining only: I am not defending. My contention is that this dimming of our moral awareness constituted the most regrettable and perhaps the only interesting element in our deterioration. I wish to explain how it occurred that in the dust of incessant argument, amid the by-paths of unceasing detail, we strayed away from the main avenues of our intention: and how it was unconsciously, rather than consciously, that we boasted, on arrival, to have come the way we meant.

The point is, I think, of some importance. If future generations come to believe that the Paris Conference was, in every single point, deliberately and exceptionally hypocritical, they will (when they also come to attend Congresses) be less on their guard against the tired falsity which is inseparable from any attempt to adjust high general principles to low practical detail. In every discussion between sovereign States claiming equality with each other, decisions can only be taken by a unanimous and not by a majority vote. This inevitable curse of unanimity leads to the no less inevitable curse of compromise. All compromises have an element of falsity, but when they have to be referred back to governing principles or generalisations a double falsity is introduced. I do not deny the ghastly hypocrisy of the Paris Treaties: I contend only that this hypocrisy was not, in every case, conscious or deliberate; that it was not, in every case, humanly avoidable; and that similar hypocrisy may not, in every case, be humanly avoidable in the future.

It will be contended by any intelligent reader that the above analysis of the nature of our hypocrisy is not, after all, an explanation, but is merely a lame and empty excuse. Yet the explanation is none the less implicit in my argument. It is this. The Paris negotiators were from the very first in a false position. This falsity increased during the whole time that the German Treaty was being discussed. It was the root-case of the whole failure, of the rapid deterioration in moral awareness. It requires to be analysed into its component parts. . . .

I have . . . indicated the acute difficulty experienced by the negotiators in Paris in reconciling the excited expectations of their own democracies with the calmer considerations of durable peace-making. . . . The main problem of democratic diplomacy . . . is [that] of adjusting the emotions of the masses to the thoughts of the rulers. The new diplomacy may be immune to some of the virus of deception which afflicted the old: yet it is acutely sensitive to its own peculiar virus—to the virus of imprecision. What the statesman thinks today, the masses may well feel tomorrow. Yet in conditions such as those of the Peace Conference, requiring extreme rapidity of solution, the time-lag between the emotions of the masses and the thoughts of the statesmen is a most disadvantageous factor. The attempt rapidly to bridge the gulf between mass-emotion and expert reason leads, at its worst, to actual falsity, and at its best to grave imprecision. The Paris Peace Conference was not a sample of democratic diplomacy at its best. It was thus by actual falsity that the gulf was bridged.

This general type of falsity, inseparable from all attempts at democratic diplomacy, was in Paris complicated and enhanced by special circumstances which require in their turn to be stated and analysed. The contrast between mass-emotion and expert reason was stated for us in acute and difficult terms. It took the form—the unnecessary and perplexing form—of a contrast not only between the new diplomacy and the old, but between the new world and the old, between Europe and America. I do not say that this contrast was, in all its implications, fully realised at the time. I contend only that it was determinant throughout the whole Conference: that it was, in fact, an unreal and not a real contrast: and that the attempt to reconcile these two unrealities was the essential misconception of the Conference, and the root cause of all resultant falsity. Let me state the contrast in quite simple terms.

On the one hand you had Wilsonism—a doctrine which was very easy to state and very difficult to apply. Mr. Wilson had not invented any new political philosophy, or discovered any doctrine which had not been dreamed of, and appreciated, for many hundred years. The one thing which rendered Wilsonism so passionately interesting at the moment was the fact that this centennial dream was suddenly backed by the overwhelming resources of the strongest Power in the world. Here was a man who represented the greatest physical force which had ever existed and who had pledged himself openly to the most ambitious moral theory which any statesman had ever pronounced. It was not that the ideas of Woodrow Wilson were so apocalyptic: it was that for the first time in history you had a man who possessed, not the desire merely, not the power alone, but the unquestioned opportunity to enforce these ideas upon the whole world. We should have been insensitive indeed had we not been inspired by the magnitude of such an occasion.

On the other hand you had Europe, the product of a wholly different civilisation, the inheritor of unalterable circumstances, the possessor of longer and more practical experience. Through centuries of conflict the Europeans had come to learn that war is in almost every case contrived with the expectation of victory, and that such an expectation is diminished under a system of balanced forces which renders victory difficult if not uncertain. The defensive value of armaments, strategic frontiers, alliances, and neutralization, could be computed with approximate accuracy: the defensive value of "virtue all round" could not be thus computed. If in fact Wilsonism could be integrally and universally applied, and if in fact Europe could rely upon America for its enforcement and execution, then indeed an alternative was offered infinitely preferable to the dangerous and provocative balances of the European system. . . . But were they certain that America would be so unselfish, so almost quixotic, as to make Wilsonism safe for Europe? Were they certain, even, that the European Powers would, when it came to the point, apply Wilsonism to themselves? The Fourteen Points were hailed as an admirable method of extracting motes from the eyes of others: would any great and victorious Power apply them for the purposes of extracting beams from their own body politic? The most ardent British advocate of the principle of self-determination found himself, sooner or later, in a false position. However fervid might be our indignation regarding

Italian claims to Dalmatia and the Dodecanese it could be cooled by a reference, not to Cyprus only, but to Ireland, Egypt and India. We had accepted a system for others which, when it came to practice, we should refuse to apply to ourselves.

Nor was this the only element of falsity by which the gospel of Woodrow Wilson was discredited from the start. The Anglo-Saxon is gifted with a limitless capacity for excluding his own practical requirements from the application of the idealistic theories which he seeks to impose on others. Not so the Latin. The logical precision of the French, and to a less extent the Italian, genius does not permit such obscurantism. The Anglo-Saxon is apt to accuse the Latin of "cynicism" because he hesitates to adhere to a religion which he would not be prepared to apply to his own conduct as distinct from the conduct of others. The Latin accuses the Anglo-Saxon of "cant" because he desires to enforce upon others a standard of behaviour which he would refuse to adopt himself. The contrast between the two is not, in fact, one between cynicism and hypocrisy, it is one between two divergent habits of mind. The Anglo-Saxon is apt to feel before he thinks, and the Latin is apt to think before he feels. It was this divergence of habit, this gap between reason and emotion, which induced the Latins to examine the Revelation of Woodrow Wilson in a manner more scientific, and therefore more critical, than we did ourselves. . . .

They observed, for instance, that the United States in the course of their short but highly imperialistic history, had constantly proclaimed the highest virtue while as constantly violating their professions and resorting to the grossest materialism. . . . They observed that such principles as the equality of man were not applied either to the yellow man or to the black. They observed that the doctrine of self-determination had not been extended either to the Red Indians or even to the Southern States. . . . They observed that, almost within living memory, the great American Empire had been won by ruthless force. Can we blame them if they doubted, not so much the sincerity as the actual applicability of the gospel of Woodrow Wilson? Can we blame them if they feared lest American realism would, when it came to the point, reject the responsibility of making American idealism safe for Europe? Can we wonder that they preferred the precisions of their own old system to the vague idealism of a new system which America might refuse to apply even to her own continent?

It is only fair to record that on the American Delegation themselves this unfortunate disparity produced a sense of impotence. The President himself was able to dismiss from his consciousness all considerations which might disturb the foundations of his mystic faith. Colonel House, being a man of robust intelligence, might have been able, had he possessed supreme control, to bridge the gulf in a wholly scientific manner, to evolve an honest triumph of engineering. Yet upon the other members of the delegation, who were ardent and sincere, the suspicion that America was asking Europe to make sacrifices to righteousness which America would never make, and had never made, herself, produced a mood of diffidence, uncertainty and increasing despair. Had President Wilson been a man of exceptional breadth of vision, of superhuman determination, he might have triumphed over all these difficulties. Unfortunately neither the will-power nor the brain-power of President Wilson were in any sense superhuman.[1]

Its Pharisaism, its hypocrisy, may have been the Treaty's gravest fault, as Sir Harold claims. But, on the other hand, that very hypocrisy was also the one ingredient which saved the Wilsonian parts of the Treaty from becoming as eroded as its concrete, materialist provisions. In public life hypocrisy has a positive function. The well-born cliché has it that "hypocrisy is the compliment that vice pays to virtue." If that be so, then the hypocrite must, outwardly at least, accept the value of the virtue to which he pays his hypocritical compliments. In private life an individual may, if he is lucky, get away with being a hypocrite until he is put six feet underground. In public life, however, it does not work that way. Once a public body, be it an organization, a nation, or a civilization, accepts certain principles and starts paying lip service to them even while it violates them in its day-to-day behavior, it will not long be able to avoid behaving as if it actually did believe in these concepts, and will, sooner or later, end up by sincerely embracing them.

Take but one example: In his diary Sir Harold Nicolson recounts a slight brush he had with his Foreign Office chief, Sir Eyre Crowe.

January 22, Wednesday

Work all morning. Crowe is cantankerous about Cyprus and will not allow me even to mention the subject. I explain (1) That we acquired it by a trick as disreputable as that by which the Italians collared the Dodecanese. (2) That it is wholly Greek and under any interpretation of Self-Determination would opt for union with Greece. (3) That it is no use to us strategically or economically. (4) That we are left in a false moral position if we ask everyone else to surrender possessions in terms of Self-Determination and surrender nothing ourselves. How can we keep Cyprus and express moral indignation at the Italians retaining Rhodes? He says, "Nonsense, my dear Nicolson. You are not being clear-headed. You think that you are being logical and sincere. You are not. Would you apply self-determination to India, Egypt, Malta and Gibraltar? If you are *not* prepared to go as far as this, then you have not right to claim that you are logical. If you *are* prepared to go as far as this, then you had better return at once to London." Dear Crowe—he has the most truthful brain of any man I know.[2]

Nicolson's young and tender conscience was obviously bothered by the idea of applying two different standards to the colonial claims of Britain and Italy. But in 1919 the nineteenth-century concepts of colonialism were so firmly established that Nicolson paled when he was confronted with the very thought of applying self-determination to India, Egypt and other jewels in Britain's imperial crown. He did not pack his bags, return to London and resign from the Foreign Service. He swallowed his scruples and went along with his beloved chief. There was nothing else he could do in 1919.

At Paris the Colonial Powers accepted the Wilsonian concept of administering mandates "in the interests of the populations concerned." In order to evade the restrictions which the Covenant placed upon mandatories, they also accepted the provisions of the Smuts memorandum, which, in retrospect, reads almost like a blueprint for the development of backward colonies to self-determination and independence.

The Colonial Powers did not accept Wilson's edicts because they believed in them, but because they had to, if they wanted to be awarded the mandates they craved. Their minds still considered colonies "territories developed and exploited for the benefit of the mother country," the proper nineteenth-century definition of the word.

The Wilsonian concept ran counter to the interests of all Colonial Powers. Yet they accepted it, for they had no choice. They made no bones about their hypocrisy and when mandates were finally awarded, Lloyd George walked away from the meeting chuckling: "Well, he has saved his precious principles, but we got our colonies." Yet today, less than half a century after Nicolson's little talk with Crowe, there is not a single colonial empire left in the world.

It would be naïve to maintain that acceptance of the mandate principle and the concept of self-determination were the sole reasons for the collapse of the British, French, Italian, Belgian and Dutch colonial empires. But it would be highly unrealistic to ignore the power of an idea to force its professor to live up to the standards it sets, once it has been embraced, no matter how hypocritically.

The hypocrisy with which the colonial provisions of the Treaty were coated has preserved the Wilsonian, the anti-colonial, components of the compromises, while the concrete components, such as mandates, colonial armies, and the whole nineteenth-century concept of colonies as such, have disappeared. Today we would have to paraphrase Lloyd George: "All that is left are his precious principles."

The same line of thought applies to almost every other part of the Treaty, for we only have to look about us to realize that we live in a world that is far more Wilsonian than Woodrow Wilson ever dreamed it could be. For better or for worse, self-determination is rampant in five continents, the United Nations is a revised edition of Wilson's League, and United States isolationism has given way to the Wilsonian concept of an expanded Monroe Doctrine, whereby the United States extends its protection to the weak of this world against any foreign interference, except its own. Whereas all the "concrete" provisions of the Treaty of Versailles have been swept away by the winds of time, the Wilsonian contributions to the document have survived under the protective coating of hypocrisy.

But today's Wilsonian world has also inherited the Wilsonian problems the Big Four wrestled with. Wilson himself seems to have been quite unconscious of the fact that his Fourteen Points contained two basically contradictory doctrines, "national self-determination" and "supernational authority." Nor did any of the statesmen at the Conference ever in so many words point out the basic incompatibility of the two doctrines, although their arguments often show signs of their inability to reconcile the two.

As interpreted at Paris, "self-determination" was the acme of nationalism, whereby any ethnic group or splinter group, almost for the asking, could obtain a franchise to set up its own sovereignty, in disregard of any overriding political, geographic or economic considerations. "Supernational authority," on the other hand, as represented by the League, subjected national sovereignty to restrictions that, limited to begin with, inevitably had to encroach ever more and more on the political and economic life of its member states.

At the Paris Peace Conference the two streams of thought merged, and as the torrent of nationalism met the pristine current of supernational authority they formed a vortex of conflicting emotions and ideas from which the Western world has not yet emerged. Western civilization (indeed, the world as a whole) has not yet made up its mind whether supernational considerations, national interests, or ideological loyalties shall be given precedence in governing the minds and emotions of modern man. In consequence, none of the basic problems that the peacemakers of Paris struggled with nearly half a century ago have yet been solved. National self-determination, minority rights, supernational authority and its enforcement, disarmament and the prevention of war, are all as problematical today as they were when Wilson, Clemenceau and Lloyd George tackled them at the Peace Conference. Nor will any of these problems be solved until the fundamental question is solved: Shall national interests, supernational considerations or ideological faith command the ultimate loyalty of modern man? Until such time we shall go on living in a twilight zone of fuzzy values, mixed and shifting emotions, wallowing in a sea of unsatisfactory and transitory compromises with our own consciences and with our fellow men.

The farther the Paris Peace Conference and the resulting peace structure recede into the past, the more evident it becomes that they, together with World War I, represent a major watershed in the history of the Western world; far more definite and decisive than World War II and its aftermath, for instance. When we think of "the world before 1914" we have to think of a world almost as far removed from our own as the one that existed before the French Revolution. It was a world governed by an entirely different set of values, political, economic and moral. Compared to ours it was a pastel-colored world, utterly sure of itself and the concepts it lived by. It came to an end with World War I, and a new epoch started with the Treaties of the French châteaux. The Paris Peace Conference and "Versailles" are the beginning of the era we still live in, and its ideas, its compromises, its faults, its mistakes and its achievements are still very much part of our present lives; and our fates are its consequences.

NOTES

I. The Armistice and the Pre-Armistice Agreement

1. Deutsche Reichskanzlei, *Preliminary History of the Armistice*, Documents 21 through 26.
2. *Ibid*, Document 33.
3. *Ibid*, Document 34.
4. Alma Luckau, *The German Delegation at the Peace Conference*, Document 6.
5. Deutsche Reichskanzlei, *op. cit.*, Document 44.
6. *Ibid*, Document 59.
7. *Ibid*, Document 63.
8. *Ibid*, Document 65.
9. *Ibid*, Document 78.
10. Charles Seymour, *The Intimate Papers of Colonel House*, Vol. IV, p. 87.
11. *Ibid*, p. 192
12. *Ibid*, p. 153.
13. Edward House, *Private Diary*, Historical Manuscripts Collection, Sterling Memorial Library, Yale University, January 31, 1920.
14. Luckau, *op. cit.*, Documents 2, 3, 4.
15. House, *Diary*, October 26, 1918.
16. *Ibid*, October 28, 1918.
17. Minutes of Supreme War Council Meeting, October 29, 1918.
18. House, *Diary*, October 30, 1918.
19. Edward House, *Papers*, Historical Manuscripts Collection, Sterling Memorial Library, Yale University.
20. *Ibid*.
21. *Ibid*.
22. *Ibid*.
23. House, *Diary*, November 4, 1918.
24. Deutsche Reichskanzlei, *op. cit.*, Document 101.
25. Georges Clemenceau, *Grandeur and Misery of Victory*, p. 117ff.
26. House, *Papers*.
27. Minutes of Supreme War Council Meeting, November 1, 1918.
28. For full text of Armistice see: Great Britain, *Foreign Office Documents*; Miscellaneous No. 25, 1918.
29. Ferdinand Foch, *L'Armistice et la paix*, p. 84.
30. Seymour, *op. cit.*, Vol. IV, p. 137.
31. Deutsche Reichskanzlei, *op. cit.*, Document 107.
32. *Ibid*, Document 108.

II. Pre-Conference Positions

1. F. Seymour Cocks, *The Secret Treaties*, p. 67ff.
2. *Ibid*, p. 69
3. Ray Stannard Baker, *Woodrow Wilson and World Settlement*, Vol. I, p. 361.
4. David Lloyd George, *The Truth About the Treaties*, Vol. I, p. 132.
5. House, *Papers*.
6. David Lloyd George, *Memoirs of the Peace Conference*, p. 306ff.
7. John Maynard Keynes, *The Economic Consequences of the Peace*, p. 139ff.
8. Seymour, *Intimate Papers*, Vol. IV, p. 151.
9. David Hunter Miller, *My Diary*, Vol. I, p. 270ff.
10. Baker, *op. cit.*, Vol. I, p. 112ff.
11. *Ibid*, p. 225ff.
12. Mermeix, *Le combat des trois*, p. 82ff.

III. ORGANIZATION OF THE CONFERENCE

1. Harold Nicolson, *Peacemaking, 1919,* p. 76ff.
2. Baker, *World Settlement,* Vol. III, p. 59f, Document 7.
3. Nicolson, *op. cit.,* p. 95f.
4. *Ibid,* p. 47f.
5. Edward House, *Encyclopaedia Britannica,* 14th edition, "Paris, Conference of."
6. Nicolson, *op. cit.,* p. 114ff.
7. André Tardieu, *The Truth About the Treaty,* p. 98ff.

IV. THE COVENANT

1. Lloyd George, *Memoirs,* p. 180.
2. Lloyd George, *Truth,* p. 185f.
3. *Annales de la chambre des députés,* November 30, 1917.
4. House, *Diary,* December 19, 1918.
5. *Annales,* December 29, 1918.
6. House, *Diary,* January 7, 1919.
7. Lloyd George, *Truth,* p. 276.
8. *Ibid,* p. 277.
9. David Hunter Miller, *The Drafting of the Covenant,* Vol. I, p. 152ff.
10. Minutes of League of Nations Commission Meeting, February 6, 1919.
11. *Ibid,* February 11, 1919.
12. House, *Diary,* February 4, 5, 6, 9 & 12, 1919.
13. Miller, *op. cit.,* p. 323ff.
14. Baker, *World Settlement,* Vol. III, p. 234ff.
15. House, *Diary,* February 13, 1919.
16. Woodrow Wilson, *Public Papers, War and Peace,* Vol. I, p. 444f.
17. Miller, *op. cit.,* p. 174.
18. Baker, *op. cit.,* p. 324ff.
19. Henry Cabot Lodge, *The Lodge-Lowell Debate on the Proposed League of Nations,* p. 11ff.
20. Baker, *op. cit.,* p. 311.
21. House, *Diary,* March 16, 1919.
22. House, *Papers.*
23. House, *Diary,* March 16, 1919.
24. Miller, *op. cit.,* p. 322f.
25. *Ibid,* p. 342ff.
26. *Ibid,* p. 337f.
27. House, *Diary,* March 27, 1919.
28. Miller, *op. cit.,* p. 425.
29. Baker, *op. cit.,* Vol. I, p. 325ff.
30. Miller, *op. cit.,* p. 442ff.
31. *Ibid,* p. 459ff.
32. *Ibid,* p. 461ff.

V. GERMAN COLONIES

1. Lloyd George, *Truth,* p. 190ff.
2. Baker, *World Settlement,* Vol. III, p. 250ff.
3. *Ibid,* p. 254ff.
4. *Ibid,* p. 229ff.
5. Lloyd George, *Truth,* p. 525ff.
6. Lloyd George, *Memoirs,* p. 306ff.
7. Baker, *op. cit.,* p. 255.
8. *Ibid,* p. 256.
9. *Ibid.*
10. Wiseman, *Papers,* Historical Manuscripts Collection, Sterling Memorial Library, Yale University.
11. House, *Diary,* January 27, 1919.
12. House, *Papers.*

13. House, *Diary,* January 28, 1919.
14. Lloyd George, *Memoirs,* p. 357.
15. Seymour, *Intimate Papers,* Vol. IV, p. 319f.
16. House, *Diary,* January 29, 1919.
17. *Ibid.*
18. Baker, *op. cit.,* Vol. I, p. 274f.
19. Secret Minutes of the Council of Ten, January 30, 1919.
20. Baker, *op. cit.,* Vol. I, p. 270f.
21. *Ibid,* p. 241ff.
22. *Ibid,* Vol. II, p. 266.

VI. Germany's Eastern Frontiers

1. Baker, *World Settlement,* Vol. III, p. 37f.
2. Lloyd George, *Truth,* p. 304ff.
3. House, *Papers.*
4. Lloyd George, *Memoirs,* Vol. I, p. 188f.
5. Lloyd George, *Truth,* p. 978ff.
6. *Ibid,* p. 990.
7. *Ibid,* p. 990ff.
8. Lloyd George, *Memoirs,* p. 276.
9. Miller, *Drafting,* p. 208f.
10. Secret Minutes of the Council of Four, April 1, 1919.
11. *Ibid,* April 3, 1919.
12. *Ibid,* April 9, 1919 (Editor's translation from the French).
13. *Ibid,* April 12, 1919 (Editor's translation from the French).
14. *Ibid,* April 18, 1919 (Editor's translation from the French).

VII. Germany's Western Frontiers

1. Tardieu, *Truth About Treaty,* p. 242ff.
2. *Ibid,* p. 145ff.
3. House, *Diary,* February 9, 1919.
4. Secret Minutes of the Supreme Council, February 12, 1919.
5. House, *Papers.*
6. *Ibid.*
7. Secret Minutes of the Supreme Council, February 22, 1919.
8. Baker, *World Settlement,* Vol. III, p. 299ff.
9. House, *Papers.*
10. *Ibid.*
11. *Ibid.*
12. Tardieu, *op. cit.,* p. 147ff. (These points have been excerpted from the original.)
13. *Ibid,* p. 167.
14. House, *Papers.*
15. House, *Diary,* March 7, 1919.
16. Lloyd George, *Memoirs,* p. 188.
17. House, *Papers.*
18. House, *Diary,* March 10, 1919.
19. Tardieu, *op. cit.,* p. 172ff.
20. House, *Diary,* March 12, 1919.
21. Edith Bolling Wilson, *My Memoir,* p. 245f.
22. Tardieu, *op. cit.,* p. 181f.
23. House, *Papers.*
24. Miller, *Drafting,* Vol. I, p. 337.
25. Tardieu, *op. cit.,* p. 250ff.
26. House, *Diary,* March 28, 1919.
27. Seymour, *Intimate Papers,* Vol. IV, p. 396.
28. Tardieu, *op. cit.,* p. 265.
29. *Ibid,* p. 269.
30. House, *Diary,* April 3, 1919.

31. Tardieu, *op. cit.*, p. 271.
32. *Ibid*, p. ·272.

VIII. Reparations

1. Lloyd George, *Memoirs*, p. 118f.
2. House, *Diary*, January 6, 1919.
3. Miller, *My Diary*, January 17, 1919.
4. Bernard M. Baruch, *The Making of the Reparation and Economic Clauses of the Treaty*, p. 289ff.
5. *Ibid.*
6. *Ibid.*
7. *Ibid.*
8. *Ibid*, p. 21f.
9. Philip Mason Burnett, *Reparations at the Paris Peace Conference*, Vol. I, Document 137.
10. Baruch, *op. cit.*, p. 26.
11. Lloyd George, *Truth*, Vol. I, p. 559.
12. House, *Diary*, February 28, 1919.
13. *Ibid*, March 6, 1919.
14. Lloyd George, *Truth*, Vol. I, p. 286.
15. House, *Diary*, March 10, 1919.
16. Burnett, *op. cit.*, p. 689ff.
17. House, *Diary*, March 16, 1919.
18. *Ibid*, March 17, 1919.
19. Burnett, *op. cit.*, p. 26f.
20. His Majesty's Stationery Office, *Treaty of Peace Between the Allied and Associated Powers and Germany*, p. 101ff.
21. Burnett, *op. cit.*, p. xff.
22. Baruch, *op. cit.*, p. 29ff.
23. Burnett, *op. cit.*, Document 210.
24. *Ibid*, Document 211.
25. *Ibid.*
26. Baruch, *op. cit.*, p. 26ff.
27. *Ibid*, p. 45ff.
28. *Ibid*, p. 32ff.
29. Burnett, *op. cit.*, Document 219.
30. *Ibid*, Document 230.
31. *Ibid*, Document 235.
32. *Ibid*, Document 237.
33. House, *Diary*, April 5, 7 & 8, 1919.
34. H.M. Stationery Office, *op. cit.*, p. 102.

IX. Negotiations with the Germans

1. Herbert Hoover, *Years of Adventure*, p. 461f.
2. Luckau, *German Delegation*, Document 30.
3. *Ibid*, Document 29.
4. *Ibid*, p. 118ff. (The concluding remarks obviously refer to Leon Trotsky's "no war—no peace" formula that so disconcerted the Central Powers at Brest-Litovsk.)
5. *Ibid*, Document 21.
6. *Ibid*, Document 31.
7. *Ibid*, Document 37.
8. *Ibid*, Document 44.
9. *Ibid*, Document 51.
10. House, *Papers*.
11. Baker, *World Settlement*, Vol. III, Document 69.
12. Lloyd George, *Truth*, p. 992ff.
13. Luckau, *op. cit.*, Document 60.
14. *Ibid*, Document 63.

15. *Ibid*, Document 64.
16. *Ibid*, Document 66.
17. Nicolson, *Peacemaking*, p. 365ff.
18. Hoover, *op. cit.*, p. 252.

X. United States Refusal to Ratify the Treaty

1. *Congressional Record*, 66th Congress, 1st session, p. 1430.
2. *Ibid*, p. 2336ff.
3. Washington *Post*, April 29, 1925.
4. Senate Documents, 66th Congress, 1st session, Document 76.
5. *Congressional Record*, 66th Congress, 1st session, p. 6425f.
6. *Ibid*, 2nd session, p. 4599f.
7. *Ibid*, 1st session, p. 8781ff.
8. *Ibid*, p. 8791f.
9. R. R. Palmer, *History of the Modern World*, p. 702.
10. *Congressional Record*, 66th Congress, 2nd session, p. 7747f.
11. *Ibid*, 67th Congress, 1st session, House Joint Resolution 74.
12. Clemenceau, *Grandeur and Misery*, p. 120f.

XI. Conclusion

1. Nicolson, *Peacemaking*, p. 187ff.
2. *Ibid*, p. 246.